Praise for *On The O*

"I like the idea of mental synthesis very much ... I quite agree that language evolved in a way that facilitates synthesis and transmission of the synthesized mental image. ... I don't think there can be much doubt, purely conceptually, that language was a late arrival. Whatever mutation provided the key to it would have had no selectional advantage at all, and would have just been a useless "organ," if it could not have linked up to pre-existing thought systems."

> —NOAM CHOMSKY, Professor Emeritus of Linguistics, MIT

"Boston University's Andrey Vyshedskiy brings a neuroscientist's perspective to the discussion of human mental history in *On the Origin of the Human Mind*."

> —*Scientific American Mind* (July 2009)

"I found the prefrontal synthesis theory stimulating and provocative. The author puts forward an explanation for the evolution of the human mind based on predator detection that led to increased visual prefrontal analysis which set the stage for visual mental syntheses. The author presents an impressive array of recent research on the brain with up to date references that are highly relevant to his case and the origin of mind. For me, the most interesting aspect of the book centers on the significance of imagination for understanding the evolution of the mind, which, as the author states, has not been given enough attention in academic circles. This book brings forth a great deal of interesting new research that would be of interest both to the informed reader and the general public."

> —DEREK HODGSON, Prof. of Cognitive Archaeology, Univ. of York

"I strongly recommend this book to everyone interested in the human evolution, primarily on the strength of (1) the author's original thesis that detecting hidden motionless predators was a driving force for the evolution of prefrontal synthesis, and (2) the author's overall coherence and clarity in integrating a sufficiently wide range of evidence for his prefrontal synthesis theory (such as research on language, vision science, neuroanatomy, evolutionary history of primates, and archaeological/paleontological evidence of tool and art creation and usages)."

> —RICHARD J. HARRINGTON, Professor of Anthropology

"It is with great enthusiasm I recommend this book to everyone interested in the study of the human mind. The theory of integration of neuronal ensembles allowing for a uniquely human experience of "prefrontal synthesis" is fascinating and is presented in a clear and easy-to-understand language. Author's diverse background in neuroscience, bioengineering, and humanities allowed him to integrate all these fields into a coherent and fascinating text. His contribution to our common knowledge of evolutionary neurobiology will be extremely valuable to established neuroscientists, medical and graduate students and interested people of all professions alike."
—MARIA K. HOUTCHENS, M.D., MMSc, Professor of Neurology,
Harvard Medical School

"I read the book in one sitting, which was an easy task owing to the author's concise writing and knack of explaining science with simple clarity."
—NICHOLAS J MULCAHY, Hon Research Fellow, Univ. of Queensland,
Australia

"I enjoyed reading Vyshedskiy's book a lot. I'm impressed by the quality of the book on its main topic: qualitative differences between human and animal brains and the role of 'prefrontal synthesis'. The book devotes a lot of pages to the importance of neural synchronisation. This is a strong point to my view, as I share with the author the idea that (group/phase) synchronisation plays a major role in feature binding and consciousness. The book also makes a strong point about prefrontal synthesis. I made a similar point (though with less emphasis) in Why we talk (2007; 2000, French version). The book is very didactic and well-documented on various topics, especially brain functional anatomy. It is also excellent on evolutionary facts. I learned from it, and I will certainly recommend it to my students at least for this reason. One can only admire the author for the breadth of his knowledge and the clarity of his account."
—JEAN-LOUIS DESSALLES, Professor at Telecom ParisTech,
author of *Why We Talk: The Evolutionary Origins of Language*

"I like this book very much. Like the first edition, it is engagingly written and beautifully illustrated. I have to say that I am not entirely convinced that prefrontal synthesis is what distinguishes the human mind, but the author does make a good case."
—MICHAEL CORBALLIS, Professor Emeritus of Psychology,
University of Auckland, author of *The Recursive Mind*

=

"I thoroughly enjoyed reading the book. I think the idea about "prefrontal synthesis" is brilliant and that it should enter the literature as an alternative to the other theories that explain the origin of humans."
— FREDERICK E WASSERMAN, Professor of Biology, Boston University

"The value of Vyshedskiy's book may rest on his highly original concept of prefrontal synthesis and its possible neural basis. I am not a neuroscientist and cannot judge the plausibility of the neural mechanisms proposed by the author for linking sensory areas of the brain with the prefrontal cortex. But he marshals an impressive body of empirical evidence and develops a persuasive argument. If this work holds up to neuroscientific scrutiny, it will prove a valuable contribution to an account of the neural basis for displaced reference, and a nice complement to Derek Bickerton's recent work, "More than Nature Needs" (Harvard, 2014)."
— MICHAEL STUDDERT-KENNEDY, Professor Emeritus of Psychology, Univ. of Connecticut, Professor Emeritus of Linguistics at Yale University,

"This is a book with a sweeping scope and a grand vision. It incorporates insights from neuroscience, linguistics and paleoanthropology, which can only be achieved by someone with rigorous scientific training who is at the same time courageous enough to cross many boundaries between academic disciplines."
—JEN-WEI LIN, Professor of Neuroscience, Boston University

"The book is well written, and serves to stimulate consideration of what factors contributed to the emergence of 'behaviourally modern' *Homo sapiens.*"
— FRANCIS THACKERAY, Professor of Anthropology, University of the Witwatersrand

"I had an opportunity and pleasure to read one of the first copies of this exciting book. This is one of the few successful attempts to present a coherent model of the human mind in an engaging and fascinating manner. I've enjoyed the discussion of numerous animal and human intelligence experiments, as well as comprehensive analysis of the development of the visual system on the evolutionary timescale. I found the neurobiological explanation of visual object representation in human minds convincing. The book is a captivating read that ultimately leads to a well thought out theory of what makes us humans."
—ALEX GANELIS

"... the theory of the evolution of prefrontal synthesis through a refinement of the visual system and the theory of conscious thought and the voluntary synchronization of neuronal ensembles were enlightening for me because they showed that a credible scientific explanation of these two facts is possible. ... I do believe now that they are within the reach of current science. Previously, these two fields were as enigmatic to me as a light bulb might have been to an Australopithecus."

— MARTIN GORNER

"... The book presents a very logical theory of the human mind. This logic is easy to understand and follow. I recommend this book to anyone who is curious, who always wants to get to the bottom of things. The book is a lot of fun to read."

— EDWARD KHOKHLOVICH

"On the Origin of the Human Mind is a highly important work because it sheds light on that most defining, yet elusive, quality of our nature -- the imagination. I agree with Einstein's view that imagination is more important than knowledge. I have believed this for many years, even before really being able to articulate why. Dr. Vyshedskiy's book has been a great asset to me (as well as a pleasure) because it provides a more concrete explanation for what most people only know by intuition -- namely, that the human mind is unique. By bringing together the evidence from both our species' evolutionary history as well as the latest in neurological research, I think he makes a highly compelling case for the theory of prefrontal synthesis. This is one of those rare books that I wish I could get everybody to read!"

— DANE WOLF

ON THE
ORIGIN
OF THE
HUMAN
MIND

THIRD EDITION

ANDREY VYSHEDSKIY

Published by MobileReference

Third edition, 2021
The first edition was published in 2008 by MobileReference.
The second edition was published in 2014 by MobileReference.

ISBN: 978-1611988888

Audience
The book speaks best to readers who want to approach the
mind from a scientific perspective. The book is written in easy-
to-read engaging style. No previous knowledge in psychology,
paleoanthropology, or neuroscience is necessary.

Front cover
"Lion-man" statuette carved out of mammouth-tusk, H 31 cm
Site: Hohlenstein-Stadel-cave in the Lone valley, Asselfingen,
Baden-Württemberg, Germany
Upper Paleolithic period, approx. 40 000 years old
Inv. Ulmer Museum Prä Slg. Wetzel Ho-St. 39/88.1
Photo Thomas Stephan © Ulmer Museum, Ulm, Germany

I pondered deeply ... over the adventures of the jungle. And after some work with a colored pencil I succeeded in making my first drawing. My Drawing Number One. It looked something like this:

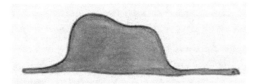

I showed my masterpiece to the grown-ups, and asked them whether the drawing frightened them. But they answered: "Frighten? Why should anyone be frightened by a hat?" My drawing was not a picture of a hat. It was a picture of a boa constrictor digesting an elephant. But since the grown-ups were not able to understand it, I made another drawing: I drew the inside of a boa constrictor, so that the grown-ups could see it clearly. They always need to have things explained. My Drawing Number Two looked like this:

ANTOINE DE SAINT-EXUPÉRY, *The Little Prince* (1943)

Contents

Foreword

While studying the neuroscience of imagination, I was struck with certain facts about imagination that seemed to shed some light on the process of the evolution of the human mind. The origin of the human mind remains one of the greatest mysteries of all times. The last 150 years, since Charles Darwin proposed that species evolve under the influence of natural selection [1], have been marked by great discoveries. Molecular biology described the genetic principles underlying species evolution and identified specific changes in the human genome since our lineage split off from the chimpanzee line about six million years ago [2]. Great paleontological discoveries have filled that span of six million years of human evolution with a number of intermediate species that display both human- and ape-like characteristics. However, the discussion of the evolution of the human intellect and specific forces that shaped the underlying brain evolution is as vigorous today as it was in Darwin's times.

At the center of the predicament about the origin of the human mind lies the question of human uniqueness. Most scientists agree that humans possess a unique intellect that sets us apart from other animals. However when any individual skill is considered, researchers invariably point to a comparable skill among non-human primates. Scientists used to think that only humans made and used tools. Sherwood Washburn, the great American physical anthropologist, has even suggested that the use of tools was the main driving force of human evolution. He wrote, "It was the success of the simplest tools that started the whole trend of human evolution and led to the civilizations of today" [3]. Washburn felt that tools were responsible for the changes in hominid teeth, hands, brain, and pelvises; tools, in effect, changed the pressures of natural selection and thus formed the man. However since the late 1960s, researchers have found numerous examples of animals using tools in the wild [4-7]. Scientists used to think that only humans could have an expanded vocabulary, but it is now known that chimpanzees, bonobos, and gorillas can learn hundreds of words [8-10]. Scientists used to think that only humans could count, but it has been discovered that chimpanzees have arithmetical skills [11]. Many social functions, such as altruism, understanding another person's cognitive state, social cooperation, and cultural transmission, which were once thought to be human-specific, have recently been described in various forms in chimpanzees, bonobos and other great apes [6,12]. These findings cast doubts on the "social brain hypothesis," which argues that human intelligence evolved primarily as a means of surviving and reproducing in large and complex social groups [13]. At the start of the 21st century, there is still no consensus as to what makes the human intellect unique.

Over three decades ago, when the question of human uniqueness was first presented to me by a colleague, it occurred to me that I should look for the difference between humans and other animals in respect to imagination. I have been interested in the physical properties of imagination since I was nine years old, and was involved in related research since my undergraduate studies. Having been trained in neuroscience, I set out to understand the neurological basis of imagination pertaining to the differences between humans and other animals. In 2008, after fifteen years of research, I allowed myself to speculate on the subject, and published the first edition of "On the Origin of the Human Mind." From that period to the present day, I have continued to work on the same subject. In 2014, I published the second edition. As the theory evolved, I had to update the book. The third edition is being published in 2021.

Henri Poincaré, a French mathematician and a philosopher

of science, wrote, "Science is built with facts, as a house is built with stones; but a collection of facts is no more a science than a pile of stones is a house. ... Above all, the scientist must make predictions" [14]. Paleontology, molecular biology, and neuroscience have provided a great number of "facts" concerning human evolution. This book uses that scientific data to conjecture a thesis on the origin of the human mind. The proposed model connects the dots between the archeological and genetic findings, explains the evolution of stone tools, language, and culture and yields testable, often counter-intuitive predictions. In the time period from the first edition of the book many predictions have been confirmed. For example, we have confirmed that training voluntary imagination improves language in children with autism. In a 3-year clinical study of 6,454 children with autism, language score in children who engaged with voluntary imagination exercises has increased to levels, which were 120% higher than in children with similar initial evaluations [15]. This difference was statistically significant (p<0.0001).

In this book, I will follow the format of the "Neuroscience of consciousness and the evolution of language" course that I have been teaching at Boston University over the past decade. I will start by sketching out a neurobiological model of what happens in the human mind when we imagine something that we have never seen before, such as an apple on the back of a whale. This process involves the **syntheses** of two existing mental images into a new one and it is conducted by a part of the brain called the **prefrontal cortex** (located just behind one's forehead). Therefore, this process is called *prefrontal synthesis*.

Part 1. Neuroscience of imagination

Chapter 1: Voluntary versus involuntary imagination

> ...internal experiences like imagery can be divided into two
> types of imagery-like experiences, where one is voluntary
> and the other involuntary.
> JOEL PEARSON, *Nature Reviews Neuroscience*, 2019 [16]

1.1 Imagination during dreaming and waking

A vivid and bizarre dream conjures up a myriad of novel mental images. The same exact images can be created volitionally when awake. The neurological mechanisms of these two processes are different. Voluntary combination of mental objects is mediated by the lateral prefrontal cortex (the part of the frontal cortex located just behind one's forehead) and patients with damage to the lateral prefrontal cortex often lose this ability. Conversely, the combination of mental objects into novel images during dreaming does not depend on the lateral prefrontal cortex: the lateral prefrontal cortex is inactive during sleep [17,18] and patients whose lateral prefrontal cortex is damaged do not notice a change in their dreams [19].

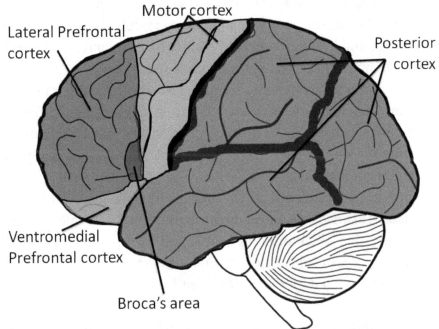

Figure 1.1 The neocortex: the lateral view. The posterior cortex includes occipital, parietal, and temporal cortices. The frontal cortex includes the motor cortex (that contains primary motor, premotor, and supplementary motor areas), Broca's area, the lateral prefrontal cortex and the ventromedial prefrontal cortex.

Paradoxically, few scientists are aware of the difference between mechanisms of imagery during dreaming and waking. Furthermore, neither colloquial English nor scientific jargon have an established way to report on the origin of a conjured up mental image: the term "imagination" is regularly used to describe any experience generated internally whether voluntarily (in waking) or involuntarily (in dreaming). Failing to distinguish between voluntary and involuntary imagination leads to confusion in developmental psychology, neurolinguistics, and paleoanthropology. For example, in a single paragraph Darwin uses both voluntary imagination and dreaming as examples of imagination: "The imagination is one of the highest prerogatives of man. By this faculty he unites former images and ideas, . . . and thus creates brilliant and novel results . . . Dreaming gives us the best notion of this power" [20].

Darwin's comments suggest how misleading it can be to lump all imaginative experiences into a single category. Darwin notes that many animals dream and on this basis attributes to them a power of imagination that could reasonably be understood to include voluntary imagination: "As dogs, cats, horses, and probably all the higher animals, even birds have vivid dreams . . . we must admit that they possess some power of imagination" [20]. While dogs, cats, and horses might very well conjure up novel images in their dreams, the mechanism of imagination in dreaming is different from voluntary imagination of humans.

Only recently have attempts been made to differentiate voluntary and involuntary imagination. Joel Pearson writes:

"When people talk about the mind's eye, they typically refer to the voluntary experience of creating a conscious sensory experience at will. However, there are many examples of involuntary sensory experiences that are equally decoupled from direct sensory input. For example, in synaesthesia and in many visual illusions individuals can experience vivid color without color information stimulating the retina. In post-traumatic stress disorder (PTSD), individuals experience flashbacks or vivid, intrusive memories of trauma experienced as involuntary imagery. ... One proposed overarching framework is that internal experiences like imagery can be divided into two types of imagery-like experiences, where one is voluntary and the other involuntary" [16].

While many people intuitively distinguish between voluntary and involuntary imagination, few people—even among scientists—recognize the difference between their mechanisms on the neurological level. The human neocortex consists of two functionally different parts. Its back part, called the *posterior cortex* (including occipital, parietal, and temporal cortices), is dedicated to sensory functions; its front part, called the *frontal cortex*, is dedicated to motor functions (Figure 1.1). Joaquin M. Fuster, a distinguished neuroscientist from UCLA and the leading expert on the prefrontal cortex explains that "the entirety of the frontal cortex, including its prefrontal region, is "action cortex" in broadest terms. It is cortex devoted to action of one kind or another, whether skeletal movement, ocular movement, the expression of emotions, speech or visceral control; it can even be the kind of internal, mental action that we call reasoning. The frontal cortex is 'doer' cortex, much as the posterior cortex is 'sensor' cortex" [21]. In the cortex analogy to a theater, the posterior cortex provides the actors, costumes and colors (sensory content), while the frontal cortex schedules the actors' performance (motor content).

The word "voluntary" is always associated with activity initiated in and controlled by the frontal cortex. Voluntary muscle contraction is initiated in and controlled by the motor cortex [22], voluntary thinking is initiated in and controlled by the lateral prefrontal cortex [21,23-27], and voluntary talking initiated in and controlled by the Broca's area [28]. When activity is initiated outside of the frontal cortex, it is never described as voluntary. In contrast to voluntary muscle contractions, spasmatic skeletal muscle contractions are neither initiated by not controlled from the frontal cortex: their origin results from spontaneous action potentials in muscle fibers. Involuntary swearing that can be observed in patients with expressive aphasia is initiated by the subcortical structure called basal ganglia [29]. Similarly, involuntary imagery perceived during REM-sleep dreaming is neither initiated nor controlled by the lateral prefrontal cortex. The dramatic decrease of blood flow to the lateral prefrontal cortex [17] and reduction of EEG power in the lateral prefrontal cortex [18] demonstrate that the lateral prefrontal cortex is inactive during sleep: the dreaming hallucinations are the result of spontaneous activation of neuronal ensembles in the posterior cortex. A stroke affecting the motor cortex commonly results in paralysis of voluntary movement, but cannot prevent involuntary muscle spasms. A stroke in the lateral prefrontal cortex often results in paralysis of voluntary imagination, but does not affect dreaming [19]. Thus, the neurological difference between the voluntary and involuntary imagination is in the lateral prefrontal cortex: the voluntary imagination is controlled by the lateral prefrontal cortex and the involuntary imagination is lateral prefrontal cortex-independent.

If few scientists recognize the neurological difference between voluntary and involuntary imagination, fewer still specify clearly the mechanism of voluntary imagination. GoogleScholar Search for "voluntary imagination" in March, 2020 has found only 157 references. The majority of scientists either refer to "voluntary imagination" simply as "imagination" or create new terms such as "ability to invent fiction" [30], "episodic future thinking" [31], "mental scenario building" [32], or "creating new internal representations" [33]. These new terms are equally ambiguous with respect to the role of the lateral prefrontal cortex in generating novel images.

Voluntary imagination, but not involuntary imagination, is an essential component of language. To understand the difference between "the cat on the mat" and "the mat on the cat," it is not enough to understand the words and the grammar, but it is necessary to *imagine* the cat and the mat together to appreciate their relations. When reading the two phrases, one visualizes the two situations in their mind's eye and places the image of the cat on top of the image of the mat. Similarly, if the phrase was modified to become "big black cat on a tiny wet mat," one would immediately adjust the mental image to reflect the additional details. When the new phrase is rearranged to "big black mat on a wet cat," the same process of disassembly and reassembly takes place. Thus, a completely new image is constructed, despite the fact that most people have never seen a mat on a cat.

Linguists refer to this property of human languages as recursion, since it can be used to build nested (recursive) explanations. E.g., a sentence "a snake on the boulder, to the left of the tall tree, that is behind the hill," forces the interlocutor to use voluntary imagination to combine four objects: a snake, the boulder, the tree, and the hill. Comprehension of spatial prepositions and recursion is impossible without the capacity for voluntary imagination.

1.2 Misleading intuition of imagination

Most people intuitively assume that all individuals have the capacity for voluntary imagination. We are accustomed to measure other people by ourselves and since voluntary imagination is so natural to us, we project this ability on to others. Symptoms of *voluntary imagination paralysis* are less obvious than those of muscle paralysis, and affected individuals find ways to avoid putting their disability on display. Voluntary imagination paralysis is, however, easily revealed in special tests. Affected individuals commonly exhibit a selective and catastrophic deficit in matrix reasoning tasks requiring mental integration of multiple objects [24], such as those shown in Figure 1.2, Tower of London test [34] and the mental 2-digit number multiplication [35]. Similarly, individuals with voluntary imagination paralysis have difficulty combining objects in a sentence: they show dramatically reduced ability to understand spatial prepositions [21] making them incapable of following simple instructions such as 'draw a triangle above a circle.' Joaquin Fuster calls their alteration in language "prefrontal aphasia" [21] and explains that "although the pronunciation of words and sentences remains intact, language is impoverished and shows an apparent diminution of the capacity to 'prepositionize.' The length and complexity of sentences are reduced. There is a dearth of dependent clauses and, more generally, an underutilization of what Chomsky characterizes as the potential for recursiveness of language" [21].

Alexander Luria calls this condition "frontal dynamic aphasia" [36] and reports that as long as a conversation does not involve a combination of objects, these patients look unremarkable. They do not lose their vocabulary and can keep a conversation going:

> Patients with this type of lesion have no difficulty articulating words. They are also able to retain their ability to hear and understand most spoken language. Their ability to use numerical symbols and many different kinds of abstract concepts also remains undamaged. . . . these patients had no difficulty grasping the meaning of complex ideas such as 'causation,' 'development,' or 'cooperation.' They were also able to hold abstract conversations. . . . They can repeat and understand sentences that simply communicate events by creating a sequence of verbal images.

Luria explains that this disability manifests itself only when patients have to imagine several objects or persons in a *novel* combination:

> But difficulties developed when they were presented with complex grammatical constructions which coded logical relations. . . . Such patients find it almost impossible to understand phrases and words which denote relative position and cannot carry out a simple instruction like 'draw a triangle above a circle.'. . .Their particular kind of aphasia becomes

apparent only when they have to operate with groups or arrangements of elements. If these patients are asked, 'Point to the pencil with the key drawn on it' or 'Where is my sister's friend?' they do not understand what is being said. As one patient put it, 'I know where there is a sister and a friend, but I don't know who belongs to whom'.

In our research, we have found that simple non-canonical relational inquiries can quickly elucidate voluntary imagination paralysis: questions, such as "If a cat ate a dog, who is alive?" and "Imagine the *blue* cup inside the *yellow* cup, which cup is on top? can be consistently answered by four-year-old children but commonly failed by individuals with voluntary imagination paralysis [37].

Both Fuster and Luria focus on linguistic deficits in prefrontal patients and call their condition "prefrontal aphasia" and "frontal dynamic aphasia" respectively. Aphasia, however, is translated from Greek as "speechless" and these patients have normal articulate speech. Furthermore, as pointed above, patients commonly exhibit a related deficit in nonverbal tasks requiring voluntary imagination [24,34,35]. Thus, their condition is better described as *voluntary imagination paralysis.*

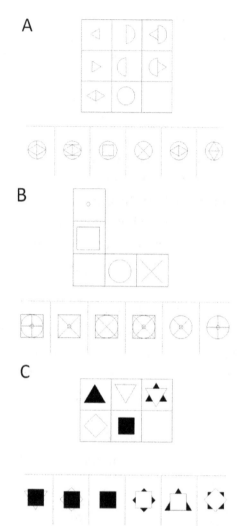

Figure 1.2 *Voluntary imagination paralysis* **goes beyond problems with understanding recursive language.** Nonverbal tasks requiring imagining a novel combination of two or more objects is impossible in this condition. Typical IQ test tasks that require combination of several objects: (A) The top two rows of the matrix indicate the rule: "the object in the right column is the result of the combination of the two objects shown in the left and middle row" (the solution in the 5th square). (B) shows a question that relies on a combination of four objects. (C) shows a question in which a combination of two objects has to be conducted according to the following rule specified in the top row: "the object in the middle column goes on top of the object in the left column" (the solution in the second square).

1.3 Voluntary imagination acquisition in children

Normal ontogenetic development of most neurological systems–from muscle innervation to the development of all sensory systems–requires genetic instructions to be complemented by adequate experience: normal development of vision requires light, normal development of hearing depends on auditory stimulation, normal development of somatosensory cortex is the function of tactile input, etc. What is highly unusual about the ontogenetic acquisition of voluntary imagination is that the necessary experience is only provided by the exposure to a purely cultural phenomenon. For the normal development of vision, light reflected from surrounding objects has to reach the retina, but that occurs whenever it is light, independent of cultural exposure; for the normal development of the muscular system, the trophic factors released by muscles have to reach their neurons, but that occurs whenever a child is moving—the stimulation to neurons comes naturally even when a child is growing alone in a forest [38]. However, this is not the case with voluntary imagination. The development of neurological networks necessary for normal voluntary imagination requires a community of humans using recursive language to communicate with a child. Modern children who experience fewer recursive dialogs show significant reduction of frontoposterior fiber tracts mediating voluntary imagination [39] and complete lack of recursive conversations (in feral children and deaf linguistic isolates) is associated with voluntary imagination paralysis [40].

In developmental psychology the problem of voluntary imagination paralysis is traditionally described as *stimulus overselectivity, tunnel vision*, or *lack of multi-cue responsivity* [41-43]. Affected children have difficulty accomplishing seemingly trivial tasks, such as an instruction to "pick up a blue straw that is under the table," which requires them to combine three different features, i.e. the object itself (*straw*), its color (*blue*), and its location (*under the table*). These children may "over-select" the word "straw" and ignore both its location and the fact that it should also be blue, therefore picking up any available straw; alternatively, they can "over-select" on the color, therefore picking up any blue object. (The name of the phenomenon is erroneous. It is not that a child "over-selects" on one feature, rather it is the failure of mental integration. In other words, it is not an attention or focus problem [37], but paralysis of voluntary imagination.) These children are known to benefit from special exercises that develop voluntary imagination. Speech language pathologists use the techniques of "combining adjectives, location/orientation, color, and size with nouns," "following directions with increasing complexity," "building the multiple features/clauses in the sentence" [44] and ABA therapists use "visual-visual and auditory-visual conditional discrimination" [45-48], "development of multi-cue responsivity" [42], and "reduction of stimulus overselectivity," [43] that are training voluntary imagination.

1.4 Voluntary imagination acquisition has a strong critical period

Most language and cognitive functions have weak critical periods. A familiar example is acquisition of a second language. While learning French or German is much harder after puberty [49], phoneme tuning [50,51], grammar processing [52], articulation control [53], and vocabulary acquisition [54] —all can be significantly improved by training at any age [55,56], and therefore have weak critical periods.

Strong critical periods, that make learning impossible after a certain age, are less common and therefore counterintuitive. The most famous examples of strong critical periods in central nervous system development include monocular deprivation [57], filial imprinting in birds [58], and monaural occlusion [59]. Filial imprinting in birds occurs only during several hours after birth [58]. Monocular deprivation in cats during the first postnatal month (in primates during the first several years) results in life-long loss of vision in one eye [57]. Similarly, plugging one ear in owls during the first two postnatal months results in lifelong inability to localize sounds [59]. Neural circuits underlying strong critical periods are programmed to be shaped by experience during short periods of early postnatal life; later development is impossible.

Voluntary imagination seems to have a strong critical period that ends shortly after the age of five. This idea was popularized by Lenneberg and is known as "Lenneberg's language acquisition critical period hypothesis" [60]. Lenneberg's conjecture about the strong critical period was based on a few cases of childhood traumatic aphasia and hemispherectomy. When the left hemisphere is surgically removed before the age of five (to treat cancer or epilepsy), patients often attain normal cognitive functions in adulthood (using the one remaining hemisphere). Conversely, removal of the left hemisphere after the age of five often results in significant impairment of recursive language and voluntary imagination.

Recently Lenneberg's hypothesis has received more experimental support. The randomized controlled study of institutionalized Romanian children demonstrated a significant difference in voluntary imagination tasks at the age of eight between children placed in foster care and therefore exposed to recursive dialogs before the age of two and children who have been placed in foster care after the age of two [61].

Deaf individuals communicating using formal sign language from an early age develop normal voluntary imagination. However, in the absence of early communication, or when the sign language is lacking spatial prepositions and recursion, deaf individuals show clear deficits of voluntary imagination. Deaf individuals who had learned American Sign Language (ASL) early in life were found to be more accurate than later learners at identifying whether two complex-shape figures presented at different degrees of rotation were identical or mirror images of each other [62]. Individuals who learned ASL earlier were also faster than later learners at identifying whether two-dimensional body-shaped figures (bears with one paw raised) presented at different rotations were identical or mirror images of each other [63]. Even after decades of signing experience, the signers who learned ASL earlier were better at mental rotation accuracy [64]. Among deaf individuals who acquire sign language at the same age, the richness of "spatial" language makes a difference. First cohort of signers acquired the emerging sign language in Nicaragua when this language was just invented and had few spatial prepositions, while the second cohort of signers acquired the language in a more complex form with more spatial prepositions. Predictably, the second cohort of signers (tested when they were in their 20s) outperformed the first cohort of signers (tested when they were in their 30s) in several mental rotation tasks [65]. Finally, deaf individuals never exposed to formal sign language until puberty invariably suffer lifelong voluntary imagination paralysis despite learning significant vocabulary through intensive post-pubertal language therapy [40].

1.5 Confusing imagination terminology

Among individuals diagnosed with autism, the prevalence of lifelong voluntary imagination paralysis is 30 to 40% [66]. This problem is exacerbated by confusion between voluntary and involuntary imagination and a misunderstanding of the strong critical period. It is not uncommon for parents to brush off their child's language delay until elementary school, at which time, for most children it is too late to develop voluntary imagination. It is also common for parents to mistake drawing, Lego constructions, and jigsaw puzzle assembly for manifestation of voluntary imagination. In children developing atypically some aspects of creativity can be driven exclusively by involuntary imagination and do not reflect the development of voluntary imagination.

While clinicians are usually aware of the critical period and normally recommend early intervention at the time of diagnosis, they are often reluctant to emphasize the urgent nature of the problem to the parents [67]. Again, most clinicians are uncertain about the distinction between voluntary and involuntary imagination and have never learned the difference between weak and strong critical periods.

Even when intensive therapy ensues early, the success is hindered by ambiguous goals. Many techniques used by speech language pathologists and ABA therapists are aimed at improving voluntary imagination. However, voluntary imagination exercises are usually just a small part of intervention that primarily focuses on building up a child's vocabulary. Vocabulary is easier to train and most tests rely exclusively on a child's vocabulary to measure success (e.g., Peabody Picture Vocabulary Test (PPVT-4) [68], Expressive Vocabulary Test (EVT-2) [69]), thus encouraging focus on vocabulary training.

Thus, ambiguous imagination terminology and lack of appreciation for the strong voluntary imagination critical period have a clear negative effect on the education of vulnerable children. A better understanding of the strong critical period for voluntary imagination will result in greater effort toward language therapy in very young children and eventually in many more high-functioning productive lives.

1.6 Dreaming imagination benefits survival

The greatest fallacy of natural philosophy is the assumption of evolutionary permanence of imagination. Components of involuntary and voluntary imagination rely on multiple neurological mechanisms that evolved over time. Dreaming, the simplest mechanism of involuntary imagination, evolved 140 million year ago (ya) when marsupials and placentals diverged from the monotreme line [70]. Periods of REM-sleep, the best marker for dreaming, have been observed in marsupials and placentals but not in the monotremes. Since REM-sleep in humans is associated with vivid dreaming, it is assumed that animals could experience similar incidence of dreaming during REM-sleep [71]. Novel combinations of mental objects during dreaming present possible scenarios to our judgment. An envisioned juxtaposition of mental objects can provide a solution of heretofore unexperienced problem important for future survival.

Dreaming simulations work for humans as well as rodents. What kind of future do rodents dream about? An ingenious experiment conducted by Freyja Ólafsdóttir et al. (2015) comes as close as possible to interrogating the content of an animal's mind (Figure 1.3). [72] The technique involves recording neuronal "preplay" of events that never happened with an animal and therefore provides evidence of an animal's forming a novel experience in their mind. Hippocampal "place" neurons encode the location of an animal in space. When the animal is in one location, a few neurons fire; when the animal moves to a new spot, other "place" neurons fire instead. Each time the animal returns to the same spot, the same "place" neurons fire. Thus, as the animal moves, a place-specific pattern of firing emerges which can be used to reconstruct the animal's position. By the same token, when the animal is not moving, but the "place" neurons are firing, their place-specific firing pattern can be used to reconstruct the animal's mental experience. In the Ólafsdóttir experiment, rats were allowed to run up to the junction in a T-shaped track. The animals could see into each of the two arms, but not enter them. Food was then placed in one of the arms, therefore making this arm of the track important for the animal. Will the animal "dream" of visiting this arm of the track during sleep?

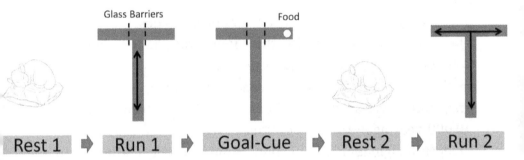

Figure 1.3. Preplay of the future recorded in a rat during sleep. Preplay of the future events may allow animals to remember the outcomes of their mental simulations and therefore improve their adaptive behavior by preselecting the best outcome.

Researchers recorded the firing of "place" neurons when animals were on the track and during sleep afterwards. After the sleep, the rats were allowed to return to the track and enter both arms, and again their brain activity was recorded. Now that researchers knew the "place" neurons firing pattern corresponding to both arms of the track, they could compare those patterns to the "place" neurons firing during sleep. Researchers report that in the sleep period after the rats first viewed the inaccessible arms, the "place" neurons pattern that would later form the mental map of a journey to the food-containing arm was in fact activated. The "place" neurons pattern that would become the mental map of the other inaccessible arm was not activated. An implication of these findings is that the brain was able to simulate future experience. Furthermore, the brain preferentially simulated the experiences that was functionally significant, since that experience was associated with reward [72]. If neuronal preplay in rats is homologous to dreaming simulations in humans, then this sleep-time component of imagination must have evolved before the primate line split from the mammals line 70 million years ago.

Thus, dreaming is the evolutionarily oldest adaptation, that **simulates future in the neocortex**. Components of voluntary imagination were acquired in multiple steps over millions of years. The most advanced component of voluntary imagination was acquired by humans relatively recently, around 70,000 year ago [30,73] and resulted in the birth of humans with modern imagination. Acquisition of modern imagination is the topic of this book.

1.7 Conclusions

On the neurobiological level, *voluntary* imagination is different from *involuntary* imagination as voluntary muscle contractions are different from muscle spasm. The difference is in the lateral prefrontal cortex: the voluntary imagination is controlled by the lateral prefrontal cortex and the involuntary imagination is lateral prefrontal cortex-independent.

Neither colloquial English, nor scientific jargon defines this distinction clearly. This distinction is neither taught in school, nor emphasized in university programs. Without education on this issue, scientists and non-scientists alike default to an intuition that assumes little distinction between voluntary and involuntary imagination, the presence of voluntary imagination abilities in all people, and a weak critical period for language acquisition. Until heliocentricity was taught in school, people also assumed that the sun and the planets were circling the Earth. When intuition is failing, education is the only way to progress.

The ambiguous definition of imagination is a good illustration of the Whorfian conjecture, that vocabulary affects its speakers' cognition. It is impossible to discuss neurobiology of imagination, language evolution, and children's education, without a clear understanding of the differences between voluntary and involuntary imagination. Terms such as "mental storytelling" [74], "internal mentation" [75], "mentally playing with ideas" [76], "creative intelligence" [77], "prospective memory" [78], "memory of the future" [79], "integration of multiple relations between mental representations" [24], "the ability to form nested scenarios" [80], "an inner theatre of the mind that allows us to envision and mentally manipulate many possible situations and anticipate different outcomes" [80] are ambiguous in terms of the role of the lateral prefrontal cortex in the generation of novel images; they do not communicate whether the images were created voluntarily or involuntarily.

The success of humans is primarily due to dramatic improvement of voluntary imagination. In order to understand human evolution, we must understand the evolution of voluntary imagination on the neurological level.

Chapter 2: Neuroscience of imagination

... how can a brain perform difficult tasks in one hundred steps that the largest parallel computer imaginable can't solve in a million or a billion steps? The answer is the brain doesn't "compute" the answers to problems; it retrieves the answers from memory. In essence, the answers were stored in memory a long time ago. It only takes a few steps to retrieve something from memory. Slow neurons are not only fast enough to do this, but they constitute the memory themselves. The entire cortex is a memory system.

JEFF HAWKINS, *On intelligence* (2004)

2.1 How are objects encoded in the brain?

One of the most exciting experiments that delves into the neuroscience of mental imagery was conducted at the turn of the millennium by Gabriel Kreiman, Christof Koch, and Itzhak Fried at UCLA and Caltech [81]. The researchers were involved in identifying areas of the brain responsible for abnormal electrical activity in patients with intractable epilepsy. To achieve this goal, surgeons implanted electrodes inside the patient's brain, in and around the hippocampus. The hippocampus is a group of specialized neurons located deep inside the temporal lobe essential for forming long-term memories of people, places and events. The electrodes remained in the patient's brain for approximately a week, and were used to monitor neuronal activity. During this time, the scientists were able to interact with the patients by having them go through a number of specific tasks. This allowed the researchers to directly observe the activity of these patients' neurons.

The study, which recorded from hundreds of neurons, found that in the majority of cases, neurons that were activated during vision of a particular object were again activated during the recall of the same object. The patients were shown objects from nine categories, one at a time, and their neuronal activity was recorded. The researchers were able to find 49 neurons that were activated during vision, most of which (44) responded selectively to only one of the nine objects. Later, the patients were prompted to recall each one of the objects with their eyes closed. This time researchers were able to pinpoint 33 neurons that fired during visual imagery, 23 of which were selective to exactly one of the recalled objects. Of the 16 neurons that fired during both vision and visual imagery, 14 neurons fired selectively during vision and recall of the **same** object.

For example, a single neuron in the entorhinal cortex of one of the patients showed an increased firing rate when the patient was shown a picture of a baseball, and not when the patient was shown any other object (such as an emotional face or a food item). Later, the same patient was asked to recall each one of the objects, one at a time, and the same neuron responded with increased firing only when the patient was recalling the baseball. In another patient, a neuron in the left amygdala increased its firing rate exclusively when the patient viewed a picture of an animal and then again when the patient (now with eyes closed) was prompted to mentally recall the same animal.

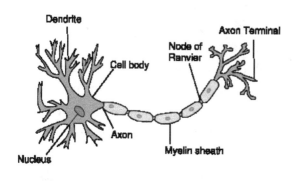

Figure 2.1 A simplified drawing of a typical neuron found in the brain. The human brain contains about 100 billion neurons and each neuron can be linked to as many as 10,000 other neurons. All neurons are small cells with a cell body that is about 0.02 millimeters wide (that's just a bit thinner than an average human hair) and long branch-like projections that can be up to one meter in length. These long projections allow neurons to exchange information over long distances. Neurons exchange information by firing action potentials, which are short 1 millisecond (0.001 seconds) spikes in voltage from a resting membrane potential of negative 70 millivolt (0.070 Volt) to positive 40 millivolt. Some neurons fire action potentials as often as 100 times per second, while others can go minutes without firing. These spikes in voltage can be measured by electrodes implanted in the brain.

The findings of this remarkable study imply that the mechanisms in the human brain that encode objects may be the same as the mechanisms that allow us to recall that object. In other words, this experiment supports the notion that your brain is acting in a very similar way when you use your eyes to recognize an object in an image as when you close your eyes and imagine the object in your "mind's eye." A number of other experiments that also support this hypothesis will be discussed later on, but first let us look more closely at exactly how the neurons in our brain encode an object.[a]

---

[a] Understanding the evolution of the human mind is impossible without knowing the fascinating and complex way in which our brain is organized. If you haven't studied neuroscience before, you can benefit from taking a look at Appendix 2 which will get you acquainted with some of the basic neuroscience topics essential for the purposes of our discussion.

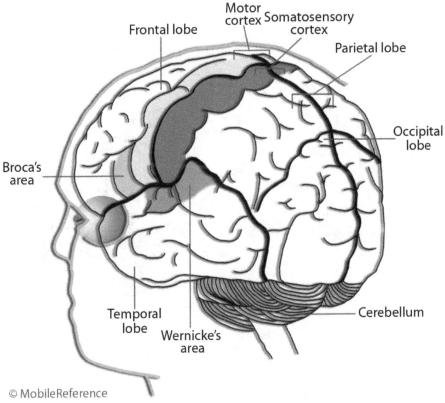

© MobileReference

Figure 2.2 Functional organization of the cerebral cortex. Neurons in the cerebral cortex are organized territorially based on their function. Motor neurons that control muscle movement are located in the motor cortex. Neurons sensitive to touch are located in the somatosensory cortex. Neurons responsible for language comprehension are concentrated in Wernicke's area. Neurons responsible for language production are located in Broca's area. If you think of a brain as a company, then functional cortical areas correspond to different departments. Each department minds its own business.

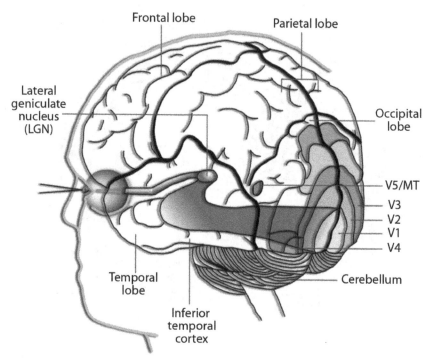

Figure 2.3 Organization of the visual system. The visual system, which makes up about half of the entire cortex [82], also consists of multiple departments. The primary visual cortex, V1, is located in the occipital lobe. V1 receives information from the retina via the lateral geniculate nucleus in the thalamus. The primary visual cortex is the first *cortical* area that receives visual information. There is a specialization hierarchy along the visual information pathways. The departments become more specialized the farther the information moves along the visual pathway. Neurons in the lateral geniculate nuclei can be activated by visual stimulation from either one eye or the other but not both eyes. They respond to any change in activity of the retinal neuron that they are connected to. Neurons in V1 can usually be activated by either eye. Neurons in V1 are sensitive to specific attributes, such as the orientation of line segments, color, and binocular disparity. Visual information is transmitted from V1 to cortical areas with greater specificity. Neurons in V4 respond selectively to aspects of visual stimuli critical to shape identification. Neurons in the inferior temporal lobe may respond only when an entire object (such as a face) is present within the visual field. The perception of motion is the major function of the visual area V5, also known as visual area MT.

2.2 Objects are encoded by ensembles of neurons

Our visual world appears to consist of meaningful, unified, and stable objects that move in spatially and temporally predictable ways. Similarly when we close our eyes and imagine a visual scene, that scene is also populated by unified and stable objects. "Objects," therefore, constitute the functional units of perception. Finding object-selective neurons is a great first step, but a full understanding of object encoding requires considering all the neurons in the brain that represent a particular object, not just the single neuron recorded by scientists. Few neuroscientists believe that objects are encoded by single neurons. The so-called "grandmother cell" theory, which asserts that every object (such as your grandmother, hence the name of the theory) is represented by a single cell, was discredited in its pure form. Rather, most neuroscientists think that the perception of each object is associated with firing of tens of thousands to millions of neurons located throughout the brain [83]. In the Kreiman experiment, for example, the "baseball neuron" would have been only one of thousands of neurons that fired when the patient perceived a baseball; it just happened to be the only one that was being recorded during the experiment.

These thousands of neurons encode the various characteristics of the baseball, such as its shape, color, texture, etc. [84,85]. The majority of the neurons activated by the baseball image are located in the primary visual area (usually called V1), which is located in the back of the brain. A smaller number of neurons are activated in the extrastriate areas such as V2 and V4, and an even smaller number of neurons are activated in the temporal lobe where scientists placed their recording electrodes.

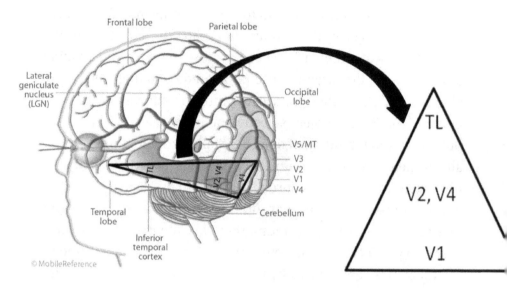

Figure 2.4 Neuronal ensembles encode objects and events in memory. This illustration shows a schematic representation of an object-encoding neuronal ensemble (objectNE) overlaid over the ventral visual path. An objectNE pyramid includes a high number of relatively non-selective neurons in V1 (at the base of the pyramid) that encode the contours of the object, its color, the spatial depth, etc.; a fewer number of relatively more selective cells in the extrastriate areas such as V2 and V4 that encode simple shapes; and an even fewer number of very selective neurons in the temporal lobe (the top of the pyramid). It is important to understand that a significant number of selective neurons in the temporal lobe are associated with any single objectNE. ObjectNEs include neurons located throughout the cerebral cortex, not limited to V1, V2, V4, and the temporal lobe, but this simplified representation makes it easier to conceptualize a neuronal ensemble. The layers of the pyramid are connected by axons going in both directions that enable the neurons of the ensemble to activate into a common resonant mode.

This neuronal arrangement is best represented by a pyramid. The base of the pyramid represents the high number of neurons located in the primary visual area (V1) that encode the contours of the object, its color, spatial depth (by means of binocular disparity), etc. These neurons at the base of the pyramid are relatively non-selective; they are involved in the encoding of a great number of different objects. The middle of the pyramid represents the fewer number of relatively more selective cells in the extrastriate areas such as V2 and V4 that encode simple shapes. The top of the pyramid represents an even fewer number of very selective neurons in the temporal lobe. The firing of these selective neurons in the temporal lobe is often associated with a single face, object, or event. For example, the baseball neuron recorded in Kreiman's experiment was one of these selective neurons. It responded to an image of a baseball but not to any other images presented to the patient.

In addition to the baseball neuron, researchers recording the activity of single neurons in the medial temporal lobe of patients have identified neurons selectively activated by animals (such as spiders and seals), people (such as Bill Clinton, Halle Berry and Jennifer Anniston) and places (such as the Sydney Opera House and the Tower of Pisa) as well as hundreds of other objects [83,84]. These neurons were activated by objects in an invariant, stable, and explicit manner. This means that the object's neuron was activated whenever the patient was shown any image of the particular object even if it displayed the object in a novel position, from another angle or in a different context. For example, the Bill Clinton neuron would react strongly whenever Bill Clinton was shown, be it from the front or from the side, whether it was his whole body or just his face, and even when he was in the company of other dignitaries. Remarkably, that same neuron would be activated even when the patient saw the written name of the object, heard the spoken name of the object or even simply recalled the object from memory. That same neuron would stay silent when the patient was exposed to photographs, written or spoken names of other objects.

There is significant scientific evidence that all neurons encoding an object, such as a baseball, activate *synchronously* when a person perceives that object (discussed below). Tens of thousands of neurons in various parts of the brain fire one or more action potentials in synchrony. For this reason, neuroscientists call this collection of neurons a *neuronal ensemble.*

Donald Hebb first developed the theoretical concept of neuronal ensembles in 1949. He defined "cell assembly" as "a diffuse structure comprising cells in the cortex and diencephalon, capable of acting briefly as a closed system, delivering facilitation to other such systems" [86]. Hebb suggested that, depending on functional requirements, individual neurons could participate in different neuronal ensembles.

Hebb also suggested a mechanism responsible for the integration of neurons into a resonant structure of an ensemble. "Neurons that fire together, wire together" was a phrase coined by Hebb to explain "associative learning," in which simultaneous activation of neurons leads to pronounced increases in synaptic strength between those neurons [86]. Hebb wrote: "... any two cells or systems of cells that are repeatedly active at the same time will tend to become 'associated,' so that activity in one facilitates activity in the other. ... When one cell repeatedly assists in firing another, the axon of the first cell develops synaptic knobs (or enlarges them if they already exist) in contact with the soma of the second cell." (Work by Eric Kandel and others has further provided direct support for the involvement of Hebbian learning in the mechanisms of memory [87]). The neurons within the neuronal ensemble that encode the baseball in the Kreiman experiment have, over time, increased the connection strength between all the cells in the ensemble. In other words, the memory of the baseball is physically stored in connections between the various neurons throughout the brain that encode the baseball. In summary, **the *object-encoding neuronal ensemble* (objectNE) is a group of neurons with**

enhanced connections that make them prone to activate together and fire synchronously. Once the neurons within an objectNE self-organize into a synchronous activity, the object encoded by the ensemble is perceived by the person.

This tendency of neuronal ensembles to activate together and fire synchronously is essentially responsible for our perception of "meaningful, unified, and stable objects" and can be demonstrated by electrical stimulation of the selective neurons at the top of the 'objectNE pyramid.'[b] Neurosurgeon Wilder Penfield invented a procedure in which it was possible to treat patients with severe epilepsy by destroying the nerve cells in the brain where the seizures originated. Before operating, Penfield stimulated the brain with electrical probes while the patients were conscious on the operating table, and observed their responses. In this way, he could more accurately target the responsible areas of the brain, reducing the side-effects of the surgery. Penfield reported that stimulation of the temporal

---

[b] These selective neurons in the temporal lobe seem to play an especially important role in bonding neurons of the neuronal ensembles into a resonant system. For example, damage (particularly bilateral damage) to the fusiform gyrus of the inferior temporal lobe may result in prosopagnosia (Damasio AR, 1982), a complete inability of a subject to identify faces (prosopagnosia comes from the Greek *prosopon* meaning "face" and *agnosia* meaning "non-knowledge"). In the absence of bonding neurons in the fusiform gyrus, the neuronal ensembles encoding faces cannot activate into synchronous firing that is necessary for face recognition.

Prosopagnosia is one type of visual agnosia. Patients with visual agnosia are able to attend to the object and perceive the fragment, however they are unable to group the fragments together in order to *experience* the complete object; they cannot make sense of the object or name it. Visual agnosia was made famous by Oliver Sacks' essay, *The Man Who Mistook His Wife for a Hat* [88]. It tells the story of the patient named Dr. P who cannot recognize the common objects around him, including a shoe, a foot, his wife, or even his own face. Because of this complete lack of recognition, Dr. P thinks that his wife's head is a hat and grabs it in order to put it on his head.

lobes could lead to vivid recall of events from memory [89].[c] Conversely, when non-selective neurons in the primary visual area (area V1, at the bottom of the pyramid) were electrically stimulated, subjects only reported seeing a flash of light [89,90]. Since neurons in V1 are part of a great many objectNEs, stimulation of one cell does not evoke activation of any complete objectNE and the subjects do not experience seeing any specific objects or events. A significantly larger proportion of V1 neurons need to be stimulated to trigger activity of the complete objectNE (as happens when a visually presented object is recognized).

2.3 Visual recognition of an object and memory recall of an object activate the same neuronal ensemble

There are two ways in which an objectNE is normally activated leading to the perception of the particular object encoded by that ensemble:

(1) An image of an object presented to our eyes triggers activation of an objectNE from the bottom-up by stimulating neurons in the primary visual area (V1). This process is referred to as "visual recognition."

(2) When an object is recalled from memory (with eyes shut) the same objectNE is activated from the top down. This process is referred to as "memory recall."

---

[c] See Appendix 3 for a detailed description and a discussion of Penfield's observations.

Visual recognition   Memory recall

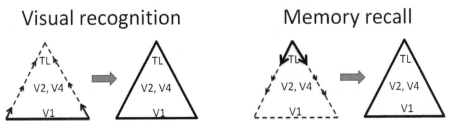

Figure 2.5 Visual recognition and memory recall. Recognition and recall can be defined as: *self-organization of an objectNE into a synchronously firing unit.* When the process of self-organization is triggered from the base of the pyramid by a few visual cues, a sound, or a familiar smell, it is called "recognition" (bottom-up recognition initiated by firing of neurons at the base of the pyramid, primary visual area V1). When the self-organization is triggered from the top of the pyramid by associative thinking or active planning, the process is called "visual recall" (top-down recall initiated by the firing of neurons at the top of the pyramid, temporal lobe, TL).

Kreiman's experiment recorded from single neurons located at the top of the pyramid, in the medial temporal lobe. These neurons were activated during *both* the visual recognition of a baseball (left panel) and during its recall from memory (mental image, right panel). There is growing scientific evidence that visual recognition and memory recall share underlying neural processes [91]. In other words, it's not just the neurons in the temporal lobe but rather the complete objectNE which is activated during visual recognition of a particular object, and which is again re-activated during recall of that object from memory. Of course this model is a bit of an oversimplification, but it's a good starting point, and it holds true at least in some experimental paradigms (as discussed below). In Kreiman's experiment, this means that when a patient saw the picture of a baseball, the baseball's objectNE activated to fire synchronously yielding a perception of the baseball; when the subject's eyes were closed and the image of the baseball was recalled, it was recalled by activating the same objectNE to fire synchronously, which again yielded a perception of the baseball.

As mentioned above, Kreiman's experiment is part of a growing body of scientific experimental evidence that supports the notion that visual recognition and memory recall share underlying neural processes: object perception is mediated by activation of the same objectNE, independently of whether the physical or recalled object is perceived. Let's take a quick look at some other notable experimental evidence that supports this seminal notion:

Researchers led by Hagar Gelbard-Sagiv and Itzhak Fried recorded from hundreds of neurons in and around the hippocampus of 13 epilepsy patients [92]. As in the Kreiman experiment, the patients were undergoing operations to treat epilepsy. In the course of the operation, surgeons had to introduce electrodes into the brain in order to locate the source of the seizures. During the experiment, the patients were shown a number of short (10 second) television clips consisting of audiovisual sequences. The first time the patients saw the clips, some of their neurons were selectively activated only by certain episodes and not by others. For example, one patient's neurons were activated by a clip from *The Simpsons* but not by any other clip including a clip of Michael Jordan playing basketball. As discussed in the previous section, this means that the researchers were able to find just one of the neurons which is part of the objectNE that encodes *The Simpsons*. Since the objectNE representing *The Simpsons* is different from the one representing Michael Jordan, the scientists were able to record from the single neurons that were exclusively part of one of the objectNE pyramids and not the other.

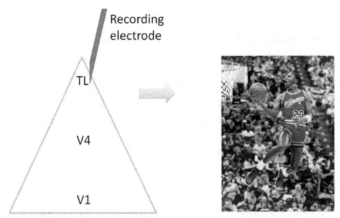

Activation of the neuronal ensemble pyramid encoding
Michael Jordan results in recall of *Michael Jordan*.

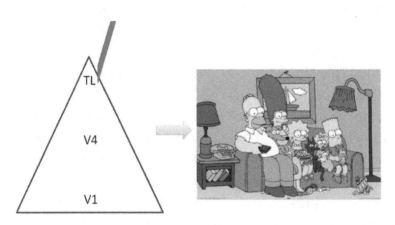

Activation of the neuronal ensemble pyramid encoding
the *Simpsons* results in recall of the *Simpsons*.

Figure 2.6 Activation of an objectNE results in perception of that object.
The patients were shown a number of short television clips consisting of
audiovisual sequences. The first time the patients saw the episodes, some of
the neurons in the hippocampus were selectively activated only by certain
episodes and not by others. For example, some neurons were activated by a
clip from *The Simpsons* but not by a clip of Michael Jordan playing basketball.
In other words, the objectNE representing *The Simpsons* was different from
the one representing Michael Jordan, and the scientists were able to record
from the single neurons that were part of one objectNE pyramid and not the
other.

Note that during these operations, only local anesthesia was used. No general anesthesia is needed because the brain does not have pain receptors. Subjects remained conscious and completely aware of their environment. As a result, most patients were able to easily remember nearly all of the clips and were able to verbally describe the content of the clips. Several minutes after showing the episodes, the researchers asked the patients to recall the clips as they came to mind. The sequence of recalled episodes was freely chosen by the patient and therefore random. Scientists continued to record the neuronal activity during the free recall and observed that **the same neurons that were active during the viewing of a particular clip would be reactivated just before the recall of that particular clip**. The neuronal activity in the temporal lobe was able to predict which clip the patient would talk about next. The neurons active during The Simpsons clip were reactivated a second or two before the verbal recall of The Simpsons clip. The neurons active during the Michael Jordan episode were reactivated a second or two before the verbal recall of the Michael Jordan episode. In other words, the scientists were able to observe the formation of a mental image represented by an objectNE corresponding to a particular episode, and a few seconds later listened to the patient describing the content of that mental image.

The experiments discussed above were limited in that they were only able to record the activity of single neurons, a few at a time. Recording from multiple electrodes positioned to cover most cells of an objectNE is not possible because such an intrusive setup would obviously be detrimental for the patient. This limitation in human experiments is overcome by the use of functional magnetic resonance imaging, commonly known as fMRI. The fMRI device makes images showing the location of increased blood-flow, which is normally associated with increased neuronal activity. Let's take a look at some experiments that use fMRI imaging to record the activity in the brain:

Researchers Leila Reddy, Naotsugu Tsuchiya, and Thomas Serre used fMRI scans in their experiment which set out to answer three important questions about the nature of neuronal activity during both visual recognition and visual recall [93]. First of all, the researchers asked if it was possible to determine what kind of object someone was imagining simply by observing their neuronal activity. In other words, can we tell if someone is imaging a tool as opposed to a face? Secondly, the researchers wondered whether the same regions of the temporal cortex were active during viewing and imagining of a particular category of objects. Finally, and most importantly, the researchers were interested in determining whether visually perceived and imagined objects actually shared the same neuronal pathways within the ventral temporal cortex.

The subjects in this study were 10 healthy individuals (in contrast to the studies discussed above, where subjects were patients with epilepsy). Each subject underwent fMRI scans while performing both visual recognition tasks and memory recall tasks (recalling mental images of objects from memory). During the visual recognition task, subjects viewed common images of objects from the following four categories: tools, food, famous people, and famous buildings. For example, the "food" category consisted of images of fruits and vegetables, such as an apple, a banana, and a tomato. During the memory recall task, subjects were asked to recall detailed mental images of a specific object, such as an apple, upon hearing the name of that object ("apple") through a set of headphones.

The researchers were successful in answering all three of their questions. First of all, they observed that it is possible to determine which category of objects someone was imagining simply by observing the neuronal activity in the ventral-temporal cortex. In addition, the authors were able to conclude that the same region in the temporal cortex is responsive during both the viewing of objects in a particular category, and the recall of objects within the same category. Finally, the authors found that largely the same neuronal patterns were activated during both visual recognition and memory recall of the same object categories. It is interesting to note that these results were more substantial for objects from the "famous people" and the "famous buildings" categories than from the "food" and "tools" categories.

In a similar experiment, Radoslaw M. Cichy and colleagues from the Bernstein Center for Computational Neuroscience used a combination of fMRI and multivariate pattern classification to assess whether recall and recognition encode the category of objects in a similar fashion [94]. Their results indicated that the fMRI response patterns for different categories of recalled objects could be used to predict the fMRI response patterns for viewed objects.

In yet another experiment, Isabelle Klein and colleagues asked six subjects to visualize *bow tie* patterns. These patterns were oriented either vertically or horizontally. Once again, the activation of the visual cortex was monitored by fMRI. The pattern of activation during the visualization task closely matched the pattern of activation during visual recognition of similar objects. The patterns of visual cortex activation differed significantly between the horizontal and the vertical imagined stimuli, and "colocalized with the horizontal and vertical visual field meridians, as determined for each individual using a retinotopic localizer task" [95].

The results of these studies, as well as additional studies listed in Appendix 4, support the hypothesis that the mental activity involved in the process of viewing an object and recalling the same object with eyes closed is largely the same.

Or, as Jared F. Danker and John R. Anderson from Carnegie Mellon University put it, "Remembering an episode involves literally returning to the brain state that was present during that episode" [96]. In fact, this seems to be a fundamental principle of the brain across motor and sensory modalities: neural processes that underlie motor and sensory perception are also used in imagery of that modality. The experimental evidence is summarized in Table 1.1.

MODALITY	EXPERIMENTAL EVIDENCE
Motor	Mental rehearsal of a movement - that is, the use of visual imagery to plan a movement - invokes the same patterns of activity in the premotor and posterior parietal cortical areas as those that occur during the actual performance of the movement. For example, since the right motor cortex is responsible for raising your left arm, when you simply *imagine* raising your left arm (but do not actually raise it), it is the right motor cortex which is activated [97]. In another experiment, pianists who played music on a silent keyboard activated the same part of their brain as when they simply imagined playing the music [98].
Somato-sensory	Real and imagined cutaneous stimulation activates similar areas of primary and higher-level somatosensory areas [99].
Auditory	The same activity that occurs in the temporal lobe when a person hears a word or a phrase being spoken, also occurs when the person simply imagines that same word or phrase being spoken [100].
Visual - faces	Cortical area activated during visual presentation of faces was also activated during the recall of those faces [93,94]. Patients who are impaired at face recognition often have difficulty imagining faces [101,102].

Table 1.1 A summary of experimental evidence illustrating the principle of brain organization across motor and sensory modalities. Neural processes that underlie motor and sensory perception are also used in imagery of that modality.

Visual - buildings	Cortical area activated during visual presentation of famous buildings was also activated during recall of those buildings [93,94].
Visual - tools	Cortical area activated during visual recognition of tools was also activated during recall of those tools [93].
Visual - food items	Cortical area activated during visual presentation of food items was also activated during recall of those food items [93].
Visual objects - other	Individual neurons increased their firing rate when a subject saw a picture of an object such as a baseball and also when the subject recalled the same object [81]. An fMRI study confirmed that the patterns of visual cortex activation differed significantly between the horizontally and the vertically visualized bow tie, and "colocalized with the horizontal and vertical visual field meridians, as determined for each individual using a retinotopic localizer task" [95]. Parallel deficits were reported in mental image formation and in visual recognition in patients with brain damage [103].
Visual - motion	Visual motion cortical area MT is activated during observation and imagery of moving stimuli [104].
Video clips	Individual neurons increased their firing rate when a subject saw a video clip and also when the subject recalled the same video clip [92].

The relationship between mental imagery and perception across auditory, motor, and visual modalities was reviewed in great detail by Stephen Kosslyn, the chair of the Department of Psychology at Harvard University [103]. The authors conclude that there is converging evidence that, "most of the neural processes that underlie like-modality perception are also used in imagery; and imagery, in many ways, can 'stand in' for (re-present, if you will) a perceptual stimulus or situation. Imagery not only engages the motor system, but also affects the body, much as can actual perceptual experience."

What is the importance of this conclusion? The two processes — visual recognition and imagery — were thought to be disparate since the time of Descartes. Descartes, in his *Passions of the Soul* and *The Description of the Human Body*, suggested that the body works like a machine and that it has material properties. The mind (or soul), on the other hand, was described as being nonmaterial and therefore not following the laws of nature. Though we have come far in our understanding of both the body and mind since the time of Descartes, some of the biases laid out in his work have remained with us to this day. Accordingly, visual recognition (a function of the body) was normally studied by neuroscientists, while subjective imagery (a function of the soul) was primarily studied by psychologists. [d] Recent understanding that visual recognition of a physical object and recall of the same object from memory activate substantially the same objectNE may have a powerful effect on

---

[d] The body mind distinction also resonates in medicine, where we have two different fields for treating brain disease. Neurology mostly deals with motor and perceptual abnormalities that are considered to be "body " problems. Psychiatry, on the other hand, mostly deals with the problems of the "mind." In reality, there is no biological reason to divide brain science.

scientific progress toward understanding of the human mind.[e]

Now that the cortical location of neurons involved in the formation of mental images[f] has been established, the next chapter will discuss the pattern of neuronal activity necessary for conscious awareness of those images. There is strong evidence that for a subject to be consciously aware of any experience (including mental images), neurons representing that experience must fire synchronously.

---

[e] Looking back at the history of science one can see that similar unification theories of phenomena previously thought to be unrelated have heralded some of the greatest breakthroughs in science. For example, in the mid 19th century light was considered completely unrelated to other electromagnetic phenomena. While lecturing at Kings College in 1862, James Clerk Maxwell calculated that the speed of propagation of an electromagnetic field is approximately that of the speed of light. He considered this to be more than just a coincidence, and commented, "We can scarcely avoid the conclusion that light consists in the transverse undulations of the same medium which is the cause of electric and magnetic phenomena." Working on the problem further, Maxwell showed that the equations predict the existence of waves of oscillating electric and magnetic fields that travel through empty space at a speed that could be predicted from simple electrical experiments. In his 1864 paper "A dynamical theory of the electromagnetic field," Maxwell wrote, "The agreement of the results seems to show that light and magnetism are affections of the same substance, and that light is an electromagnetic disturbance propagated through the field according to electromagnetic laws." Understanding that X-rays, light, thermal radiation, microwave radiation and radio waves had the same underlying mechanism greatly facilitated development of our understanding of all electromagnetic phenomena.

[f] One interesting question is whether or not each recalled image activates a complete objectNE. Specifically, when one is asked to remember a scene and to describe it verbally, does one always activate a complete objectNE pyramid comprised of neurons in the temporal lobe, V4, V2, and V1? It seems that the selective neurons at the top of the pyramid are essential for perception of an object. It is possible, however, that the neurons at the base of the pyramid are not always activated in the recall process but only when the mind focuses on finer details of the vivid mental image. The question of whether or not V1 directly contributes to visual consciousness is not critical for our discussion.

2.4 Neuronal binding by synchronization

Until the 1990s, the brain was viewed as a collection of neurons that fire in asynchrony. The synchronous firing of cortical neurons was only associated with epileptic seizures (wavelike electrical activity of a large number of neurons, often associated with a loss of consciousness and involuntary body movement). New evidence indicates that neurons often communicate by firing near-synchronous action potentials (for a review see [105]. This proposal has evolved from the evidence that cortical neurons, when engaged in processing, often get entrained into oscillatory activity [106]. Distinct networks of inhibitory interneurons serve as pacemakers for these oscillations [107]. The synchronous firing is thought to be involved in binding neurons of a neuronal ensemble together (again following the principle of "fire together - wire together"). This hypothesis is referred to as "binding-by-synchronization" [108].

There is a significant body of experimental data consistent with the "binding-by-synchronization" hypothesis [109]. For example, Andreas K. Engel and colleagues reported direct observation of synchronicity of neurons belonging to a single object. The investigators recorded from multiple neurons in the primary visual cortex of a cat. They observed that two neurons synchronized their firing *only* when their activating stimulus belonged to a single object [110]. In other words, neurons synchronized *only* when they were part of the same neuronal ensemble.

Converging data were obtained by Hirabayashi and Miyashita from the University of Tokyo's. The scientists recorded activity of pairs of neurons located in the inferior temporal cortex (responsible for face recognition) in alert monkeys [111]. The monkeys were shown pictures from two different sets. In the first set, the nose, mouth, and eyes were organized into a face-like combination. In the second set, the facial fragments - nose, mouth, and eyes - were shown scrambled up (e.g. mouth could be on top, nose on the left, one eye on the bottom, and another eye on the right). The neurons were selected in such a way that both cells in a pair responded significantly to facial fragments shown one at a time. Thus both neurons would significantly increase their activity when presented with either the face-like pictures or the scrambled face pictures. Was there any difference in the neuronal activity between the face-like pictures and a scrambled collection of facial features? The study found that there was no difference in terms of firing rate, but a clear difference was observed in the *timing* of the neuronal firing: neurons responding to the features transiently synchronized their responses when the monkeys recognized that the component features of a face actually formed a face. Thus, the neuronal firing phase was modulated by the feature configuration in a face-like picture, whereas the firing rates did not reveal configuration-dependent bias. In other words, the recognition that component features of a face formed an actual face was associated with the synchronization of neurons encoding the individual facial features.

The synchronous firing of neurons may be controlled on both the local and global levels [112]. On the local level, groups of neurons within one cortical area often synchronize in order to "vote on a particular issue." In this case, local groups of neurons undergo low amplitude depolarization waves with a frequency of around 40 Hz (range: 30 to 100 Hz). These waves are called gamma-frequency waves or, simply, gamma waves. The gamma wave depolarization does not make each neuron in the local group fire an action potential. However, neurons are more likely to fire an action potential at the peak of the depolarization wave because, at the peak, the threshold for action potential firing is reduced. This mechanism ensures that voting neurons fire action potentials at the same time.

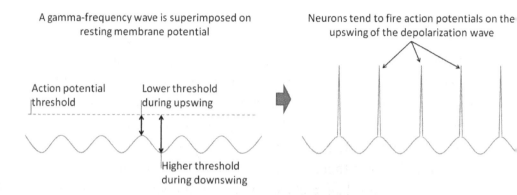

Figure 2.7 Cortical depolarization waves promote synchronous firing of neurons by influencing the timing of action potentials. When a gamma-frequency wave is superimposed on the resting membrane potential, neurons are more likely to fire action potentials on the upswing of the depolarization wave.

One may wonder: how can the brain operate on such a fast time scale? When thinking about this question, consider the body's ability to control movement. A tennis player needs to coordinate hand movement down to the millisecond in order to hit the ball in the correct direction. Other activities such as batting, juggling, and driving are no less demanding. The execution of such precisely coordinated movements indicates that the brain is able to accurately time the activity of groups of neurons. In fact there are numerous examples of neuronal networks capable of submillisecond precision.

2.5 Global synchronization

In addition to the local depolarization wave, a global wave with a frequency of 16 Hz (range: 15 to 25 Hz) ensures effective communication between neurons in different cortical areas (analogous to a company-wide meeting). This wave is called a beta-frequency wave. Both beta-frequency and gamma-frequency cortical neuron synchronizations are observed for consciously perceived stimuli [113,114] and for conscious perception in binocular rivalry [115,116]. These findings have inspired the hypotheses that synchronized oscillations play a role in consciousness [99,117,118]. In fact, there is strong experimental evidence that conscious perception is associated with the global synchronization of objectNEs in the beta-frequency. Pejman Sehatpour used intracranial electrodes to record from three human subjects (who were undergoing medical tests for intractable epilepsy) as they performed a challenging visual object recognition task that required them to identify barely recognizable fragmented line-drawings of common objects. Neuronal activity recorded during the "recognition" moment (also called *perceptual closure*) was compared to the "non-recognition" event when scrambled (nonsensical) versions of the same images were shown [119]. Sehatpour and colleagues simultaneously recorded from several areas thought to be involved in visual recognition: the occipitotemporal cortex, the prefrontal cortex, and the hippocampus. The analysis showed a robust coherence in the beta-band between all three brain areas when participants recognized the fragmented images. In contrast, when scrambled versions of the same images were presented, a significantly lower coherence was observed. These results suggest that object-encoding neuronal ensembles are distributed through the posterior cortex and that neurons of the ensemble synchronize when the encoded object is consciously perceived.

Similar results were recorded by Eugenio Rodríguez, in a study that focused on the perception of 'Mooney' faces, high-contrast pictures of a human faces which are easily recognized as faces when presented upright orientation, but usually seen as meaningless black and white shapes when presented upside-down [120]. An electroencephalogram (EEG) was used to record from healthy human subjects. A consistent pattern of synchrony was established during face recognition around 200 ms after presentation of an upright face. This synchrony corresponds to the synchronization between the neurons of the neuronal ensemble of the face. When the upside-down faces were presented, the faces were not recognized and no synchrony was observed.

Convergent results have been reported by Joerg F. Hipp, who used high-density EEG recordings from human subjects to analyze the synchronization of cortical networks [121]. EEG electrodes are placed on the surface of the skull and can cover the entire skull. The authors developed a new analysis method that allows an unbiased search for synchronized networks across the *entire* human brain. The subjects' task was to judge the configuration of an ambiguous stimulus which consisted of two bars that approach, briefly overlap and move apart from each other. The perception of this stimulus spontaneously alternates between two distinct alternatives. In half of the trials, the two bars are perceived as two independent objects passing one another. In the other half of trials, the two bars are perceived as a single object with bouncing sides.

Note that while perception is drastically different between the trials, there is no difference in the visual information presented to the subject's eyes. The difference in perception therefore must come from integration of the two bars into a single object. Encoding two independent moving bars may be accomplished by neurons in the extrastriate cortex. On the other hand, integration of the two moving bars into a single bouncing object (think of a slinky) is expected to involve a significantly greater number of neurons distributed over multiple areas of the cortex. In fact, Hipp's analysis revealed a highly structured cortical network comprised of the extrastriate cortex, as well as the posterior parietal, temporal and prefrontal cortex, which showed enhanced beta rhythm synchrony during stimulus processing. More importantly, the synchronicity between regions in beta frequency predicted the subjects' perception of the stimulus even on a single-trial level. In other words, when beta frequency synchronization was enhanced, subjects were more likely to perceive the same sensory stimulus as a single bouncing object (encoded by a single synchronized neuronal ensemble) rather than two bars passing each other (encoded by two independent unsynchronized neuronal ensembles).

In summary, there is significant experimental evidence that long-range synchronization of neurons encoding an object plays an important role in the binding of multiple features into one integrated percept. This integration is involuntary. It is driven by the resonant activation of the objectNE stored in memory as enhanced connections between neurons of the ensemble. The complete objectNE of the baseball is automatically activated and the baseball is perceived whether the recollection is triggered by seeing a partially visible baseball, hearing about a baseball, or just thinking of a baseball. The complete objectNE of the baseball is activated because the neurons of the ensemble have preexisting enhanced connections.

In the next chapter, I will discuss a different process in which two objectNEs with no preexisting enhanced connections between them are voluntarily synchronized into a single percept.

Chapter 3: Prefrontal Synthesis

Imagination is the cornerstone of creativity. It's pretty hard to conceive that anyone could be creative without a rich imagination.

ANTONIO DAMASIO, *A panel on creativity and the brain at the Society for Neuroscience's annual meeting, San Diego* (2013)

3.1 Combinations of mental objects

Close your eyes and imagine your favorite cup somewhere where you have never seen it before: standing on top of your computer's keyboard.

Figure 3.1 What happens in your brain when you imagine a new mental image? Recalling the image of the cup or the image of a keyboard one at a time does not produce a new image of a cup standing on top of the keyboard. Some magical event must happen in the brain for you to perceive the cup and the keyboard together in one mental frame.

What happens in your brain when you imagine this new, never-before-seen mental image? Let's take a closer look:

Well, the first part is undisputed: you recall an image of your favorite cup (step 1) by activating the objectNE of the cup. The second step is also undisputed: you recall an image of the keyboard by activating the objectNE of the keyboard. But recalling one of these images at a time does not produce a new image of a cup standing on top of the keyboard. Some magical event must happen in the brain in order for you to perceive the cup and the keyboard together in one mental frame. This monograph is based on the hypothesis that this magical event involves the synchronization of the objectNE of the cup with the objectNE of the keyboard [122]. **The cup is perceived standing on top of the keyboard only when the objectNE of the cup and the objectNE of the keyboard fire at the same time at least once (the Neuronal Ensembles Synchronization hypothesis or NES [123]).**

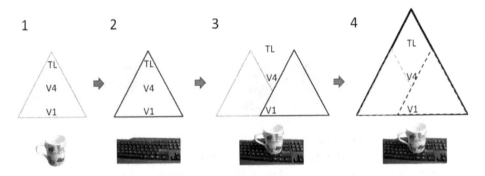

Figure 3.2 Imagination of the cup on top of the keyboard:

Step 1: Recall of the cup: the brain activates the ensemble of neurons representing the cup to fire synchronous actions potentials. The cup is perceived.

Step 2: Recall of the keyboard: the brain activates the ensemble of neurons representing the keyboard to fire synchronous actions potentials. The keyboard is perceived.

Step 3: The two objectNEs are synchronized together by the prefrontal cortex. At that moment a new, never-before-seen mental image of the cup on top of the keyboard is perceived.

Step 4: The connections between the synchronously activated neurons are strengthened and, thus, the new objectNE representing the cup on top of the keyboard is formed (black pyramid). This ensemble will be stored in memory and can be activated at a later time as one unit.

The NES hypothesis predicts that synchronization of objectNEs is fundamental to both involuntary and voluntary imagination. The vivid and bizarre novel mental scenes perceived during dreaming involve **involuntary spontaneous synchronization of objectNEs**. Voluntary juxtaposition of mental objects (e.g., the cup on the keyboard) involves synchronization of objectNEs that is purposefully intentionally orchestrated by the lateral prefrontal cortex.

To emphasize the role of the lateral prefrontal cortex in the process of voluntary juxtaposition of mental objects, I named it *prefrontal synthesis* or PFS. PFS is the process we use to imagine the cup on top of the keyboard, an apple on top of a whale, a sofa on top of an armchair or any other never-before-seen image that is described to us. For example, as you read a fictional book such as "Pinocchio," and get to the part where Pinocchio is swallowed by the Terrible Shark, your mind actively imagines a wooden boy inside a shark. This is a brand new, never-before-seen image freshly created in your mind (unless, of course, you have actually seen such an illustration). In order to manufacture an image of Pinocchio inside a shark, your mind had to synthesize a brand new image by synchronizing the objectNEs of Pinocchio with that of a shark. Since you could not simply recall such an image (having never seen it before), you must have used PFS to construct it.

PFS feels easy and natural to us, since it is something we do all the time. PFS makes it possible for us to read a work of fiction as we synchronize disparate objectNEs into an entire mental movie that we have never actually seen before. PFS makes it possible for us to plan out how the furniture should be arranged in the room, how to rebuild the house, or what new path to take on our way to work. PFS allows us to imagine things that we cannot physically see, such as the structure of DNA, the model of an atom, and nuclear chain reaction.

3.2 Definition of prefrontal synthesis

Prefrontal synthesis (PFS) is the voluntary process of juxtaposing mental objects. The NES hypothesis predicts that PFS is mediated by the prefrontal cortex-dependent synchronization of two or more objectNEs.

What is the difference between PFS and imagination, fantasizing, and mental imagery? Imagination, fantasizing and mental imagery are all defined as the experience of perceiving objects or events when those objects or events are not real but occur in the mind. However, imagination, fantasizing, and mental imagery do not necessarily require the creation of a new mental image. They may simply be a recollection from memory of something already seen. While recalling an image from memory only requires activating a single objectNE, PFS requires the additional step of synchronizing two or more objectNEs, thus combining the recalled images into a unique and novel creation. The process of synchronization is mediated by the lateral prefrontal cortex that changes the timing of the firing of one objectNE in order to synchronize it with the firing of another objectNE.

Furthermore, remembering an image that your mind had synthesized in the past and memorized, does not involve PFS either. Once an image comprising several objectNEs has been synthesized (in the past), the connections between neurons become stronger and a new objectNE is formed. Thus, when you now think of a mermaid, you simply activate the objectNE for mermaid, even though originally (the first time you heard of a mermaid) you have synchronized the ensemble of a fish with the ensemble of a woman. Similarly with Pinocchio inside a shark (or any other composite image): once you think about this scene, it becomes its own objectNE building block that you can use to make more and more complicated images (e.g. you can picture a mermaid holding Pinocchio inside a shark's belly).

Additionally, as discussed above, imagination, fantasizing, and mental imagery can be involuntary (i.e. lateral prefrontal cortex-independent). Critically, PFS always includes voluntary (i.e. lateral prefrontal cortex-dependent) synthesis of new mental images.

PFS is also a distinct component of executive function. Conventionally, executive functions include inhibition and attention, working memory, and cognitive flexibility – all mediated by the lateral prefrontal cortex [124]. PFS is also mediated by the lateral prefrontal cortex [21,23-27], but the mechanism of PFS is different from inhibition, attention and working memory, that do not involve synchronization of multiple objectNEs. PFS is also different from cognitive flexibility that is commonly investigated using task-switching and set-shifting tests [124]. Such tests, e.g., Wisconsin Card Sorting Task, involve category-sorting rules identification, that do not require the synchronization of objectNEs and visuospatial synthesis of PFS.

PFS is also different from abstract thinking. There is no clear definition of abstract thinking on either a psychological or a neurological level. When abstract thinking is defined narrowly as "the process of generalization by reducing the information content of a concept or an observable phenomenon," it is clearly very different from PFS. One does not need abstract concepts to perform PFS. For example when you imagine your favorite cup standing on top of your computer's keyboard, you use PFS to integrate the mental image of the cup with the mental image of the keyboard. You did not imagine an abstract cup but a very specific one. On the neurological level, you synchronized the objectNE representing the cup with the objectNE representing the keyboard. For this to happen, you do not need the neuronal representation of an abstract cup or an abstract keyboard. Defined narrowly, abstract thinking has nothing to do with PFS. However, abstract thinking can also be understood more broadly as a mental process detached from physical reality. In that case abstract thinking is in fact close in its meaning to imagination and mental imagery which include both PFS and memory recollection.

The closest scientific term I have been able to find in literature that has the same meaning as PFS is "future thinking" [125]. The logic goes that since one cannot "recall" the future, thinking about the future always involves synthesizing new images. This sounds like a valid philosophical argument, but neurologically it may not always be true for two reasons. 1) Suppose you are thinking of coming back to your hometown and visiting your childhood house. While this experience may be charged by new emotions, it is possible that no new juxtapositions of mental objects are created in the process. Rather, the brain is just recalling your childhood memory of the house. 2) If future thinking occurs in dreaming it is involuntary (i.e. the lateral prefrontal cortex-independent) and thus has nothing to do with the process of PFS. For example, a person with PFS paralysis can dream about the future. Thus, "future thinking" may not *always* involve PFS.

To discuss human evolution rigorously we must avoid ambiguous definitions of imagination. Thus, we will stick to the strict definition of PFS based on neuroscience.

3.3 External manifestations of prefrontal synthesis

PFS permeates through just about every aspect of human behavior and is an integral part of many of our everyday tasks. Below, I will discuss nine commonly exhibited external manifestations of PFS:

1. Language: When we speak we use PFS to describe a novel image ("My house is the second one on the left, just across the road from the red gate") and we rely on the listener to use PFS in order to visualize the novel image.

2. Storytelling: When we tell stories, we are often describing things that the listener has never seen before ("That creature has three heads, two tails and can run faster than a cheetah") and we rely on the listener to imagine the story in their mind's eye.

3. Active Teaching: When we teach, we do so actively, using language ("Imagine you have 5 cookies. You eat 2 of them.

How many do you have left?") and we rely on the student's ability to use PFS to mentally simulate the instructions, construct a new mental image, and arrive at an answer.

4. Figurative art: We use PFS to create novel objects of art that look like real objects.

5. Creativity and Innovation: We use PFS to engineer new objects such as car engines, drug molecules, and nuclear reactors.

6. Design and Construction: We use PFS to create a plan that will allow us to make new objects (such as a house) or to consider a new configuration (such as whether a new piece of furniture will fit in our living room).

7. Natural Sciences: As we actively seek to understand the forces in the natural world, we use PFS to create models, often for phenomena that are invisible to us (such as the atomic model, nuclear chain reaction, model of DNA, etc.)

8. Strategy Games: As we grow older, our games become more complex. We continue exercising our imagination through chess, Sudoku and crosswords.

9. Religion: We use PFS to create an imaginary world that answers the questions: Why? and How?

3.4 All human languages facilitate communication of novel images

Let's first take a look at language. All human languages allow the speaker to create novel mental images in the mind of a listener. If I were to ask you to picture the house you live in, you would simply recall an image that you have seen countless times. If, however, I were to ask you to picture an elephant standing on top of the roof of the house you live in, you could not rely on simple recall, but would instead need to create, or synthesize, the image in your mind. As discussed above, this process involves you recalling the image of an elephant, then recalling the image of your house, and finally synthesizing a new mental image of the elephant on top of your house. This is just one example of how I am able to use language to direct synthesis of a new image in your mind from images that you already have in your memory.

Let's try another example. Imagine the number seventy-seven. Now, flip the first digit horizontally and move the two digits together until their edges are connected. What does the newly synthesized figure look like? Don't yet read the answer. Try to synthesize the new image from the two parts.

example of horizontal flipping

Figure 3.3 An example of horizontal flipping

Answer: the new mental image should look like a triangle. Note, that again, I was able to use language to manipulate your mind into creating a new mental image in the process of PFS.

Similarly, I can make you imagine a word by spelling it out one letter at a time (no writing allowed, of course, since my goal is to have you *synthesize* the word in your mind). Let's try it. Imagine an H. Now add an O, then a U, an S, and finally an E. I have just used language to synthesize the complete word in your mind. One thing that is important to notice is that, unlike the first example where you imagined something that you probably have never seen before, in the second and third examples you have seen the final image (a triangle and the word "HOUSE") numerous times. All three examples, however, required PFS, since you had to synchronize separate objectNEs until one cohesive image emerged.

Language allows us to communicate things that we have never seen: you can read about and understand the complex structure of the brain, the organization of distant stars, the physical model of the universe and the structure of DNA, amongst countless other things. As a teacher of human physiology, I use words to help my students take the images that they already have stored in their memories and synthesize them into new images. My students then use these new images to practice medicine, so, hopefully these new images are put to good use.

We often use words to describe to our listeners something that they have never seen. When you recount last night's football game to a friend who missed the match, you try to portray a play-by-play picture that they have not seen but must imagine. When you describe a particularly long throw that was intercepted by the opposing team at their 20 yard line, you rely on your friend to recall previously seen images (such as the quarterback, the intercepting defender, the ball, and the position on the field) and then to synthesize a new image based on *your* story. Moreover, the image is most likely not a static snapshot, but rather a mental movie that was assembled based on your story, and which your friend can literally watch in his or her mind. In fact, some people actually prefer to follow a game over the radio, rather than watching it on TV. Similarly, many people prefer *reading* a fictional story to watching a film adaptation. Reading, of course, relies primarily on PFS: to understand what you are reading, you must create a running "movie picture" in your mind as you go through the text.

Using words for the transmission of novel images is analogous to moving a building to a new location. The images (just like buildings) are transmitted piece by piece with little degradation. I was once involved in moving a log house. We numbered each log, disassembled the house at the old location, then moved all the logs one by one, and then reassembled them into an identical building at the new location.

Similarly, to describe a theatre to someone who has never seen one, I would go through the same kind of process. First I would imagine a theatre, and mentally disassemble the image into the following fragments: (1) the stage, (2) the orchestra pit, and (3) the seating area in a large hall. Then I would use words to transfer the fragments to the mind of my listener, one fragment at a time. I would say: "a theatre consists of (1) a stage on which actors perform, (2) an orchestra pit where musicians play their musical instruments, and (3) a large hall, from where spectators are watching the performance." The listener imagines these three images one at a time, and then assembles them into a complete mental image of a theatre. The newly formed image can now be stored in his memory. When he visits a theatre at a later time, he will be able to recognize the theatre from the image stored in his memory, even though it may not be exactly as he imagined.

Clearly, words, which constitute the communication system of the language, evolved to be tools for synthesis of new images in a listener's mind. As Steven Pinker put it, "the speaker has a thought, makes a sound, and counts on the listener to hear the sound and to recover that thought" [126]. The evolutionary benefit of a communication system capable of synthesizing novel images in the mind of a listener seems obvious. It complements PFS in communicating an action plan. It is not enough for me to simply imagine a new and creative animal trap. If I cannot build the trap on my own, I need to explain my mental plan to my fellow hunters, so we can build the trap together (by digging a deep pit, for example, and camouflaging it with twigs and branches, so that an unwitting animal would fall right in). In other words, after I use PFS to come up with a worthwhile plan, I then have to use a communication system in order to converse my plan to my buddies, who must mentally synthesize an image of the new trap as well as understand the step-by-step process of building it. To communicate my idea, I can use gestures, signs or words — the exact means of communication are not important. What's important is that the communication system should effectively transfer any number of novel images from the mind of the speaker to the mind of the listener. To accomplish this goal, the communication systems of all human languages have a set of common properties, or as Charles F. Hockett put it "design features," of language [127]. Let us quickly look at some of these common properties.

3.5 Semantically-reversible sentences is the hallmark of all human languages

The existence of semantically-reversible sentences is an essential quality of *all* human languages. A change in the word-order often completely changes the image synthesized in the mind of a listener upon hearing the words. Consider the following two sentences:

-The cat ate the mouse.

-The mouse ate the cat.

The sentences use identical words and the same grammatical structure. Appreciating the drama of the first sentence and the absurdity of the second sentence depends on the lateral prefrontal cortex ability to synthesize the mental object of the cat and the mental object of the mouse into a novel scene. (Sentences in which swapping the subject and the object result in a new meaning are called semantically-reversible sentences. By contrast, in a nonreversible-sentence (e.g., "The boy writes a letter") swapping the subject and the object results in a sentence with no real meaning ("A letter writes the boy").

A simple exchange of two words in a sentence completely changes its meaning. The image synthesized in the mind as a result of the first sentence is that of a big cat that ate a small mouse. The image synthesized as a result of the second sentence is that of an abnormally large mouse that ate an abnormally small cat.

3.6 Prepositions exists in all human languages

Spatial prepositions (words such as *behind, in front of, on* and *under)* are a class of words that express the relationship of one object to another in space. Just like semantically-reversible sentences, prepositions facilitate the capacity of language to communicate an infinite number of novel images with a finite number of words. Children begin to understand prepositions between the ages of three and four. Given a cup and a bowl, a four year old child, following a command, is normally able to spatially arrange the objects on the table. They should be able to put:

- the bowl *behind* the cup
- the bowl *in front of* the cup
- the bowl *on top of* the cup
- the bowl *under* the cup

It is important to note that to accomplish the correct arrangement, the child first needs to simulate the process in her mind. She needs to mentally synthesize the novel image: for example, a bowl *behind* the cup by synchronizing the independent objectNEs of the bowl and the cup into one mental frame. After completing the mental simulation, the child can spatially arrange the physical objects into the structure that represents her mental image. Without PFS it would be impossible to understand the difference between the task of "putting a bowl *behind* a cup" and the task of "putting a bowl *in front of* the cup."

All human languages have spatial prepositions. In many languages (e.g. Korean, Japanese, Turkish, Hindi, and Urdu), prepositions come after the complement. However this does not change their role.

Semantically-reversible sentences, prepositions, adjectives, verb tenses, and other common elements of grammar, all facilitate the human ability to communicate an infinite number of novel images with the use of a finite number of words. One thousand nouns can communicate one thousand images to a listener. Adding just one spatial preposition allows for the formation of three-word phrases (such as: 'a bowl *behind* a cup' or 'a cup *behind* a bowl') and increases the number of distinct images that can be communicated to a listener from one thousand to one million.[g] Adding a second spatial preposition

---

[g] In general, the number of distinct images communicated by three-word

and allowing for five-word sentences of the form *object-preposition-object-preposition-object* (such as: a bowl *on* a cup *behind* a plate) increases the number of distinct images that can be communicated to four billion (1000x2x1000x2x1000). The addition of a third spatial preposition increases the number of distinct images to nine trillion, and so on. A typical language with 1000 nouns and 100 spatial prepositions can theoretically communicate 1000^{101} x 100^{100} distinct images. This number is significantly greater than the total number of atoms in the universe. For all practical purposes, an infinite number of distinct images can be communicated by a language with just 1000 words and a few prepositions.

Prepositions, adjectives, and verb tenses dramatically facilitate the capacity of a communication system with a finite number of words to communicate an infinite number of distinct images. To further increase the infiniteness of language we use recursive statements with nested explanations: e.g., "a snake on the boulder, to the left of the tall tree, that is behind the hill". Such statements force the interlocutor to use PFS to combine objects (a snake, the boulder, the tree, and the hill) into a novel scene. For this reason, linguists refer to modern full human languages as recursive languages.

The "infiniteness of this system has been explicitly recognized by Galileo, Descartes, and the 17th-century 'philosophical grammarians' and their successors, notably von Humboldt" [128]. The magic of using a finite number of words to communicate an infinite number of images completely depends on the PFS ability. A person lacking PFS ability is unable to construct novel mental images according to the rules imposed

---

sentences of the structure *object-preposition-object* equals the number of object-words times the number of prepositions times the number of object-words.

by spatial prepositions and, therefore, will not understand the meaning of spatial prepositions.

3.7 Recursive communication systems arise spontaneously in a group of humans

Communication systems used by humans around the world employ all kinds of tones, clicks, words, gestures and signs to describe objects. The Chinese language is tonal (the same word can have a different meaning just by varying the pitch); the Japanese language has a relatively small sound inventory and a pitch-accent system; the Khoisan languages of southern and eastern Africa are known for their use of click consonants as phonemes; the Jul'hoansi language, spoken by about 30,000 people in the northeast of Namibia, has five vowels, but these may be nasalized, glottalized, murmured, or any combination of these three. Of course sign languages do not rely on verbal expression at all, however they are full, complex, recursive languages, equivalent in all important aspects to spoken languages. While the signs used in human languages vary from language to language, the capacity to synthesize novel images in the mind of a listener is universal among all human languages.

Since the earliest recorded history, people have felt that the development of a new language by an isolated group of people could provide a window into the fundamental nature of all human languages. The Greek historian Herodotus conveyed a story about an experiment conducted by the Egyptian Pharaoh Psammetichus (664-610 BC). The Pharaoh gave two newborn babies into the care of a shepherd with the instructions that neither he nor anybody else should speak to either of the babies. The king was interested in finding out whether two children left alone and deprived of any external communication would develop their own language. In addition, Psammetichus sought to discover the origin of language. The shepherd was asked to listen to the children and to record their first words. According to the story, the children did in fact develop their own language and their first word was "bekos," which sounded like the Phrygian word for "bread." Thus, Psammetichus concluded that the Phrygians were an older people than the Egyptians, and that Phrygian was the original language of men. Though Herodotus' account may simply be a legend, he presents a valid scientific question: would a language arise spontaneously in an isolated group of people?

While such an experiment cannot be conducted for obvious reasons, there is in fact clear evidence that a recursive language arises spontaneously in any group of modern humans, even when the group is isolated from the outside world. For example, deaf children in Nicaragua were able to spontaneously develop an original sign language. In 1980, following the Sandinista revolution, the Nicaraguan government opened several vocational schools for deaf children. By 1983 there were over 400 students in the two schools. The school program emphasized spoken Spanish and lip reading, and discouraged the use of signs by teachers. The program failed and students were unable to learn the Spanish language in such a manner. However, the school provided fertile ground for deaf students to communicate with each other. In this process, children spontaneously generated a new recursive sign language. The school teachers were unaware of the developing sign language and considered the children's gesturing as mime. A failure to acquire the Spanish language triggered the teachers to call for help. By 1987, Dr. Judy Kegl, a linguist from MIT, arrived in Nicaragua and began to analyze the new sign language. Judy realized that the children had developed a language of great complexity, with verb agreement and other conventions of grammar [129-131].

The spontaneous development of a structured language has been observed in two other isolated deaf communities. In the early 18th century, the deaf community of Martha's Vineyard island spontaneously created their own sign language [132]. Unfortunately, this sign language disappeared over 60 years ago and was never properly described. Another example comes from an isolated endogamous Al-Sayyid Bedouin community with approximately 150 deaf individuals born within the past three generations, who have, over the past 70 years, also created their own distinct sign language. The Al-Sayyid Bedouin sign language was recently studied by Wendy Sandler and her colleagues. The researchers reported that the Al-Sayyid Bedouin sign language has "a conventionalized word order," and that signers "readily use their language to relate information beyond the here and now, such as descriptions of folk remedies and cultural traditions, some of which are no longer in force." The researchers have documented "personal histories of deaf members of the community and witnessed conversations about topics as diverse as social security benefits, construction techniques, and fertility" [133].

The spontaneous development of distinct recursive languages in Nicaragua, Martha's Vineyard, and amongst the Al-Sayyid Bedouin community is consistent with Noam Chomsky's theory that complex language is innate and will arise spontaneously in any group of humans. Noam Chomsky, the distinguished linguist at MIT, suggests that linguistic ability manifests itself without being purposefully taught, and that there are properties that all natural human languages share [128]. The neurological evidence presented in this monograph suggests that the innate and most important part of human language is PFS.

A species in which individual organisms are capable of PFS

would benefit immensely from being able to share and communicate novel images between individuals. Not surprisingly, all human languages are complex **recursive communication systems, that is, languages optimized for synthesizing never-before-seen images in the mind of a listener**. Three characteristics of all human communication systems are important in regards to PFS:

1. *Creation of novel images*: all human communication systems allow transmission of *novel* images from the mind of a speaker to the mind of a listener (i.e. images never-before-seen by the listener).

2. *High fidelity transmission*: enough details can be transmitted so that the image is not significantly degraded, that is, the image synthesized in the mind of a listener is similar to the original image in the mind of the speaker.

3. *Infinite number of images can be described by a finite number of words*. This is possible because changing the word order, adding prepositions, adjectives, and verb tenses can dramatically change the meaning of a sentence [128]. All human languages use complex grammar.

The following statement combines the three concepts: **all human communication systems allow *high fidelity transmission* of an *infinite* number of *novel* images with the use of a *finite* number of words**.

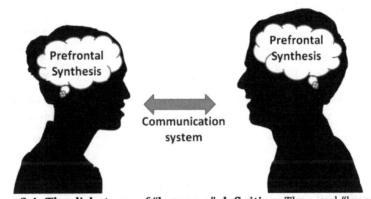

Figure 3.4 The dichotomy of "language" definition. The word "language" has highly divergent meanings in different contexts and disciplines. In informal usage, a language is usually understood as a culturally specific communication system: "Peter learned three new languages: German, French, and American Sign Language." On the other hand, in linguistics, the term "language" is used quite differently to refer to "an internal component of the mind/brain" [128] — the faculty that mainly corresponds to the process of PFS. Fitch, Hauser, & Chomsky [134] further explain the dichotomy of the "language" definition: "It rapidly became clear in the conversations leading up to HCF [128] that considerable confusion has resulted from the use of "language" to mean different things. We realized that positions that seemed absurd and incomprehensible, and chasms that seemed unbridgeable, were rendered quite manageable once the misunderstandings were cleared up. For many linguists, "language" delineates an abstract core of computational operations, central to language and probably unique to humans. For many biologists and psychologists, "language" has much more general and various meanings, roughly captured by "the communication system used by human beings." Neither of these explananda are more correct or proper, but statements about one of them may be completely inapplicable to the other." Thus for linguists, "language" primarily means the innate faculty of PFS, while for the general public "language" means a culturally acquired communication system, and for physiologists "language" can be a mixture of both. To avoid confusion, this monograph will differentiate between the two meanings of "language": 1) language as the process of PFS and 2) language as a culturally acquired communication system. PFS is defined as the ability to juxtapose mental objects at will (such as: an apple *on top of* a dolphin), while a culturally acquired communication system primarily involves knowing the meaning of individual words within a specific language (such as French or Latin). When one learns a new communications system (e.g. French or Latin), one learns new associations between words and images; the PFS ability is unchanged.

3.8 Prefrontal synthesis acquisition age

Recently, our group has developed and validated a 5 minute test for PFS called "Language Evaluation of Prefrontal Synthesis" or LEPS [37]. The 10-item LEPS test uses spatial prepositions and non-canonical syntax to present participants with a set of novel questions that children have never encountered before:

1) Give me a *small red* straw;
2) Put the *blue* cup inside the *red* cup;
3) Inside the *green* cup, put the *orange* cup;
4) Show me: the *monkey* ate the *lion*;
5) Show me: the *giraffe* was eaten by the *elephant*;
6) Put the *lion* on the *giraffe*;
7) Place the *monkey* on top of the *lion* and under the *giraffe*;
8) Imagine an *elephant* and a *chicken*. Which one is bigger?
9) If a *lion* was eaten by a *tiger*, which one is still alive?
10) Imagine the *green* cup inside the *red* cup, which cup is on top?

The sum of 10 items results in the LEPS total score that ranges from 0 (no PFS ability was demonstrated) to 10 (full PFS ability). LEPS test can be used to diagnose PFS paralysis and to monitor PFS acquisition. LEPS norms were calculated in 50 neurotypical children age 2 to 6 years [37]. All children older than 4 years received the LEPS score 7/10 or greater and all children younger than 3 received the LEPS score less than 3/10, indicating that PFS is acquired between the ages of 3 and 4 years.

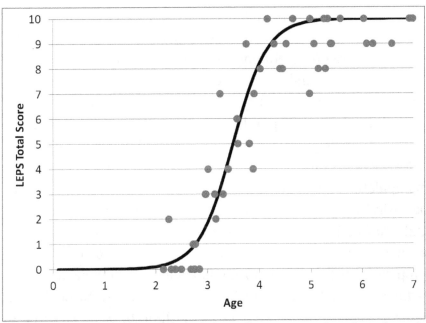

Figure 3.5 Scatter plot of the LEPS total score as a function of age in neurotypical children. Markers indicate LEPS total scores of individual children. Reprinted from Ref. [37].

3.9 Predilection for storytelling

Storytelling involves creating a story in the process of PFS and then sharing it with others by means of a communication system (listeners, of course, must also use PFS to understand the story). Most storytelling requires the listeners to imagine creatures and scenarios that they have never seen before [135]. This is especially true in fairy tales, which are filled with fantastical characters such as fairies, elves and mermaids. Therefore, storytelling is yet another major manifestation of PFS.

Greek mythology in particular is teeming with fantastical creatures, which interestingly are often hybrids of actual creatures. Greek mythological figures include fantastical hybrids such as the centaur (half-man, half-horse), the Chimera (a three headed monster which blends lion, goat and serpent into one monstrous creature), Hippocampi (sea creatures with the fore-parts of a horse and the tails of a fish) and many others. It's important to note that fairy tales and Greek myths were both widely circulated as a purely verbal tradition, without reliance on accompanying illustrations. Listeners had to imagine a never-before-seen creature in their mind's eye. Storytellers were manipulating the mental images of familiar creatures that would be easily recognizable to their listeners (such as a man, a horse, and a rooster) and combining them into creative hybrids such as a man-horse (the centaur), and horse-rooster (called Hippalectryon). Listeners formed new images in their minds by segmenting and synchronizing familiar images through the process of PFS. Fairy tales and Sci-Fi literature, by their very nature, describe objects, places and situations that the reader has never seen. Authors rely on readers' ability to use PFS to synthesize new images in their minds.

3.10 Active teaching

Kindergarten teachers and university professors employ PFS in the process of teaching: they talk and hope to synthesize new images in their students' minds. "An atom consists of a dense central nucleus surrounded by a cloud of negatively charged electrons." Students are familiar with an image of a cloud, so teachers use that image to aid students in forming the image of a cloud of electrons around a centrally located nucleus. "Gas in a closed container generates pressure because gas particles bombard the walls of the container similar to billiard balls." Teachers use their students' familiarity with billiards to explain the concept of gas pressure.

Parents warn a small child: "Do not cross the road without

me. A car may hit you." They expect the child to imagine the collision in hopes that the gruesome image will deter him from crossing by himself.

Before entering a fast-food restaurant, parents may have a dialog with a child: "What is the first thing you need to do after you enter Wendy's?" "Look for the line." "Then order food. What would you say?" "What would you say afterwards? Say thank you." After you place your food on the tray? Leave without bumping into the person behind you." PFS allows the child to prepare his action mentally.

When explaining an arithmetic problem to a child, parents also rely on the child's PFS. "How much is four minus one? ... Imagine mom has four apples. Then she gives one apple to your brother. How many apples does mom have now?" Parents expect the child to imagine his mom holding four apples by synchronizing objectNEs of mom and apples in one mental frame. Parents then expect him to imagine mom giving one apple away, and then to actually count the remaining apples in the resulting mental image.

Humans are rarely allowed to use any machinery without first mentally simulating the process. Student drivers have to learn the rules and pass the exam where they are tested on theoretical situations before they are allowed behind the wheel of a car.

When you have been driving a car for years and decide to receive a license for a motorcycle, you again will be asked to attend a series of lectures. An instructor will challenge your mind to simulate situations specific to motorcycle driving. Only after passing the theoretical course will you be allowed to drive an actual motorcycle.

Amongst humans, active teaching nearly always involves an instructor-guided simulation of the material in the process of PFS.

3.11 Figurative art

Now let's shift gears from the realm of verbal linguistic expression of PFS, to the realm of creativity in which we pursue manufacturing of tangible objects borne out of our imagination.

Consider some particularly striking examples of human artwork depicting objects that don't exist in nature and therefore could not have been seen by the artist who first created them.[h] The art world is brimming with fantastical, mythological creatures such as centaurs, dragons, cyclopes, and mermaids, amongst many other examples in both sculpture and painting. Let's take a closer look at the neurological activity involved in drawing one such imaginary creature: the centaur. Since live centaurs are notoriously difficult to come by, the image of a centaur must have been created in the artist's mind by fusing the image of a human upper body with an image of a horse's lower body. This never-before-seen image must have been *synthesized* in the artist's mind using the following recipe:

1) Recall an objectNE of a human and segment that objectNE into two objectNEs: one representing the upper body and one representing the lower body.
2) Recall the objectNE of a horse and segment that ensemble into an upper and lower body.
   ... and finally, here's where the magic happens:
3) Synchronize the ensemble representing the human upper body with the ensemble representing the horse's lower body.

———————————

[h] It is important to note that I am talking about the original artist, who created the work of art without ever having previously seen an analogous image.

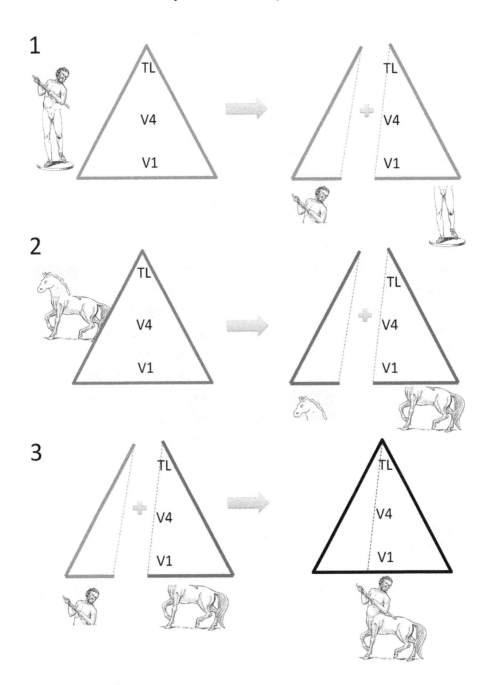

Figure 3.6 Prefrontal synthesis of a centaur. Description in text.

Though the drawing of a centaur may be an obvious example of PFS at work, I would go so far as to argue that most original figurative art involves the process of PFS. After all, when someone is drawing an object from memory such as a running horse, they cannot just stamp a completed image of that horse on paper. The drawing process is much more complex. After observing a number of people drawing a horse, I noticed that their drawing styles could be classified into three styles. Some people clearly drew one fragment at a time: first the mane, then the ears, the muzzle, the top part of the body, the tail, the legs with the hoofs, and finally the lower part of the body contour. Others drew the complete body contour first (slowly) and then added the fragments (the mane, the ears, the tail). The third group of artists avoided long lines all together. They drew with short strokes. They still drew one fragment at a time but their fragments were shown with strokes and shadows.

All the artists drew a horse one fragment at a time, though the fragments themselves and the sequence of drawing were different. Despite different drawing styles, the final image of the horse consisted of multiple fragments put together (and it couldn't have been otherwise since drawing is not stamping), and all these fragments had to be drawn in the correct relationship to each other in order for the image to make sense. An artist has to segment the imaginary horse into its component fragments, concentrate on one fragment at a time, and then, using PFS, combine those fragments on paper into a recognizable image of a horse.

1. Disassemble an object into pieces (mental analysis)

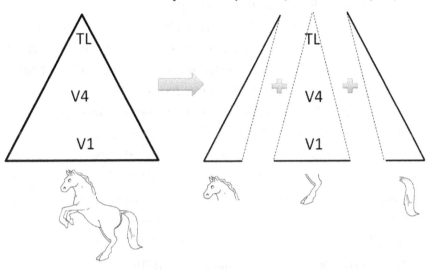

2. Synthesize those pieces on paper (mental synthesis)

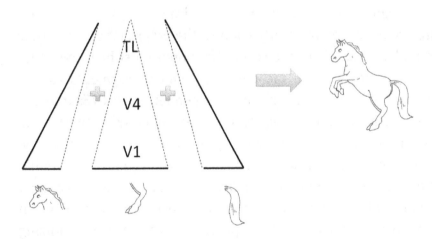

Figure 3.7 A schematic illustration of the drawing process. To draw a figurative picture, an artist first mentally disassembles an object into elements and then synthesizes the elements on paper.

For those of you like me, who have a difficult time drawing a horse, let's stick to a simpler example; let's see what happens in the brain when we try to draw a basic representation of an eye consisting of two arcs and a circle.[i] Like any other mental image, the image of an eye is encoded by an objectNE that fires synchronously when we recall an eye from memory. That's all in the brain. But what actually happens on paper? On paper, most of us will draw an eye in three strokes: top arc, bottom arc, and a circle in the middle. Therefore to draw the eye, we must segment the objectNE of the eye into three fragments, each fragment corresponding to a single stroke: top arc, bottom arc, and the circle. Each fragment is now encoded by its own neuronal ensemble. To draw the first arc, we must focus on its objectNE and translate the visual image of the arc into the motor cortex. The motor cortex is then responsible for the actual movement of the hand. All that just to draw the first arc! Now comes the intriguing second step, in which the second fragment (the bottom arc), which has been held in memory, is fitted to the first fragment that has already been drawn. To add the second arc, we must first **mentally** connect the two fragments in order to understand where the second fragment must be drawn. The only way to perceive the two independent fragments as one entity is to synchronize the two independent objectNEs into one mental frame. In other words, we must mentally synthesize the two fragments (the arc already drawn on paper with the imaginary arc) by synchronizing the two ensembles encoding the fragments. Now that we have drawn the two arcs, we must again use PFS to place the circle in its correct location between the two arcs. Again, this process involves synchronizing

---

[i] Let's imagine that an eye is being drawn for the first time, otherwise the process may have already become automated. Doodling does not involve PFS.

objectNEs; the objectNE encoding the circle will need to be synchronized with the objectNE encoding the arcs.

By definition, the process of synchronizing two independent objectNEs involves PFS. Therefore, PFS is involved in the drawing of complex figurative art. The resulting image of a horse is **not** an exact "photograph" of the horse that the artist has seen in real life. It is a completely new image that resulted from first decomposing the mental image of a horse into multiple fragments, transferring those fragments on paper one at a time, and in the process synthesizing the figurative drawing of a horse. This new drawing was created through the process of mentally synthesizing the various fragments that make up the image, each fragment encoded by an independent neuronal ensemble.[j]

---

[j] Mechanical drawing and copying an image from another picture may involve a different neurological process that does not rely on PFS. One can copy a figurative picture one fragment at a time while mechanically preserving the relationship between the fragments. Although one still needs to be able to break the picture into fragments (to copy one fragment at a time) one may not need to synthesize those fragments in the mind and consequently one does not need to use PFS for copying.

Interestingly, most art schools do not accept drawings that were made by copying photographs or other paintings. Art schools, though not aware of PFS, are looking for original artists, who can generate novel concepts (in the process of PFS) rather than simply copying someone else's work.

People with visual agnosia, who are impaired in recognition of visually presented objects, can often copy without any understanding of what they are copying. For example, Humphreys & Riddoch describe patient John who could copy a picture, but could not draw from memory [136].

Figure 3.8 Children's drawings. Benny, 3 years 6 months, chalk on asphalt, described as a lion.

There is a considerable amount of research focusing on the developmental aspects of children's spontaneous drawing. According to this body of work, young children begin with (abstract) scribbling and only acquire the ability to produce figurative drawings by the age of three or four. At this age, their drawings may not be perfect representations but they are "preplanned" by the child and are often clearly recognizable. It is important to note that children start drawing figurative objects at the same age as when they acquire PFS (3 to 4 years) [37]. Most parents are familiar with this stage, as they all of a sudden find themselves bombarded by a barrage of inquisitive questions such as: "how does this thing work?", "what is Mom doing?" and "where did Dad go?" When you tell your child that "Dad is walking the dog" and "Mom is reading a book," your child is most likely synthesizing the images of Dad with the dog and Mom with the book in his or her mind.

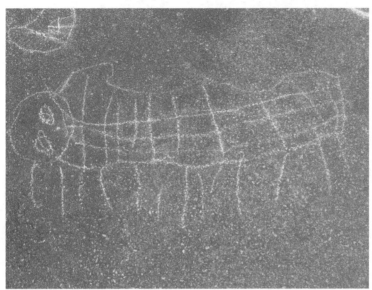

Figure 3.9 Children's drawings. Benny, 3 years 6 months, chalk on asphalt, described as a horse.

Figure 3.10 Children's drawings. Max, 3 years 8 months, pencil on paper, described as a hedgehog, Max also said that "these are not wings, these are spines."

Figure 3.11 Children's drawings. Emma, 3 years 2 months, pencil on paper, described as a self-portrait.

Figure 3.12 Venus of Hohle Fels. Venus of Hohle Fels is one of the earliest Venus figurines dated to be between 35,000 and 40,000 years old. It was found in the Swabian Alp region, which has yielded other famous mammoth-ivory artifacts including the lion-man figure.

Since PFS is associated with creation of figurative art, it is interesting to go back in time to see when hominins first started to create figurative art, and thus shed light on the time frame in which hominins first developed PFS.

The archeological record does not contain any figurative art objects until about 40,000 year ago, when some of the earliest behaviorally modern humans populated Europe. At this time there was a sudden explosion of artwork including spectacular multicolor images of animals painted on cave walls. In fact, hundreds of caves around the world contain figurative drawings dated to be between 40,000 and 15,000 years old. For example, the cave paintings of northern Spain have been dated to 40,000 years ago [137], those of Chauvet, France, to 32,000 years ago and those at Lascaux, France, to 17,000 years ago. In addition to the figurative cave paintings, paleoanthropologists also found various "Venus figurines" of well-endowed females as well as other figurative statuettes.

Figure 3.13 Exquisite sculptures created by early modern humans. Left to right: Venus of Willendorf, Oolitic limestone (24,000 BC) Naturhistorisches Museum, Vienna, Austria; Venus of Dolní Vestonice, ceramic (26,000 BC); Venus of Lespugue, tusk ivory (25,000 BC) Musée de L'Homme, France.

Figure 3.14 Spectacular multicolor animal images painted by early modern humans on the walls of caves. Left: Aurochs, horses, and deer from the cave of Lascaux, France (16,000 BC) Right: Bison from the cave of Altamira, Spain, (33,000 to 13,000 BC). It is said that following a visit to the

Altamira cave in Cantabria (Spain), Picasso was so impressed by the modernity of its paintings that he declared, "after Altamira, all is decadence."

Further proof of PFS in early modern humans comes from evidence of their elaborate burials. Grave goods, such as decorative artifacts, were often included in the burials along with the corpse. Also included were objects from daily life that could be desirable for the deceased in the afterlife, suggesting the existence of religious beliefs. One example of an elaborate early human burial site was found in Sungir (near Vladimir, Russia) and dates back to about 30,000 years ago. The site holds the remains of an adult male and two juveniles carefully buried with an astonishing variety of objects, both decorative and functional. The adult male wore a tunic adorned with thousands of drilled and polished mammoth–tusk beads.

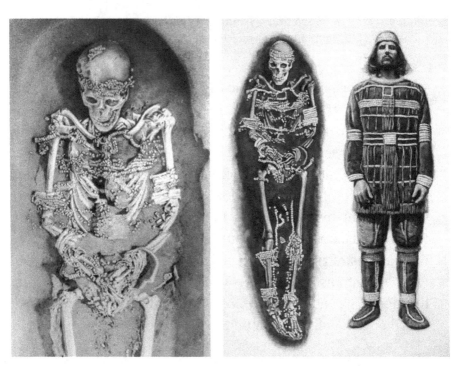

Figure 3.15 An elaborate burial of a 60-year-old found in Sungir, Russia.
The man is wearing bracelets, necklaces, pendants, and a tunic adorned with
thousands of mammoth-ivory beads. Two juvenile burials were found at the
same site. The site and the skeletons date back to 28,000 years ago.
Photograph Source: Novosti Photo Researchers, Inc., Illustration: © Libor
Balák

Figure 3.16 The lion-man statuette. Carved from mammoth ivory, the lion-man (Lowenmensch) was found in the Hohlenstein-Stadel cave of the Lone valley near Vogelherd in southern Germany. It was carbon-dated to around 39,000 B.C., when the earliest known modern humans populated Europe. Height: 31 cm. Ulmer Museum Prä Slg. Wetzel Ho-St. 39/88.1 Photo Thomas Stephan © Ulmer Museum, Ulm, Germany. A color photograph of the lion-man is shown on the front cover of the book.

A particularly striking example of early art is the sculpture of a Lowenmensch (literally 'lion-man'), found in the Hohlenstein-Stadel cave of the Lone valley in Germany [138]. The lion-man, dated to around 39,000 B.C., is a composite object combining the head of a lion with the body of a man. As discussed in the beginning of this chapter, an image that does not exist in nature must have been created through PFS. The sculptor must have imagined this lion-man by synthesizing the head of a lion and the body of a man and then executing the product of PFS in ivory. This figurine provides direct evidence that early modern humans were capable of PFS.

In addition to the lion-man from Germany, other composite images have been found elsewhere. Paintings at Lascaux show depictions of strange beasts that are half-human and half-bird, as well as those similar to the lion-man that blend human with lion. The only painting of a human in the Chauvet cave morphs a woman's lower body with the head of a lioness. An engraving in the Spanish cave of Hornos de la Peña shows a man with a horse's tail and a bird's head.

Note that the first direct evidence of PFS in hominins (the composite images of a lion-man from Germany, a bird-man from Lascaux, a lion-woman from Chauvet, and the engraving of a bird-horse-man from Hornos de la Peña) appears in the archeological record *at the same time* as other early figurative art objects such as cave paintings and Venus figurines. It seems that as soon as hominins started to produce figurative art objects they also began creating composite objects. Since PFS is clearly a prerequisite to production of composite objects then this observation supports the conjecture that PFS may be a prerequisite to the production of any figurative art.

3.12 Creativity and innovation

Let's now expand beyond the creation of figurative art to the more general creativity required for the creation of any new objects. In general, creativity involves the PFS of new objects. For example, we can invent a bicycle, because we can imagine a frame, wheels and pedals put together. Humans have invented the steam powered spinning and weaving machines, the internal combustion engine, and nuclear reactors. We have been able to put ourselves in orbit around the Earth, fly to the moon and even send probes to Mars. Humans are good at innovation because we can imagine objects that we have never seen. This imagination is a direct result of PFS, which then greatly accelerates technological progress. In the absence of PFS, any innovation has to come through trial and error. Trial and error is a slow and random process. One has to be lucky to manufacture an object by accident and also happen to remember the steps involved in making that object.

PFS, on the other hand, allows one to mentally simulate all the possible solutions to a problem, select the best solution and then mentally test multiple manufacturing processes. It is difficult to avoid the analogy to fast computers. When Boeing was developing the 767 series planes in the 1980s, engineers physically assembled and tested 77 wing prototypes in the wind tunnel. When Boeing was developing the 787 Dreamliner in 2005, engineers tested only 11 wing prototypes. What happened between the 1980s and 2005? Boeing got access to fast supercomputers. Instead of testing physical wing structure in a wind tunnel, Boeing switched to virtual computer simulations. Computer simulations are increasingly used by all kinds of companies in product development to save time and money.

Mental simulations facilitate technological progress in three major ways:

1. PFS allows one to imagine the best solution to a problem.
2. PFS allows one to simulate steps involved in the manufacturing process of the object.
3. PFS allows one to quickly disseminate the knowledge about the manufacturing process through a recursive communication system.

Archeological records show a dramatic acceleration of

technological progress occurring approximately 30,000 years ago. The Neanderthals, who inhabited Europe and parts of western and central Asia from 400,000 to 30,000 years ago, left very few artifacts: Mousterian stone tools and wooden spears. That's about it. Early modern humans, on the other hand, left plenty of functional artifacts, including kiln-baked ceramics, projectile spears, bows and arrows (which have been dated back to 64,000 years ago), and even bone needles with eyes (which have been dated back to 26,000 years ago) [139-141].k

3.13 Design and Construction

An integral part of design and construction is visual planning, which involves the PFS of a plan. Do you recall the last time you moved into a new house or apartment? You probably spent hours planning the configuration of furniture in your new living room: "would the sofa look better next to the fireplace? Neh. It would look better next to the armchair beside the coffee table. But the armchair is a different color. Well, then I will have to buy a rug that will incorporate the colors of the sofa and the armchair..." As hypothesized in this monograph, this kind of visual planning is based on the synchronization of objectNEs of the sofa, the fireplace, the armchair, the rug, and the coffee table with the neuronal ensemble of your living room. When objectNEs are synchronized, you perceive the encoded objects in one mental frame and can judge how the objects will fit and look together.

Human dwellings are not built by reflex or trial and error. An architect first generates a mental plan, consults with the

---

k There is little doubt that Neanderthals processed animal skins, which were presumably used for clothing. However the absence of any bone needles among Neanderthal artifacts is consistent with the hypothesis that skins were not sewn together.

client ("do you want the stairs to the right or to the left of the fireplace?"), and then draws up the plans. Thanks to PFS, human houses take on a multitude of forms ranging from rudimentary huts of nomadic tribes to complex structures composed of many systems, to castles and skyscrapers. Whether you look inside or outside of the house, human imagination and planning is clearly on display.

Design and construction are not limited to adults either. Children use building blocks such as Legos starting at an early age of two or three years old. Initially they just stack these blocks one on top of the other, but sometime between the ages of three and four, construction projects turn into buildings, palaces, castles, and battlefields clearly displaying the newly acquired propensity for voluntary imagination.

Figure 3.17 An example of wooden blocks used by a four-year-old boy to build a fortress.

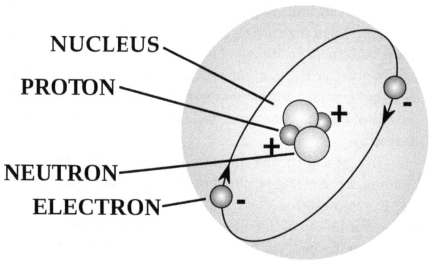

Figure 3.18 A model of an atom

3.14 Natural sciences

Do you remember the illustration of an atom that you studied in high school physics? It probably looked something like the image above, with a nucleus replete with spherical protons and neutrons, as well as circling electrons. Well, I'm going to let you in on a secret: no human has ever seen a proton, a neutron or an electron. Protons, neutrons, and electrons are part of the visual model of an atom. With the help of this model, physicists visually understood the process of a nuclear chain reaction and created a nuclear reactor. If you ask a physicist to explain the nuclear chain reaction, he will paint a colorful picture of neutrons flying into nuclei and nuclei exploding. You might almost believe that he has actually seen this reaction with his own eyes, but of course he hasn't; he has seen the action only in his imagination by mentally synthesizing the events of a nuclear chain reaction. Similarly, nobody has ever seen a black hole (since it absorbs all the light which hits it), but we can use

PFS to imagine a super-dense mass pulling all kinds of radiation and material towards its center. Also, no one has ever seen the structure of DNA; Watson and Crick only saw the results of the X-ray crystallography. They had to use PFS to put Adenine, Thymine, Guanine, and Cytosine together into a beautiful double-stranded DNA structure. They mentally synthesized the four nucleotides into polymers and then imagined how those polymer configurations would project onto an X-ray film. Science is a continuous exercise in PFS. Here is one final example: to come up with the equivalence principle that would be the foundation of the General Relativity theory, Einstein imagined himself in an elevator falling freely towards the ground; it was a mental experiment. Progress in scientific research is due largely to provisional explanations which are developed through PFS. Albert Einstein famously said, "Imagination ... is more important than knowledge. Knowledge is limited. Imagination encircles the world" [142].

Humans have an uncanny propensity towards seeking explanations for unobservable forces. We ask "why?" and "how?" starting at an early age and these common questions remain in the daily vocabulary of most adults, scientists in particular. By the age of four, children form hypotheses and are able to produce explicit explanations for events acting much like scientists who are engaged in theory formation [143].

The search for explanation is universal across cultures and recorded human history. Alison Gopnik, a professor of psychology at Berkeley, speculated that seeking causal explanations is a fundamental drive of our species' psychological make-up [143]. From an early age until the end of our lives, we humans are natural scientists, seeking an explanation and generating visual models for invisible forces in the process of PFS.

3.15 Predilection for strategy games

Another behavioral manifestation of PFS that has transcended time and cultures is the human predilection for strategy games. One of the oldest known board games is Senet. It has been found in several Egyptian burial sites starting as early as 3500 BC; it was painted in the tomb of Merknera (c. 3300 BC), the tomb of Hesy (c. 2686–2613 BC) and the tomb of Rashepes (c. 2500 BC). This popular strategy game was played everywhere from Egypt to Levant, and even as far as Cyprus and Crete. The Royal Game of Ur (thus named because it was found in the Royal Tombs of Ur in Iraq) was dated back to before 2600 BC. An early variant of "tic-tac-toe," called Terni Lapilli, was played in the Roman Empire, from around the first century BC. The famous strategic game of "Go" originated in China more than 2,500 years ago.

The ultimate strategy game, requiring intensive visual planning, is exemplified by the game of chess. Players visually imagine the position of figures several moves ahead (by mentally synthesizing figures in the new positions) and deciding if that position is advantageous. Even more impressive is the game of blindfold chess wherein the players do not see the positions of the pieces and cannot touch them. This forces players to maintain a mental model of the chessboard during the entire game. Moves are communicated via a recognized chess notation. Blindfold chess was considered miraculous for centuries, but today it is accepted that any strong player should be able to play blindfolded, and many can keep track of more than one simultaneous blindfolded game. In 1924 at the Alamac Hotel of New York, the Russian World Champion Alexander Alekhine played 26 simultaneous blindfold games against very strong opponents (Isaac Kashdan and Hermann Steiner among them), with the score of 16 wins, 5 losses, and 5 draws. In February of the next year in Paris, he faced 28 teams of four players each, with the impressive result of 22 wins, 3 losses, and 3 draws. On July 16, 1934 in Chicago, Alekhine set the new world record by playing 32 blindfold games, with 19 wins, 5 losses, and 5 draws.

Children can learn chess moves before the age of four. Chess prodigies José Raúl Capablanca (1888–1942), who became World Champion, and Samuel Reshevsky (1911–1992), one of the top players in the world, learned chess moves at the age of four. According to Capablanca, he learned the rules of the game by watching his father play, pointing out an illegal move made by his father, and then beating him twice. Reshevsky was giving simultaneous exhibitions at the age of six. At age eight he was already beating some accomplished players.

In general, all strategy games require thinking that relies on branch logic conducted by using the process of PFS. From antiquity to the present, strategy games undoubtedly existed to satisfy the human hunger for PFS gymnastics.

Figure 3.19 Samuel Reshevsky, at age eight, defeated several chess masters in France.

3.16 Religious beliefs

Humans have been using PFS to make sense of their everyday worlds, and this has manifested itself in various forms of religious beliefs. The origin of religious beliefs can be traced through beliefs in an afterlife. As noted above, elaborate human burials have been commonplace for the last 40,000 years. As was previously mentioned, the ancient burial site found in Sungir (near Vladimir, Russia), which holds the remains of an adult male and two juveniles, is evidence of the antiquity of human religious practices. The deceased were buried along with an astonishing variety of decorative and functional objects that could be useful in the afterlife. Other early known burials include the 42,000 years old ritual burial of a man at Lake Mungo in Australia (the body of the man was sprinkled with copious amounts of red ochre), as well as an abundance of elaborate burials found throughout Europe.

The ancient Egyptian civilization was based on religion; the belief in an afterlife was the driving force behind the funeral practices. Bodies of the deceased dignitaries were preserved through mummification, put into a sarcophagus, and provided with statuary and other funerary equipment. The earliest Egyptian pyramid that served as a tomb for a king, the Pyramid of Djoser, was constructed over 4,600 years ago.

The Ancient Greeks had a special god of the underworld called Hades, who protected a place where souls went to live after death. The messenger of the gods, Hermes, would take the dead soul of a person to the underworld. Hermes would leave the soul on the banks of the River Styx, the river between life and death. Charon, the ferry-man, would take the soul across the river to Hades.

Beliefs about an afterlife are the ultimate creations of PFS.

Chapter 4. Components of imagination

... it has been proposed that conscious perception depends on the transient synchronization of widely distributed neural assemblies. The neural signature of ... conscious perception would require global coordination of widely distributed neural activity by long-distance synchronization....

LUCIA MELLONI et al., *Synchronization of Neural Activity across Cortical Areas Correlates with Conscious Perception* (2007)

... synchronization is a ubiquitous phenomenon in cortical networks and likely to serve a variety of different functions in addition to feature binding at early levels of sensory processing.

PETER J. UHLHAAS et al., *Neural synchrony in cortical networks* (2009)

So far we have discussed two components of imagination: the completely involuntary REM-sleep dreaming and completely voluntary prefrontal synthesis. Other components of imagination include amodal completion, integration of modifiers, mental rotation, and many others. These components have different neurological mechanisms that evolved at different times and are acquired by children at different ages.

4.1 Integration of modifiers and mental rotation.

Close your eyes and recall your car. Now imagine your car in different colors: blue, red, yellow. The mechanism of changing the color does not fall under the definition of PFS since only a single object is involved – your car. Under the Neuronal Ensemble Synchronization (NES) hypothesis, integration of modifier, such as a color, involves the lateral prefrontal cortex-orchestrated synchronization of a single objectNE and another group of neurons encoding its color in the ventral visual cortex [144]. When the lateral prefrontal cortex shifts the neurons encoding the color to fire in-phase with the objectNE, synchronized neurons encoding the color {blue/red/yellow} and the shape of the car are experienced as a complete image of a car in blue, red, or yellow color and this novel image is stored in memory, Figure 4.1.

A similar mechanism is theorized by the NES hypothesis to be responsible for purposeful mental metamorphoses of an object's size, number, and rotation [40,145].

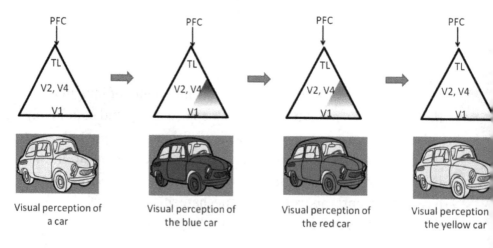

Visual perception of a car   Visual perception of the blue car   Visual perception of the red car   Visual perception the yellow car

Figure 4.1 Integration of modifiers. According to the NES hypothesis, imagining a car in blue, red, or yellow color requires the lateral prefrontal cortex-orchestrated synchronization of the car-encoding objectNE and various color encoding neurons in V4.

4.2 Prefrontal Analysis

While following the steps of Alice in Wonderland, recall your kettle and imagine a broken handle. Magically, the good old kettle turns in your mind into a broken stump with no handle. Under the NES hypothesis, this transformation involves *desynchronization* of the part of an **objectNE** encoding the handle from the rest of the **objectNE** of the kettle, Figure 4.2. Since this process is mediated by the lateral prefrontal cortex, we call it *Prefrontal Analysis* (PFA, *analysis* involves the disassembly of an object into parts as opposed to *synthesis*, which involves combining two or more objects together). lateral prefrontal cortex-driven shift of a part of the **objectNE** *out-of-phase* with the rest of the ensemble, results in the perception of a *new* object encoded by those neurons that remain firing synchronously. The new object is a novel imaginary object since you have never physically observed it.

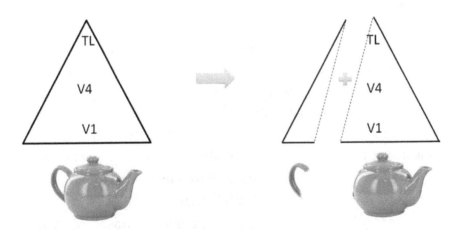

Figure 4.2 Prefrontal Analysis of a tea kettle. According to the NES hypothesis, mentally breaking off a handle from a tea kettle involves desynchronization of the handle-encoding neurons from the kettle objectNE.

4.3 REM-sleep dreaming

PFS, integration of modifiers, mental rotation, and PFA are all examples of top-down lateral prefrontal cortex-controlled imagination. Conversely, during REM-sleep, when the lateral prefrontal cortex is inactive [17,18] and the communication between neocortex and hippocampus is disrupted by high ACh level [146], objects appearing in one's perception must be mediated by activation of *previous* memories encoded in objectNEs in the posterior cortex. It is unclear how exactly those objectNEs jump up into activity. A common explanation is that objectNEs, primed by previous activity or current sensory or subcortical stimulation, activate spontaneously, triggered by the ponto-geniculo-occipital waves that characterize REM-sleep [147]. In the words of Hobson & McCarley, the neocortex is making "the best of a bad job in producing even partially coherent dream imagery from the relatively noisy signals sent up from the brain stem" [148]. It is also commonly accepted that the intensity of dreams during REM-sleep can be dialed up or down by the dopaminergic cells of the ventral tegmental area. For example, drugs that block activity in the dopaminergic activity (e.g., haloperidol) inhibit unusually frequent, and vivid dreaming, while increase of dopamine (e.g., through l-dopa) stimulates excessive vivid dreaming and nightmares [149].

We are not concerned with the exact reason why a specific objectNE is activated during REM-sleep. The main issue herein is how those objectNEs hybridize into *novel* images. The NES hypothesis predicts that objectNEs that spontaneously activate *in-synchrony* will be perceived together as novel combined objects or scenes. In other words, the objectNEs firing asynchronously from each other are perceived as *separate* objects; however, if by accident, two disparate objectNEs fire in-sync with each other, they are perceived as a *novel* hybrid object. In this process, an unlimited number of bizarre hybrid mental images can form during REM-sleep.

4.4 Amodal completion

Another mechanism of bottom-up imagination involves so-called amodal completion. In the example shown in Figure 4.3, most people easily perceive scattered letters 'B' covered by spilled ink. The missing parts of contours are filled in or imagined (involuntarily) by the posterior cortex.

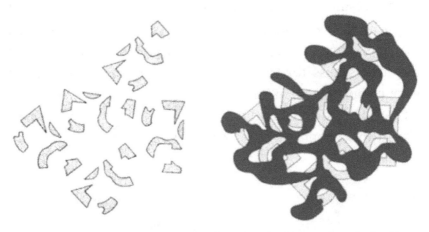

Figure 4.3. The visual system has an obsessive desire to make whole objects from fragmentary evidence. We look for complete objects!

4.5 Categorically-primed spontaneous imagination

In addition to clearly top-down (PFS, integration of modifiers, mental rotation, and PFA) and unambiguously bottom-up (REM-sleep dreaming, amodal completion) types of imagination, the NES hypothesis anticipates hybrid mechanisms as well. For example, the lateral prefrontal cortex, known to encode categorical features (such as 'things that protect you from the rain') [150,151], can prime the whole category of objectNEs, without activating any specific objectNE, Figure 4.4. Just as in a dream, primed objectNEs fire randomly; the objectNEs that happen to fire in synchrony, are predicted to be perceived as unified complete hybrid novel mental images and scenes. Conspicuous examples of categorically-primed spontaneous imagination include racing thoughts about an upcoming exam, spontaneous sexual fantasies, compulsive jealousy, impulsive fantasizing about food or drugs, an anxiety over a missing child, and many other obsessions. When such an obsession overtakes the brain, one category of objectNEs is primed and imagery is a fantasy, resulting from spontaneous firing of these primed objectNEs in the posterior cortex. This phenomenon is often called "mind-wandering" or "spontaneous thought" [152], but these terms miss the important point: the objectNEs firing is never completely spontaneous as some categories are always more likely to fire than others. To capture this observation we refer to this phenomenon as *categorically-primed spontaneous imagination* [153].

Figure 4.4: Most people hesitate to recognize an object displayed in this figure. However, once one category of objectNEs is primed by the lateral prefrontal cortex, the object is easily recognized. When you are ready to be primed by reading the object's category, please scroll to Figure 4.5.

Categorically-primed spontaneous imagination seems to be the default mode of a relaxed mind. Consequently, the brain areas mediating categorically-primed spontaneous imagination are called the Default Mode Network [152,154]. The categorically-primed spontaneous imagination is also one of the common mechanisms of scientific thinking: instead of serial purposeful PFS, one can let their mind wander while priming fantasies along a few categories of interest. The resulting semi-spontaneous neuronal firing results in synchronization of previously independent objectNEs and provides new ideas for scientific inquiry. Sometimes we may even experience the "Aha!" moment alike to Archimedes who shouted "Eureka!" when he suddenly discovered that water displacement could be used to calculate density.

Contemporary research on insight uses a variety of verbal and physical tasks [155-157]. Mark Jung-Beeman and colleagues have examined the neural bases of these Eureka moments and reported increased activity associated with insight moments in the right hemisphere temporal cortex [158]. Interestingly, just prior to reporting the insight, individuals had a sudden burst of high-frequency gamma-band neural activity in the same area. This increased gamma-band neural activity may be associated with synchronization of objectNEs that allows individuals to see connections that previously eluded them.

Earl K. Miller brilliantly summarized these "Aha!" moments of scientific inquiries when he was asked how he was finding his inspiration: "I don't. Inspiration finds you, most often when you're not trying to find it. Many times, inspiration and decision-making are the result of unconscious processes churning away at something. Your conscious mind then receives the result. In fact, your conscious mind can often get in the way by forcing you down the same well-worn paths. Inspiration often comes when your conscious mind is not engaged by the question at hand. This is why we often get ideas when we are drifting off to sleep, or walking to work in the morning, etc. One of the central ideas of my most cited paper [159] came to me suddenly at a bar in Vancouver. Good thing there was a cocktail napkin nearby." [160]

4.6 Dissociation of top-down and bottom-up imagination mechanisms in patients with lateral prefrontal cortex lesions.

Perhaps the most striking feature of dreaming is how similar the experience generated by dreams is to the real world. In fact, at times, the dreamer might be in doubt whether they are asleep or awake. The reason for this is straightforward: PFS and dreaming hallucinations share the neurological substrate that generates the sensory experience with all its video-spatial and auditory features, namely the posterior cortex. Accordingly, lesions in the posterior cortex often result in parallel decline in waking visuo-spatial abilities and dreaming [161]. For example, lesions in specific regions of the posterior cortex that underlie deficits in visual perception are associated with corresponding deficits in dreaming [149]. Individuals with lesions in the V4 region who do not perceive color, dream in black-and-white; those who do not perceive motion as a consequence of V5/MT lesion do not dream of motion; and subjects with impaired face perception as a consequence of fusiform gyrus lesion, do not dream of faces [19,149]. Furthermore, global cessation of dreaming commonly follows large lesions in or near the temporo-parieto-occipital junction [149], the region where a large part of objectNEs are located. The logical consequence of damage to temporo-parieto-occipital junction is a significant reduction of the ability of objectNEs to organize into resonant synchronous activity essential for sensory recollection of these objects. Predictably, this at the same time results in inability to recall those objects and also inability to dream about them.

While the posterior cortex is shared by waking and dreaming imaginations, other brain regions are essential for one, but not the other imagination mechanism. As discussed in Chapter 1, patients with damage to the lateral prefrontal cortex sparing most of Broca's area often present a very specific PFS deficit, that affects both their language and ability to reason. Joaquin Fuster calls this alteration in language "prefrontal aphasia" [21] and explains that "although the pronunciation of words and sentences remains intact, language is impoverished and shows an apparent diminution of the capacity to 'propositionize.' The length and the complexity of sentences are reduced. There is a dearth of dependent clauses and, more generally, an underutilization of what Chomsky characterizes as the potential for recursiveness of language" [21].

Alexander Luria calls this condition "frontal dynamic aphasia" [36] and reports that "these patients had no difficulty grasping the meaning of complex ideas such as 'causation,' 'development,' or 'cooperation.' They were also able to hold abstract conversations. But difficulties developed when they were presented with complex grammatical constructions which coded logical relations. ... Such patients find it almost impossible to understand phrases and words which denote relative position and cannot carry out a simple instruction like 'draw a triangle above a circle.'" [162].

In addition to language alterations, individuals with lateral prefrontal cortex lesions often show deficit in reasoning revealed by nonverbal IQ tests. These individuals may have normal full-scale IQ, but commonly exhibit a selective and catastrophic deficit in tasks relying on PFS, such as matrix reasoning tasks requiring integration of multiple objects [24], such as those shown in Figure 1.2. Individuals with PFS paralysis invariably fail these integration tasks and, therefore, typically perform below the score of 85 in non-verbal IQ tests [163].

Crucially, individuals with lateral prefrontal cortex damage and the associated PFS paralysis do not report changes in their dreaming [19]. They continue to experience the same vivid REM dreams that they experienced before the lesion. This observation is consistent with neurobiological dissociation between mechanisms of the top-down voluntary imagination (e.g., PFS) and the bottom-up involuntary imagination (e.g., REM-sleep dreaming).

4.7 Six different mechanisms of imagination

At least six different mechanisms of imagination are predicted by the NES hypothesis. On an axis of their dependence on the lateral prefrontal cortex, imagination mechanisms range from completely lateral prefrontal cortex-independent spontaneous REM-sleep dreaming to the lateral prefrontal cortex-dependent PFS. In between these extremes lies a panoply of mechanisms with gradually increasing role of the lateral prefrontal cortex: amodal completion, categorically-primed spontaneous insight, integration of modifiers and mental rotation, and prefrontal analysis (Figure 4.5).

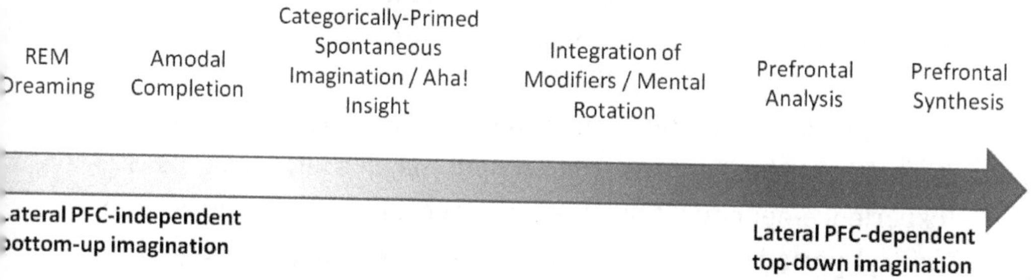

Figure 4.5 The six different mechanisms of imagination as a function of their dependence on the lateral prefrontal cortex. Note related to Figure 4.4. The bird displayed in Figure 4.4 is an eagle.

4.8 Prefrontal synthesis is a distinct component of executive function

PFS was not previously identified as a separate component of executive functions. Conventionally, executive functions include inhibition and attention, working memory, and cognitive flexibility – all mediated by the lateral prefrontal cortex [124]. PFS, defined as the process of juxtaposing multiple mental visuospatial objects, is also mediated by the lateral prefrontal cortex [21,23-27]. PFS, however, is mediated by a mechanism separate from other executive functions – synchronization of objectNEs: the lateral prefrontal cortex phase-shifts firing of two or more objectNEs, synchronously firing objectNEs are perceived as a novel hybrid object. ObjectNEs' firing in synchrony with each other results in enhanced synapses between these objectNEs; the Hebbian "fire together–wire together" [86]. This mechanism of PFS is different from inhibition, attention and working memory, that do not involve synchronization of multiple objectNEs. PFS is also different from cognitive flexibility that is commonly investigated using task-switching and set-shifting tests [124]. Such tests, e.g., Wisconsin Card Sorting Task, involve category-sorting rules identification, that do not require the synchronization of objectNEs and visuospatial synthesis of PFS.

In addition to differences in the underlying neurology, PFS is distinguished by its phenotypic properties, such as its experience-dependent acquisition mechanism and the strong critical period. Inhibition and attention, working memory, and task-switching are acquired by children independent of their use of language. Feral children and deaf linguistic isolates often exhibit normal inhibition, attention, working memory, and task-switching [164-167]. Conversely, acquisition of PFS requires use of recursive language in early childhood. Recursive conversations, story-telling, and fairy tales are essential for acquisition of PFS.

The myelination of frontoposterior fiber tracts mediating PFS [168] depends on early childhood conversations [39,164]. "Non-recursive" communication systems devoid of spatial prepositions and recursion, such as homesign (that spontaneously arises in families of congenitally deaf children) do not result in PFS acquisition [40].

The second important difference is the presence of the strong critical period for PFS acquisition. Inhibition and attention, working memory, and cognitive flexibility can all be improved at any age [124,169]. They have weak critical periods. PFS, however, cannot be learned after early childhood. Case studies of feral children and deaf linguistic isolates show that post-pubertal intensive therapy does not result in PFS acquisition even after many years of intervention [40]. Strong critical periods are common in the central nervous system development. Neural circuits underlying strong critical periods are programmed to be shaped by experience during short periods of early postnatal life; later plasticity is impossible. The PFS strong critical period has many well-studied analogs, e.g., 1) filial imprinting in birds [58], 2) monaural occlusion [59], 3) post-childbirth bonding in mammals [170], 4) the vestibulo-ocular reflex [171], 5) song dialects learning in male white-crowned sparrows [172], and 6) monocular deprivation [57]. The closure of one eye for the duration of the critical period causes a permanent loss of vision through that eye. Cats which had one eye sewn shut from birth until 3 months of age, fully developed vision only in the open eye. Loss of vision occurs despite there being no damage to the sensory receptors in the eye, the thalamus, or the cerebral cortex. The simple act of covering an eye can profoundly alter the physical structure of the brain. The duration of this critical period lasts from weeks in mice to months in cats and years in primates [38].

PFS is not congruent to planning or fluid intelligence. A lot of planning is not visuospatial and therefore does not involve

PFS (e.g., planning by ants, planning by bees, planning by people with PFS paralysis). Furthermore, some visuospatial scenario-playing planning occurs during REM-sleep dreaming [72]. Dreaming visuospatial synthesis can be vivid and can be remembered upon waking up, thus, serving its adaptive function [173]. This type of planning, however, is involuntary and occurs without the control from the lateral prefrontal cortex (that is inactive during REM-sleep [17,18]) and, therefore, is distinct from PFS that is defined as a voluntary process completely controlled by the lateral prefrontal cortex [123]. Finally, most PFS that occurs to understand recursive language ("the cat on the mat" vs. "the mat on the cat") is not planning. In other words, all planning is not PFS and all PFS is not planning.

PFS is also defined more narrowly than fluid intelligence. A lot of fluid intelligence tasks can be accomplished without PFS. These tasks can be solved using amodal completion, integration of color and size, mental rotation, and patterning [145]. PFS always involves a combination of two or more mental visuospatial objects. The narrow definition of PFS is essential for understanding human evolution.

4.9 Prefrontal synthesis is a distinct component of language

Most components of language have weak critical periods: vocabulary acquisition [54], articulation control [53], grammar processing [52], and phoneme tuning [50,51] — all can be significantly improved by training at any age [55,56]. PFS, however, has a strong critical period that ends between the age of five and puberty [40]. This idea was popularized by Lenneberg and is known as "Lenneberg's language acquisition critical period hypothesis" [60]. Lenneberg's conjecture about the strong critical period was based on a few cases of childhood traumatic aphasia and hemispherectomy. When the left hemisphere is surgically removed before the age of five (to treat cancer or epilepsy), patients often attain normal cognitive functions in adulthood (using the one remaining hemisphere). Conversely, removal of the left hemisphere after the age of five often results in PFS paralysis.

PFS ability is essential for understanding sentences describing novel combinations of objects. For example, the semantically-reversible sentences "The dog bit my friend" and "My friend bit the dog" use identical words and grammar. Appreciating the misfortune of the first sentence and the humor of the second sentence depends on the lateral prefrontal cortex ability to faithfully synthesize the two objects – the friend and the dog – into a novel mental image. Similarly, understanding of spatial prepositions such as *in, on, under, over, beside, in front of, behind* requires a subject to synthesize several objects in front of the mind's eye. For example, the request "to put a green box {inside/behind/on top of} the blue box" requires an initial mental simulation of the scene, only after which is it possible to correctly arrange the physical objects. An inability to produce a novel mental image of the green box {inside/behind/on top of} the blue box would lead to the use of trial-and-error, which in the majority of cases will result in an incorrect arrangement.

To conduct PFS and to synchronize objectNEs encoded in the posterior cortex, the lateral prefrontal cortex relies on its frontoposterior connections, such as arcuate fasciculus. Patients with damage to any component of this circuit—the lateral prefrontal cortex [24], or the frontoposterior fibers [168], or temporal-parietal-occipital junction [174]—often lose access to the full extent of PFS. As discussed above, Fuster calls their condition "prefrontal aphasia" [21] and Luria "frontal dynamic aphasia" or "semantic aphasia" [36]. I prefer to call this condition 'PFS paralysis' since aphasia is translated from Greek as "speechless" and these patients may not experience any speech deficit.

Thus, PFS is a distinct component of both language and executive functions, different on both neurological and phenotypic levels. On the neurological level it is characterized by the lateral prefrontal cortex-controlled phase-shift of two or more objectNEs into synchronous activity. On the phenotypic level it is characterized by a distinctly strong critical period and an unusual dependence on early childhood cultural experience: exposure to spatial prepositions, recursive conversations, story-telling, and fairytales. Furthermore, the symptoms of PFS paralysis are different from other types of aphasia, dementia, and memory deficits.

4.10 Prefrontal synthesis and Chomskyan Merge

Chomskyan Merge [175] is defined linguistically as a combination of any two syntactic objects to create a new one. Several components of imagination can be utilized by the Merge operation. Processing of spatial prepositions and semantically-reversible sentences rely on PFS, combination of an adjective and a noun uses integration of modifiers, and processing a familiar sentence (e.g., 'ship sinks') can be understood via memory recall (i.e., by *remembering* of a previously seen picture of a sinking ship). These components of imagination are neurologically distinct. Memory recall is the simplest operation that primarily involves the posterior cortex and only minimally involves the lateral prefrontal cortex; integration of modifiers relies on the lateral prefrontal cortex ability to control the activity in the ventral visual cortex [144] (areas V2 and V4 near the temporal-occipital junction); and PFS depends on the lateral prefrontal cortex ability to control the activity of nearly half of the posterior cortex (visual areas in the temporal, parietal and occipital cortices) [176-180].

Intelligence tests have been primarily developed to classify individuals by their voluntary imagination abilities. To score above 73 on a standardized IQ test individuals usually have to demonstrate memory recall ability; to score above 77, have to demonstrate integration of modifiers; and to score above 85, have to demonstrate the PFS ability [145]. In other words, the Merge operation is not a unitary all-or-none ability, but an assembly of several skills that rely on neurologically distinct mechanisms that differ in individuals with different IQ.

Thus, PFS is defined more narrowly than the Merge operation. PFS is one of several voluntary imagination mechanisms that is used in some (but not all) Merge operations.

Another difference between the Merge and PFS definitions is that PFS is defined independent of language. Merging of objects in visuospatial mental space does not directly depend on knowledge of any language. An individual does not need to know the names of objects in order to combine them mentally into a novel hybrid object or scene. One can mentally combine objects of strange geometrical shape that do not have names in any language.

Part 1. Neuroscience of Imagination

Part 2. Evolution of imagination

While it is clear that all mechanisms of imagination are available to modern humans, it is also clear that not all mechanisms of imagination were available to our ancestors. The goal of this part of the book is to analyze when different components of imagination were acquired based on the available archeological artifacts.

Chapter 5. A Quick Guide to Paleoanthropology

The human brain is a bizarre device, set in place through natural selection for one main purpose – to make decisions that enhance reproductive success.

MICHAEL S. GAZZANIGA, *Human: The Science Behind What Makes Us Unique* (2009)

5.1 The human family tree

All living primates are related to a common evolutionary ancestor. The closest living human relatives include the chimpanzees, bonobos, gorillas, and orangutans (collectively referred to as the great apes). Genetic studies indicate that the last common ancestor of humans and orangutans lived about 12 million years ago. At that time, orangutans diverged from the lineage that includes humans, chimpanzees, bonobos, and gorillas. For 12 million years, orangutans developed independently; their genes did not intermix with the rest of the great apes. About 10 million years ago, gorillas diverged from humans, chimpanzees, and bonobos [181] and about 6 million years ago, humans diverged from chimpanzees and bonobos [182]. Since then, hominins, a group that includes modern humans and their extinct ancestors (all of the *Homo* species, all of the australopiths and other ancient forms like Paranthropus and Ardipithecus) followed their own evolutionary path.

Nature experimented widely with the human form. The hominin family includes such diverse species as the two meter tall *Homo erectus* (nicknamed "Goliath"), the one-meter-short *Homo floresiensis* (nicknamed "hobbit") found on the Indonesian island of Flores, the strong-jawed Paranthropus, and the strong-boned Neanderthals.

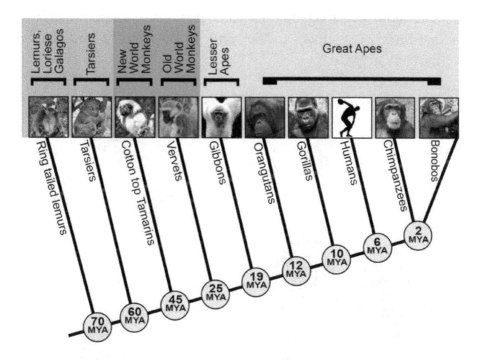

Figure 5.1 All living primates are related to a common evolutionary ancestor. Apes diverged from monkeys about 25 million years ago. The great apes then parted ways with the lesser apes, a group that includes modern gibbons, about 19 million years ago. Dozens of species of great apes lived during the Miocene, but now only humans, chimpanzees, bonobos, gorillas and orangutans remain. About 10 million years ago, Gorillas diverged from humans, chimpanzees, and bonobos [181] and about 6 million years ago, humans diverged from chimpanzees and bonobos [182]. Since then, hominins have followed their own evolutionary path: their genes did not intermix with the rest of the great apes. Bonobos diverged from chimpanzees approximately 2 million years ago [183]. Some key features of the primates include: forward facing eyes that provide good stereoscopic vision with depth perception, a relatively large brain, and a long childhood.

However, all but one branch of the hominin evolutionary tree have died out. The *Homo sapiens*, known for their intelligence, is the only surviving species of the genus *Homo*. As Ian Tattersall eloquently reminds us: "In pondering our history as human beings we should never forget that we are simply the sole surviving twig on this ramifying bush, rather than the products of a slow, steady, and single minded process of perfection" [139].

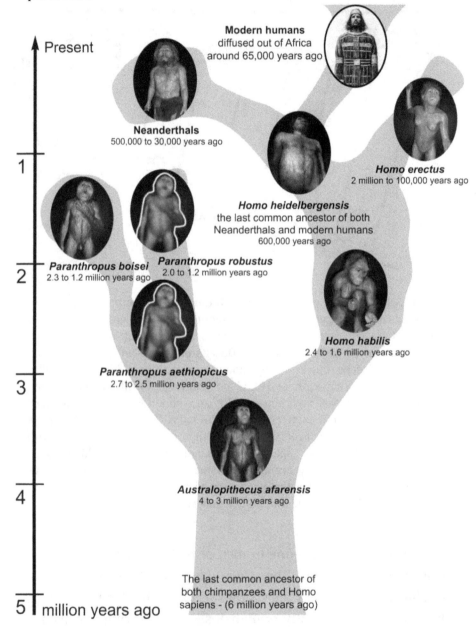

Present

Modern humans
diffused out of Africa
around 65,000 years ago

Neanderthals
500,000 to 30,000 years ago

1

Homo erectus
2 million to 100,000 years ago

Homo heidelbergensis
the last common ancestor of both
Neanderthals and modern humans
600,000 years ago

Paranthropus boisei
2.3 to 1.2 million years ago

Paranthropus robustus
2.0 to 1.2 million years ago

2

Homo habilis
2.4 to 1.6 million years ago

Paranthropus aethiopicus
2.7 to 2.5 million years ago

3

Australopithecus afarensis
4 to 3 million years ago

4

The last common ancestor of
both chimpanzees and Homo
sapiens - (6 million years ago)

5 million years ago

Figure 5.2 The hominin evolutionary tree showing the timeline of the main branches of the hominin family. All but the *Homo sapiens* branch resulted in an evolutionary dead end (i.e., extinction). There is some debate as to whether some species are direct ancestors of *Homo sapiens* or whether their branch represents an evolutionary dead end.

It is likely that all or most hominin species evolved in Africa. The most successful species were able to migrate out of Africa and to colonize other continents. For example, *Homo erectus* settled most of Europe and Western Asia starting around 1.8 million years ago. The most successful species was, of course, the *Homo sapiens* who successfully colonized all the continents. There is evidence that multiple hominin species coexisted throughout Africa, Asia, and Europe. For example, Australopithecus and Paranthropus coexisted in Africa 3.2 to 2 million years ago; Neanderthals and *Homo Erectus* coexisted in Europe and Asia 500,000 to 70,000 years ago; *Homo sapiens* and Neanderthals coexisted in Europe and Asia 45,000 to 30,000 years ago.

It's important to note that an evolutionary tree is inherently an oversimplified way to look at the gene flow. Interbreeding is sometimes possible between species, even ones separated by as much as two million years of evolution. For example, a donkey can breed with a horse (resulting in a mule), even though these species diverged one to three million years ago and despite a different number of chromosomes (horses have 64 chromosomes whereas donkeys have 62). A lion can breed with a tiger (resulting in a liger); these species have the same number of chromosomes (38) and diverged one to two million years ago. While in the wild, bonobos and chimpanzees do not overlap in their current ranges, there have even been reports from a circus in Belgium of several bonobo-chimp hybrids; these species have the same number of chromosomes (48) and diverged about two million years ago. While most offspring of interspecies breeding are infertile (such as the mule and the male liger), some are fertile (such as some female ligers). As a result, genes sometimes flow between the branches. For example, a small number of Neanderthal genes crossed over into the non-African *Homo sapiens* [184].

This monograph will not attempt to cover all the species of hominins, nor will it describe all the morphological features of a particular hominin species. Rather it will concentrate on the four key species of hominins that are most interesting and best characterized: *Australopithecus afarensis, Homo habilis, Homo erectus*, and Neanderthals. It will first explore the archeological evidence associated with these four hominins, bearing in mind that, since soft tissues normally disintegrate quickly, the only surviving archeological record consists primarily of bones and stone tools.[l]

5.2 The birth of hominins (10 to 6 million years ago)

Ten million year ago, our ancestors, just like modern day chimpanzees, were primarily living in tropical rainforests. Tropical forests are warm (with an average annual temperature of 25 degrees Celsius), moist (with an annual rainfall of around 300 centimeters), and produce abundant plant growth and diversity. African jungles supplied our chimpanzee-like ancestors with everything they needed to survive. The trees served as the primary food source, providing ample fruits and leaves, as well as a convenient location to sleep at night. Amidst the tree canopies, our ancestors were protected both from ground-dwelling predators such as big cats and hyenas as well as the numerous sky-dwelling birds of prey, such as the eagle. In fact, our ancestors spent most of their time amidst the trees, easily moving from one tree to another without much need for moving around on the ground. The jungle was their evolutionary niche. About ten million years ago, however, the earth's climate entered a cooler and drier phase [187].[m] One

---

[l] Whenever DNA is available, it provides additional insights into hominin abilities. At this time, however, the oldest extinct species from which DNA was successfully extracted and analyzed is the Neanderthal [184-186]. Even when DNA is available, it is often difficult to associate the DNA sequence with particular features or abilities.

[m] Eventually, this global cooling led to the growth of permanent ice sheets in Greenland and North America around three million years ago. Technically, the Earth is still in this ice age, with tropical sea surface temperatures some 5 °C to 20 °C cooler than at their peak around 75 million years ago [187].

consequence of the cooling was that the North African tropical forest began to retreat over the course of millions of years, being slowly replaced by grasslands and eventually by desert (the modern Sahara desert). Our tree-dwelling chimpanzee-like ancestors were practically thrown off the trees into the much less hospitable grassland planes of the savanna. The reduction of their natural habitat forced some of our tree-dwelling hominin ancestors to adapt to the new environment. The australopith was the first hominin species that left the safety of the treetop canopies and began bipedal walking in the savanna.

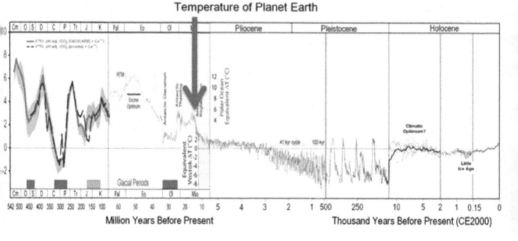

Figure 5.3A The earth's climate entered a cooler and drier phase 10 million years ago (marked by the vertical red arrow). Cooling climate resulted in changing rainfall in northern Africa: the rain forest was slowly replaced by the savanna and then by the Sahara Desert (Figure 5.3B).

10 million year ago

3 million year ago

1 million year ago

Today

Figure 5.3B The retreating tropical forest. The Saharan Desert is almost as large as the continental United States, and is larger than Australia. Ten million years ago this area was covered by rainforest. Back then hominins were safe in the treetop canopies of the rainforest. However, about ten million years ago, the North African tropical forest began to retreat. Rainforest was replaced first by patches of forest separated by expanses of grassland, and then those patches of forest were replaced by open savannas where predators were plentiful. Savannas were later replaced by open grasslands, and eventually by desert (the modern Sahara). When rainforests began to retreat, our tree-dwelling hominid ancestors were practically thrown off the trees onto the planes of the savanna.

Figure 5.4 A full reconstruction of Australopithecus on display at the Museum of Human Evolution, Burgos, Spain. With chimpanzee-like arms and a human-like walking stance, *Australopithecus afarensis* seems to have been equally at home in the trees as well as on the savanna ground.

5.3 *Australopithecus afarensis* (4 to 3 million YO)

The first australopith fossil discovered and documented was of a three-year-old child discovered in a lime quarry by workers at Taung, South Africa. The specimen was studied by Raymond Dart, an anatomist at the University of the Witwatersrand in Johannesburg. He came to the conclusion that the fossil was an early ancestor of humans and gave the new genus its name: Australopithecus from Latin *australis* "of the south" and Greek *pithekos* "ape."

The most famous australopith skeleton was found in 1974 under the direction of French geologists Maurice Taieb, Donald Johanson and Yves Coppens. The fossil was nicknamed Lucy, after the Beatles song "Lucy in the Sky with Diamonds," which was being played loudly and repeatedly on a tape recorder in the archeologists' camp. Lucy was dated to around 3.2 million years old. It was only 1.1 meters (3.6 feet) tall and estimated to weigh about 30 kilograms (66 pounds). A number of similar skeletons were found later.

In the year 2000, the most complete skeletal remains of a three-year-old *Australopithecus afarensis* female were discovered by Zeresenay Alemseged. It was named Selam and is often jokingly called "Lucy's baby." The remains have been dated to be 3.3 million years old.

The anatomy of hands, arms, and shoulder joints shows that Lucy and other *Australopithecus afarensis* were adept tree climbers. The curved finger bones and long arms, similar to that of modern-day apes, were efficient for grasping tree branches. The characteristically apelike upward-facing shoulder socket facilitated australopiths in climbing by allowing them to raise their hands above their heads (modern humans, in contrast, have laterally facing shoulder sockets) [188].

While the upper extremities of the australopiths remained apelike, the lower extremities evolved for walking. The changes in the knee portion of several skeletons as well as the human-like anatomy of the ankle joint indicate that Lucy and her *Australopithecus afarensis* relatives moved by walking upright on the ground. In addition, the Laetoli footprints, discovered in Tanzania (just south of Olduvai Gorge) in 1978 by Louis and Mary Leakey, provide the strongest evidence for bipedal walking.

Figure 5.5 The Laetoli footprints. Two lines of hominin footprints were discovered by a team headed by Louis and Mary Leakey in 1978 at the Laetoli site in Tanzania, 45 km (28 miles) south of Olduvai gorge. (Altogether the

team found over 18,000 individual prints from a variety of animals ranging from rhinoceros to ostrich.) The hominin footprints were preserved in a layer of volcanic ash deposited by an eruption of a nearby volcano. The rain falling onto the ash created something like wet cement. Animals and hominins crossing the muddy surface left footprints. The chemicals in the ash caused it to harden preserving the details of the footprints. In time, additional deposits of ash and mud covered the footprints. The Laetoli footprints were dated to 3.6 million years ago. There was absolutely no doubt that the hominins who made the tracks were walking upright. These parallel tracks were produced by two individuals, one larger than the other, walking side by side. The tracks were in step and very close together. These observations were interpreted as indicating that a male and female australopith were walking arm in arm. Based on a computer simulation of the spacing between the footprints, it appears that this couple moved at a leisurely pace of about one meter per second. Photo by John Reader. (This video describes the process of footprint formation and explains the difference between chimpanzee footprints and Laetoli footprints: http://www.youtube.com/watch?v=w1Lu4VggDH0).

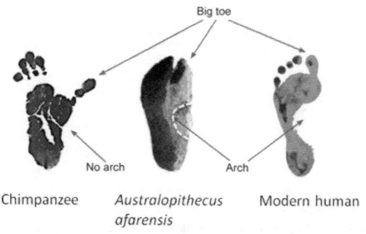

Chimpanzee   *Australopithecus*   Modern human
              afarensis

Figure 5.6 The Laetoli footprints reveal that the foot structure of the
***Australopithecus afarensis* was very similar to that of a modern human.**
The Laetoli footprints do not have the mobile big toe specialized for grasping
that is found in the chimpanzees; rather, the big toe is in line with the rest of
the toes as seen in modern humans. The Laetoli footprints also have an arch
similar to that of modern humans.

There are no knuckle impressions in the Laetoli footprints,
informing us that the hominins that left the prints did not use
arms to support the body during walking. Furthermore the feet
did not have the mobile big toe of apes (specialized for efficient
branch grasping). Rather, as in modern humans, the big toe was
in line with the rest of the toes. The footsteps also had an arch
typical of modern humans. In humans the arch serves to absorb
energy produced by the body-weight, especially important
when walking over a hard surface. The Laetoli footprints are so
similar to modern human footprints that some scientists have
had a hard time believing that the footprints were made by
Australopithecus afarensis, the only human ancestor known to
have lived at the time. The footprints clearly demonstrate that
Australopithecus afarensis had a foot adapted for supporting the
body during bipedal walking. Most scientists now agree that
Australopithecus afarensis walked upright when moving in
savannas.

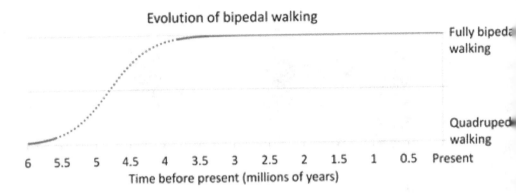

Figure 5.7 **Evolution of bipedal walking.** Our last common ancestor with the chimpanzee was primarily quadrupedal like the modern day chimpanzee. As evidenced by the Laetoli footprints and the skeletal remains such as Lucy, the *Australopithecus afarensis* were walking upright, in a human-like fashion as of 3.6 million years ago. The exact course of evolution of bipedalism between 6 and 3.6 million years ago is unknown (and is approximated by the dotted line).

In addition to the foot structure adapted for walking, hominins acquired larger knees and hip joints to better support the greater portion of body weight supported by the hind legs.

The skeletal changes and foot structure adaptations of the Australopithecus can only be understood in the context of hominins taking long trips on the ground away from the trees. They could have collected savanna grasses, herbs, and seeds, as well as dug out roots, rhizomes, and tubers. Their erect posture may have benefitted australopiths by positioning their eyes above the grass, allowing them to scan the savanna for predators such as big cats, hyenas, and now extinct sabertooths, as well as to scavenge on carcasses of dead animals (that could be signposted by vultures or other scavenging birds). In addition, bipedalism freed the hands to do something other than to support the body during walking: carrying infants or food back to a safe place, picking up stones that could prove helpful at breaking nuts and bones (filled with nutrient-rich marrow), and disassembling of a large carcass left over by other carnivores.

The *Australopithecus afarensis* did not manufacture stone tools; the oldest stone tools that were undeniably manufactured by hominins are only 3.3 million years old [189]. These tools are primarily associated with a new genus: *Homo*.

5.4 *Homo habilis* (between 2.4 and 1.6 million years ago)

One of the earliest hominin species that undoubtedly handcrafted stone tools was *Homo habilis* (literally "handy man" or "skillful person"), which appeared in East Africa during the Lower Paleolithic period about 2.4 million years ago. In appearance and morphology, *Homo habilis* was short and had disproportionately long arms compared to modern humans. This hominin, however, had a reduction of the protrusion of its face and significantly increased brain size. The cranial capacity of *Homo habilis* was slightly less than half the size of that of modern humans (about 630cm^3). Despite the ape-like morphology of their bodies, the remains of *Homo habilis* are often accompanied by primitive stone tools. The stone tools of this period are referred to as *Mode One* or *Oldowan* tools named after the Olduvai Gorge, a steep-sided ravine in the Great Rift Valley in northern Tanzania, where many of the tools have been discovered.

Mode One tools are the first tools that were clearly manufactured by hominins. They were produced starting from 3.3 to 2.6 million years ago [189,190]. Mode One choppers were manufactured from hard cobblestones that can be found in riverbeds and beaches. Any material that was hard enough to produce sharp edges was used including basalt, obsidian, quartz, flint, and chert. The cobblestone was repeatedly struck by hammerstone on the edge to remove large flakes and to produce sharp edges. The Mode One Oldowan choppers are the simplest stone tools produced by hominins.

Figure 5.8 Scientific reconstruction of a *Homo habilis* on display at the Museum of Human Evolution, Burgos, Spain.

Figure 5.9 Olduvai Gorge. Mode One or Oldowan tools take their name from Olduvai, a steep-sided ravine in the Great Rift Valley in northern Tanzania, where many of the tools have been discovered. Two million years ago, the site was that of a large lake. The waters of the lake attracted both animals and hominins. Several active volcanoes often deposited volcanic ash that covered and preserved bones and artifacts. The site was systematically excavated and both fossil bones and stone tools have been found. The layered stratification of the site allows accurate dating of the artifacts. Olduvai Gorge and other African archaeological sites have yielded thousands of Mode One stone tools.

Figure 5.10 A Mode One Oldowan chopper. Museum of Man, San Diego, California.

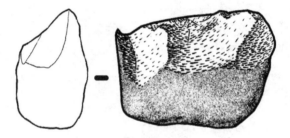

Figure 5.11 A Mode One Oldowan chopper (side and front views) that comes from the Pleistocene site of Dmanisi (Georgia). Its age is estimated at 1.9 million years old.

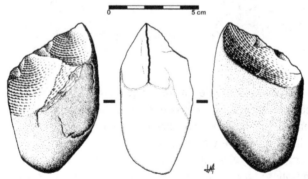

Figure 5.12 A Mode One Oldowan chopper (front, side, and back views) from an archeological site in the Valladolid province (Spain), in the Douro valley. The horizontal bar is 5 centimeters (2 inches).

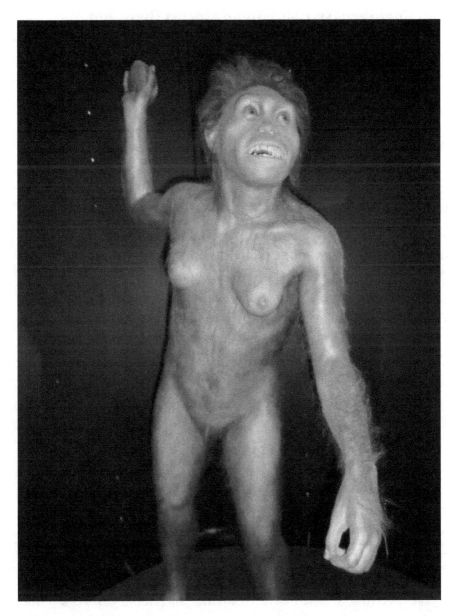

Figure 5.13 Reconstruction of a *Homo erectus* on display at the Museum of Human Evolution, Burgos, Spain

5.5 *Homo ergaster* and *Homo erectus* (between 2 million and 70,000 years ago)

Homo ergaster (from the Greek word "ergaster" meaning "workman") and *Homo erectus* (from the Latin for "upright man") are considered by many scientists to be one species. Accordingly, they will be referred to in this book as *Homo erectus*. *Homo erectus* originated in eastern and southern Africa about 2 million years ago and dispersed throughout most of Africa, Europe and Western Asia approximately 1.8 million years ago. *Homo erectus* was the first hominin to have the same bodily proportions (longer legs and shorter arms) as modern humans. Its brain volume expanded over time from 850 cm^3 to 1225 cm^3, which is still somewhat smaller than that of modern humans. *Homo erectus* hominins were tall, at about 1.8 m (5.9 ft) on average. They were also stronger than modern humans.

The most complete *Homo erectus* skeleton nicknamed "Turkana Boy" (alternatively called "Nariokotome Boy") was discovered at Lake Turkana, Kenya in 1984. The skeleton belonged to a boy who was somewhere between 8 and 15 years of age [191], and is approximately 1.5 million years old. The Turkana Boy skeleton provides the first evidence of the developing speech apparatus. The position of Turkana' Boy's larynx (voice box) is remarkably similar to that of a young, modern child, suggesting that the *Homo erectus* capability of producing complex sounds was superior to that of chimpanzees but inferior to that of modern adults [139].

More advanced *Mode Two* or *Acheulean* stone tools are typically found with the remains of *Homo erectus*. The Acheulean tools are named after the site of Saint Acheul in northern France, where some of the first examples were identified in the nineteenth century. Mode Two pear-shaped handaxes have been found over a wide area across Africa and much of West Asia and Europe. The primary innovation of these tools is that the stone was worked symmetrically on both sides indicating greater care in the production of the final product. The earliest Mode Two tools are dated to be 1.65 million years old although some of the best examples were discovered in the 1.2 million year old layer in Olduvai Gorge.

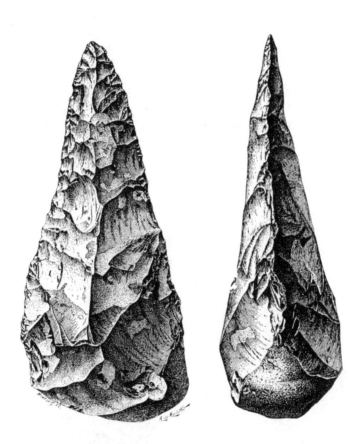

Figure 5.14 A Mode Two Acheulean handaxe found at Saint Acheul in northern France. The stone tool is 20 centimeters (8 inches) high. Drawing by A. Mortillet, end of 19th century.

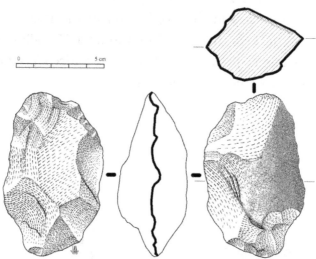

Figure 5.15 Un-reworked edge of a shape found in both Mode One Oldowan and Mode Two Acheulean tools (front, side, back, and top views). This tool is Mode One. The horizontal bar is 5 centimeters (2 inches).

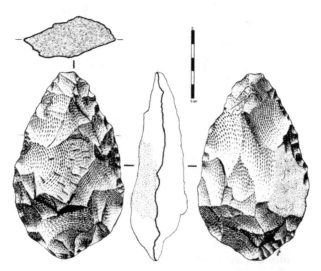

Figure 5.16 Roughly reworked edge; a scalloped effect is produced (front, side, back, and top views). This tool is Mode Two. The vertical bar is 5 centimeters (2 inches).

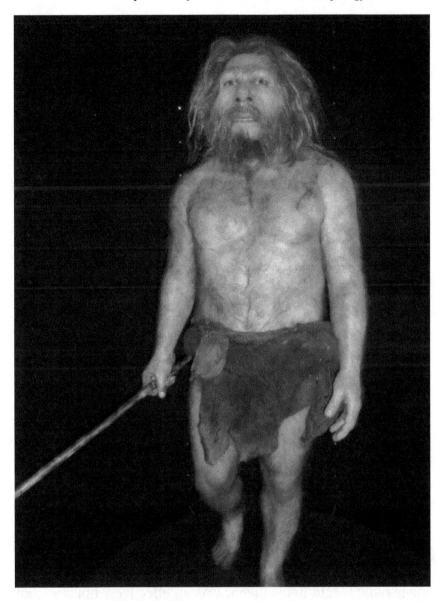

Figure 5.17 Reconstruction of a Neanderthal on display at the Museum of Human Evolution, Burgos, Spain

5.6 The Neanderthals (between 500,000 and 30,000 years ago)

The Neanderthals (*Homo neanderthalensis*) diverged from the *Homo sapiens* lineage over 500,000 years ago [185]. They flourished widely in Europe and parts of western and central Asia (at least as far east as the Altai Mountains in the northern Caucasus) from about 400,000 years ago to about 30,000 years ago [139]. The last known Neanderthals population lived in a cave system on the coast of Gibraltar between 30,000 and 24,000 years ago. Other than the Gibraltar site, there is no fossil record of the Neanderthals as of 30,000 years ago, indicating that they had become extinct.

Neanderthals were similar in height to early modern humans (160cm or 5'3" on average) but were more muscular than modern humans and had stronger bones with thicker walls. Their brain volume was slightly larger (from 1200 cm^3 to 1700 cm^3) and their faces were bigger. Compared to humans, they had lower foreheads and bonier brow ridges. Some Neanderthals had red hair and a pale skin color [192].

Neanderthals invented Mode Three or Mousterian tools. Mode Three tools were manufactured from flint using a more sophisticated Levallois or "prepared-core" technique, which provides much greater control over the size and shape of the final tool. The Levallois technique involves percussion with a soft hammer made of bone or wood, instead of a hard stone hammer. A stone is elaborately shaped in such a way that a single blow would detach what was an effectively finished tool. Mode Three tools appear in the archeological record around 300 thousand years ago during the Middle Paleolithic period. They were named after the site of Le Moustier, a rock shelter in the Dordogne region in central France. Mode Three tools have been found all over Europe and also in the Near East and North Africa.

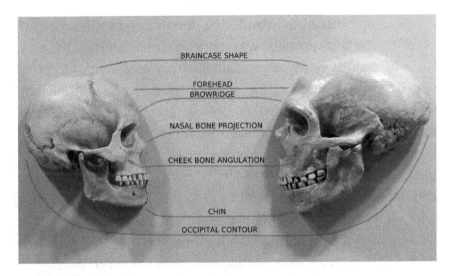

Figure 5.18 Comparison of Modern Human and Neanderthal skulls from the Cleveland Museum of Natural History. The differences in structure between the skulls are marked.

Figure 5.19 Examples of Mode Three Mousterian tools. The horizontal bar is 5 centimeters (2 inches). Source: Dan David Laboratory, Tel Aviv University.

Isotope studies of Neanderthal fossils suggest that the bulk of their dietary protein was coming from animal sources. Neanderthals hunted large animals such as mammoth using wooden spears for hunting. These spears were made of long wooden shafts, sharpened at one or both ends, which were likely used as thrusting spears [193].[n] Projectile spears are more commonly associated with *Homo sapiens*. The high frequency of bone fractures found in Neanderthal skeletons, especially in the ribs, femur, fibulae, spine, and skull, suggests that their primary hunting technique may have been to simply thrust themselves at an animal in an attempt to stab their prey rather than to attack from a safe distance using projectile spears or to trap the animal first [139].

Strikingly, Neanderthals left no symbolic objects, certainly not before contact had been made with early modern humans [139]. The Neanderthal practice of burying the dead may simply have been a way of discouraging hyena intrusion into their caves [139]. In any case, Neanderthal burials completely lack the

---

[n] Whether Neanderthals used the spears for thrusting or throwing is a matter of intense debate. For example, the eight wooden spears found in Schöningen, Germany, which date back to 300,000 years ago, could have been used as throwing spears [194]. The spears are between 1.8 and 2.5 meters long and are made from spruce stems and pine wood. The tips are worked symmetrically at both ends. The wooden Schöningen spears were found to be similar to today's tournament javelins, as far as their throwing qualities. During tests, athletes were able to throw replicas of the ancient spears up to 70 meters [195]. Of course the observation that Schöningen spears *could have been* thrown does not mean that they actually were. If it were used as a throwing spear, it is unclear why it would need to have both ends sharpened (sharpening hardwood with stone tools must have been an arduous procedure). On the other hand, sharpening both ends of a spear becomes more understandable if it was used in close combat for thrusting directly into an animal no matter which direction it may be coming from. Consult Churchill SE [196] for further discussion on this interesting topic.

"grave goods" that would indicate the belief in an afterlife [139].

It is likely that Neanderthals had a developed vocal apparatus. The Neanderthal hyoid bone (which connects the musculature of the tongue and the larynx) found at the Kebara Cave in Israel is virtually identical to that of modern humans [197].

Further support for a well-developed speech apparatus in Neanderthals is provided by DNA analysis. The FOXP2 gene is the first identified gene that, when mutated, causes a specific language deficit in humans. Affected people have mostly normal motor coordination and cognitive abilities, but they are unable to correctly pronounce words, form words into grammatically correct sentences, and have trouble understanding complex language. For example, many members of the English family known as KE (abbreviation is used for privacy) with a single mutation in FOXP2 exhibit great difficulties in controlling their facial movements, as well as with reading, writing, grammar, and understanding others [198]. (The protein encoded by the FOXP2 gene is a transcription factor. It regulates genes involved in the production of many different proteins. Therefore it is not surprising that KE-family exhibit several abnormalities.)

Recently the Neanderthal DNA sequence was extracted from two bones (of two different individuals) excavated from the El Sidron Cave in Asturias, northern Spain. The DNA analysis showed that humans and Neanderthals have an identical FOXP2 protein sequence [186]. This indicates that the common ancestor of *Homo sapiens* and Neanderthals already had a FOXP2 protein sequence that was identical to that of modern humans.

5.7 Hominin brain volume increased over time

Over the course of hominin evolution, the volume of the brain nearly quadrupled from 350cm^3 to 1,350cm^3. A large brain is a very "expensive" device: at rest, brain tissue burns 16 times as much energy as the same volume of muscle tissue [199]. In modern humans, the brain accounts for 2% of body weight but is responsible for 20% of energy consumption in a resting body [200]. All the skeletal muscles, which account for 42% of body weight, generate the same amount of heat (at rest) as the brain. For comparison, the brains of other vertebrates use (nearly uniformly) 2 to 8% of that animal's caloric intake [201].° Furthermore, the brain burns so much energy that keeping it cool is a problem. A human brain at rest generates as much heat as a 15-watt incandescent bulb [202]. The cooling function is primarily performed by the circulating blood. As the hominin brain increased in size, cooling became a greater problem and new blood vessels had to evolve before the brain was capable of growing further. The network of emissary veins along the parietal and mastoid brain regions acquired by australopiths created an additional radiator that allowed for a more rapid cooling of the human brain (the so-called "radiator theory" [203]).

Despite these problems, the brain evolved faster than any other part of the body. Noel Boaz, Director of the International Institute for Human Evolutionary Research, writes: "*Homo* clearly has a larger brain than earlier hominids ... We know of no other anatomical character in any part of the body that is changing so rapidly in human evolution" (1997).

° In fact, with the exception listed below, the only vertebrates known to possess brains consuming more than 10% of resting energy consumption are some primates (11–13 %) and humans (Mink JW, 1981). A very special exception to this rule was found in Africa among weakly electric fish. The brain of the *Gnathonemus petersii* holds a record for the highest energetic cost of a vertebrate brain. It is responsible for a whopping 60% of body energy consumption (Nilsson G, 1996). The exceptionally high energetic cost of the *G. petersii* brain appears to be a consequence both of the brain being very large and of the fish being ectothermic ("cold-blooded").

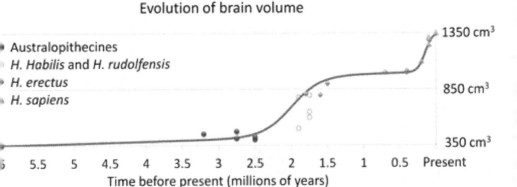

Figure 5.20 **Evolution of hominin brain volume.** Plotting brain volume (as measured by endocranial volume) against the estimated age of fossil specimens reveals that the brain size increased relatively slowly in australopiths from 350 cm³ to 450 cm³ over 3.5 million years, but then increased significantly in two major growth spurts: around 1.8 million years ago and again about 70,000 years ago (for review, see Ref. [202], page 315)

At the same time muscle strength decreased. Chimpanzee muscle exceeds human muscle in maximum dynamic force and power output by about 1.35 times[p] [204]. Clearly the role that the brain played in the survival of our ancestors increased disproportionately over the last six million years. Our ancestors survived because they became smarter, not because they became stronger or faster.

---

[p] This is primarily due to a different balance between fast – and slow-twitch muscle fibers. The higher content of the fast-twitch fibers in chimpanzees, rather than exceptional maximum isometric force or maximum shortening velocities, is responsible for the greater dynamic force. It is likely that greater ratio of slow to fast-twitch muscle evolved in hominins in response to selection pressure for repetitive, non-fatiguing contractile behavior such as walking.

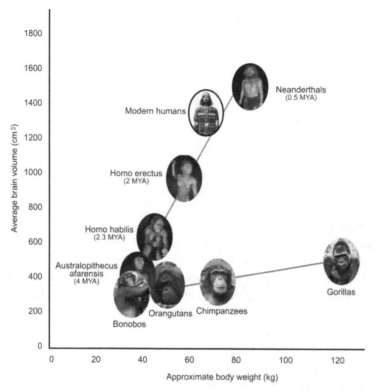

Figure 5.21 The brain volume in mammals is related to body weight. Bigger mammals commonly have bigger brains. Apes are no exception. Bigger apes (e.g. gorillas) have a greater brain volume than smaller apes (e.g. bonobos). The hominin brain, however, is significantly bigger than that of an ape. The volume of the human brain is three times greater than what you would expect for an ape of the same size; data points are averages based on data compiled from Ref. [205].

5.8 Modern humans diffuse out of Africa (around 65,000 years ago)

The converging archeological and genetic evidence indicates that all modern humans descend from a small population that lived in sub-Saharan Africa about 70,000 years ago. Let's first consider the genetic data. Human DNA has about six billion base pairs. DNA accumulates mutations over time at a relatively predictable rate. These mutations, which may be neither beneficial nor harmful, allow scientists to use DNA as a molecular clock. By counting the differences in the number of mutations between any two lineages, scientists can trace back to a common ancestor.

DNA samples have been collected from thousands of people around the world and DNA analyses have been performed separately on mitochondrial DNA, on the Y-chromosome, and on the complete human genome. All mitochondria are passed from mother to offspring. Mutations accumulated in the mitochondrial DNA can be used to trace back to the most recent maternal common ancestor for all currently living human beings. Mitochondrial Eve is traced back to between 160,000 years ago [206] and 124,000 years ago [207]. Mitochondrial Eve was not the only woman living at the time, however all people are descendents of that one woman.

Similarly, Y-chromosomal Adam, the most recent, common paternal ancestor from whom all Y-chromosomes in living men are descended, is traced back to around 138,000 years ago [207] (other smaller, less reliable studies range between 190,000 [208] and 62,000 years ago [207]. The most reliable data are obtained from analysis of the complete human genome. This analysis indicates that all modern humans are descendents of a small population that existed in sub-Saharan Africa between 70,000 and 140,000 years ago [209].

Humans made their first journey out of Africa sometime between 70,000 and 65,000 years ago [206,209]. The Andaman Islands in the Indian Ocean were settled some 65,000 years ago [210], and Australia may well have been settled as early as 62,000 years ago [211]. The DNA analysis indicates that *Homo sapiens* arrived in Europe between 55,000 and 30,000 years ago [206]. The skeletal remains and artifacts left by *Homo sapiens* date back to 45,000 years ago [212], which supports the conclusions of the DNA analysis.

Hominin species	Chimpanzee	*Australopithecus afarensis*	*Homo habilis*
Known time of existence	7 million years ago to now	5 to 2.5 million years ago	2.4 to 1.6 million years ago
Territorial distribution	Africa	Africa	Africa
Most famous skeleton	*Currently living species*	Lucy (3.2 million year old skeleton)	Olduvai Hominid 7 discovered by Jonathan and Mary Leakey
Reconstruction			
Walking	Quadrapedal	Bipedal	Bipedal
Associated tool culture	Chimps use natural stones to break nuts	Possibly spit stones or used natural sharp-edged stones	Mode One: Oldowan chopper
Stone tools			
Average height	1 m (3.3 ft)	1.2 m (4 ft)	1.3 m (4.3 ft)
Approximate body weight	45 kg (99 lb)	32 kg (71 lb)	45 kg (99lb)
Average brain volume	350 cm^3	350 cm^3	630 cm^3
Proposed top-down control of mental imagery	Little control. Mental images are limited to natural objects	Developing mental analysis	Primitive mental analysis. Ability to generate a primitive mental template
Speech apparatus	Primitive	Primitive	Primitive
Communication system	Non-syntactic communication system with about 30 vocalizations	Non-syntactic communication system with few vocalizations	Non-syntactic communication system with few vocalizations

(Sidebar text: Hominin species and associated tool culture)

Table 5.1 Hominin species and associated tool culture

Homo ergaster and Homo erectus	Neanderthal	Homo sapiens	Hominid species
2 million to 100,000 years ago	500,000 to 30,000 years ago	Diffused out of Africa around 65,000 years ago	Known time of existence
Africa, Europe, Asia	Europe, Asia	All continents	Territorial distribution
Turkana boy (1.5 million year old skeleton)	Neanderthal 1 discovered in Neanderthal, Germany	Currently living species	Most famous skeleton
			Reconstruction
Bipedal	Bipedal	Bipedal	Walking
Mode Two: Acheulean symmetrical handaxe	Mode Three: Mousterian prepared-core tools	Ornamented tools	Associated tool culture
			Stone tools
1.8 m (5.9 ft)	1.6 m (5.2 ft)	1.5 m (4.9 ft)	Average height
50 kg (110 lb)	70 kg (154 lb)	60 kg (132 lb)	Approximate body weight
1000 cm^3	1500 cm^3	1350 cm^3	Average brain volume
Advanced mental analysis. Ability to generate an advanced mental template	Advanced mental analysis. Ability to generate an advanced mental template	Mental analysis and mental synthesis	Proposed top-down control of mental imagery
Developing	Nearly modern	Modern	Speech apparatus
Non-syntactic communication system with a significant number of words	Non-syntactic communication system with a large number of words	Syntactic communication system	Communication system

Chapter 6. Acquisition of prefrontal synthesis 70,000 years ago

... if there is one single thing that above all else unites all human beings today, it is our symbolic capacity: our common ability to organize the world around us into a vocabulary of mental representations that we can recombine in our minds in an endless variety of new ways. This unique mental facility allows us to create in our heads the alternative worlds that are the very basis of the cultural variety that is so much a hallmark of our species. Other creatures live in the world more or less as Nature presents it to them; and they react to it more or less directly, albeit sometimes with remarkable sophistication. In contrast, we human beings live to a significant degree in the worlds that our brains remake.... [I]t is entirely without precedent. Not only is the ability for symbolic reasoning lacking among our closest living relatives, the great apes; such reasoning was apparently also absent from our closest extinct relatives— and even from the earliest humans who looked exactly like us.

IAN TATTERSALL, *Masters of the Planet: The search for our human origins* (2012)

6.1 External manifestations of prefrontal synthesis

Once we realize that prefrontal synthesis (PFS) is a neurologically separate component of imagination, we must then ask when PFS was acquired by hominins [153]? Archeological records indicate gradual, piece-meal process of accretion of symbolic artifacts such as perforated shells [213], use of pigments presumably in body decoration [213], and intentional burials [214], over hundreds of thousands of years [215]. However, symbolic thinking is not congruent to PFS. The symbolic use of objects can be accompanied by PFS in modern individuals, but PFS is not necessary for using an object as a symbol. For example, the use of red ochre may be highly symbolic due to its association with blood. However, this association may be entirely based on memory of an emotional event such as a bloody battle, as well as spontaneously formed imagery of a battle. Crucially, memory recall and spontaneously formed imagery (like in a dream or during an insight) do not rely on PFS [153] and therefore use of red ochre is not an indication of the PFS abilities in hominins. Similarly, simple personal ornaments such as perforated shells [213,216-218] could have been used as symbols of social power. However, neither their manufacturing nor their use signify the PFS ability. The line marks on stones and shells [219], as well as geometrical figures and hand stencils painted on cave walls are undoubtedly associated with general improvement in the lateral prefrontal cortex function and voluntary imagination in their creators, but there is nothing in these artifacts indicating the presence of the most advanced component of imagination, the PFS ability [153].

The first definitive evidence of PFS appears in the archeological record around 65,000 to 40,000 years ago and it emerges simultaneously in six modalities: (1) composite figurative arts, (2) bone needles with an eye, (3) construction of dwellings, (4) elaborate burials, (5) lightning-fast colonization of the globe and migration to Australia (presumably by boats), and (6) demise of the Pleistocene megafauna (presumably with the aid of animal traps).

6.2 Figurative art

Let's start with figurative art. The archeological record has few objects that can be classified as art until about 80,000 year ago. There is always heated debate on whether some ancient item, like a bone or a stone with regular incisions, was produced by nature or by the hand of a hominin (e.g. Ref. [220]). The first undisputed art objects include pierced marine shells, found in various locations in Africa, Asia, and Europe, which were probably used as beads. For example, the earliest pierced shells from eastern Morocco were dated to around 82,000 years ago [216]. The famous shells from the Blombos Cave in South Africa were dated to around 70,000 years ago, and include over 65 shells that were brought from rivers located 20 km from the cave and then pierced by inserting a small bone tool through the aperture to create a "keyhole perforation" [217,218]. In addition to beads, archeologists have also discovered several ochre plaques with cross-hatched patterns engraved over a smoothed surface [219]. The plaques were dated to approximately 75,000-70,000 years ago.

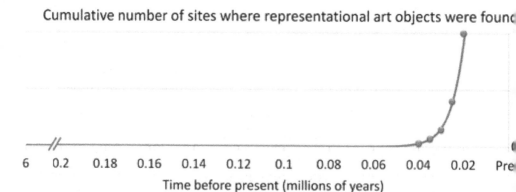

Figure 6.1 **Evolution of figurative art.** The graph shows the approximate cumulative number of sites where figurative art objects were found as a function of time. The archeological record has few objects that can be classified as art until about 80,000 years ago. The earliest objects of figurative art date back to around 40,000 years ago.

Figure 6.2 Picture of a half-animal half-human in a Paleolithic cave painting in Dordogne, France.

Figure 6.3 Venus of Laussel, a one-and–a-half foot tall limestone bas-relief of a female figure, painted with red ochre. It was carved into a large block of limestone in a rock shelter (abri de Laussel) in southwestern France. The female holds a bison horn clearly marked with 13 notches that may symbolize the number of moons or the number of menstrual cycles in one year. The female's other hand is placed on her womb. The carving is dated to approximately 25,000 years ago.

The earliest figurative art appears in the archeological record around 40,000 years ago in multiple different forms: cave paintings drawn using charcoal and ochre or even carved into the walls, and various figurines, such as the voluptuous "Venus figures," made out of bone and stone. What's interesting is that this early art appeared nearly simultaneously in hundreds of locations spread around the globe [137]. The figurative art objects are undeniably associated with early modern humans often referred to as Cro-Magnons (after the cave of Crô-Magnon in southwest France, where the first specimen was found). As was discussed in Chapter 3.11, composite objects such as the Lowenmensch ("lion-man") sculpture from the caves of Lone valley in Germany, depictions of bird-man and lion-man hybrids from the Lascaux cave in France, an engraving of a man with a horse's tail and a bird's head from the cave of Hornos de la Peña in Spain, all undeniably show the presence of PFS in early modern humans.

6.3 Religious beliefs

As noted in Part 1, the origin of religious beliefs can be traced through beliefs in the afterlife. Beliefs in the afterlife, in turn, are often associated with adorned burials. Therefore the development of religious beliefs may be inferred by studying the time period when humans first buried their deceased in elaborate graves with accompanying "grave goods."

The oldest known human burial, dated to 500,000 years ago and attributed to *Homo heidelbergensis*, was found in the Sima de los Huesos site in Atapuerca, Spain, and consists of various corpses deposited in a vertical shaft. A significant number of burials are also associated with Neanderthals: La Chapelle-aux-Saints, La Ferrassie, and Saint-Cesaire in France;

Teshik-Tash in Uzbekistan; Shanidar Cave in Iraq. However, whether or not these sites constitute actual burial sites is hotly disputed. Their preservation could well be explained by natural depositions [221]. Even if those burials were made deliberately, the goal may have been to simply toss the bodies away in order to discourage hyena intrusion into their caves [139]. In any case, these early burials completely lack the "grave goods" that would indicate the belief in an afterlife [139].

The earliest undisputed *deliberate* human burial occurred approximately 70,000 years ago. Human skeletal remains that were intentionally stained with red ochre and buried with "grave goods" were discovered in the Skhul and Qafzeh caves, in Levant. One of the burials contains a skeleton with a mandible of a wild boar in the arms, another contains a woman with a small child at her feet, and another a young man with a possible offering of deer antlers and red ochre. While these burials are clearly intentional, whether or not they indicate the belief in an afterlife is uncertain. The ochre by itself is inconclusive evidence. For example, if the local nobility were marking themselves with ochre during their lifetime as a sign of superiority over their kinsmen, or simply to protect their skin from insects, they may have died and been buried still bearing the ochre marks. The small number of "offerings" found in these burial sites may have simply been objects that fell into the burial pit accidentally. In any case, there is not enough conclusive evidence from these early burials to judge the occupants' beliefs in an afterlife.

The number of known *adorned* burials and the sophistication of the offerings significantly increased around 40,000 years ago. To date, over one hundred graves of *Homo sapiens* have been discovered that date back to the period between 42,000 and 20,000 years ago. In many cases several bodies were interred in a single grave. Burial offerings were commonplace and ochre was used abundantly. Examples include: a burial in Lake Mungo, Australia of a man sprinkled with red ochre, dating back to 42,000 years ago; an elaborate burial in Sungir, Russia that includes two juveniles and an adult male wearing a tunic adorned with beads and carefully interred with an astonishing variety of decorative and useful objects, dating back to 30,000 years ago; a grave in Grimaldi, Italy, which contains the remains of a man and two adolescents along with burial offerings; and a site in Dolni Vestonice, in the Czech Republic where a woman was buried between two men and all three skulls were covered in ochre.

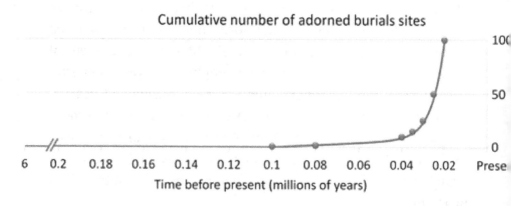

Figure 6.4 Evolution of religious beliefs traced through beliefs in an afterlife. The graph shows the approximate cumulative number of adorned burials sites as a function of time. The earliest undisputed human burial dates back to 70,000 years ago. The number of known *adorned* burials significantly increased around 40,000 years ago.

6.4 Design and construction

There is little evidence of hominins constructing dwellings or fire hearths until the arrival of *Homo sapiens*. While Neanderthals controlled the use of fire, their hearths were usually very simple: most were just shallow depressions in the ground. There is almost a complete lack of evidence of any dwelling construction [222]. The arrival of *Homo sapiens*, on the other hand, is marked by plentiful constructed structures including stone-lined and dug-out fireplaces, as well as unambiguous remains of dwellings, which all flourished starting around 30,000 years ago. The examples include: foundations for circular hut structures at Vigne-Brune (Villerest) in eastern France, dating back to 27,000 years ago; postholes and pit clusters at a site near the village of Dolní Věstonice in the Czech Republic, dating back to 26,000 years ago, and mammoth bone structures at Kostienki, Russia and Mezirich, Ukraine. As early as 12,000 years ago, *Homo sapiens* introduced agriculture and started to build permanent villages [139] [141].

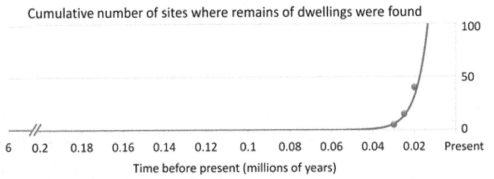

Cumulative number of sites where remains of dwellings were found

Time before present (millions of years)

Figure 6.5 Evolution of design and construction. The graph shows the approximate cumulative number of sites where constructed structures and unambiguous remains of dwellings were found as a function of time. There is little evidence of hominin construction of dwellings or fireplaces until the arrival of *Homo sapiens*. Plentiful constructed structures and unambiguous remains of dwellings appear in the archeological record starting around 30,000 years ago.

6.5 Creativity and innovation

As noted in Part 1, creativity and innovation involves *PFS* of new objects. It is pretty difficult to come up with a new type of tool without first thinking through various possible designs. Therefore, the hominin propensity for creativity and innovation can be inferred by looking at the number and quality of the different types of tools they manufactured. The number of different types of tools used by hominins will be reviewed first and the evolution of tool quality will be reviewed separately.

Jane Goodall and other scientists have been able to observe and record an extensive list of over thirty types of tools used in the wild by chimpanzees [4-6]. Most tools, such as stones used to break nuts, are used in their natural form, but there are a few tools that are manufactured by chimpanzees. For example, chimps prepare sticks for termite-fishing by trimming twigs; they also make a sort of spear for hunting bushbabies by biting on one end of a stick [7].

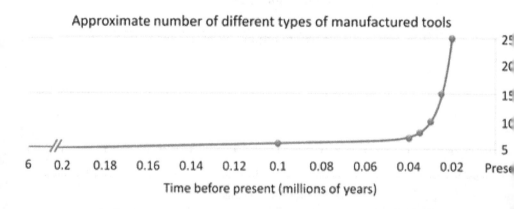

Figure 6.6 Evolution of creativity and innovation can be traced by counting the number of different types of tools manufactured by hominins. The graph shows the approximate number of different types of manufactured tools as a function of time. The number of different types of manufactured tools in the archeological record significantly increased about 40,000 years ago. The numbers have been increasing exponentially ever since.

Hominins expanded on the chimpanzee repertoire by adding Mode One stone choppers 3.3 million years ago. Around 2 million years ago, *Homo ergaster* added Mode Two handaxes. Around 400,000 years ago, Neanderthals added Mode Three stone tools, which consisted of sophisticated stone-flakes and task-specific tools such as large scrapers created from flint flakes. These tools were produced using soft hammer percussion, using hammers made out of materials such as bones, antlers, and wood, as opposed to hard hammer percussion, which uses stone hammers. As discussed above, Neanderthals also manufactured wooden spears. This list pretty much includes all the types of tools manufactured by primates before the arrival of *Homo sapiens.*

In comparison to the relative stasis of tool development by our ancestors, tool development by modern humans seems lightning fast. As early as 65,000 to 30,000 years ago, *Homo sapiens* introduced kiln-baked ceramics, projectile spears, the bow and arrow[q], musical instruments[r], and even bone needles; as early as 12,000 years ago, *Homo sapiens* introduced agriculture and built permanent villages [139,141].

---

[q] The earliest quartz-tipped arrows have been dated to about 64,000 years ago [140].

[r] The oldest flute was discovered at Divje Babe in Slovenia and dates back to about 43,000 years ago. It is made out of the femur of a juvenile cave bear, with several holes. The next oldest flute was found in the Geißenklösterle cave and dates back to 42,000-43,000 years ago [223]. The five-holed flute made from the wing bone of a vulture dates back to 35,000 years ago, and was discovered in Hohle Fels cave near Ulm, Germany [223]. More flutes were found in the Geißenklösterle cave in southern Germany: one made from a mammoth tusk (dating back to 37,000-30,000 years ago), and another one made from swan bones (dating back to about 36,000 years ago). While the implications of humans manufacturing musical instruments could be a subject of a separate discussion, for our purposes they are just another type of tool: a tool for facilitating the process of producing pleasing sounds.

6.6 Fast colonization of the globe and migration to Australia.

Hominins diffusing out of Africa had been colonizing the Europe and Asia long before the arrival of *Homo sapiens*: the remains of *Homo erectus* have been found as far as in Spain [224] and Indonesia [225] and Neanderthals remains have been found in Europe and Asia [226]. However, both the extent and the speed of colonization of the planet by *Homo sapiens* 70,000 to 65,000 years ago are unprecedented. Our ancestors quickly settled Europe and Asia and crossed open water to Andaman Islands in the Indian Ocean by 65,000 years ago [210] and Australia as early as 62,000 years ago [211]. Migration to Australia is consistent with the use of boats by early modern humans further underlying their propensity for technological innovations.

6.7 Building animal traps and demise of the Pleistocene megafauna.

Without PFS one cannot envision the building of an animal trap, e.g. pitfall trap, which requires digging a deep pit and camouflaging it with twigs and branches. PFS aids trap building in three ways. First, a leader can use PFS to mentally simulate multiple ways to build a trap. Second, a leader could use PFS to think through the step-by-step process of building a trap. Finally, a leader could communicate the plan to the tribe: "We will make a trap by digging a large pit and covering it with tree branches. A mammoth will then fall into the pit; no need to attack a mammoth head on." In fact, early modern humans are known for building traps; traps for herding gazelle, ibex, wild asses and other large animals were found in the deserts of the Near East. Some of the traps were as large as 60km (37miles) in length [227]. Funnel-shaped traps comprising two long stone walls (up to 60 kilometers in length!) converged on an enclosure or pit at the apex. Animals were probably herded into the funnel until they reached the enclosure at the apex surrounded by pits, at which point the animals were trapped and killed. Some traps date back to as early as the 7th millennium BC [227]. The building process must have been pre-planned by a tribe leader (or several leaders) and then explained to all the workers. Each worker, in turn, would have had to understand exactly what they needed to do: collect proper stones, assemble stones into a wall, and have the two walls meet at the apex 60 km away from where they started.

The correlation of human migration with the demise of the Pleistocene megafauna [228,229] is consistent with PFS that would have enabled mental planning of sophisticated attack strategies with the use of animal traps [227].

6.8 Conclusions: Prefrontal synthesis acquisition results in cognitive revolution

In Part 1, nine external manifestations of PFS were identified: a recursive communication system; predilection for story-telling, strategy games; the ability to create figurative art, as well as to design and construct new structures; an inclination towards active teaching, natural sciences, and religious beliefs; and a tendency towards creativity and innovation. While five of these do not leave an archeological record, four manifestations, namely figurative arts, design and construction, creativity and innovation, and religious beliefs are often associated with tangible artifacts. There is no evidence of the PFS ability in hominins before 65,000 years ago and there is an *abundance* of clear and unambiguous evidence of the PFS ability in all four previously identified manifestations of PFS in hominins after 62,000 years ago: composite objects executed in bone and cave paintings, bone needles with an eye, construction of dwellings, and appearance of adorned burials, Together with steadfast colonization of the planet and migration to Australia and demise of the Pleistocene megafauna, the archeological evidence unambiguously indicates acquisition of the PFS ability in hominins around 70,000 years ago.

Evolution of figurative arts, religious beliefs, design and construction, and creativity and innovation are highly correlated with each other. All four traits flourished simultaneously across multiple geographical locations 65,000 to 40,000 YA. This phenomenon has been characterized by paleoanthropologists as the "Upper Paleolithic Revolution," [139,230,231] the "Cognitive revolution," [232] and the "Great Leap Forward" [233]. Furthermore the archeological indicators of PFS are correlated geographically: at the sites where paleoanthropologists find adorned burials and remains of human dwellings, they also often find figurative art objects and multiples bone and stone tools. Finally, the physical evidence of all four traits is commonly discovered alongside the skeletal remains of *Homo sapiens.* The considerable temporal and geographical correlation of clear PFS artifacts is consistent with the single event of PFS acquisition by hominins.

Let's try to pin down the exact timeframe for the first acquisition of PFS. The lower boundary of the timeframe is provided by evidence of the first settlers outside of Africa who possessed PFS. It has been reported that the Andaman Islands in the Indian Ocean were settled some 65,000 years ago [210], and Australia may well have been settled as early as 62,000 years ago [211]. As the Andaman Islanders have been genetically isolated for 65,000 years, and have the capacity for PFS, acquisition of PFS must have occurred before the genetic isolation of the inhabitants of the Andaman Islands. Adding 5,000 years for migration from Africa to the Andaman Islands, **the first PFS acquisition date can be estimated around 70,000 years ago**.

This date conforms to the genetic analysis of the complete human genome indicating that all modern humans are descendants of a small population that existed in sub-Saharan Africa between 140,000 and 70,000 years ago [209]. The date also conforms to the genetic analysis of the Y-chromosome, which places the most recent, common, paternal ancestor to 138,000 years ago [207] (other smaller, less reliable studies range between 190,000 [208] and 62,000 years ago [234]) and mitochondrial DNA, which places the most recent, common, maternal ancestor to between 160,000 years ago [206] and 124,000 years ago [207].

Acquisition of PFS ability increases the competitive advantage of a tribe in many ways. First, by changing hunting strategy from persistence hunting to building traps, hominins could have obtained nearly unlimited quantity of food resulting in increased fertility and decreased mortality. Second, tribe's losses to predation must have come down since hominins no longer had to expose themselves to predators during persistence hunting and foraging [235]. Third, the number of wounds received in close combat with large animals had to come down as a result of preferential use of trapping of megafauna. Fourth, PFS must have dramatically increased cohesion between tribe members through religion and syntactic language [236]. Fifth, PFS facilitated the process of discovery of new tools, such as spear throwers and bow-and-arrows [140]. Thus, it is likely that a tribe that first acquired PFS would have quickly increased in size and overcome the rest of hominins. The genetic bottleneck that has been detected around 70,000 [237] is likely associated with the "founder effect" of a few individuals who acquired PFS and imposed their genes on the rest of hominins.

Chapter 7. Evolution of voluntary imagination leading to prefrontal synthesis acquisition

The intellectual resource that allows us to process such knowledge is our symbolic cognitive style. This is a shorthand term for our ability to mentally dissect the world around us into a huge vocabulary of intangible symbols. These we can then recombine in our minds, according to rules that allow an unlimited number of visions to be formulated from a finite set of elements. Using this vocabulary and these rules we are able to generate alternative versions or explanations of the world – and of ourselves. It is this unique symbolic ability that underwrites the internalized self-representation expressed in the peculiarly human sense of self. In between the two ends of the spectrum, linking the primordial and the symbolic styles of self-awareness, there presumably exists a near-infinite array of states of self-knowledge. Yet because alien cognitive states are among the few things human beings find it impossible to imagine, let alone to experience, any discussion of such intermediate forms of self-knowledge – such as that possessed by our early ancestors – is fraught with huge risks of anthropomorphizing. When we try to understand how other organisms comprehend particular situations, or their place in society, or indeed their place in the world, our tendency is always to impose our own constructs. The temptation is to assume that beings of other kinds are seeing and understanding the world somehow as we do, just not as well or as fully. Yet the truth is that we simply cannot know, still less feel, what it is subjectively like to be any organism other than ourselves, modern Homo sapiens.

IAN TATTERSALL, *Masters of the Planet: The search for our human origins* (2012)

While PFS acquisition and appearance of behaviorally-modern humans 70,000 thousand years ago was abrupt, neurological mechanisms of voluntary imagination were gradually improving over the 6 million years of hominin evolution. In this chapter we will follow improvement of voluntary imagination in hominins using the evidence from the stone tools.

7.1 Following improvement of voluntary imagination by watching the quality of manufactured stone tools

It is likely that our ancestors handled stones for quite some time. Even modern day chimpanzees from the Tai Forest in the Ivory Coast (Côte d'Ivoire) are known to often carry stones when walking bipedally. Tai Forest chimpanzees use stones for cracking nuts. This tendency must have grown in bipedal australopiths whose hands were not used for walking. Stones could assist australopiths in protection against some predators and could have been used to improve access to food: breaking nuts and getting marrow out of bones, as well as the disassembly of large carcasses left over by other carnivores. It would have been only natural for australopiths to carry a stone with them at all times, since one may not have been readily available whenever it became necessary.

At some point, australopiths may have discovered that sharp-edged stones work better than dull ones for breaking up carcasses and bones (there is some evidence of cut marks on bones as early as 3.3 million years ago). Australopiths could have discovered that striking a cobble with a hammerstone splits the cobble into two sharp-edged stones. (After all, even birds are known to drop shells on a pebble beach to extract the meat from inside the shell.) Australopiths may have also selected naturally sharp stones. However, australopiths did not manufacture Mode One choppers at least not until around 3.3

million years ago [189]. It seems that they lacked some important brain function that would have allowed them to manufacture the choppers. As previously mentioned, the first Mode One chopper appears in the archeological record 3.3 million years ago and it is associated with *Homo habilis*. Since then, hominin evolution is closely linked with the improvement of stone tools.

How does the quality of stone tools reflect the hominin cognitive development? The first observation from the stone tool record is that the species capable of manufacturing finer, more symmetrical and sharper stone tools were also more successful evolutionarily: Mode Two tools are sharper and more symmetrical than Mode One tools and *Homo erectus*, the manufacturer of Mode Two tools, succeeded over *Homo habilis*, the manufacturer of Mode One tools. Neanderthals, armed with Mode Three stone tools that are even finer than Mode Two tools, succeeded over *Homo erectus*. In other words, the species that was capable of attending to smaller and finer details in the final product, was the clear evolutionary winner.

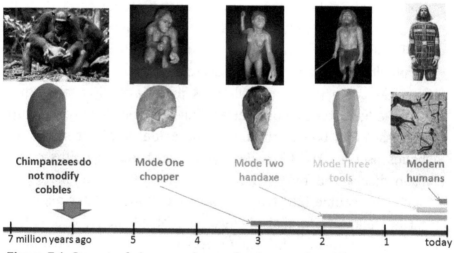

Figure 7.1 Stone tools improved very slowly over time. The great puzzle of paleoanthropology: why is each hominin species associated with only a single stone tool culture? Why is there so little progress within each species?

The second observation is that the use of each particular type of stone tool is primarily associated with a particular hominin species: Mode One Oldowan choppers with *Homo habilis*, Mode Two Acheulean handaxes with *Homo erectus*, and Mode Three Mousterian advanced stone-flakes and spearheads with the Neanderthals. Such a stepwise evolution creates the impression that each hominin species started at a higher level than the previous one, but once that phase had started, further development was impossible. *Homo habilis* had over half a million years of evolution to stumble upon a better technique for manufacturing stone tools, but this never happened. What was easy for *Homo erectus* (Mode Two Acheulean tools) was impossible for *Homo habilis*. In turn, *Homo erectus* did not do much to improve its tools for nearly two million years (!) of evolution. Mode Three Mousterian stone-flakes manufactured by Neanderthals in great quantity were beyond the reach of *Homo erectus*. Even the Neanderthal's stone tool kit remained relatively unchanged for several hundred thousand years.

The constant refinement of technology by modern humans contrasts markedly with a pattern of slow technological innovation observed in the evolution of *Homo* species, where each improvement took nearly a million years. Modern humans improve tools with every generation. In 60,000 years that have passed since modern humans began spreading around the planet, we have created civilizations, produced artwork, built cities and reached for outer space. This is a remarkably short period of time compared to the several million years that other homo species inhabited the planet. What prevented hominins from making better tools over hundreds of thousands of years? Clearly it was not the lack of transmission of knowledge between generations, since all primates are able to pass on complicated skills to their kin (think of chimpanzee termite fishing and nut cracking [238]. Neither can you satisfactorily explain the lack of tool development by limitations in the structure of the hand. The Neanderthal hand structure, for example, was very similar to that of modern humans, except for greater robustness, and the range of manipulative movement was also comparable [239,240].

The stasis in tool development within each *Homo* species is consistent with the cognitive limitations of those species [241]. It appears that, within each species, hominins were not smart enough to make stone tools of better quality. In other words, each species of hominins produced the best tools they were able to manufacture. A major evolutionary shift that created a new species (one that was different neurologically) was required to improve the tools. Thus, studying the neurobiology of chopper manufacturing may shed light on the following question: what quality of mind developed stepwise from one *Homo* species to another which allowed the new species to manufacture better stone tools? Furthermore, we shall be able to make a conjecture as to what new quality of mind allowed hominins to make the first stone tools 3.3 million years ago.

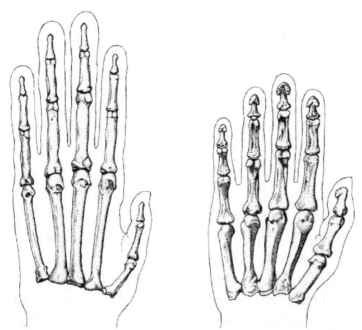

Figure 7.2 Comparison of a chimpanzee hand (left) to a modern human hand (right). In chimpanzees, the thumb is weak and short. The hand is adapted for suspension on tree branches and not adapted for the kind of firm grip that is easily generated by a modern human hand. The hands of *Australopithecus afarensis* (not shown) were still effective for tree-climbing, but the fingers were shorter than those of the chimpanzee and the thumb was longer. The hand of *Homo habilis* (not shown) had an even longer thumb, with a more human-like grip. Finally, the modern human hand (right) has a longer opposable (or prehensile) thumb, shorter fingers, and some additional muscles, which result in a more flexible, precise, and stronger grip than that of the other hominins. Note that the Neanderthal hand (not shown) was very similar to the modern human hand.

7.2 Neurobiology of chopper manufacturing

Let's examine the neurobiology behind the manufacturing of a stone chopper. The best way to start is to physically manufacture a Mode One Oldowan chopper. I invite you to step outside, find a cobblestone, an anvil, and a hammerstone and to actually make one yourself. You can make it from nearly any material: basalt, obsidian, quartz, flint, or chert. ....

Figure 7.3 Chopper manufacturing. Turning an unformed stone into a sharp tool requires hitting the stone at just the right angle and in just the right location.

... Ok, now let's discuss your experience. The first strike of the hammerstone probably broke the cobblestone into a shape similar to that shown in Figure 8.15B. Where did you hit next? In order to make a chopper you probably hit the cobblestone approximately where the dashed line is in Figure C. How did you know where to hit it? What were you thinking before the strike? You probably did the following:

1. imagined the future chopper,
2. overlaid that mental template onto the cobblestone,
3. visualized the part of the cobblestone that needs to be removed, and then
4. aimed your hit for that part of the stone.

With every strike you had to think about the best place to aim your hammerstone so that the cobblestone would get closer to your mental template of a chopper. If you did not have the mental template and just randomly hit the cobblestone, you would end up with a broken cobble, not a chopper. According to Ian Tattersall, author of *Becoming Human: Evolution and Human Uniqueness,* "To make a carefully shaped hand ax from a lump of rock not only demanded a sophisticated appreciation of how stone can be fashioned by fracture, but a mental template in the mind of the toolmaker that determined the eventual form of the tool" [139].

What is this "mental template" in neurologic terms? Let's

start with a very simple listing of facts.

1. The mental template of a chopper is encoded in the brain by a neuronal ensemble.

2. The objectNE encoding the future chopper is different from the objectNE of the cobble. (If they were the same you would have perceived the cobble, not a chopper.)

3. The mental template of the future chopper that you generate before each strike in order to understand where to apply force is different from anything you've seen before simply because each strike results in a half-finished-product with an unpredictable shape. In other words, the mental template (objectNE of the future chopper) was not recalled from memory but must have been a creation of your own mind.

4. The mental template of the chopper is generated based on the physical cobblestone.

Recall how the brain encodes physical objects. When you find a cobblestone, neurons encoding its shape (color, texture, 3D disparity, etc.) get activated into synchronous firing. There is no voluntary aspect to this process: you see a cobblestone -> neurons encoding the cobblestone fire in synchrony -> neurons grow new connections and get consolidated into an objectNE encoding the cobblestone -> this objectNE is stored in memory.

There is of course a voluntary element in the recall process: when you recall the cobblestone, the objectNE is activated into synchronous firing so that you perceive a cobblestone. However, the objectNE was formed automatically by the sensory input with no voluntary contribution.

Thus the difference between the formation of the objectNE of a cobblestone and the formation of the mental template of a chopper is the presence of a *voluntary* process that mentally reduces the cobblestone neuronal ensemble. Simplistically speaking, you must turn off the parts of the cobblestone objectNE that correspond to the future flakes. These neurons corresponding to the flakes must be turned off (probably by desynchronization with respect to the cobble's neuronal ensemble) so that only the remaining synchronized part of the objectNE is perceived. Neurons in one part of the brain (presumably, in the prefrontal cortex, as discussed in Part 3) must act upon neurons in another part of the brain to remove them from the objectNE of the cobblestone in a *voluntary* process. It follows that *Homo habilis* was capable of *voluntarily* eliminating parts of objectNEs. *Homo habilis* looked at a cobblestone, voluntarily shifted neurons representing the flakes *out-of-phase* with the rest of the cobble neurons and perceived the remaining synchronously firing neurons as the chopper. *Homo habilis* was then able to strike the cobblestone with a hammerstone multiple times at the location of choice to make the physical chopper that was similar to his mental template of the chopper.

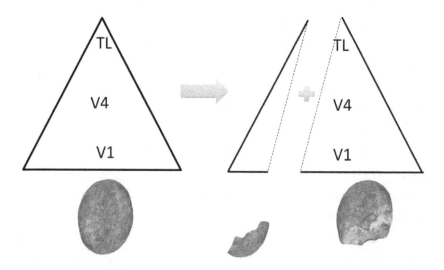

Figure 7.4 Prefrontal analysis. Mental decomposition (analysis) of the objectNE of a cobble (on the left) into the mental template of a chopper and the mental template of a flake.

We have previously defined the process of the disassembly of an objectNE into parts as prefrontal analysis (breaking down of an objectNE into fragments – fragment 1 is the objectNE of the future chopper and fragment 2 is the objectNE of the flakes). The result of prefrontal analysis is shifting part of the ensemble *out-of-phase* with the rest of the ensemble and the perception of a *new* object encoded by those neurons that remain firing synchronously. The new object is an imaginary object since you have never physically observed or touched it.

Mode One Oldowan choppers are crude. *Homo habilis* was only able to break out large flakes from a cobble. If the size of the flake reflects the size of the part of an objectNE that was voluntarily removed from the cobblestone neuronal ensemble, then *Homo habilis'* control of prefrontal analysis was quite crude: he was only capable of desynchronizing large chunks of objectNEs. *Homo erectus*, on the other hand, was able to break off much smaller flakes and produce fine symmetrical Mode Two handaxes. It's therefore reasonable to conclude that *Homo erectus* had acquired more advanced prefrontal analysis; he was capable of finer voluntary control of his objectNEs. Neanderthals were capable of even finer control. They manufactured Mode Three Mousterian tools. **The succeeding species were capable of desynchronizing finer and finer fragments of an objectNE and exhibiting better voluntary control of their perception (mental template).**

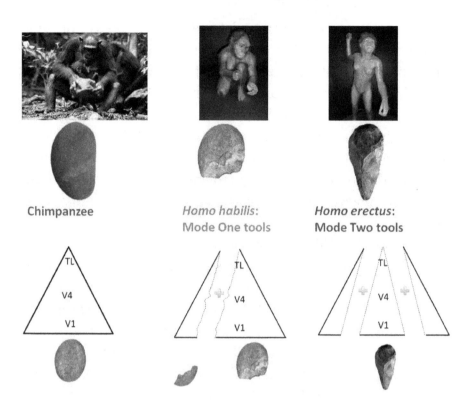

Figure 7.5 Evolution of prefrontal analysis and the corresponding stone tool culture. Chimpanzees make use of cobbles to break nuts but they do not modify them. *Homo habilis* was one of the earliest hominin species that intentionally modified cobbles to manufacture the crude, Mode One choppers. *Homo habilis* was only able to break out large flakes from a cobble; its voluntary control of its mental template was quite crude: it was only capable of desynchronizing large chunks of objectNEs. *Homo erectus*, on the other hand, was able to break off much smaller flakes and produce the fine, symmetrical, Mode Two handaxes; therefore, *Homo erectus* was most likely capable of finer voluntary control of its mental template.

To summarize, the understanding of the neurological mechanism of prefrontal analysis allows one to make a connection between the cognitive development of hominins and the evolution of stone tools. The improvements in the ability to perform prefrontal analysis by successive *Homo* species seems to be associated with their increasing ability to manufacture better stone tools. *Homo habilis* was not yet Michelangelo, who famously said, "every block of stone has a statue inside it and it is the task of the sculptor to discover it." However, *Homo habilis* was able to see the chopper inside a cobble; he had a *mental template* of the chopper. He was able to desynchronize, i.e. to shift, the firing phase of parts of the cobble's objectNE that correspond to the flakes. In this process he was able to voluntarily change his perception of the cobble into the mental template of the chopper.

Were *Homo habilis*, *Homo erectus* and Neanderthals capable of voluntarily *synchronizing* independent objectNEs into one mental frame? In other words, were they capable of PFS? From what can be observed about the behavior and customs of these species, it is logical to conclude that they had not acquired this ability. If they had acquired PFS, they would likely display this ability through some of the manifestations of PFS that were discussed above. They would be expected to create widespread figurative art objects, design and construct novel dwellings, exhibit creativity and innovation, and develop religious beliefs. The archeological record shows no figurative art objects, no adorned burials that could indicate religious beliefs, no dwelling constructions, and no signs of creativity or innovation (rather there is a stasis in tool development for each of the three hominin species) until the arrival of *Homo sapiens*. However, as was just discussed, manufacturing of stone tools indicates that *Homo habilis* and *Homo erectus* were capable of prefrontal analysis (voluntarily shifting chosen neurons *out-of-phase* with the rest of the neuronal ensemble), and it is not much of a stretch to link this ability with the future ability to voluntary shift chosen independent objectNEs *in-phase* with each other (*PFS* acquired by *Homo sapiens*). Both processes involve voluntary top-down regulation of the neuronal firing phase of existing objectNEs and as a result both create a percept different from anything previously seen by a subject: an imaginary percept!

Neurologically it must be much easier to knock neurons *out-of-phase* than to tune multiple neurons *in-phase* with each other. The top-down voluntary control of the neuronal firing phase that could only desynchronize parts of the neuronal ensemble, which is evident in *Homo habilis* and *Homo erectus*, culminated in the finest top-down control of the neuronal phase, which later enabled *Homo sapiens* to synchronize independent objectNEs into one mental frame.

Acquisition of prefrontal analysis was an evolutionary stepping-stone on the road towards PFS. *Homo habilis* had greater control of its mental image than its ancestor, the Australopithecus. Similarly, *Homo erectus* had an even greater control of its mental image than its ancestor, *Homo habilis*. Finally, we, *Homo sapiens,* are capable of the greatest control of our mental image: we can imagine anything we want.

Figure 7.6 (next page). On an axis of their dependence on the lateral prefrontal cortex, imagination mechanisms range from completely lateral prefrontal cortex-independent spontaneous REM-sleep dreaming to the lateral prefrontal cortex-dependent Prefrontal Synthesis defined as voluntary juxtaposition of various mental objects. In between these extremes lies a panoply of mechanisms with a gradually increasing role of the lateral prefrontal cortex: amodal completion, categorically-primed spontaneous imagination, integration of modifiers and mental rotation, and prefrontal analysis. Adapted from [153].

Imagination Mechanisms by their Dependence on the Lateral Prefrontal Cortex		Phylogenesis of imagination	Ontogenesis of imagination
LPFC-Dependent	Prefrontal Synthesis	70,000 years ago by *Homo sapiens*	36 – 48 months; direct testing
	Integration of Modifiers / Mental Rotation	No data	24 – 36 months; direct testing
	Prefrontal Analysis / Stone Tools Manufacture	3.3 million years ago by australopithecines	No data
	Categorically-Primed Spontaneous Imagination	70 million years ago with acquisition of the LPFC by primates	18 – 24 months; pretend play and spontaneously recounted stories
	Amodal Completion	>100 million years ago by mammals	4-7 months; direct testing
LPFC-Independent	REM Dreaming	140 million years ago by mammals	Third trimester of gestation

7.3 Evolution of imagination conclusions

First of all, it is important to understand that most thinking is not constructive imagination at all, but recalling of previous events and other memories associated with those events (driven by hippocampal ripples re-reactivating previously recorded objectNEs in the posterior neocortex). This process has nothing to do with constructive imagination. This recall mechanism is probably shared by all vertebrates who acquired the cortex and the hippocampus 525 million years ago.

Different mechanisms of constructive imagination were acquired by our ancestors at different times. Predictably, the involuntary bottom-up mechanisms of imagination, that minimally rely on the lateral prefrontal cortex, are phylogenetically oldest and ontogenetically first to develop, Figure 7.6.

The first constructive imagination was acquired by mammals 140 million ya, when REM-sleep dreaming (the simplest form of constructive imagination) has evolved[s]. Mammals gained the adaptive ability to simulate the future in their neocortex, albeit involuntarily (in dreams). Children likely experience REM-sleep dreaming as early as the third trimester of gestation [242]. Another bottom-up mechanism of imagination, amodal completion, has probably also been acquired early in mammalian evolution as it has been observed in mice [243] and primates [244]. Children seem to acquire amodal completion at about 4–7 months of age [245]. Categorically-primed spontaneous imagination has probably improved in primates with the acquisition of the lateral prefrontal cortex [202,246] around 70

---

[s] REM-sleep dreaming was acquired by mammals 140 million ya, when marsupials and placentals diverged from the monotreme line. Monotremes do not exhibit REM-sleep, while marsupials and placentals do.

million year ago and continued to improve with increasing size of the lateral prefrontal cortex in apes and hominins. In children, the development of categorically-primed spontaneous imagination can be easily observed via pretend play and spontaneously recounted stories around ages of 1.5 to 2 [247]. Since PFS is only acquired by children between the ages of 3 and 4 years, categorically-primed spontaneous imagination precedes voluntary imagination by about two years.

Top-down voluntary imagination significantly improved after hominins split from a chimpanzee line around 6 million year ago as the ability to flexibly integrate modifiers has not been demonstrated in any animal and mental rotation, that has been demonstrated in animals, may be utilizing a neurobiological mechanism that is different from humans [248]. In children, top-down imagination is clearly exhibited around the age of 3 when they become capable of following a direction to find a *long red straw* among many straws of different sizes and colors [37]. Prefrontal analysis acquisition by hominins can be easily followed by looking at the stone tools culture that was slowly improving from about 3.3 million year ago [189]. The most advanced mechanism of imagination, PFS, was acquired phylogenetically only 70,000 year ago [236] and develops in children between ages of 3 and 4 [37].

Chapter 8. Evolution of the speech apparatus

In a forest habitat an adept climber, particularly a biggish one such as an Ardi [an early hominin], would have been menaced by few predators, at least as an adult. Its food supply would have fluctuated seasonally, but in a relatively predictable way; and its basic lifestyle was underwritten by many tens of millions of years of primate evolution. In contrast, the expanding areas of forest edge, woodland, and grassland would have teemed with ferocious killers such as lions and sabertooths; and at the same time an entirely new foraging strategy would have been required to obtain the unfamiliar resources these habitats offered. For any primate to move into these novel environments meant entering a fundamentally unfamiliar and difficult ecological zone, and for the first hominids it was certainly a huge gamble—albeit one that eventually paid off in spades. ... The ecological move to these more open environments brought with it new opportunities for hominids, as well as extraordinary future possibilities; but it also came at a huge immediate cost. This penalty was, of course, vulnerability to woodland predators. It is impossible to overstate the significance of this new factor: no new force could have had anything close to the impact on small-bodied bipeds, venturing away from their ancestral habitat, that the ubiquity of predators must have had.

IAN TATTERSALL, *Masters of the Planet:*
The search for our human origins (2012)

The articulate speech of humans is unique among primates. The vocal tract of our closest relatives, chimpanzees, is extremely limited in its ability to modulate sound. While there is no theoretical limit on the number of different vocalizations nonhuman primates can generate [249], attempts to teach chimpanzees articulate speech have failed [250] and the range of distinct vocalizations observed in the wild is limited to between 20 and 100 [251-254]. On the contrary, human languages contain tens of thousands of different words easily generated by the modern human vocal apparatus. If the development of articulate speech could have triggered PFS acquisition, that would explain the human cognitive revolution 70,000 years ago. Unfortunately, the dates do not match.

Evolutionary changes in the vocal tract have been extensively studied by paleoanthropologists [139,255,256]. The modern vocal apparatus developed as a result of changes of the structure and the position of many organs that play a role in generating and modulating vocalizations: larynx, tongue, musculature of the mouth, lips, and diaphragm as well as the neurological control of the associated musculature. While cartilaginous and soft tissue is not preserved in the fossil record, we can draw conclusions about the evolution of vocal apparatus from the bony structures which do survive. Dediu and Levinson cite five lines of converging evidence pointing to acquisition of modern speech apparatus by 600,000 years ago [257]: (1) the changes in hyoid bone, (2) the flexion of the bones of the skull base, (3) increased voluntary control of the muscles of the diaphragm, (4) anatomy of external and middle ear, and (5) the evolution of the FOXP2 gene.

8.1 The changes in hyoid bone

This small U-shaped bone lies in the front of the neck between the chin and the thyroid cartilage. The hyoid does not contact any other bone. Rather, it is connected by tendons to the musculature of the tongue, and the lower jaw above, the larynx below, and the epiglottis and pharynx behind. The hyoid aids in tongue movement used for swallowing and sound production. Accordingly, phylogenetic changes in the shape of the hyoid provide information on the evolution of the vocal apparatus.

The hyoid bone of a chimpanzee is very different from that of a modern human [258]. The australopith hyoid bone discovered in Dikika, Ethiopia, and dated to 3.3 million years ago closely resembles that of a chimpanzee [259]. The *Homo erectus* hyoid bone recovered at Castel di Guido, Italy, and dated to about 400,000 years ago reveals the "bar-shaped morphology characteristic of *Homo*, in contrast to the bulla-shaped body morphology of African apes and *Australopithecus*" [260]. Neanderthal hyoids are essentially identical to that of a modern human in size and shape: these have been identified in Kebara, Israel [261] and El Sidrón, Spain [262]. At the same time these are also identical to hyoid of *Homo heidelbergensis* from Sima de los Huesos, Spain [263] suggesting that the latter was a direct ancestor of both *Homo neanderthalensis* and *Homo sapiens* and had already possessed a nearly modern hyoid bone [197,257]. The similarities between Neanderthal and modern human hyoid make it likely that the position and connections of the hyoid and larynx were also similar between the two groups.

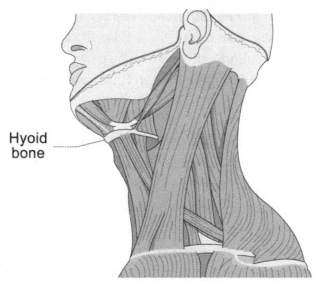

Hyoid
bone

Figure 8.1 The hyoid bone. (Illustration on the opposite page) The hyoid bone connects the musculature of the tongue and the larynx. In human neonates, the larynx is positioned as high as in other mammals, so infants can drink and breathe at the same time. In both humans and chimpanzees, the larynx descends during postnatal development. However, the human larynx descends significantly lower than the larynx of chimpanzees. The lower larynx allows humans to produce a wider range of sounds than other animals, but also makes choking easier.

Both the structure and the position of the hyoid bone are important factors when assessing the ability for complex speech. However, the position of the hyoid bone in the vocal tract cannot be determined in skeletal remains since it is not attached to any other bones in the body.

8.2 The flexion of the bones of the skull base

Laitman [264,265] has observed that the roof of the vocal tract is also the base of the skull and suggested that evolving vocal tract is reflected in the degree of curvature of the underside of the base of the skull (called basicranial flexion). The skull of *Australopithecus africanus* dated to 3 million years ago shows no flexing of the basicranium, as is the case with chimpanzees [266].

The first evidence of increased curvature of the base of the basicranium is displayed in *Homo erectus* from Koobi Fora, Kenya, 1.75 million years ago [264]. A fully flexed, modern-like, basicranium is found in several specimens of *Homo heidelbergensis* from Ethiopia, Broken Hill 1, and Petralona from about 600,000 years ago [267].

8.3 Increased voluntary control of respiratory muscles

Voluntary cortical control of respiratory muscles is a crucial prerequisite for complex speech production [268]. Greater cortical control is associated with additional innervation of the diaphragm, which can be detected in fossils as an enlarged thoracic vertebral canal. *Homo erectus* from 1.5 million years ago (Turkana Boy) has no such enlarged canal, but both modern humans and Neanderthals do [257], providing converging evidence for acquisition of modern-like vocal apparatus by 600,000 years ago.

8.4 The anatomy of external and middle ear

Modern humans show increased sensitivity to sounds between 1kHz and 6kHz and particularly between 2kHz and 4kHz. Chimpanzees, on the other hand, are not particularly sensitive to sounds in this range [263,269]. Since species using complex auditory communication systems tend to match their broadcast frequencies and the tuning of perceptual acuity [270], it was argued that changes in the anatomy of the external and middle ear in hominins are indicative of the developing speech apparatus. Data from several Neanderthal and *Homo heidelbergensis* fossils indicate a modern-human-like pattern of sound perception with highest sensitivity in the region around 4kHz, that is significantly different from that of chimpanzees [269,271].

8.5 The evolution of the FOXP2 gene

The most convincing evidence for the timing of the acquisition of the modern speech apparatus is provided by DNA analysis. The FOXP2 gene is the first identified gene that, when mutated, causes a specific language deficit in humans. Patients with FOXP2 mutations exhibit great difficulties in controlling their facial movements, as well as with reading, writing, grammar, and oral comprehension [198].The protein encoded by the FOXP2 gene is a transcription factor. It regulates genes involved in the production of many different proteins. The FOXP2 protein sequence is highly conserved. There is only one amino acid difference in the chimpanzee lineage going back some 70 million years to the common ancestor with the mouse [272]. The FOXP2 proteins of chimpanzee, gorilla and rhesus macaque are all identical. This resistance to change suggests that FOXP2 is extraordinarily important for vertebrate development and survival. Interestingly, there is a change of two amino acids in FOXP2 that occurred over the last 6 million years, during the time when the human lineage had split off from the chimpanzee. These two amino acid substitutions predate the human-Neanderthal split. Both amino acid substitutions were found in two Neanderthals from Spain [186], as well as in Neanderthals from Croatia [184], and in Denisovans, an extinct Asian hominin group related to Neanderthals [273]. This indicates that *Homo heidelbergensis,* the common ancestor of *Homo sapiens* and Neanderthals, already had the two "human specific" amino acid substitutions. Despite evidence of possible further evolution of FOXP2 in *Homo sapiens* [274], the comparatively fast mutation rate of FOXP2 in hominins indicates that there was strong evolutionary pressure on development of the speech apparatus before *Homo sapiens* diverged from Neanderthals over 500,000 years ago [185].

8.6 Conclusions on acquisition of articulate speech

Based on these five lines of evidence — the structure of the hyoid bone, the flexion of the bones of the skull base, increased voluntary control of the muscles of the diaphragm, anatomy of external and middle ear, and the FOXP2 gene evolution — most paleoanthropologists conclude that the speech apparatus experienced significant development starting with *Homo erectus* about two million years ago and that it reached modern or nearly modern configurations in *Homo heidelbergensis* about 600,000 year ago [139,257].

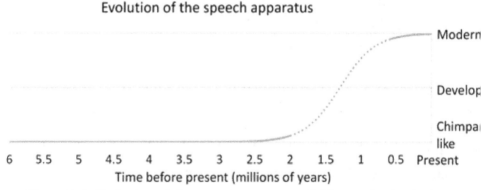

Figure 8.2 Evolution of the speech apparatus. Evidence of a developing speech apparatus is present in *Homo erectus* who lived 2 million years ago. The vocal apparatus virtually reaches its modern configuration 600,000 years ago in *Homo heidelbergensis* [139]. The exact course of evolution of speech apparatus between 2 and 0.6 million years ago is unknown (and is approximated by the dotted line).

Dediu and Levinson write: "there is ample evidence of systematic adaptation of the vocal apparatus to speech, and we have shown that this was more or less in place by half a million years ago" [257]. We will never know the extent of *Homo heidelbergensis* neurological control of their speech, however, considering that chimpanzee communication system already has 20 to 100 different vocalizations [251-254], it is likely that the modern-like remodeling of the vocal apparatus in *Homo heidelbergensis* extended their range of vocalizations by orders of magnitude. In other words, by 600,000 years ago the number of distinct verbalizations used by hominins for communication was on par with the number of words in modern languages. Thus, by 600,000 years ago the number of words in the lexicon could **not** have been holding back acquisition of PFS and recursive language. Articulate speech likely has been an important prerequisite to, but could not be the trigger for PFS acquisition 70,000 years ago. It also follows that hominin groups with fluent articulate speech must have existed for hundreds of millennia before acquisition of PFS. In many regards these hominins must have been similar to patients with prefrontal aphasia discussed in the introduction who have fluent speech, but completely limited to non-recursive dialogs due to PFS paralysis.

What can explain the 500,000-year gap between acquisition of the modern speech apparatus and acquisition of PFS and recursive language 70,000 years ago? As discussed above, a genetically modern tribe is expected to invent recursive elements and acquire PFS within several generations similar to the Nicaraguan deaf community who spontaneously generated a new sign language, complete with *syntax*, verb agreement and other conventions of grammar [129,275-277]. It follows that PFS acquisition must have been precluded by a genetic factor. Next part of the book is a quest to find the exact mutation that triggered PFS acquisition.

Part 2. Evolution of Imagination

Part 3. The mutation that triggered prefrontal synthesis acquisition

In previous chapters, I have tried to make complex neural systems understandable to non-specialists. It is possible, however, that the simplified technical information I have provided is still too much for many who are not versed in basic neuroscientific jargon. If that is the case, it might help to draw attention to the three most important points: 1) Objects are represented in the brain by networks of neurons referred to as objectNEs. Neurons of an objectNE are bound together by enhanced synaptic connections. 2) These enhanced connections make objectNEs prone to fire in synchrony, as a resonant system. An object is perceived when an objectNE synchronously fires one or more action potentials. While points 1 and 2 are generally accepted in the scientific community, the third point is the main theory put forth in this book: 3) The process of mentally morphing two or more objects into one imaginary object which had never been previously seen, involves the synchronization of the objectNEs encoding those objects. I called the neurological process of synchronizing two independent objectNEs *prefrontal synthesis* or PFS.

Chapter 9. The role of the prefrontal cortex in the process of prefrontal synthesis

... our strange intellectual faculty is attributable to a novel neural conformation, a change in the internal organization and wiring of our brains. Acquisition of such a novelty would not in itself be unprecedented; after all the human brain has a long and largely accretionary history going right back to the earliest vertebrate brains half a billion years ago—and beyond. Nothing inherently new there. But the results of this acquisition were revolutionary: in today's jargon, they were "emergent, whereby an adventitious change or addition to a pre-existing structure led to a whole new level of complexity in function.

IAN TATTERSALL, *Masters of the Planet: The search for our human origins* (2012)

9.1 Neuropsychological techniques for testing prefrontal synthesis

Neuropsychology uses all kinds of clever techniques to study how different areas of the brain relate to specific psychological processes and behaviors. In fact, PFS has been studied in humans by many researchers under a number of other names: "ability to invent fiction" [30], "episodic future thinking" [31], "mental scenario building" [32], "mental storytelling" [74], "internal mentation" [75], "mentally playing with ideas" [76], "creative intelligence" [77], "prospective memory" [78], "memory of the future" [79], "counterfactual thinking" [278], "integration of multiple relations between mental representations" [24], "the ability to form nested scenarios" [80], "an inner theatre of the mind that allows us to envision and mentally manipulate many possible situations and anticipate different outcomes" [80], "mental exercises that require tracking and integration of what, in the subject's mind, are temporally separate items of information" [21]. Several standard neuropsychological techniques primarily test PFS. These include, for example, the *Tower of London Test*, complex mental arithmetic, as well as parts of the common IQ test. Let's take a look at these techniques in some detail:

1. **The *Tower of London Test*** was originally developed by the neuropsychologist Tim Shallice [34]. The test consists of two boards, each one with three vertical pegs, and colored rings made to slide up and down the pegs. The pegs are of different heights, so that the first can accommodate three rings on top of one another, the second can accommodate two rings, and the third just one. The configuration of the beads is different on the two boards. The subjects are asked to move the rings from a given "start position" on the first board in order to achieve the particular ring arrangement shown as the "goal position" on the second board, and to do so in as few moves as possible. In

addition, the subjects are instructed to first plan their moves mentally before physically starting the task. Obviously, this test requires visual planning of a series of moves. For example, to find the correct sequence of moves on the test shown in Figure 9.1, the subject must first imagine the starting board with the top black ring removed. Now the subject must visualize the black ring separately from the rest of the board, and then to re-combine the two images (the starting board without the black ring, and the separate image of the black ring) into a new image with the black ring in its new position either on the 2nd peg (correct move) or on the 3rd peg (incorrect move). The subject must then perform the same task with the white ring, and mentally place it either on the 2nd or 3rd peg. Each new mental image corresponds to a new configuration of rings, which gets the subject closer to the end goal. These new mental images, which combine images of rings and the ever-changing board, are constructed in the mind in the process of PFS. Of course, we humans have gotten so good at PFS that all of these steps happen very quickly in the brain. So quickly, in fact, that we hardly even notice the many distinct steps our brain must take to solve such a problem.

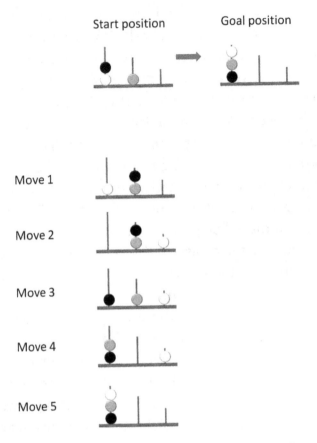

Figure 9.1 The *Tower Of London* test. The *Tower Of London* test consists of two boards with three vertical pegs and colored rings made to slide up and down on the pegs. The pegs are of different heights, so that the first can accommodate three rings on top of one another, the second two rings, and the third just one. The configuration of the beads is different on the two boards. The subjects are asked to move the rings on one board in order to achieve the ring arrangement of the second board (the "goal position"). The subjects are instructed to plan internally and to achieve the goal arrangement in as few moves as possible. The test requires visual planning of a series of moves in order to reach the goal position. The prefrontal cortex, particularly the left lateral prefrontal cortex, is believed to be uniquely important for the task of visual planning. Strong activation of the left lateral prefrontal cortex is observed in normal subjects performing the Tower of London test [27]. Converging evidence comes from frontal patients. Patients with lesions to the prefrontal cortex, particularly to the left prefrontal cortex, are severely impaired in their performance of the Tower of London test [34,279].

2. **IQ tests** nearly inevitably include deductive and inductive reasoning problems that require "integration of relations" [24,153]. The solution to these problems is normally obtained through visual integration of objects in the process of PFS. Below are a few problems borrowed from a standard IQ test. Try the problems for yourself, but make sure to solve them mentally (without the aid of paper and pencil). While working through the questions, monitor the mental imagery you use to solve the problems. Notice that it is impossible to solve these problems mentally without synthesizing *novel* mental images:

Question 1. Mary is taller than Julia. Jennifer is taller than Mary. Therefore, Julia is the shortest girl. Answer: True / False

Question 2. A round wall clock that has been rotated until it is hanging upside down will have a minute hand that points to your right when it is two forty. Answer: True / False

Question 3. If the word, "BOM," is written under the word, "PRY," and the word, "KOK," is written under "BOM," then the word, "POK," is formed diagonally. Answer: True / False

Question 4. Six identical triangles can be formed by drawing two straight lines through an octagon's center point. Answer: True / False

Question 5. If a doughnut shaped house has two doors to the outside and three doors to the inner courtyard, then it's possible to end up back at your starting place by walking through all five doors of the house without ever walking through the same door twice. Answer: True / False

Question 6. The angle formed by the two hands of a clock is larger than 90 degrees when the time is 6:20. Answer: True / False[t]

---

[t] Answers to IQ test questions. Question 1: True; Question 2: True; Question 3: True; Question 4: False; Question 5: False. Question 6: False.

3. Mentally finding the solution to a **complex arithmetic problem** also relies on PFS. Assuming that you still remember your multiplication table, calculating the product of, say, 4 and 6 does not require PFS. You have already memorized this as a fact and simply *remember* that the product is 24 by easily retrieving this fact from memory [35]. However, consider calculating the product of 32 and 24, and please do so mentally, without the use of any aids such as paper and pencil or a calculator.

Again, monitor the mental imagery you use to solve the problem. For most people, it is impossible to mentally calculate the product of two two-digit numbers without visualizing each step of the calculation. You must break apart one of the numbers, say 32, into tens and ones: 32 = 30 + 2. You must then multiply both the tens and the ones by the other number: 30 × 24 and 2 × 24. Finally, you will have to add these two products together mentally to get the final answer: 720 + 48 = 768. At every step, you are imagining and re-combining new numbers with the help of PFS.

9.2 Functional imaging of the prefrontal cortex in healthy subjects

Recently, there has been a plethora of evidence provided by brain imaging that implicates the prefrontal cortex in tasks that involve PFS in healthy individuals. Neuropsychological and neuroimaging studies have established that the lateral prefrontal cortex plays a major role in problem solving that relies on PFS. For example, significant activation of the lateral prefrontal cortex has been demonstrated in subjects conducting mental transformations to solve algebraic problems [96]. Strong prefrontal cortex activation has also been reported when subjects performed complex arithmetic operations internally [35,280,281], or imagined themselves walking through different places [280]. Strong activation of the left lateral prefrontal cortex was observed in all subjects performing the Tower of London test [27]. The activation was greater in subjects that found the task more difficult and consequently took more time to perform it. A greater mental effort in these tasks is associated with greater activation of the lateral prefrontal cortex and recruitment of a greater portion of the lateral prefrontal cortex [282].

In contrast, no appreciable prefrontal activation is observed when subjects solve simple arithmetic problems such as calculating the sum of numbers smaller than seven or retrieving simple arithmetic facts from memory (i.e., 2×4) [35]. This observation suggests that once a complex task has become automatic, and as a result does not rely on PFS, activation of the prefrontal cortex during task performance diminishes [21].

Christoff and Gabrieli compiled a comprehensive review of published imaging studies that "intentionally studied reasoning processes and employed standard problem-solving tasks" in healthy subjects [23]. Their literature evaluation found evidence of significant activity in the prefrontal cortex. The authors also concluded that, in particular, the anterior lateral prefrontal cortex (the part of the lateral prefrontal cortex located right behind the forehead, also called the frontopolar cortex or Brodmann area 10), became recruited during more complex cognitive tasks, such as the Tower of London Test [27], inductive and probabilistic reasoning tasks [282] and the Raven's Progressive Matrices Test [283].

Thus, functional brain imaging studies in healthy subjects are consistent with the hypothesis that the prefrontal cortex plays the central role in the process of PFS.

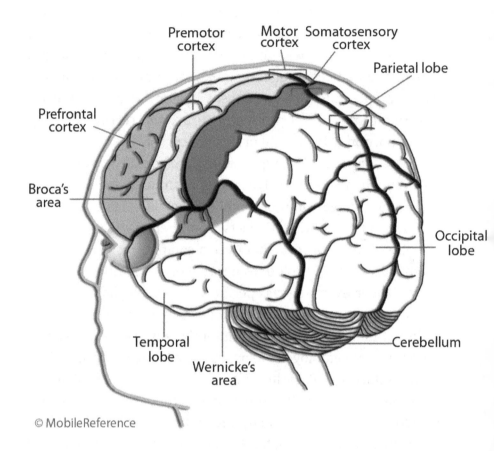

Figure 9.2 The prefrontal cortex is the very frontal part of the brain; it is in front of the motor and premotor areas. It is located right behind your forehead. In terms of its cellular composition, the prefrontal cortex is defined by the presence of an internal granular layer IV (in contrast to the agranular premotor cortex). The prefrontal cortex is responsible for executive functions, which include planning complex cognitive behavior, personality expression and moderating correct social behavior.

9.3 Neurological deficits associated with lesions of the prefrontal cortex

Compelling evidence that links the prefrontal cortex to the execution of PFS can be found in the plethora of research that has been conducted on patients who suffer from lesions of their prefrontal cortex. These patients often struggle on neuropsychological tests that require PFS, and this enables us to infer which brain areas are associated with PFS.

Patients with prefrontal cortex damage, particularly damage in the left prefrontal cortex, are severely impaired in the performance of the Tower of London test [34,279]. Patients with lesions of the left prefrontal cortex have also been found to exhibit impaired performance in other tasks that, like the Tower of London test, require internal visual planning through PFS, such as the Tower of Hanoi test.

Frontal patients, especially patients with lesions to the lateral prefrontal cortex can also be impaired on tests of intelligence, such as IQ tests [284,285]. However intelligence is a complex function that depends on attention, memory, verbal understanding, and verbal expression, in addition to PFS. All these capabilities are components of intelligence and if any of them is deficient in a frontal patient, intelligence measured by an IQ test can suffer. Some components of the IQ test are more sensitive to damage in the prefrontal cortex. These include assessments of "fluid intelligence" that test a patient's ability to solve new problems [25] as well as tests that involve "integration of relations," such as Question 1 of the "IQ tests" section which requires integrating the heights of Mary, Julia and Jennifer [24]. Patients with prefrontal damage that have near normal scores on a general IQ test such as the Wechsler Adult Intelligence Scale, exhibit a selective and catastrophic deficit in tasks that require mental integration of objects [24] and mental planning [25], i.e. tasks that rely on the process of PFS.

Figure 9.3 Brodmann's cytoarchitectonic map of cortical areas. (Illustration on the opposite page) The human prefrontal cortex is usually divided into three structurally and functionally separate regions: the **lateral prefrontal cortex** (Brodmann areas 8, 9, 10, 45, 46, 47), the **medial prefrontal cortex** (also called the anterior cingulate cortex, which includes Brodmann areas 25, 12, 32, 33, 24), and the **ventral prefrontal cortex** (also called the orbital prefrontal region, that includes Brodmann areas 11 and 13). Neurons in the ventral prefrontal cortex respond preferentially to external stimuli that are likely to be rewarding or otherwise significant.

Neurons in the medial prefrontal cortex are primarily concerned with processing information about the body's internal state. Together, the medial and ventral prefrontal cortices are predominantly involved in such emotional and social functions as the control of impulse, mood, and empathy [21]. Finally, the lateral prefrontal cortex is predominantly, but not exclusively, involved in time integrating and organizing functions [21], such as working memory and PFS. The lateral prefrontal cortex is present in all primates but is absent in other animals including other mammals [202].

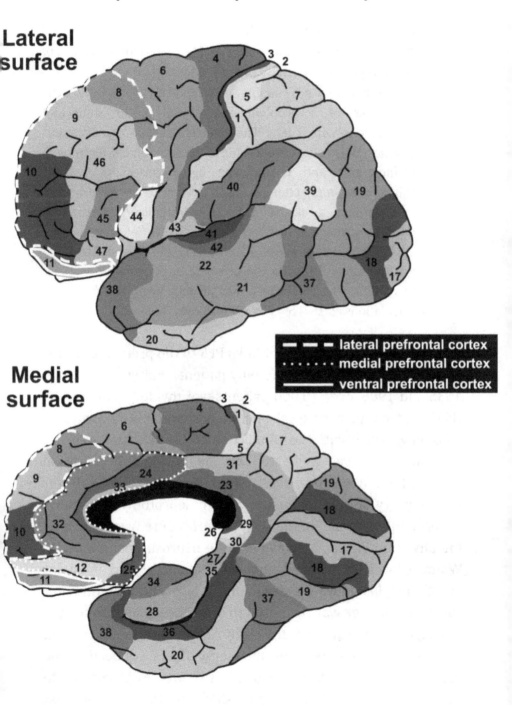

The famous neuropsychologist Alexander Luria provides us with an excellent analysis of the particular type of impairment in patients with prefrontal cortex damage:

These patients are unable to systematically analyze the conditions of a problem and to select the important connections within it ... The selective system of operations that normally successively leads to the solution of the problem disintegrates and is replaced by a series of isolated, fragmentary connections, not subservient to the general plan and without a clearly defined hierarchical structure. ... Complex problems, such as 'A son is 5 years old; in 15 years his father will be twice as old as he. How old is his father now?' are completely beyond the grasp of such patients. Without listening to the conditions, they at once begin to make such calculations as $15 \times 5 = 75$ or $3 \times 15 = 45$. [26]

Additional evidence that links PFS to the prefrontal cortex can be found in studying lobotomy patients. Between the years 1935 and 1986, over 70,000 patients worldwide (40,000 in the USA) underwent a surgical operation commonly known as a lobotomy, which cuts the connection to the prefrontal cortex. The operation was pioneered by the Portuguese physician António Egas Moniz, who received the Nobel Prize in 1949 "for his discovery of the therapeutic value of leucotomy [lobotomy] in certain psychoses." In the USA, the procedure was refined by the physician Walter Freeman and the neurosurgeon James W. Watts. It involved lifting the upper eyelid and placing the point of a thin stylus under the eyelid and against the top of the eye socket. A hammer was then used to drive the stylus through the thin layer of bone and into the brain. The stylus was then moved from side to side to sever the nerve fibers connecting the prefrontal cortex to the deeper brain structures. According to the Psychiatric Dictionary published in 1970: "Prefrontal lobotomy was found of value in the following disorders, listed in a descending scale of good results: affective disorders, obsessive-compulsive states, chronic anxiety states and other non-schizophrenic conditions, paranoid schizophrenia, undetermined or mixed type of schizophrenia, catatonic schizophrenia, and hebephrenic and simple schizophrenia."

Dr. Freeman personally performed over 3,000 lobotomies. Amongst famous patients who underwent lobotomy was Rosemary Kennedy, the sister of President John F. Kennedy, who was born a year after her brother. In 1941, at the age of 23, she underwent a lobotomy when her father, Joseph Kennedy, complained to doctors about her "mood swings that the family found difficult to handle at home." Reportedly, Joseph Kennedy was also uncomfortable with Rosemary's low intellectual abilities and promiscuity. Dr. Watts personally performed the procedure with Dr. Freeman observing.

With connections between the prefrontal cortex and the rest of the cortex destroyed, most lobotomy patients suffered from passivity, blunted emotions, and a reduced capacity to plan. Dr. Walter Freeman, acknowledging these side-effects, wrote: "What the investigator misses most in the more highly intelligent individuals is the ability to introspect, to speculate, to philosophize, especially in regard to the self... Creativeness seems to be the highest form of human endeavor. It requires imagination, concentration, visualization, self-criticism, and persistence in the face of frustration, as well as trained manual dexterity.... Theoretically, on the basis of psychologic and personality studies, creativeness should be abolished by lobotomy.... On the whole psychosurgery reduces creativity, sometimes to the vanishing point" [286]. In many cases, the procedure was thus less a cure than a pacifier, and reduced many patients to post-operative vegetables. Rosemary Kennedy was one such example. The lobotomy reduced her to an infantile mentality that left her incontinent and staring blankly at walls for hours. She became largely detached from the Kennedy clan, and spent most of the time in institutions until her death in 2005. The practice of lobotomy ceased in the 1970s with the introduction of antipsychotic drugs.

Joaquin Fuster, concludes that creative intelligence (which depends on PFS to "invent the future") almost inevitably suffers in patients with lateral prefrontal cortex damage [21]. He writes, "the failure to formulate plans, especially new plans, is generally accepted as being a common feature of prefrontal syndromes. Remarkably, the symptom appears unique to dysfunction of the prefrontal cortex. It is not associated with clinical damage to any other neural structure — in the absence of concomitant dementia or disorder of consciousness" [21]. Fuster reports that prefrontal patients lead a life "without much display of imagination, let alone creativity... This deficit in temporal integration pervades all activities and prevents the patient (who lives 'here and now') from constructing new sequences of behavior, speech and reasoning" [21].

To sum up, observations in patients with lesions of the prefrontal cortex as well as functional brain imaging studies in healthy subjects indicate that the prefrontal cortex, especially the left lateral prefrontal cortex, plays an essential and unique role in the process of PFS.

9.4 A model of the prefrontal cortex

Joaquin M. Fuster has put together a simple but sensible model of the neocortex. Fuster divides the neocortex into the primarily sensory posterior section (occupying the back of the brain, i.e. the occipital, temporal, and parietal lobes) and the frontal cortex (including the prefrontal cortex as well as motor and premotor areas), which is primarily concerned with action [21].

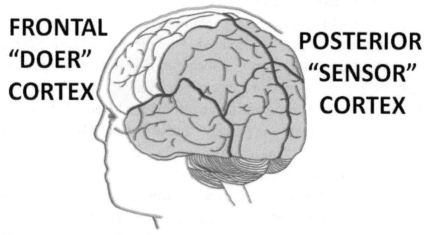

FRONTAL "DOER" CORTEX

POSTERIOR "SENSOR" CORTEX

Figure 9.4 Joaquin M. Fuster's model divides cerebral cortex into the frontal ("doer") cortex primarily concerned with actions and the posterior ("sensor") cortex primarily concerned with storing long-term memory. Fuster writes: The entirety of the frontal cortex, including its prefrontal region, is "action cortex" in broadest terms. It is cortex devoted to action of one kind or another, whether skeletal movement, ocular movement, the expression of emotions, speech or visceral control; it can even be the kind of internal, mental action that we call reasoning. The frontal cortex is "doer" cortex, much as the posterior cortex is "sensor" cortex. Most certainly, however, the frontal cortex does nothing by itself; all it does is in cooperation with other cortices, with subcortical structures, and with certain sectors of the sensory and motor apparatus and of the autonomic system [21].

While the premotor and motor cortical areas are directly concerned with muscle movement, the prefrontal cortex does not directly influence muscle movements, but works in accord with the posterior sensory cortex to select and organize the most appropriate actions. Fuster's model places the prefrontal cortex on top of the "perception-action cycle" where, according to Fuster, "there is no true origin, cortical or subcortical." In other words, "the prefrontal cortex works as an integrator of current inputs from cortical and subcortical sources" [21]. Fuster also claims that the function of the prefrontal cortex "cannot be understood in isolation, but as part of integrative sensory-motor operations that transcend modalities of either sensation or movement.[u] Those integrative operations are constituents of the figurative and dynamic substrate for the perception-action cycle — that is, the circular flow of information between the organism and its environment that takes place in all forms of adaptive behavior. Prefrontal networks at the higher levels of the cycle are capable of integrating percepts and actions of a high order of complexity and abstraction" [21]. In this regard Fuster underscores the unique role of the prefrontal cortex in organizing the timing of neurological processes: "One important aspect of sensory-motor integration is the bridging of time at the top of the perception-action cycle, in the cortex of association [the prefrontal cortex]. In that time-bridging process, motor acts are coordinated with sensory inputs that for whatever reason, are not contemporaneous with them; in other words, inputs that have occurred in the recent past or are expected to occur in the near future. Electrophysiological data show that for this form of cross-temporal integration — the integration of the temporally separate acts and percepts — the prefrontal cortex can be essential" [21].[v]

The integrative and organizing function of the prefrontal cortex is often referred to as an *executive function*. Fuster defines it as " the ability temporarily to organize purposive behavior, language, and reasoning" and considers it to be "the

---

[u] The prefrontal cortex is distinguished from other comparable areas of the cortex by a higher number of connections between the neurons, and a considerably lower density of neurons. A significantly greater number of inputs received by each neuron in the prefrontal cortex indicates that these neurons are involved in integration of more information than the neurons in any other comparable area of the cortex.

[v] Temporal organization of neuronal ensembles is undoubtedly aided by the cerebellum. The lateral prefrontal cortex receives extensive connections from the cerebellum and sends reciprocal connections to the cerebellum.

principal function of the prefrontal cortex" [21]. In Fuster's model, all executive functions of the prefrontal cortex operate on and with the neuronal networks distributed throughout the cortex [21]. "These networks [objectNEs] are made of connective associations between neuronal assemblies, in some cases widely dispersed from one another, which represent simpler and more concrete items of knowledge and long-term memory" [21].

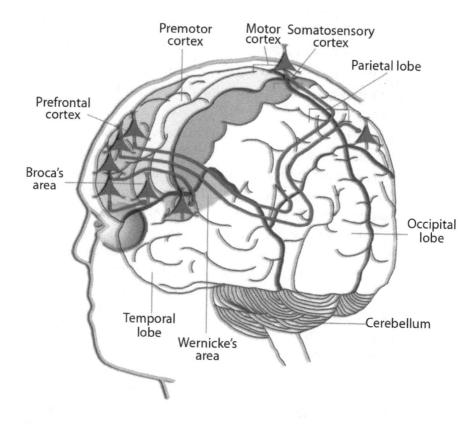

Figure 9.5 All executive functions of the prefrontal cortex operate on the neuronal networks distributed throughout the cortex. The length of connections between the prefrontal cortex and these neuronal networks varies significantly.

Fuster's model does not attempt to seek neurological differences between humans and other primates. Rather it is built based on the similarities between human and animal prefrontal cortices. Within this framework it is perfectly fine to avoid the question of synchronization of independent objectNEs. This question simply does not arise until one tries to understand the neurological differences between humans and other primates. If, however, the goal is to understand the differences between the human brain and the brains of non-human primates the theory must build upon Fuster's model and describe not only how the prefrontal cortex retrieves and holds an objectNE in working memory, but also how the prefrontal cortex builds novel objectNEs. Fuster does not provide direct answers to that question but he offers a general framework for such a theory:

> Any series of purposive actions that deviates from rehearsed automatic routine or instinctual order necessitates the functional integrity of the lateral prefrontal cortex. The longer the series, the greater is the need for that cortex. ... Time, however, is the single most important attribute placing a complex and novel sequence of behavior under the physiological purview of the lateral prefrontal cortex. Only this part of the cerebral cortex can provide that "temporal gestalt" with the coherence and coordination of actions that are essential for the organism to reach its goal. Both coherence and coordination derive from the capacity of the prefrontal cortex to *organize actions in the time domain*, which, in my view is the most general and characteristic of all prefrontal functions in the primate. The importance of this temporal organizing function in mammalian behavior cannot be overstated. Without it, there is no execution of new, acquired, and elaborate behavior, no speech fluency, no higher reasoning, and no creative activity with more than minimal temporal dimension; only temporal concreteness is left, the here and now, in anything but instinctual sequence or

automatic routine. [21]

Joaquin M. Fuster later calls the prefrontal function of temporal organization the "syntax of action": "All cognitive functions of the lateral prefrontal cortex are determined, we might say 'caused,' by goals. If there is a unique and characteristic feature of that part of the brain, it is its ability to structure the present in order to serve the future... "[21].

All functions that rely on temporal coordination of *novel* sequences of behavior, whether that behavior is directed outward in the form of movement, or directed inward in the form of imagination depend on intact networks in the prefrontal cortex. Sequences of habitual and reflexive movement routines are primarily encoded in deep subcortical structures (such as basal ganglia) and do not rely on the prefrontal cortex for their temporal organization. Similarly, long-term memories of places, people and events are encoded by objectNEs distributed in the posterior cortex. Those objectNEs can activate, and the corresponding memory can be consciously perceived without the active role of the prefrontal cortex. However voluntary synthesis of *novel* visual images requires temporal organization of independent objectNEs and therefore depends on the lateral prefrontal cortex, which "plays a major role in all decisions that are the result of temporal integration, working memory, and planning" [21]. Without PFS, mental objects cannot be voluntarily combined into a novel image, but will remain as separated entrants. Without PFS, mentation is limited to memory recall and spontaneous dreaming hallucinations. A major role of the lateral prefrontal cortex is to "manufacture" novel images by pulling objectNEs into working memory and synchronizing them in time. These "manufactured" novel images allow humans to simulate the future and form the basis for such functions as language and reasoning.

While the central role of the lateral prefrontal cortex in planning and mental simulation has been recognized for several decades, the specific neurological mechanism of those functions has been understood only in general terms. Planning and mental simulation are thought to rely on such lateral prefrontal cortex functions as working memory and "time-integration" [21], but specifics of time-integration are lacking. Current models of the lateral prefrontal cortex do not explicitly talk about synchronization of independent objectNEs as a specific mechanism of planning and mental simulation in humans. This monograph is the attempt to pinpoint a specific neurological mechanism responsible for planning and mental simulation. Rather than describing the process in general terms of "time-integration," the Neuronal Ensembles Synchronization (NES) model offers synchronization of independent objectNEs as the mechanism of PFS organized by the lateral prefrontal cortex [123].

While this monograph does not aim to build an exhaustive model of the prefrontal cortex, I would like to share with you a simplistic view of the lateral prefrontal cortex in regard to PFS. I view the lateral prefrontal cortex as a puppeteer and the existing memories encoded in objectNEs and stored in the posterior cortex as its many puppets. By pulling the strings, the prefrontal cortex changes the firing phase of the retrieved objectNEs thus synchronizing them into new mental constructs [119,121]. In this process, the lateral prefrontal cortex synthesizes novel mental objects and mediates visual simulations.

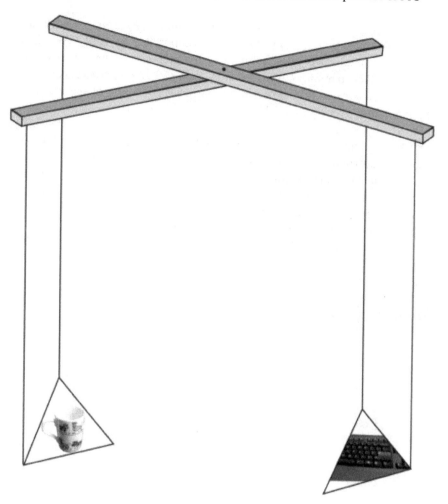

Figure 9.6 The prefrontal cortex puppeteer. The prefrontal cortex can be viewed as a puppeteer controlling its puppets (memories encoded in neuronal ensembles stored in the posterior cortex). By pulling the strings connecting the puppeteer to its puppets (an analogy for phase-shifting of target activity), the prefrontal cortex changes the firing phase of the retrieved neuronal ensembles. Phase-synchronized neuronal ensembles are consciously experienced as a whole novel object or scene.

For example, to imagine your favorite cup on top of your keyboard, your prefrontal cortex (1) activates the objectNE of the cup, (2) activates the objectNE of the keyboard, and then (3) synchronizes the two ensembles in time.

Top-down control of memory retrieval: It was conjectured in this monograph that PFS involves two processes: retrieval of objectNEs from memory and their synchronization in time. While it is impossible to study the latter process in animals, it is possible to study the memory retrieval part of the process. Similar to humans, primates store their visual memories encoded on the neural substrate of the posterior sensory cortex (temporal, parietal, and occipital lobes). Neurons encoding a memory of an object are bound into an objectNE by enhanced inter-neuron connections. Memory retrieval is mediated by activation of the corresponding objectNE and is under the executive control of the prefrontal cortex (reviewed by Miyashita [150]). Direct proof of the existence of top-down signaling was provided by single cell recordings from the temporal cortex of monkeys [287]. A considerable number of inferior temporal cortex neurons receive both top-down signals from the frontal cortex as well as bottom-up signals from the retina via the visual cortical areas in the occipital and temporal lobes. The response latency of the top-down input was about 100ms longer than the latency of the bottom-up input, reflecting the multi-neuron conduction path within the frontal cortex [287]. In summary, the single-cell recordings in primates reveal that top-down signals from the frontal cortex trigger the activation of memory representations stored in the posterior sensory cortex during the active memory retrieval process.

The lateral prefrontal cortex is connected to the posterior cortex via frontoposterior connections, such as arcuate fasciculus and superior longitudinal fasciculus (Figure 9.7). These long fiber tracts connect executive cortical areas in the front (e.g., Broca's area) with sensory areas in the back (e.g., Wernicke's area) and have been implicated in various language-related processes in both hemispheres (syntax, semantics, prosody) [168,288,289]. Patients with damage to the lateral prefrontal cortex [24], or the frontoposterior fibers [168], or to the temporal-parietal-occipital junction [174] (where objectNEs are encoded) often experience PFS paralysis.

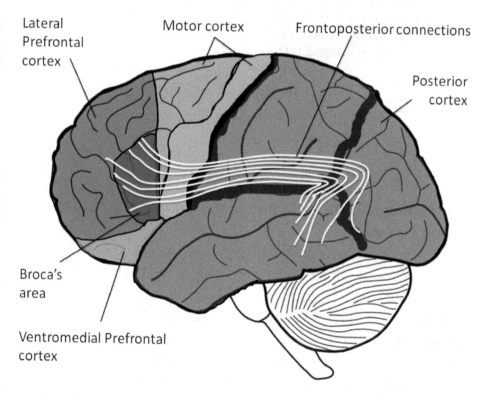

Figure 9.7 The lateral prefrontal cortex mediates PFS by exercising it control over the posterior cortex via frontoposterior connections, such as arcuate fasciculus and superior longitudinal fasciculus

Chapter 10: Evolution of the prefrontal cortex

The extraordinary human cognitive style is the product of a long biological history. From a non-symbolic, non-linguistic ancestor (itself the outcome of an enormously extended and eventful evolutionary process), there emerged our own unprecedented symbolic and linguistic species, an entity possessing a fully-fledged and entirely individuated consciousness of itself. This emergence was a singular event, one that involved bridging a profound cognitive discontinuity. For there is a *qualitative* difference here; and, based on any reasonable prediction from what preceded us, the only reason for believing that this gulf *could* ever have been bridged, is that it *was*.

IAN TATTERSALL, *Masters of the Planet: The search for our human origins* (2012)

10.1 Human brain evolution in the context of primate brain evolution

Since the lateral prefrontal cortex plays such a central role in PFS in humans, it would be interesting to see if a homologous brain area was present in other animals. It turns out that the lateral prefrontal cortex (Brodmann areas 8, 9, 10, 45, 46, 47) is present in all primates but is absent in non-primate mammals [202]. Georg F. Striedter, the leading expert in the field of comparative neuroanatomy, explains that in nonprimate mammals, the prefrontal cortex consists of only two major regions: the *orbital prefrontal region* and the *anterior cingulate cortex*:

Nonprimate mammals do have a prefrontal cortex, but it apparently consists of only two major regions, rather than three as in primates. The two conserved prefrontal regions are the *orbital prefrontal region*, whose neurons respond preferentially to external stimuli that are likely to be rewarding or otherwise significant, and the *anterior cingulate cortex*, which mainly process information about the body's internal state. Collectively, these two regions contribute to what we might call the "emotional" aspect of decision making . The third prefrontal region, which is generally known as the lateral, or granular prefrontal cortex, is apparently unique to primates and is concerned mainly with the "rational" aspects of decision making. Its neurons respond less rapidly than orbitofrontal neurons to rewarding stimuli and are more selective for the physical attributes of the stimuli, such as their spatial location. Without those lateral prefrontal neurons, primates become less able to retrieve and manipulate information about objects in the outside world. In the context of decision making, this probably means that the lateral prefrontal cortex helps primates to consider alternative interpretations of external objects and to construct alternative scenarios of how to interact with them. ... The notion of the lateral prefrontal cortex being a primate innovation originated with Brodmann and has recently been championed by Todd Preuss. Central to their argument is that small celled granular layer that characterizes the lateral prefrontal cortex in primates is lacking in most other mammals. This finding does indeed suggest that the lateral prefrontal cortex is unique to primates. [202]

What is so special about primates? What was the evolutionary driving force for their acquisition of the lateral prefrontal cortex? To answer these questions, we need to look at the evolution of primates. The primate lineage separated from the rest of mammals some 70 million years ago, when dinosaurs still roamed the Earth.[w] The mammalian ancestors of primates were small nocturnal animals who spent most of their time underground [202] (p.261). Following the demise of dinosaurs some 66 million years ago, the competition for aboveground resources diminished and primates evolved into diurnal arboreal animals. Primates came to occupy the evolutionary niche that heavily depends on vision rather than olfaction for food search and predator avoidance.[x] Reliance on an enhanced sense of vision became the defining feature of *all* primates [291]. Georg F. Striedter reports that most primate-typical features reflect the development of the visual system. For example, primate eyes evolved to a more frontally placed position (presumably to improve depth perception) and eye projections to the superior colliculi (the major visual center in the brainstem) also evolved to project in roughly equal proportion to both superior colliculi [292], which further improved depth perception. Primates also acquired an additional color receptor to better differentiate red from green [202].[y] Primates occupied the

---

[w] A recent discovery of a tiny 55-million-year-old primate fossil in China supports the notion that the primate lineage separated from the rest of mammals around the time of the demise of dinosaurs. The ancient primate, dubbed Archicebus Achilles, is the oldest most complete skeleton of a tree-dwelling primate ever discovered.

[x] Primates primarily use vision to direct skilled movements, as well as to search for food and avoid predators. Rodents can also grasp and manipulate objects using the tips of their digits, however rodents are much less visual. Their skilled movements are primarily directed by the sense of touch and olfaction: rats without vision are able to locate and reach for food as quickly as they did before being blinded, but rats without olfaction, who therefore rely more on vision, are significantly slower [290].

[y] Most placental mammals, from which primates evolved, have only two different kinds of color receptors. These receptors have peak sensitivity in the blue and in the yellow-green regions of the spectrum. Thus, most placental

"fine-branch niche" collecting ripe fruits and leaves, and hunting for insects. Primates also acquired more direct corticospinal projections (connections between the cortical neurons and the motor neurons in the spinal cord, which increase fine control over muscles) and an additional cortical area (called the ventral premotor cortical area) specialized for arm and mouth movements [293]. Furthermore, the control of hand and foot movement benefited from an increased somatosensory cortex, which, in primates, added several cortical areas that have no homologues in non-primates [292]. Striedter concludes that "diverse evolutionary changes in the visual, motor and somatosensory systems all interacted to give early primates exceptionally good hand-eye coordination, which must have come in handy in the fine-branch niche" [202]. Thus, acquisition of the lateral prefrontal cortex by primates may be associated with the evolution of the visual system. What role does the prefrontal cortex play in the visual system?

A primate's survival in the "fine-branch niche" depended on its ability to visually detect predators, prey, and edible objects. Consequently, primates were under constant evolutionary pressure to recognize those objects faster and from a greater distance. Visually identifying ripe fruits, leaves, and insects relies on a primate's ability to separate those objects from the background and from other objects. Fruits are normally hidden under leaves, leaves in the rainforest merge into thick foliage, and insects tend to camouflage their appearance. Predators are also often camouflaged and therefore

---

animals, including dogs and cats, cannot distinguish green and red colors. The additional color receptor acquired by primates helped them to select ripe fruit, which tends to be red or orange against the background of green leaves as well as to pick out the young leaves, which tend to be red in Africa and are more nutritious and digestible.

merge into the background. Furthermore fruits, leaves, insects, and predators often remain motionless, and visual detection of motionless objects is significantly more difficult than detection of moving objects [294]. Finally, primates frequently move from one tree branch to another changing their perspective and making detection of visually ambiguous objects (that look different from different perspectives) significantly more difficult. Consider the illustration of the frog hidden amongst the dead leaves. To detect this frog and similar small camouflaged animals (a common primate prey), the brain needs to organize the fragments encoding the frog into synchronously firing objectNEs. According to the *binding-by-synchronization* hypothesis, detection of the frog involves phase-shifting of individual visual fragments: neurons that encode the frog have to be phase-shifted in-synchrony with each other, while fragments that are not part of the frog have to be phase-shifted out-of-synchrony. The voluntary re-arranging the visual features can only be accomplished by the lateral prefrontal cortex.

Figure 10.1 Can you find a camouflaged frog amongst the dead leaves in this illustration? (The color version of this photograph is shown on the back cover of the book.) The frog, motionless on the rainforest floor, disappears completely amongst the dead leaves. If you are seeing this picture for the first time, you are unlikely to find the frog. It looks like just a bunch of dead leaves, right? The dead leaves are numbered in the illustration on the next page.

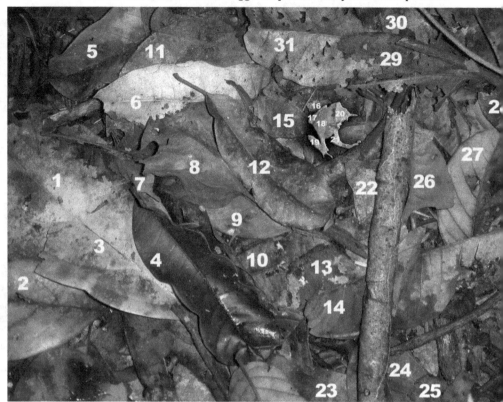

Figure 10.2 When the fragments (numbered 1 through 31) are perceived separately, each is perceived as a fragment of a dead leaf. According to the *binding-by-synchronization* hypothesis, to interpret fragments 17 through 21 as belonging to a frog (a single entity), neurons encoding these fragments have to be organized into synchronous activity. If you still do not see the frog, please turn the page to see the frog highlighted.

Fragments 1 through 30 are interpreted independently and all you perceive are fragments of dead leaves. It stands to reason that the neuronal ensembles encoding these fragments fire asynchronously. According to the *binding-by-synchronization* hypothesis, to interpret fragments 17 through 21 as belonging to a frog (a single entity), neurons encoding these fragments have to be transiently organized into synchronous activity.

Figure 10.3   The frog from the illustration on the previous page is highlighted.

While the *dead leaves frog* illustration may seem like an extreme example of visual recognition, it is important to remember that in the rainforest all objects are visually ambiguous. Recognition of fruits, leaves, and camouflaged animals (prey or predator, insect or mammal) involves the active process of selecting and organizing ambiguous visual fragments into a recognizable object.

A remarkable experiment by Sabine Windmann and colleagues emphasized the active role of the prefrontal cortex in ambiguous image perception [295]. Consider the *Rubin's Vase* pattern developed by the Danish psychologist Edgar Rubin. When looking at the pattern, perception tends to fluctuate spontaneously and unpredictably between the two mutually exclusive interpretations: the vase and the two faces. This phenomenon is dubbed bistable perception.

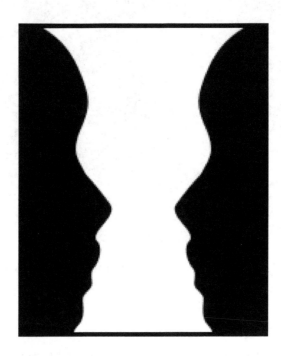

Figure 10.4 *Rubin's Vase* is an example of a bistable pattern. When staring at the pattern, the percept spontaneously switches between the vase and the faces every few seconds.

The researchers selected six bistable patterns including the *Rubin's Vase* and compared perceptual reversals in patients with lesions of the prefrontal cortex to that of healthy controls. The participants were asked to either maintain the dominant view as long as they could or to voluntarily induce as many perceptual switches as possible (in the *Rubin's Vase* example, this meant switching between perception of the vase and perception of the two facing profiles). The participants reported the reversals in their perception by pressing a button. Patients with lesions of the prefrontal cortex were able to hold the dominant view as long as the healthy control subjects: for approximately six seconds.[z] However, frontal patients struggled considerably on the second test, in which they were asked to voluntarily switch their perception as fast as they could. The healthy participants were able to switch perception every second, while frontal patients could only influence their perception minimally: they reported perception reversal approximately every 5 seconds [295]. These results suggest that the prefrontal cortex is necessary to bias the selection of perception in accordance with current goals, but that it is less essential for maintaining the dominant interpretation of the environment.

Conceptually, top-down control of bistable perception is similar to recognition of the camouflaged frog hidden amongst the dead leaves — the brain must pick and choose which visual fragments (from all the visual fragments present on the retina) are part of the percept and which aren't. The two phenomena, therefore, likely share the same neurological mechanism for top-down control of the selection process. The results of Windmann's experiment implicate the prefrontal cortex in selecting and intentionally switching between competing object representations in accordance with current goals. It follows that the prefrontal cortex is also likely involved in visual recognition of other ambiguous objects (such as the *dead leaves frog* or a camouflaged predator hiding in the grass). To succeed in an environment where prey and predators were often motionless,

---

[z] After six seconds the perception spontaneously switched to an alternative interpretation. The holding times varied somewhat between the six different ambiguous patterns used in the test. The time values cited here correspond to the *Rubin's Vase* pattern (Windmann S, 2006).

camouflaged, and partially hidden, primates had to rely heavily on their prefrontal cortex to interpret ambiguous sensory input throughout the 70 million years of their evolution. The prefrontal cortex of diurnal arboreal animals, who relied on their sense of vision to detect prey and predator from afar, was under constant evolutionary pressure to improve its ability to actively steer perception to coordinate subjective goals with objective reality.

To sum up, since their origin some 70 million years ago, primates occupied the evolutionary niche that relied primarily on the sense of vision for detection of both food and predators (rather than other mammals who primarily relied on their sense of smell, such as cats, dogs, and herbivores, or on their auditory system, such as bats). Visual perception, especially perception of motionless ambiguous objects is an active process wherein the brain seeks to interpret what is giving rise to the current patterns of sensory stimulation. Such active interpretation is a computationally expensive process. Recall that some animals cannot visually detect a still object even when it is unambiguous. That is why ceasing all movement in order to avoid detection by predators ("freezing") is a common strategy observed in many animals [235]. For example, rabbits that sense the presence of a predator snake will remain motionless and therefore completely disappear from the snake's visual perception. To counter this strategy, vipers and rattlesnakes acquired an additional heat sensitive system to detect motionless live targets. For these reptiles it was evolutionarily "easier" to acquire this additional system rather than to develop computational support for the existing visual sensory input. Visual primates, on the other hand, "chose" to expand their computational system in order to improve detection of motionless ambiguous objects. Primates experienced a continuous evolutionary pressure on all neurological structures responsible for active object interpretation in the context of the animal's current goals. The lateral prefrontal cortex at the top of the perception-action cycle [21] underwent the greatest transformation under this evolutionary pressure. It is therefore unremarkable that the size of the prefrontal cortex increases with phylogenetic development of primates and reaches its greatest proportions in humans. Or does it? Let us investigate.

10.2 Do humans have a disproportionately larger prefrontal cortex?

The human brain is approximately three times larger than expected for a primate of comparable body size. However the intriguing fact is that different brain areas are scaled up differently. For example, the volume of the olfactory bulb in humans is only 30% as large as would be expected in a primate brain of our size, and the volume of the primary visual cortex (area V1) is only 60% as large as expected [296,297]. Remarkably, the volume of Brodmann area 10 (part of the anterior lateral prefrontal cortex, also called the frontopolar cortex) is nearly 200% as large as expected for a primate brain of our size [298]. Because neural tissue is metabolically expensive, changes in relative proportions of different brain areas are likely to be behaviorally adaptive. Accordingly, paleoneurobiologists often deduce that the survival benefit provided by the olfactory sense did not change or has reduced in hominins, while the survival benefit provided by Brodmann area 10, has increased significantly. What about the rest of the prefrontal cortex?

The eminent neurologist Korbinian Brodmann (famous for his division of the cerebral cortex into 52 distinct areas, now known as Brodmann areas), measured the sizes of various brain regions using the cytoarchitectonic method, which provides the best quantitative measure of the relative sizes. Brodmann concluded that the prefrontal cortex constitutes 29% of the total cortex in humans, 17% in the chimpanzee, 11.5% in the gibbon and the macaque, 8.5% in the lemur, 7% in the dog, and 3.5% in the cat [299]. Brodmann also reported that the relative size of the frontal cortex (which includes the prefrontal cortex, premotor, motor, and limbic cortices) was significantly larger in humans. He found that the surface of the frontal cortex constitutes 36.3% of the total surface of the cerebral hemispheres in the human brain, 30.5% in the chimpanzee, 22.5% in the cebus, and 21.4% in the gibbon [299]. However, Brodmann's conclusions on the disproportionately large human frontal cortex were recently put into doubt. The problem is that Brodmann analyzed only a few specimens and did not include a significant number of apes, human's closest relatives. A significantly larger study of the frontal cortex in humans and apes detected a significant overlap in the two groups [300]. Semendeferi and colleagues reported that the surface of the frontal cortex constitutes 37.7±0.9% of the surface of cerebral hemispheres in humans, 35.4±1.9% in the chimpanzee, 34.7±0.6% in the bonobo, 36.9% and 35.0% in the two gorillas, 37.6±1.1% in the orangutan, 29.4±1.8% in the gibbon, 30.6±1.5% in the macaque, and 31.5 and 29.6% in the two cebus [300]. In this study, there was a significant overlap between humans and the great apes, with 50% of the humans having a proportionally smaller frontal cortex than in the one chimpanzee who had the greatest proportion of the frontal cortex. While Semendeferi's analysis relied on a significantly greater number of specimens than Brodmann's, the study used a different methodology (magnetic resonance imaging) that was unable to analyze the prefrontal cortex separately from the rest of the frontal cortex. Since the prefrontal cortex and the rest of the frontal lobe could enlarge differently, the two studies are not necessarily contradictory.

A recent study considerably clarifies the picture. Paul

Thomas Schoenemann and colleagues (2005) studied the size of the prefrontal cortex in eleven primate species using magnetic resonance imaging, the same method used by Semendeferi [300]. Schoenemann however focused on a proxy for the prefrontal cortex, defined as "all portions of the frontal cortex in front of the corpus callosum" [301]. The researchers found that, in fact, the volume of the prefrontal cortex is disproportionately larger in humans than in other primates. Furthermore the researchers were able to measure the volume of gray matter (neurons) separately from white matter (connections between neurons). According to their results, there was no significant difference between humans and other primates when it came to the portion of the cortical volume occupied by gray matter (14.4±0.3% in humans, 14.1±1.1% in the chimpanzees, 11.9±0.4% in the bonobos, 13.7±0.8% in the gorillas, 14.1±0.5% in the orangutan, 12.3±1.2% in the gibbon, 8.8±0.3% in the macaque, and 11.4±0.5% in the cebus), but a large difference when it came to the volume of white matter (10.9±0.4% in humans, 8.3±0.7% in the chimpanzees, 6.8±0.4% in the bonobos, 8.3±0.2% in the gorillas, 7.5±0.6% in the orangutan, 6.9±0% in the gibbon, 7.3 ±0.9% in the macaque, and 8.6±0.2% in the cebus). This means that, while the volume of neurons in the prefrontal cortex did not change significantly, the connections between the neurons increased disproportionately in humans compared to other primates.

In a different study, Semendeferi and colleagues focused on Brodmann area 10 [298], and arrived at a similar conclusion as that of Thomas Schoenemann [301]. Using a precise cytoarchitectonic method, the researchers counted the neurons in Brodmann area 10 and concluded that neuronal density in humans was around half of that of other primates [298]. This finding indicates that Brodmann area 10 in humans has a significantly greater portion of its volume dedicated to connections between neurons.

To sum up, all the studies point toward the same fact: there has been a disproportional increase in volume of the prefrontal cortex in humans, particularly in the one part of the lateral prefrontal cortex, Brodmann area 10, which occupies a space that is twice as large as expected for a primate with a comparable brain size [298]. It has long been known that differences in behavior amongst species are generally reflected in differences in their cortical maps. For example, echolocating bats have greatly expanded cortical areas dedicated to processing of auditory signals (in the ghost bat *Macroderma gigas* this cortical area accounts for more than half the cortex), whereas primarily subterranean mole species have markedly reduced visual cortical areas [302]. Among modern humans, the volume of the white matter in the prefrontal cortex has been found to be positively correlated with cognitive tasks known to be mediated by the prefrontal cortex (e.g., the Stroop test, which tests the ability to extract and focus on relevant cues in the face of distractors). Thus, it is reasonable to assume that the disproportional increase in the volume of the lateral prefrontal cortex had behavioral implications during human evolution, specifically involving the increased importance of the kinds of behaviors mediated by the prefrontal cortex. Since PFS is a function of the lateral prefrontal cortex, a disproportional increase in the volume of the lateral prefrontal cortex may very well be associated with greater top-down control of the posterior (primarily sensory) cortex in general and with acquisition of PFS in particular. Furthermore, as PFS involves synchronization of independent objectNEs located elsewhere in the cortex, the process depends on the isochronous connections between the lateral prefrontal cortex and the rest of the cortex. In this regard, the disproportionate increase in the white matter of the prefrontal cortex may have played an essential role in making the networks synchronous, a necessary prerequisite for acquisition of PFS. The next section discusses the role of myelin (the whitish substance that gives white matter its name and occupies the bulk of white matter's volume) in establishing isochronicity of neuronal networks.

10.3 Isochronicity in neural networks

A central concept in memory development is the importance of the temporal coincidence of firing among multiple synaptic inputs onto a neuron with respect to firing of the postsynaptic neuron (Hebbian learning: 'neurons that fire together, wire together' [86]). If neuron A is being activated by two neurons B and C that are located at different distances from neuron A, the synaptic signals from neurons B and C will not arrive simultaneously. To arrive simultaneously, the action potential speed of transmission (called conduction velocity) must be accelerated in the axon of the neuron located farther away and slowed down in the axon of the neuron located closer to neuron A. If the action potentials from neurons B and C arrive simultaneously, the postsynaptic potentials produced by each excitatory input will add together, creating a larger depolarization in neuron A. Once the depolarization in neuron A reaches a critical threshold voltage, neuron A fires an action potential and initiates molecular events that reinforce synapses between neuron A and the neurons B and C. Millisecond precision in the arrival of action potentials is necessary for the summation of synaptic signals. Therefore, axonal conduction velocity is a critical variable for optimal mental performance and learning.

Consistent with this view, conduction velocity varies widely among different axons. The transmission time from one hemisphere of the human brain to another is less than 30ms through the fastest axons and more than 300ms through the slowest axons. The conduction velocity is significantly greater in axons that have multiple extra layers of electrical isolation provided by an oily substance called myelin. Myelin increases conduction velocity through axons by fundamentally changing the way action potentials are propagated. Rather than an uninterrupted wave of depolarization amplified continuously along the axon, the action potentials in myelinated axons are amplified at isolated points along the axon called nodes of Ranvier. Conduction velocity in myelinated axons can be as much as 100-fold faster than conduction velocity in unmyelinated fibers. The degree of myelination varies greatly, with some of the fastest axons having up to 160 layers of myelin. In fact, myelin occupies the bulk part of white matter, which, in turn, comprises over half of the human brain, a far greater proportion than in other animals.

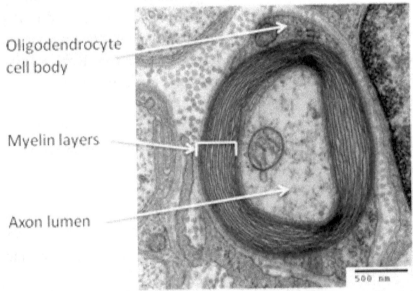

Figure 10.5 Electron micrograph of a cross-section of a myelinated axon. The myelin-producing oligodendrocyte cell wrapped itself eight times around this axon adding 16 layers of myelin.

Only vertebrates have myelin, probably due to the necessity of packing a large number of fast connections into a small space. In unmyelinated axons, the conduction velocity is proportional to the square root of the axon diameter. To have a conduction velocity that is 10 times faster, the diameter of an unmyelinated axon needs to be 100 times larger. Accordingly, invertebrates often solve the problem of fast connection by using axons with large diameters. For example, *squid giant axons* which mediate its escape response have a diameter of up to 1mm, which is about 1000 times greater than the diameter of a typical vertebrate axon (normally only 1μm in diameter). Furthermore, by variably changing the diameter of the giant axons that run between the stellate ganglia and the mantle musculature, a squid achieves faster conduction velocity for longer axons, and, as a result, the activation of the whole mantle takes place synchronously, allowing for a hasty and effective escape.

In the vertebrate brain, increasing the axonal diameter is an inferior option since it is packed with a large number of neurons and an even larger number of connections; myelination is the preferred way to accelerate conduction velocity. In axons that must travel over different distances to reach the same target, isochronicity is often achieved by changes in the conduction velocity. For example, action potentials must arrive simultaneously through axons of widely varying path lengths to activate the electric organ of an electric fish. This is achieved by increasing the conduction velocity in axons from neurons located farther from the organ, and decreasing conduction velocity through shorter axons innervating the organ [303]. Similarly, in the cat retina, axons from peripheral regions have a greater conduction velocity than axons from neurons at the center of the retina to assure simultaneous arrival of impulses in the brain [304]. Experiments in rats show that myelination is the primary factor producing uniform conduction time (to within 1ms) in connections between the inferior olive nucleus in the brainstem and the cerebellar cortex, despite wide variation in axon length [305].

Isochronous activation of groups of cells distributed in distant cortical locations has been shown in the visual cortex [106] and even between the two hemispheres of the brain [110]. In the cerebral cortex, the layer V pyramidal neurons in the ventral temporal lobe innervate various subcortical regions. Taylor Chomiak and colleagues showed that isochronous action potential delivery to target regions located in the ipsilateral hemisphere is based on the differential conduction velocity in each fiber branch [306]. Chomiak's observation on isochronicity appears to be best explained by differential myelination [307]. The amygdala connections to the perirhinal cortex play an important role in establishing fear memory. While the perirhinal cortex is an elongated structure, the small nucleus of the lateral amygdala is isochronically connected with a large portion of the perirhinal cortex [308]. Neurons in the thalamus send axons to a wide area of the somatosensory cortex through different trajectories of various travelling lengths. Nevertheless, action potentials in the thalamic neurons arrive almost simultaneously at each target cortical neuron. This isochronicity (to within 2ms) is achieved by changing the conduction velocity within the individual axons by differential myelination [309].

Reviewing the available literature, Fumitaka Kimura and Chiaki Itami of Saitama Medical University conclude: "myelination plays a major role in creating isochronicity. In other words, myelination is not merely insulation among neighboring cells, but is a method of regulating the timing of postsynaptic activations" [307].

10.4 Experience changes myelination in humans

Myelination is nearly completed by birth in most species in which the young are relatively mature and mobile from the moment of birth, such as wild mice [310] and horses [311]. However, in humans, myelination is delayed considerably. Few fibers are myelinated at birth and some brain regions continue myelination well into mid-life. The prefrontal cortex region is the last region to complete myelination. Myelination of frontoposterior fibers does not reach full maturation until the third decade of life or later [312]. One study demonstrates that the volume of white matter in the prefrontal cortex increases until the age of 45 implying that myelination of the prefrontal cortex continues until that age [313]. Humans' delayed maturation of myelination raises the possibility that experience determines myelination in a manner that optimizes isochronicity in neural networks.

There is significant evidence that neural activity can affect myelination. The number of myelin-forming cells in the visual cortex of rats increases by 30% when the rats are raised in an environment that is enriched by additional play objects and social interaction [314]. Premature eye opening in neonatal rabbits increases myelin production presumably by increasing activity in the optic nerve [315]. In contrast, rearing mice in the dark reduces the number of myelinated axons in the optic nerve [316]. The proliferation of myelin-forming precursor cells in the rat's developing optic nerve depends on electrical activity in neighboring axons [317]. In neuronal cell culture, induction of action potentials with electrical stimulation affects axonal myelination [318,319].

Environmental effects on axonal myelination extend beyond animal studies. In human infants, early experiences increase myelination in the frontal lobes in parallel with improved performance on cognitive tests [320]. On the contrary, children suffering from abuse and neglect show on average a 17% reduction in myelination of the corpus callosum, the structure comprised of connections between the neurons of the left and the right hemispheres of the brain [321]. In an important study, Bengtsson and colleagues demonstrated that extensive piano practice in childhood was accompanied by increased myelination of axons involved in musical performance [322]. The researchers report that the white matter thickening increased proportionately to the number of hours each subject had practiced the instrument.

To sum up, isochronicity in at least some neuronal networks seems to be achieved via differential myelination and myelination may be experience-dependent. In fact, considering the many variables affecting conduction delays in an adult brain, genetic instruction alone would seem inadequate to specify the optimal conduction velocity in every axon.

At the center of this monograph lies the conjecture that the mechanism of PFS involves voluntary synchronization of independent objectNEs. As discussed above, these objectNEs (encoding physical objects onto the neuronal substrate) are located in the posterior sensory cortex (occipital, temporal and parietal lobes), while the process of synchronization is executed by the prefrontal cortex (located in the frontal lobe). The only way the prefrontal cortex could be capable of synchronizing ensembles of neurons distributed over the large area of the posterior sensory cortex is if the prefrontal cortex had isochronous connections to those cortical areas.[aa] Therefore

───────────────

[aa] Isochronicity here has to be understood in terms of synchronicity of the arrival of action potentials to a target neuron rather than absolute equality of action potential conduction times over different paths. Consider the following example: suppose neuron A is receiving excitatory input from neurons B and C via two different pathways (neuron A is the target neuron for both neurons

isochronicity is expected to develop in an experience-dependent manner via differential myelination during a limited period of prefrontal cortex plasticity [307,323].

What experience might be involved in the development of PFS? What system do we, humans, use to manipulate mental images stored in our memory into novel mental pictures? The human system of choice is, of course, recursive language — whether it be internal language when we are thinking to ourselves, or external language when we are involved in conversation. As discussed above, recursive language is a communication system that allows the *transmission* of an *infinite* number of *novel* images with the use of a *finite* number of words.

B and C). Suppose that the action potential conduction time is 2ms from neuron B to neuron A and 22ms from neuron C to neuron A (i.e. the axonal pathway B-A has a significantly shorter conduction time than the axonal pathway C-A). Does it mean that the connections B-A and C-A are always asynchronous? The answer depends on the predominant neural activity rhythm in this network. At the firing rate of 50Hz (inter-spike interval of 20ms that correspond to Gamma rhythm), neurons B and C can actually be considered isochronous in relationship to neuron A: consider a train of action potentials synchronously fired by neurons B and C. The first action potential from neuron B will reach neuron A in 2ms and the first action potential from neuron C will reach neuron A in 22ms. Obviously, there would be no coincidence in the arrival times of the 1st action potentials from neurons B and C. However the second action potential from neuron B will arrive to neuron A in 22ms, concurrently with the 1st action potential from neuron C. Thus, starting with the second action potential, neuron A will receive isochronous activation from neurons B and C. The synchronous activation has a significantly greater probability of enhancing synaptic connections between neurons A and B, and A and C (Hebbian learning: 'neurons that fire together, wire together' [86]). Thus, isochronicity does not need to imply absolute equality in the conduction time over different pathways. Rather isochronicity implies near-zero phase-shift between the two firing trains of action potentials at the postsynaptic cells. The phase-shift, of course, depends on both conduction times over each pathway and the dominant firing frequency in the neural network.

Might the recursive language be that very mechanism that provides the training necessary for the development of PFS? If the answer to this question is "yes," then it might be expected that the lack of recursive language during the sensitive period of prefrontal cortex plasticity would result in an underdevelopment of PFS. The next section investigates this very scenario: what happens if children are not exposed to recursive language during the sensitive period of prefrontal cortex maturation?

10.5 Critical period for prefrontal synthesis acquisition

Although learning is possible throughout life, there is no doubt that neural plasticity is enhanced during specific windows of opportunity early on in childhood and diminishes greatly at the end of the critical period. Real and significant changes in cortical structure reflect those differences. Critical periods have been found to exist in virtually all species, from humans to Drosophila [324].

Most people are familiar with the notion of a critical period, but their familiarity is based on learning a second language in high school. While it is more difficult to learn a second language after puberty [49], it is not impossible: phoneme tuning [50,51], grammar processing [52], articulation control [53], and vocabulary acquisition [54] —all can be significantly improved by training at any age [55,56]. In other words, learning a second language has a weak critical period.

Few individuals understand that learning a first language is different from learning a second language, as learning a first language has a strong critical period. Strong critical periods, that make learning impossible after a certain age, are rarely encountered in daily life and, therefore, are counterintuitive. Strong critical periods, however, are common in the central nervous system development. Neural circuits underlying strong critical periods are programmed to be shaped by experience during short periods of early postnatal life; later plasticity is impossible. There are several mechanisms mediating the closure of critical periods. For example, myelination is known to limit the critical period for learning through inhibitory proteins that suppress axon sprouting and synaptogenesis [323]. The most studied examples of strong critical periods include 1) filial imprinting in birds [58], 2) monaural occlusion [59], 3) post-childbirth bonding in mammals [170], 4) the vestibulo-ocular reflex [171], 5) song dialects learning in male white-crowned sparrows [172], and 6) monocular deprivation [57].

Let's look at these abovementioned examples in more detail:

1) Typically the first moving object seen by baby geese is the mother, and the chick's survival depends upon learning to follow its mother [325]. Thus, chicks permanently imprint on the first moving object they see shortly after hatching.

2) Sound localization in owls depends on early access to both ears. Plugging one ear (monaural occlusion) in owls during the first two postnatal months results in a lifelong inability to localize sounds [59].

3) To distinguish their offsprings from other lambs in the flock, sheep mothers imprint on their children within a few hours of birth [170]. Later exposure cannot change the initial bonding.

4) The vestibulo-ocular reflex functions to stabilize images on the retinas during head movement. Studies in fish and tadpoles revealed that the vestibulo-ocular reflex can only be acquired during the first 10-day of life; animals who spend the first ten days in gravity deprivation during a spaceflight end up with a lifelong vestibulo-ocular reflex disability [171].

5) Marler's Sparrows have song "dialects," acquired in about the first 100 days of life by learning from older males [172].

Once the song is established, further acoustical exposure does not change the song pattern.

6) The most investigated example of the strong critical period has been monocular deprivation [57]. Cats that had one eye sewn shut from birth until three months of age, developed vision only in the open eye. This loss of vision in the covered eye occurs despite there being no damage to the cerebral cortex, the thalamus, or the sensory receptors in the eye. The simple act of closing an eye for the duration of the critical period can profoundly alter the physical structure of the brain and cause a permanent loss of vision through that eye. The duration of this critical period lasts approximately three weeks in mice, three months in cats, and three years in primates [38].

Does the acquisition of PFS have a critical period? The most dramatic evidence in favor of the existence of a critical period for the development of PFS comes from the study of feral and deaf children who were not exposed to a recursive language in their childhood.

One of the seminal cases of feral children is that of Genie (real name: Susan M. Wiley).[bb] Genie was isolated starting at 20 months of age until she was finally rescued at the age of 13 years 7 months. She was locked inside a bedroom in Los Angeles, strapped to a child's toilet during the day and bound inside a crib with her arms and legs immobilized on most nights [326,327]. She was not allowed to vocalize, was not spoken to, could not hear family conversation or any other language occurring in her home other than swearing (there was no TV or radio in the home). Genie emerged from isolation in 1970 with no development of spoken language and no comprehension of any

---

[bb] An independent film entitled *Mockingbird Don't Sing* is based on Genie's life.

238

language with exception of a few isolated words. After Genie was rescued, focused attempts were made to teach her language. Genie became the subject of an investigation (funded by NIH) to discover if there was a critical age threshold for first-language acquisition. Within a few months she had advanced to one-word answers and had learned to dress herself. Her doctors predicted complete success. Her teachers included psychologists James Kent, linguist Susan Curtiss, therapist David Rigler, and many other well-intentioned people genuinely interested in rehabilitating Genie. After seven years of rehabilitation, Genie's vocabulary had expanded to several hundred words, however she could only speak in short sentences with little use of syntax or verb tense.

Genie's comprehension of complex sentence structures remained inconsistent. Remarkably, she was unable to grasp pronouns and prepositions such as *behind, in front, on* and *under* [165,326]). Let me reiterate: Genie did not understand the difference between the simple task of "putting a bowl *behind* a cup" and "putting a bowl *in front of* a cup," despite familiarity with both objects described by the words "bowl" and "cup." Normally Genie's condition would be described as an inability to learn recursive language. However, as discussed in Chapter 3.3, understanding of recursive language is based on PFS. To put a bowl *behind* or *in front of* a cup, one first needs to simulate the process in the mind. One needs to mentally synthesize the novel image of a bowl *behind* or *in front of* a cup by synchronizing the independent objectNEs of the bowl and the cup in one mental frame. Only after completing the mental simulation, could one spatially arrange the physical objects into the correct arrangement that corresponds to their mental image. Someone who cannot simulate the process mentally would have no mental image of a bowl *behind* or *in front of* a cup and would therefore just use trial and error and probably place the cup and bowl into an incorrect arrangement. What lies at the root of Genie's failure to comprehend recursive language in general and spatial prepositions in particular is most likely "PFS paralysis." The task of "putting a bowl *behind* a cup," which is reasonably simple for a typical three and a half year old child, was beyond Genie's capability even at the age of 20 after seven years of strenuous linguistic training, presumably because the training occurred after the closure of the critical period of plasticity.[cc]

Genie's case has been extensively compared to that of Victor of Aveyron, an eighteenth-century French child whose life similarly became a case study for research in delayed first-language acquisition.[dd] Victor of Aveyron was a feral child who apparently lived a majority of his childhood alone in the woods before being found wandering the woods near Saint-Sernin-sur-Rance in France. His case was taken up by a young physician, Jean Marc Gaspard Itard, who worked with the boy for five years. Itard named the wild child Victor, and estimated that the boy was 13 years old when he initiated the study. Itard, who was interested in determining what Victor could learn, devised procedures to teach the boy words and recorded his progress [328]. Victor showed significant early progress in understanding and reading simple words, but failed to progress beyond a rudimentary level. Itard wrote, "Under these circumstances his ear was not an organ for the appreciation of sounds, their articulations and their combinations; it was nothing but a simple means of self-preservation which warned of the approach of a dangerous animal or the fall of wild fruit" [328]. In a clear parallel

---

[cc] Additional discussion of Genie's cognitive abilities can be found in Appendix 6.

[dd] Victor of Aveyron was depicted by François Truffaut's 1970 French film *L'Enfant Sauvage,* translated to English as *The Wild Child.*

to Genie's case, Victor of Aveyron failed to acquire PFS when exposed to recursive language after the closure of the period of plasticity.[ee]

Studies of feral children, however, are highly problematic: isolation and childhood abuse can result in all sorts of psychological problems, which may confound conclusions drawn about linguistic abilities. Studies of congenitally deaf people who had linguistic but not social deprivation have fewer methodological weaknesses. Up to date, there have been only eight cases reported in scientific literature of deaf subjects who were linguistically deprived for the duration of their critical period.

Gina Grimshaw and her colleagues studied a 19-year old man referred to as E.M., who has been profoundly deaf since birth and grew up in a rural area where he received no formal education and had no contact with the deaf community [329]. Although E.M. had not experienced formal language, he had not been deprived of simple communication. He and his family used home-sign (also called kitchen-sign), a system of gestures that allowed them to communicate simple commands, but lacked much in the way of syntax. This is quite typical of families with deaf children and hearing parents, which are isolated from a sign language community; instead of learning a formal sign

---

[ee] Other feral children have been mentioned in literature. Ten such children are mentioned by Carl Linneaus in his *System of Nature* published in 1735, and are included by Linnaeus under his subdivision of *Homo Sapiens* which he called *Homo Ferus* (Wild Man). One of the defining characteristics of *Homo Ferus*, according to Linnaeus, was his inability to speak. However it is not clear if a consistent effort was made to rehabilitate those children. This review focuses on cases in which a consistent rehabilitation effort was undertaken to teach language to children linguistically deprived until puberty.

language, they normally spontaneously develop a home-sign system. At the age of 15, E.M. was fitted with hearing aids that corrected his hearing loss, and he began to learn verbal Spanish. Grimshaw's tests demonstrated that E.M. had linguistic problems similar to those of Genie, Victor and other individuals who were linguistically deprived in their childhood. While E.M.'s performance on simple linguistic tests that do not rely on PFS was reasonably good, his performance on more complex tests that rely on PFS was random. Similar to Genie, E.M. had significant difficulty with spatial prepositions such as *in, on, under, over, beside, behind,* and *in front of.* E.M.'s general strategy when following a direction to "put the green box *in* the blue box," was to pick up the appropriate two boxes and to "move them through a variety of spatial arrangements, watching the examiner for clues as to which was correct" [329]. (Of course, normal performance of such a task would first involve a mental simulation of the green box *inside* the blue box in the process of PFS, followed by a demonstration of the results of the mental simulation with the physical objects.) In another task testing the understanding of simple negation, E.M. was presented with three pictures, each pair denoting a presence or absence of an object. For example, E.M. was asked to indicate a picture in which "the rabbit does not have a carrot." Note again that a typical subject would rely on PFS to imagine the rabbit with a carrot, then remove the carrot from the mental image, and only then select a physical picture fitting the mental image. Again, E.M.'s performance in this test never rose above chance.

Another example is that of Chelsea, a deaf woman isolated from recursive linguistic input until she was 32, when her first exposure to spoken English was provided by successful auditory amplification [166]. (Similar to E.M., Chelsea used home-sign to communicate until the auditory amplification apparatus was installed.) With adequate auditory amplification, Chelsea managed to learn many words. However, Chelsea never learned to put those words together into recursively meaningful phrases, and as a result she could not understand recursively complex sentences. Similar to Genie, Chelsea did not appear to comprehend or use spatial prepositions. She also did not seem to understand directions that relied on spatial prepositions such as "put a bowl *behind* a cup" (Curtiss S, personal communications).

Jill Morford studied two deaf adolescents, Maria and Marcus, as they were acquiring their first language (American Sign Language, or ASL), at the ages of 13 and a half and 12 respectively [330]. Both Maria and Marcus were born profoundly deaf. However they were not raised in isolation and already had well developed social and cognitive skills at the time of their first exposure to American Sign Language. Their first exposure to ASL happened after their families emigrated from countries with limited educational resources for deaf children to North America where public education for deaf children is mandatory. After approximately seven years of exposure to ASL, Maria and Marcus were tested by Jill Morford. Unfortunately, the comprehension of spatial prepositions was not studied (Morford J, personal communications), but the examination included another PFS test. Maria and Marcus were shown eight sentences describing events of climbing, falling, looking, biting, and licking. To show their understanding of a sentence, Maria and Marcus had to select a correct picture from a set of four pictures. The correct picture depicted the event that the target sentence described, and the three incorrect pictures depicted events that were related in path movement and/or protagonists. For example, "for the target sentence describing the boy climbing a tree, distracter pictures depicted the boy climbing a rock surrounded by trees, the frog climbing out of a jar, and the boy and the dog looking over a fallen tree" [330]. In order to select the correct response, the subjects had to mentally synthesize the scene described by the sentence and then select the picture best reflecting the result of their PFS. Chance performance for the comprehension task is 25%. Both participants selected the correct picture 38% of the time, barely above chance level. Even when the participants were allowed to review the topic sentence an unlimited number of times, Maria still selected the correct picture for only 63% of the sentences.

Daniel C. Hyde and colleagues studied the cognitive abilities of a 13-year-old deaf child named IC [331]. As a result of living in an underdeveloped country, IC received no formal sign language instruction until the age of 13 when he immigrated permanently to the United States. IC communicates his thoughts and emotions mostly through facial expression and by a home-sign gestural system developed inside the family. Following his enrollment in the residential program for deaf children, he quickly learned a great number of ASL signs. The experiments were performed using both the ASL and the home-sign system (the home-sign system was used with the help of IC's younger brother translating the tasks to IC). IC was presented with pictures containing pairs of objects: side by side or one on top of the other and was asked to describe the pictures. IC had no trouble naming the objects presented to him, but was unable to use spatial signs (left/right, on top of/underneath) to describe the relationship between the objects. Even after the experimenter prompted IC with a correct response following each attempt (for example, the experimenter signed "dog on top of cat" or "dog on the left/ cat on the right"), IC was still unable (in the following attempt) to "describe a picture in a manner that allowed the spatial relationship to be unambiguously interpreted" [331].

Naja Ferjan Ramírez and colleagues studied the acquisition of American Sign Language in three adolescents who, similarly to other deaf linguistic isolates, were deprived of a formal sign language until the age of 14 [332]. Prior to receiving training in ASL, these patients, who grew up in separate families, relied on behavior and a limited number of gestures to communicate. The researchers did not conduct any tests that could be used to judge the patients' PFS. However, patients' utterances used in spontaneous conversations are consistent with significantly diminished PFS. Despite their age, their utterances were neither long nor complex, never used lexical items indicating subordination or conditionals, and never used inflected verbs [332]. Patients "used few if any spatial prepositions or ASL classifiers describing spatial relations" (Mayberry R, personal communications).

Thus, all individuals linguistically deprived from the time of their birth until puberty exhibit clear signs of "PFS paralysis" later on in life [40]. This is despite a focused multi-year rehabilitation effort during which patients learn the meaning of hundreds of individual words.

The observations in linguistically-deprived children are not without problems. Opponents of experience-dependent acquisition of PFS might argue that these children had been cognitively impaired from birth and were unable to acquire PFS as a result of congenital neurological damage, not as a result of their linguistic deprivation. Three lines of evidence point to the contrary. First, all children linguistically deprived until puberty who have been reported in scientific literature (two feral children and eight deaf children) show signs of PFS paralysis later in life; there is no single report of a child linguistically deprived until puberty who developed normal PFS later on in life.

Second, rescued victims of childhood language deprivation who were exposed to recursive language before the age of seven eventually developed PFS comparable to their peers. For example, M.K. Mason writes about a girl named Isabelle, who was incarcerated with her deaf-mute mother until the age of six and a half [333]. As a result, Isabelle had no chance of developing speech; when she communicated with her mother, it was by means of gestures. After she was rescued, the individuals in charge of Isabelle launched a systematic program of training. As a result of this program, Isabelle was able to reach a normal linguistic level by the time she was eight and a half years old. After that, she entered a public school and appeared to be "a very bright, cheerful, energetic little girl" who "spoke well, walked and ran without trouble, and sang with gusto and accuracy" [334]. (For other examples of linguistically deprived children rescued before the age of seven see [335-337]).

Third, the extent of PFS development seems to correlate with the age of exposure to the first recursive language. Even when subjects are linguistically deprived only during the initial part of the critical period, they could end up with suboptimal performance. Elissa Newport and Rachel Mayberry studied the acquisition of sign language in deaf individuals differing in age of exposure: some were exposed to sign language from birth, while other children first learned sign language at school. These studies were conducted with adults who have been using sign language for at least twenty years. The results of the studies consistently indicated a negative correlation between the age of sign language acquisition and ultimate proficiency: those exposed to sign language from birth performed best, and late learners — worst, on all production and comprehension tests [338,339] ff

---

ff Prelingual deafness is such a serious concern that the US government has enacted laws to identify affected newborns. In 1999, the US congress passed the "Newborn and Infant Hearing Screening and Intervention Act," which gives grants to help states create hearing screening programs for newborns.

There is general consensus that early time-sensitive exposure to recursive language is critical for acquisition of the full extent of a grammatically complex language [60,340,341]. What is not known is the mechanism for this process. Here is where understanding of the dichotomy of the human language is helpful. Human language relies on both knowing the meaning of words and an ability to generate novel mental images based on words recursively mixed into sentences (in the process of PFS). Linguistically deprived children do not seem to have much of a problem learning the meanings of words; they do not have a problem with semantic ability. Rather, they seem to have a problem forming novel mental images based on words recursively mixed into sentences. Thus, observations of linguistically deprived children are consistent with an experience-dependent mechanism of PFS acquisition; recursive language seems to provide the very experience that is essential for development of neural networks that underlie PFS. Childhood usage of recursive language (both externally and internally) provides the necessary training mechanism for development of isochronous connections between the executive prefrontal cortex and the sensory memory stored as objectNEs in the posterior cortex. Without those isochronous connections developed before the closure of the period of plasticity, the prefrontal cortex executive remains forever disabled at performing precise phase control of neurons, which are located over the large parts of the posterior sensory cortex. The millions of strings connecting the puppeteer (the prefrontal cortex) to its

---

Otoacoustic Emissions Testing is usually done at birth, followed by an Auditory Brain Stem Response if the Otoacoustic Emissions test results indicated possible hearing loss. Such screening allows parents to expose deaf children to a formal sign language early and therefore avoid any delay in introduction to syntactic language.

puppets (the objectNEs in the posterior cortex) remain ill-adjusted, with the prefrontal cortex unable to control synchronization of independent objectNEs and, therefore, unable to synthesize novel mental images. A child involved in a normal recursive conversation (either with another person or with himself) internally manipulates mental images in his mind and in this process adjusts conduction velocity in his brain to achieve isochronicity in the neural networks connecting the prefrontal cortex to widespread regions of the posterior cortex. Differential myelination mediates isochronicity, with greater myelination of connections to cortical areas located farther away from the prefrontal cortex compared to connections to proximal cortical areas.

The period of plasticity for the development of PFS seems to close in several stages. The first period of plasticity seems to close around the age of five. When the left hemisphere is surgically removed before the age of five (to treat cancer or epilepsy), patients often attain normal cognitive functions in adulthood (using the one remaining hemisphere). Removal of the left hemisphere after the age of five often results in significant impairment of recursive language and tasks requiring PFS [60,342-345]. The closure of the first period of plasticity likely corresponds to a consolidation of asymmetry between hemispheres with one of the hemispheres (usually the left one) taking most of the control of the language function. The second stage of plasticity closes by the time of puberty; a lack of experience in recursive speech before puberty likely results in a consolidation of widely desynchronized networks and prevents individuals from subsequent acquisition of PFS. While parts of the prefrontal cortex network retain some plasticity for a significantly longer period of time, since myelination of the prefrontal cortex continues into the third decade of life or later [312], this plasticity seems inadequate to assist patients who were linguistically deprived until puberty in the acquisition of PFS.

Studies of linguistically deprived children have clear parallels to animal studies. As we will see in Part 4, many animals (like the gorilla Koko, chimpanzees Washoe and Nim, as well as the Bonobo Kanzi) were able to learn the meaning of hundreds of words; they were able to both comprehend those words and to use those word appropriately to achieve their goal (e.g. "Koko wants milk"). Similarly, Genie and other patients who were introduced to recursive language after puberty were able to learn hundreds of words and use those words appropriately as well. However neither animals nor humans learning individual words after the closure of the period of plasticity could acquire PFS. This observation is consistent with the notion of the dichotomy of language: human language relies on both knowing the association between words and objects/actions and an ability to generate novel mental images based on recursively mixed words in the process of PFS. Simply learning words does not ensure acquisition of the ability to perform PFS.

To sum up, it is clear that modern children isolated linguistically do not acquire PFS and recursive language on their own. (Note that children in a group, like the deaf children of Nicaragua, can come up with a recursive language spontaneously [275].) In other words, the innateness of PFS does not guarantee its ontogenetic acquisition. As is the case with ontogenetic development of many other neurological systems from muscle innervation to the development of sensory systems, nature's intent must be complemented by adequate nurture. What is unusual about the ontogenetic acquisition of PFS is that the necessary experience is provided by the exposure to a purely cultural phenomenon: a recursive language.[gg] For the

---

[gg] In a developed society, parents often augment recursive language with

normal development of vision, light reflected from surrounding objects has to reach the retina, but that occurs whenever it is light, independent of cultural exposure; for the normal development of the muscular system, the trophic factors released by muscles have to reach their neurons, but that occurs whenever a child is moving — the stimulation to neurons comes naturally even when a child is growing alone in a forest (for review see Ref. [38]). However, this is not the case with PFS. The development of PFS requires a community of humans willing to engage a child with the use of a recursive language. Only exposure to a recursive language seems to provide the adequate input for the development of PFS. Furthermore the exposure to a recursive language has to occur during the period of neural plasticity, which expires shortly before puberty. These two observations have a profound consequence for our analysis of hominid brain evolution.

---

puzzles, drawing, arithmetic exercises and strategy games (e.g. chess) that all facilitate the acquisition of PFS in children. However, 70,000 year ago, our ancestors could neither draw nor solve puzzles. For them recursive language with conspecifics was the only opportunity to develop PFS.

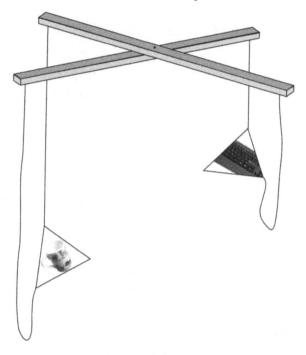

Figure 10.6 Experience-dependent acquisition of PFS. Children using recursive language internally and externally provide essential stimulation for development of isochronous neural networks. The physical distance between the prefrontal cortex puppeteer and the objectNE puppets physically located over a wide territory of the posterior cortex varies significantly. PFS, however, is based on a synchronous activation of independent objectNes. It follows that isochronicity of connections between the prefrontal cortex puppeteer and the objectNE puppets is likely essential for PFS. Considering the many variables affecting conduction delays in an adult brain, genetic instruction alone would seem inadequate to specify the optimal conduction velocity in every axon. Isochronous connections are therefore likely established in an experience-dependent manner. In our puppet-show analogy, the length of strings connecting each puppet to the puppeteer is adjusted to comfortably manipulate each of the puppet's legs and hands separately. Leave one string too long compared to other strings and the puppet's leg connected to the long string will not respond during the show; make the string too short and the leg will be continuously raised. Our objectNE puppets depend on just the right connections to the prefrontal cortex and adjustment of each connection is likely to be provided by the experience of manipulation of mental images stimulated by recursive language. Only by testing each string multiple times does the puppeteer know how to adjust the conduction time of each connection.

10.6 Implications for hominin evolution

The strong critical period for PFS acquisition observed in feral and deaf children have profound implications on hominin evolution. As discussed above, PFS does not develop in children without the concomitant development of recursive language; when children are not exposed to recursive language before puberty, they do not acquire PFS. Note that these are modern children who have all the right DNA that makes acquisition of PFS possible; they are innately predisposed to acquire PFS ontogenetically. However they do not acquire PFS unless they are engaged in conversations with the use of a recursive language. Furthermore, note that the simple non-recursive home-sign systems used by deaf children and their parents were not adequate for the acquisition of PFS.

Children who grew up with no exposure to recursive language can be used as a proxy for hominins living in a society devoid of recursive language. Let us turn back the clock and look at the hominin evolution. At some point our ancestors received all the necessary "PFS mutations." Imagine that you were the lucky person who had received that last mutation that made PFS possible (which probably happened around 70,000 years ago). You are the first child who has all the right mutations to acquire PFS ontogenetically. Your brain is innately ready to develop PFS as long as you are exposed to recursive language in your childhood. However, to acquire PFS, someone needs to converse with you using a recursive language (one that includes spatial prepositions and all other attributes of a recursive language); someone needs to tell you stories and encourage you to tell your own. As you are the first child to acquire the PFS mutation, your conspecifics do not have all the mutations necessary for PFS and, therefore, they have not yet developed recursive language. They speak to you and use many words (the speech apparatus, after all, had been developing for two million years and had reached its modern proportions by 600,000 years ago) but their communication system is non-recursive, it is void of spatial prepositions and grammar, it is a finite system akin to home-sign. In this situation, without anyone to converse with recursively, you will develop similar to a feral child: you will neither acquire PFS nor develop a recursive language on your own. As you do not acquire PFS in your childhood you do not have the competitive edge provided by PFS and your "PFS mutation" will be easily lost in a population without any evolutionary consequences. **Thus, it follows that phylogenetically, PFS must have been acquired at the same time as recursive language.** Since PFS was acquired around 70,000 years ago, then recursive language was also acquired at the same time.

Furthermore, since only children can acquire PFS, it follows that around 70,000 years ago young children must have invented the first recursive language. The parents of these children used a rich-vocabulary communication system for millennia. That system, however, contained no spatial prepositions, nesting, verb tenses or other recursive elements of language. The children may have stumbled upon recursive elements of language such as spatial prepositions (development of new words and even complete language is a common phenomena among twins and other young children living together, the process called cryptophasia [346]). With just a few spatial prepositions, their communication system would be able to communicate nearly infinite number of novel images and therefore their dialogs would have provided enough stimulation to acquire PFS [40]. Accordingly, I have named this hypothesis after the celebrated twin founders of Rome, **Romulus and Remus**. Similar to legendary Romulus and Remus whose caregiver was a wolf, the real children's caregivers had an animal-like communication system with many words but no recursion. These children were in a situation reminiscent of the condition of the children who invented the Nicaraguan Sign Language: their parents could not have taught them spatial prepositions or recursion; children had to invent recursive elements of language themselves. We can expect that each following generation expanded the recursive elements of language and, as a result, improved their PFS. Such parallel development of newly invented language and PFS is found among deaf children in Nicaragua. As newer generations of Nicaraguan Sign Language speakers expanded their language, they have also improved on multiple measures related to PFS [63-65].

10.7 The genetic trigger

The Romulus and Remus hypothesis attempts to explain the more than 500,000-year gap between acquisition of modern speech apparatus and recursive language by a low probability of an event when two or more very young children living together concurrently (1) invent recursive elements of language, (2) have enough dialogs to stimulate each other's acquisition of PFS, and (3) survive to adulthood to take advantage of their modern behavior and procreate. Unfortunately, in its pure form, the Romulus and Remus hypothesis does not survive a simple numerical test. A hominin tribe of 150 individuals spaced linearly from 0 to 30, has 5 peers. Even if we assume (1) that children younger than two could not invent any new words since they did not speak articulately enough, (2) children needed at least a year of using recursive dialogs to stimulate the formation of the neurological networks responsible for PFS, and (3) the end of the critical period for PFS acquisition occurs at the age of five, the model still yields a group of 15 children from two to five years of age per tribe. Fifteen children at the peak of their plasticity is on par with the number of deaf students, who spontaneously invented the Nicaraguan sign language (400 students in two schools) [129,275-277]. It is hard to explain why 15 children in any of the many hominin tribes have not invented recursive language in over 500,000-year period, given that they already had non-recursive communication system and only had to invent recursive elements, while the Nicaraguan deaf children invented both in a few generations.

To further refine understanding of the number of children, an evolutionary mathematical model of a hominin tribe was generated based on the Australian aboriginal population. Moody [347] reported that Australian aboriginal children experienced disproportionately higher mortality than adults with at least 28% of second-year deaths, and about 9% of deaths in the two to four years age group. This pattern of childhood mortality is best described by an exponential function of age (Mortality=const+0.4*EXP(-age/2)). After the const was calibrated to generate a stable tribe population, the model predicted the total of 207 tribesmen (100 individuals younger than 12 and 107 individuals 12 and older). Importantly the model predicted 25 children age 2 to 5, i.e. satisfying the conditions (1) to (3). Thus, the population model demonstrates that it is impossible to explain the 500,000-year gap between acquisition of modern speech apparatus and PFS by a cultural process of invention of recursive elements of language alone. Even under strict conditions (1) to (3) a genetically modern tribe is expected to invent recursive elements and acquire PFS within several generations similar to the Nicaraguan deaf community. **It follows that PFS acquisition must have been also precluded by a genetic factor.**

What may have been the genetic difference that prevented children from inventing recursive elements of language and acquiring PFS for hundreds of millennia? Inadequate vocal apparatus is commonly brought up to explain the conundrum. However, as discussed above, the improvements to the vocal apparatus amassed by hominins by 600,000 years ago must have increased vocabulary by several orders of magnitude, from 20 to 100 in chimpanzees [251-254] to thousands of different words in hominins. Modern children start acquiring PFS at the age of three [37], while using no more than few hundred words [348] and, therefore, **the number of words spoken by hominins 600,000 years ago could not have been the limiting factor to acquisition of PFS**. The PFS trigger mutation could not have been related to speech acquisition.

10.8 The mutation that triggered prefrontal synthesis acquisition

The beginning of modern molecular biology's study of human evolution can be traced to a publication by Mary-Claire King and Allan C. Wilson [349]. The researchers were surprised by the great similarity between the homologue proteins in humans and chimpanzees; the differences in the amino acid sequences known at the time amounted to only 1%. The differences in the amino acid sequence are normally significantly greater even between anatomically indistinguishable sibling species. This similarity in proteins between humans and chimpanzees puzzled the researchers, given the profound differences in the anatomy between the two species. To resolve this paradox, King and Wilson suggested that humans underwent a "relatively small number of genetic changes in systems controlling the expression of genes," yielding a large phenotypic effect with only a few genetic changes [349].

In 2005, the chimpanzee genome was published and confirmed King and Wilson's prediction: the overall DNA similarity between humans and chimpanzees was calculated to be about 96% [350,351]. For comparison, the similarity between the common mouse *Mus musculus* and rat *Rattus norvegicus* ranges from 50% to 80% [352]. These numbers, which indicate DNA similarity between two species, include both coding and non-coding DNA regions. Furthermore, most of the mutations even in the coding region likely make no contribution to a species phenotype and, therefore, are evolutionarily neutral [353]. Thus, the genetic difference between humans and chimpanzees is relatively small.

What number of DNA mutations resulted in the change of the cognition phenotype? Mehmet Somel, Xiling Liu and Philipp Khaitovich approximated the theoretical limit of the number of mutations responsible for the "evolution of human cognition" since the time when the human lineage split from the Neanderthal line [2]. They calculated that the advantageous "cognition-related" mutations that swept through the hominin population occurred once every 50,000 years or even less often. That estimate corresponds to anywhere from four to eight "cognition-related" mutations since the time when the human lineage split from the Neanderthal line. Although this number seems to be extremely small, it matches analyses of the Neanderthal genome, which found that since the species split some 600,000 to 400,000 years ago, only 88 amino acid substitutions have accumulated, and the majority of these substitutions are presumed to be evolutionarily neutral and not "cognition-related" [354]. Thus both theoretical analysis and the direct genome comparison suggest that the number of "cognition-related" mutations that took place after separation of the human and Neanderthal lineages should be on the order of ten or less [2]. Extending that number to the hominid lineage after our species split from the chimpanzees around six million years ago, yields about 120 or fewer "cognition-related" DNA mutations.

What could be the nature of these "cognition-related"

mutations? In addition to obvious mutations associated with increase in brain volume, some DNA changes can be associated with increased top-down control of perception as well as with the improved speech apparatus. The improved speech apparatus must have involved physical changes to voice-producing structures as well as more subtle changes to the organization of cortical areas controlling production of speech (Broca's area) and comprehension of speech (Wernicke's area).[hh] The majority of genetic changes, however, are probably associated with the greater top-down control of perception mediated by the prefrontal cortex and its connections to the posterior sensory cortex. As was argued above, it is the isochronicity of connections between the prefrontal cortex and the posterior sensory cortex that enables synchronous activation of independent objectNEs, which underlies PFS. Furthermore the development of isochronicity in neural fibers of variable lengths depends on repeated activation of those networks during ontogenesis. By extending the maturation period of myelination within the prefrontal cortex and connections between the prefrontal cortex and the posterior sensory cortex, these connections are provided with extra time to fine-tune their isochronicity. Therefore some genetic changes may be associated with delaying the closure of myelination plasticity. Another expected consequence of a slower maturation of the prefrontal cortex connections is the increased delay in development of synapses between both intrinsic and extrinsic prefrontal cortex connections. The slower maturation of the prefrontal cortex, its connections to the posterior cortex and its synapses would be expected to result in prolonged

---

[hh] See the illustration and the commentary on the evolution of Broca's area and Wernicke's area on the following page.

immaturity of human children, but at the same time permit more time for the development of experience-dependent top-down control of their perception. With these predictions in mind, let us turn to the genetic data.

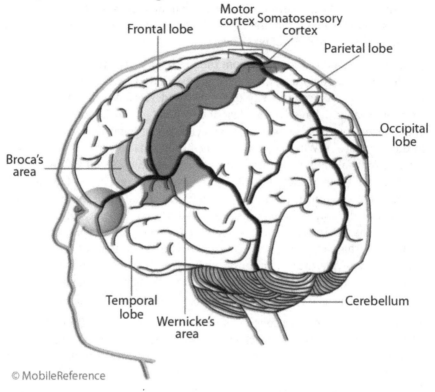

© MobileReference

Figure 10.7 Evolution of Broca's area and Wernicke's area. Two cerebral cortical areas in the left hemisphere are most commonly associated with the communicative function of language. Broca's area is the region critical for execution of spoken language, i.e. encoding of vocal signals into meaningful words and sentences. Wernicke's area is the region critical for the processing of auditory sensory information (i.e. making sense of the sounds of speech that a listener hears). However, it appears that other primates also have equivalent cortical areas. Histological studies show that there are homologues of the human Broca's area and Wernicke's area in chimpanzees [355], macaques [356] and galagos [357] and that these homologue areas are left lateralized, meaning that they are found primarily in the left hemisphere, just as they are in humans. Furthermore the imaging studies show that these cortical areas in chimpanzees may be functionally comparable to human cortical areas. The left lateralized Broca's area homologue in chimpanzees is involved in intentional communicative gestures and vocal signals [358]. The Wernicke's area homolog in the left and right hemispheres has been demonstrated to be involved in the processing of conspecific vocalizations in macaques [359] and chimpanzees [358]. Thus, the homologues of both Broca's and Wernicke's areas may have first evolved 50-60 million years ago [355] to serve the communication needs of primates.

(The figure legend is continued from the previous page.) Was the expansion of the human communication system associated with changes in the cytoarchitecture or connectivity of Broca's and Wernicke's areas? Yes, two sets of changes have been described. First, only humans (but not chimpanzees or rhesus monkeys) displayed robust hemispheric asymmetry in the structure of Wernicke's area. Specifically what is different is that the cortical minicolumns (~40 μm wide vertical columns through the cortical layers of the brain, comprising 80–120 neurons) are wider and the distance between the columns is greater on the left side of the human brain than on the right side, while in chimpanzees and rhesus monkeys the cortical minicolumns and intercolumnar spaces are the same size on both sides of the brain [360]. This asymmetry is considered an indication of the greater connectivity of Wernicke's area in humans (recall that a similar conclusion was drawn about human Brodmann's area 10: smaller neuronal density was considered to be an indication of increased connectivity of that area [298].

The second set of changes concerns the fiber tract connecting Broca's area to Wernicke's area. This fiber tract, called the arcuate fasciculus, connects the large cortical area in the frontal lobe (including Broca's area, as well as premotor and motor areas) to the large cortical area in the temporal lobe (including Wernicke's area). Lesion studies indicate that arcuate fasciculus in the left hemisphere is critically involved with human language. The recent imaging study identified human-specific changes in the structure of the arcuate fasciculus: in chimpanzees and macaques the temporal lobe projections of the pathway have been found to be much smaller or absent [361].

In conclusion: while Broca's and Wernicke's areas evolved in the hominin lineage, the identification of morphologically and functionally homologous cortical areas in non-human primates indicates continuity of their role in the communication function among primates.

Five genes have been identified that are specific regulators of brain size: *Microcephalin*, ASPM, GADD45G, NOTCH2NL, and ARHGAP11B. The evolution of *Microcephalin* was highly accelerated throughout the entire primate lineage with about 45 advantageous amino acid changes in the *Microcephalin* protein becoming fixed during the last 25–30 million years [362]. Modern humans with loss-of-function mutations in the *Microcephalin* gene have significantly reduced cranial capacities (the disease is called *Microcephaly*). As adults, their typical brain weight is 430 g, similar to the brain weight of the australopiths and threefold smaller than the brain weight in unaffected modern humans [363]. Patients with loss-of-function mutations in the *Microcephalin* gene also have a disproportionately smaller cerebral cortex. With a smaller brain and even smaller cortexes, these patients display nonprogressive mental retardation [364]. It is interesting that one genetic variant of *Microcephalin* arose only 37,000 years ago and rapidly increased in frequency in the modern human population indicating that it has spread under strong positive selection [365]. While the exact nature of the selection for that variant of the *Microcephalin* gene is unclear, it is intriguing that the gene determining the brain size in humans continued to evolve until very recently.

The second brain size gene, ASPM, experienced strong positive selection in the ape lineage leading to humans [366]. The deletion of one enhancer of the growth arrest and DNA-damage-inducible gamma (GADD45G) gene is postulated to have led to brain size expansion and it is shared with Neanderthals [367]. NOTCH2NL genes are regulators of neurogenesis. These genes increase self-renewal and expansion of radial glial cells and thereby facilitate an extended period of neurogenesis and the larger neuronal output. The genes arose in their current form roughly 3–4 million years ago [368]. ARHGAP11B gene drives proliferation of the key progenitor cells. It is found only in humans, Neanderthals, and Denisovans; not found in chimpanzees. Mice expressing this human gene during development built more elaborate brains [369].

The best-studied gene associated with human language is FOXP2 (reviewed in Preuss [293]; also discussed in Chapter 8.5 of this monograph). The protein encoded by the FOXP2 gene is a transcription factor. It regulates genes involved in the production of many different proteins. The FOXP2 protein sequence is highly conserved. There is only one amino acid difference in the chimpanzee lineage going back some 70 million years to the common ancestor with the mouse. But there is a change of two amino acids in FOXP2 in the six million years since the human lineage split from the chimpanzee lineage, indicating strong evolutionary pressure over that gene [272]. These two amino acid substitutions predate the human-Neanderthal split [186]. Among modern humans, patients with FOXP2 mutations exhibit great difficulties in controlling their facial movements, as well as with reading, writing, grammar, and understanding others [198].

A number of other cognition-related genes have been identified. The specific role of most genes is not entirely clear[ii] but an effort to understand their function is ongoing. For example, the function of one such gene has been identified recently. A human-specific duplication of a truncated version of the gene SRGAP2 (SLIT-ROBO Rho GTPase activating protein 2) is predicted to increase dendritic spine density in the cortex, leading to better connections between neurons. This mutation was dated to approximately 2.4 million years ago [370,371].

One particularly interesting line of research concerns the

[ii] E.g. PCDH11X and PCDH11Y, CDK5RAP2, SLC2A1, SLC2A4, NBPF, RFPL1, RFPL2, RFPL3, DRD5, GRIN3A, GRIN3B (reviewed in Somel [2]).

changes in the timing of brain development. A small number of genetic changes controlling developmental processes, such as shifts in the timing of events, can result in dramatically novel phenotypes. Liu X and colleagues compared gene expression in the prefrontal cortex and cerebellum of humans, chimpanzees, and rhesus macaques [372]. They collected postmortem tissue samples from healthy individuals who had suffered sudden deaths at several stages of life, from infancy to middle age, enabling the researchers to see how genetic activity changed over time in each species. The researchers demonstrated that the most prominent human-specific expression change affected genes associated with synaptic functions and represented an extreme shift in the timing of synaptic development in the prefrontal cortex, but not in the cerebellum. Peak expression of synaptic genes in the prefrontal cortex is shifted from a few months in chimpanzees and macaques to five years in humans. The researchers' observations were supported by protein expression profiles of synaptic density markers and by direct observation of synaptic density by electron microscopy. The authors conclude that "in human infants the prefrontal cortex remains in an immature state with respect to synaptogenesis in comparison to chimpanzees and macaques. Furthermore, the period of synaptogenesis in the human prefrontal cortex is stretched out over the first 3.5–10 years of childhood — a developmental window when most fundamental human cognitive abilities are formed — whereas in chimpanzees and macaques it is limited to a few postnatal months" [2].

Human-specific changes in the timing of cortical synaptic development and maturation are further supported by findings that axonal myelination rates differ between the human and the chimpanzee cortex during postnatal development and maturation. A recent study of myelination changes spanning the full period of postnatal development from birth to adulthood, in histological preparations of four cortical regions from humans and chimpanzees, demonstrated a greater fraction of mature adult-like neocortical myelination achieved before birth in chimpanzees (~20%) compared with humans (~0%) [373]. Furthermore, in chimpanzees, myelination increased steadily until adult-like levels were achieved at approximately the time of sexual maturity. In contrast, all four regions of the human cortex displayed slower myelination during childhood, characterized by a delayed period of maturation that extended well into the third decade of life [373]. The human prefrontal cortex exhibited the slowest development trajectory and matured later than the rest of the cortex [373].

Compared to chimpanzees, humans are born with an immature brain [374]. At the time of birth, human brains are relatively small in proportion to their adult size (27%) compared with chimpanzees (36%) [375]. Humans differ from chimpanzees and other primates in extending a rapid, fetal-like brain growth rate into the first postnatal year [376]. Much of that postnatal brain expansion results from increasing myelination of the cortical connections [377]. Human infants mature one and a half to two times slower than chimpanzees: molar teeth erupt three years later and humans become sexually active roughly five years after the chimps do [374]. However, the delay in synaptic maturation in the prefrontal cortex (from a few months in chimpanzees and macaques to more than five years in humans [372]) as well as the delay in axon myelination in the prefrontal cortex [373] are much more dramatic compared to this overall delay in maturation. Together, these observations indicate that this remarkable delay in the developmental schedule of the human prefrontal cortex may play an important role in the maturation of connections that contribute to PFS by providing a significantly longer time period for development of experience-dependent isochronous neural networks [378]. Notably, Liu X and colleagues report that the delay in prefrontal cortex development occurred within the last 300,000 years, which is after the separation of the human and Neanderthal lineages [372]. As was discussed in Part 2, a complete lack of external manifestations of PFS in the archeological record associated with Neanderthals suggests that Neanderthals have never acquired PFS. It is possible that the lack of PFS in Neanderthals can be associated with the faster rate of prefrontal cortex development. Such a view is concordant with reports that dental maturation and cranial development in Neanderthals was more similar to apes than to modern humans [379].

What was the last mutation that allowed acquisition of PFS? From a neuroscience perspective, it is relatively easy to imagine how a single mutation could have increased the brain volume, or the number of synapses, or the number of glial cells, or the extent of axonal myelination by a few percentage points, but those relatively small neurological differences could not have prevented children from PFS acquisition. The one neurological difference that could have a direct effect on PFS acquisition is the duration of the critical period. If the duration of critical period in pre-PFS hominins was shorter than in modern children, that would have decreased the probability of invention of recursive elements and at the same time having enough time to train their dialog-dependent neurological networks essential for PFS [39]. For example, if the critical period for acquisition of PFS was over by the age of three, hominin children would have no chances for acquiring PFS at all. A minimal critical period ending at the age of four would have provided an opportunity to acquire PFS (modern children acquire PFS between 3 and 4 years-of-age [37]).

10.9 The "prefrontal cortex delay" mutation and prefrontal synthesis were acquired simultaneously

Mutations that get selected and fixed in a population are usually associated with some survival benefits (e.g., lactase persistence is associated with the continued ability to digest lactose in milk after weaning). Mutations that decrease an organism's ability to survive and reproduce are selected against and not passed onto future generations. The "prefrontal cortex delay" mutation is inherently a strange mutation. By prolonging the critical period, the "prefrontal cortex delay" mutation increases the chances for acquisition of PFS. At the same time, this mutation carries clear disadvantages. A decrease in the prefrontal cortex development rate results in a prolonged immaturity when the brain is incapable of full risk assessment. For example, three-year-old chimps often venture away from their mother, but rarely come close to water, their decision-making prefrontal cortex prohibiting them from doing so. On the contrary, in human children under 4 years of age, drowning is the leading cause of mortality, resulting in over 140,000 deaths a year [380]. The prefrontal cortex of the four-year-old child is unable to fully assess the risk of drowning. Similarly, three-year-old children cannot be left alone near a fire, near an open apartment window, near a traffic road, or in a forest. **In terms of risk assessment, three-year-old toddlers are intellectually retarded compared to three-year-old chimpanzees**. From the point of view of risk assessment, an individual with slower prefrontal cortex maturation rate has lower chances to survive childhood, unless risks are mitigated by culture (e.g., we hold small children by hand near roads and cliffs, buckle them in a high chair, and never let them outside alone). Culture, however, could not have immediately caught up to delayed prefrontal cortex maturation. Thus, at least initially "prefrontal cortex delay" is expected to increase childhood mortality.

The evolutionary mathematical model was used to study the effect of increased childhood mortality due to prefrontal cortex maturation slowdown [73]. Decreasing childhood survival by 10% results in the collapse of tribe population to 50% within 150 years. If the "prefrontal cortex delay" mutation did not lead to an immediate survival benefit that could have balanced the increase of childhood mortality, the mutation would be expected to be weeded out from a hominin population.

How much of a post-pubertal benefit, the "prefrontal cortex delay" mutation must have resulted in order to balance out the 10% increase in childhood mortality? The population model predicts that a minimum of 26% of post-pubertal increase in survival rate is required to keep a stable tribe population. Slowing down prefrontal cortex maturation could have theoretically improved prefrontal cortex-mediated social behavior, working memory, and impulse control, but it is hard to see how these traits could have increased adult survival by 26%. On the other hand, acquisition of PFS with its associated dramatic improvement in hunting enabled by animal trapping, stratagem, and new weaponry can easily explain this dramatic increase in adult survival. I conclude that it is highly unlikely that the "prefrontal cortex delay" trait evolved for some other function, persisted in a population, and later, after many generations, was adapted for PFS acquisition. In order to balance the immediate increase in childhood mortality associated with delayed prefrontal cortex development, PFS acquisition must have happened at the same time as the "prefrontal cortex delay" mutation.

10.10 Who were the children who invented recursive elements of language and acquired prefrontal synthesis?

Who were the children who first invented recursive

elements and acquired PFS? Three conjectures are certain: (1) they must have lived together for several years, so that they could often talk to each other, (2) they must have had received the novel "prefrontal cortex delay" mutation, and (3) one of them must have survived to adulthood to have children of his own and to teach them recursive language. Other inferences are speculative: These children-inventors were unusually slow compared to their peers. Slow children do best in highly supportive environment, so maybe they were children of a chieftain. They spent a lot of time together and created their own vocabulary, so maybe they were closely spaced siblings or even twins; twin bonding and their propensity for cryptophasia are well documented [346]. The "prefrontal cortex delay" trait could have been caused by a *de novo* germline dominant mutation or combination of their parents' recessive mutations.

I attempted to reject the least probable scenario of monozygotic twins sharing the dominant *de novo* "prefrontal cortex delay" mutation. The following calculations show that the low monozygotic twins birth rate and the low probability of the specific "prefrontal cortex delay"-causing mutation are not enough to reject the monozygotic twins' hypothesis. Monozygotic twins birth rate probability is about 0.003 and is uniformly distributed in all populations around the world [381]. At a minimum, one twin had to survive to the age of 4 (probability=0.58) and another twin had to survive to the age of 20 to have children of his own and to teach them recursive language (probability=0.22). Thus, the surviving twins' probability = 3.8×10^{-4}. Assuming 1000 hominin tribes and 16 births per tribe per year, six monozygotic twins are expected to survive yearly.

Probability of any birth with a *de novo* dominant mutation affecting any transcription factor can be calculated as follows. Humans have approximately 100 new mutations per birth [382].

Conservatively assuming that only 10 out of $3x10^9$ base pairs result in the change of function of the "prefrontal cortex delay"-controlling transcription factor, the probability of the "prefrontal cortex delay" mutation = 100 x 10 / $3x10^9$ = $3.3x10^{-7}$. Again, conservatively assuming 1000 hominin tribes [383] and 16 births per tribe per year, in 500,000 years between acquisition of the modern speech apparatus and PFS acquisition, the "prefrontal cortex delay" mutation occurred in at least 2640 births. Multiplying this number by the probability of the surviving twins, we calculate that at least one set of surviving twins was born with the *de novo* dominant "prefrontal cortex delay" mutation in 500,000 years. Thus, it is possible that Romulus and Remus, the inventors of recursive language, were monozygotic twins.

One of my colleagues, Matthew Arnold, was inspired by the possibility that Romulus and Remus were twin brothers to write this short legend:

10.11 A legend of Romulus and Remus written by Matthew Arnold

Romulus and Remus were twin brothers born to Kital, the chief of a tribe of early hominins. After multiple attempts to produce a male heir, he finally got what he wanted, but soon discovered that his children were 'different.' When they were born, Romulus and Remus seemed like every other child physically, but odd enough they seemed to lack common sense. They would go near dangerous tar pits, animal dens, and rivers. At the age of 4, they even wandered out into the forest and got lost, something even younger children would not do. Most kids their age already had basic knowledge of their role in society and a simple understanding of what to do and what not to do out in the wild, but Romulus and Remus had no such understanding. While most children would understand not to go near a rushing river to gather water, the twin brothers almost drowned because they lacked the basic knowledge not to do so. Due to his children's intellectual inadequacies Kital was extremely displeased with his sons. He wanted great warriors that would grow up to lead his tribe, but unfortunately, he was growing older and after so many failed attempts to produce a male heir, he had no choice but to try and raise his children the best he could. However, as the head of his tribe he lacked the time to constantly look after his sons, so he got the tribe's medicine man to do so for him in the hope some of his wisdom would rub off on the young boys.

A few years later, while under the care of the medicine man, the brothers began to speak the primitive language of their fellow tribe members and slowly picked up on the social cues and common knowledge of others. However, the brothers went a step beyond, they started to add spatial prepositions to their language, something never done before. Even the medicine man did not know what to make of the addition of these new words to the children's language, and since he could not understand what they meant, he just assumed they were fooling around. The medicine man would also notice strange drawings around the cave where the boys spent most of their time. There were markings carved into the walls of the cave, some of which resembled animals. A normal tribe member would dismiss these drawings as pointless but not the medicine man. He thought these drawings were incredible and illustrated something special about the young boys. Just like the chief, the medicine man did not have much confidence in Romulus and Remus, but their newfound ability changed his mind, and it was not long until the medicine man deemed the boys ready to embark on a hunt on their own, a rite of passage so to speak.

The medicine man and Kital brought them to the hunting

grounds and gave them each a spear. It was now time for them to prove themselves worthy successors or die trying. Even though he was the one that agreed to this test, Kital was still terrified that his sons would not be able to catch anything or be killed by wild beasts and his last chance to have an heir would vanish, but what happened astounded him. When he told them that they would have to catch a buffalo on their own he saw them discuss a plan to catch the animal, but oddly enough, despite speaking the same language, Kital did not recognize many of the words they spoke. He could understand words like "buffalo," "run," and "rocks," but he could not understand the relationship between the words. The boys then went to a small path with steep cliffs overlooking both sides and drew a circle in the dirt and dug a hole where the circle was and covered it with leaves and branches so that it was indistinguishable from the surrounding area. Kital was confused by his sons' behavior, because normally hunters would utilize persistence hunting, which is when hunters would chase animals until the creature would die of exhaustion. After creating the hole, the brothers conversed again, and ran to find buffalo. Around half an hour later, they chased a group of them back to the corridor where they had dug the hole, and as the buffalo passed over the leaves and sticks, they fell down into the pit. Immediately after, the two brothers speared the trapped animals and pulled them out. The brothers had caught not just one wild buffalo, but many. Simply catching one buffalo would have taken a normal hunter hours to accomplish by use of persistence hunting. It was at this moment that Kital knew he had somehow succeeded in producing successful male heirs.

As years went by, the brothers improved the language they spoke, introducing more spatial prepositions and eventually developing a complete recursive language. Even though their father could not fully understand them, the brothers could work and communicate together to produce miraculous results. This led them to gain the respect of their fellow tribe members as well as their father. Together, Romulus and Remus would end up leading the tribe and conquer all the neighboring tribes with their enhanced intelligence and ability to formulate complex military tactics. Eventually, when Romulus and Remus had children, they found they were just like them when they were young, and they were able to teach them the language they had created. They would take care of their children for a longer time, but after several years, they were able to use the more complex language that their parents had created. These two brothers unknowingly started a pattern that would continue for tens of thousands of years and lead to the modern humans of today.

10.12 Discussion of Part 3

In Part 3, I presented a Romulus and Remus hypothesis of language acquisition that attempts to explain the more than 500,000-year-long gap between the emergence of the modern speech apparatus and the abundant evidence of modern imagination 70,000 years ago. I proposed that despite the acquisition of modern vocal apparatus by 600,000 years ago, hominin communication systems remained non-recursive. Spatial prepositions, verb tenses, and nesting were missing from their communication system not because there were not enough distinct vocalizations, but due to limitations of hominins' imagination.

Language is always limited by imagination. No animal can ever be taught to follow a command to bring a '*long red* straw' placed among several decoy objects including other *red* shapes (Lego pieces, small *red* animals) and *long/short* straws of other colors, not because animals cannot learn words for colors, sizes, or objects, but since they cannot purposefully imagine an object in different colors and sizes [153].

This is not to say that animals cannot imagine objects in different colors or sizes spontaneously or in their dreams. Spontaneous imagination, however, is completely different neurobiologically from voluntary imagination [153]. Voluntary imagination is always driven by the lateral prefrontal cortex and mediated by the frontoposterior fibers, while spontaneous imagination is independent of the lateral prefrontal cortex.

Many scientists make a mistake of assuming human-like imagination in hominins. In the past, many people even extended human-like imagination to animals (e.g., St. Francis preaching to the birds). Anthropomorphism is the natural intuitive fallback for the unknown, but it has to be removed from science based on experimental evidence. Imagination is not a single phenomenon but includes multiple neurobiologically distinct mechanisms [153]. This insight, clear to most therapists working to build up voluntary imagination mechanisms one by one in children with ASD, has been an enigma to many evolutionary biologists who measure hominin imagination abilities through introspection.

Once we realize the existence of multiple neurobiologically distinct mechanisms of imagination, the natural question is when these mechanisms were phylogenetically acquired? Obviously, all the distinct mechanisms of imagination could not have been acquired at the same time. The best indication of improving voluntary imagination in hominins is provided by the stone tools record as turning an unformed cobblestone into a sharp tool requires an active purposeful imagination of a previously unseen object [153]. The quality of stone tools that improved dramatically over the last 3 million years, from crude Mode One stone choppers, dated to 3.3 million years ago [189], to symmetrical Mode Two handaxes manufactured from 2 million years ago [214], to Mode Three tools manufactured from 0.4 million years ago [214] provides the time record of the increasing ability of the lateral prefrontal cortex to control the imaginary percept, but does not inform us on the Prefrontal Synthesis (PFS) ability. PFS requires significantly more complex neurobiological organization than that necessary for stone tools manufacturing and integration of modifiers [153]. PFS is the ultimate ability of modern humans, the measure stick of modern imagination, behavior, and culture. Unequivocal PFS evidence is completely missing from the archeological evidence before 70,000 years ago but is abundantly present after 62,000 years ago. Clear PFS evidence include (1) composite figurative arts, (2) bone needles with an eye, (3) construction of dwellings, and (4) elaborate burials. Together with (5) exceptionally fast colonization of the globe and migration to Australia (presumably by boats) at around 62,000 years ago and (6) demise of the Pleistocene megafauna (presumably with the aid of animal traps) this multitude of the archeological evidence indicates acquisition of PFS by some individuals around 70,000 years ago and their relentless conquest of the planet.

Since PFS is essential for comprehension of spatial prepositions and recursion, recursive modern-looking language could not have been acquired before PFS acquisition 70,000 years ago. I explained the 500,000 year-long period between acquisition of a modern speech apparatus and recursive language by the existence of two evolutionary barriers associated with a critical period for PFS acquisition. One barrier is cultural, the other is genetic. Conversations with the use of recursive language provide an essential training for formation of frontoposterior connections necessary for PFS [39]. These connections only develop as a result of experience provided in early childhood by recursive language. Modern children who experience fewer conversational turns show significant reduction of frontoposterior fiber tracts [39] and complete lack of recursive dialogs is associated with complete PFS disability [40]. Since hominin children were not involved in recursive conversations, they did not acquire PFS and, therefore, as adults, could not learn recursive language. Consequently, they could not teach recursive language to their own children, who, therefore, were not exposed to recursive conversations, continuing the cycle.

Even in genetically modern humans, this dependence of PFS on recursive language and recursive language on PFS creates an unsurpassable cultural barrier in isolated individuals. Modern children who are not exposed to recursive conversations during the critical period do not invent recursive language on their own and, as a result, never acquire PFS [40]. Considerable accumulation of young children in one place for several years is required to spontaneously invent recursive language (400 children in two schools in Nicaragua [129,275-277]).

The second evolutionary barrier to acquiring recursive language must have been a faster prefrontal cortex maturation rate and, consequently, a shorter critical period for PFS acquisition. In modern children the critical period for PFS acquisition closes around the age of five [40]. If the critical period in hominin children was over by the age of three, they would have no chance acquiring PFS. A longer critical period is imperative to provide enough time to both invent recursive language and train PFS via recursive conversations. I conjectured that the "prefrontal cortex delay" mutation that is found in all modern humans, but not in Neanderthals [2,372] was that last piece of necessary genetic makeup and that it triggered simultaneous synergistic acquisition of PFS and recursive language. The "Romulus and Remus" hypothesis calls for (1) two or more children with extended critical period due to "prefrontal cortex delay" mutation; (2) these children spending a lot of time talking to each other; (3) inventing the recursive elements of language, such as spatial prepositions; (4) acquiring recursive-dialog-dependent PFS; and (5) surviving to adulthood and spreading their genes and recursive language to their offsprings. As adults, Romulus and Remus could immediately entertain the benefits of the newly acquired mental powers. They could have engineered better weapons and planned a sophisticated attack strategy using animal traps and stratagem. They would have become more successful builders and hunters and quickly reach the position of power enabling them to spread their genes more efficiently. The genetic bottleneck that has been detected around 70,000 [237] may have been associated with the "founder effect" of a few individuals who acquired PFS and nearly completely replaced the rest of hominins.

There are clear similarities of Romulus and Remus hypothesis to Chomsky's Prometheus. Chomsky suggested that "roughly 100,000+ years ago, ... a rewiring of the brain took place in some individual, call him Prometheus, yielding the operation of unbounded Merge, applying to concepts with intricate (and little understood) properties."[384]. I argue however, that Prometheus could not have evolved alone. Modern children who are not exposed to recursive language before puberty cannot acquire PFS later in life [40]. If parents did not expose Prometheus to recursive language, the only way for Prometheus to acquire PFS was to invent recursive language himself and then use it to train his own dialog-dependent PFS. This fit can only be accomplished in a group of children. Consequently, Prometheus at the early age must have had a peer companion(s) to invent recursive elements of language and to carry out recursive conversations. Romulus and Remus better fit the role of the inventors of PFS and recursive language than the lone Prometheus.

Part 4. Evolutionary forces driving the development of speech and imagination

Chapter 11. Evolutionary pressure from predation

Predators are consistently and universally worthy of visual attention. They are always associated with death and are thus a potentially very strong selective pressure. For that reason, most predators are best detected visually from far away.

LYNNE A. ISBELL, *The Fruit, the Tree, and the Serpent: Why We See So Well* (2009)

11.1 Walking prey

To understand the forces driving early hominin evolution, it is important to remember that our ancestors evolved in an open savanna. As the African climate was becoming more arid (starting approximately 10 million years ago to as recently as 1 million years ago), the equatorial forests were shrinking. Australopiths were the first hominin species that adapted to the new environment on the edges between forest and grassland. In many ways this was an ideal environment: the patches of forest provided safety within the treetop canopies, while the savanna provided greater access to food. It is known that australopiths must have been walking in the savanna for a significant amount of time, since their foot evolved to a nearly human-like structure. Australopiths could have gathered a wide variety of edible plants growing in the grassland, scavenged for nutrient-rich leftovers or hunted for insects and small animals [235].[jj]

[jj] Modern day apes are essentially plant eaters, who occasionally supplement their diet with raw meat (anything from ants and termites to small monkeys

278

However, the 1.2 meter tall 32 kg australopiths walking upright in the savanna now had a new and serious problem to confront. They just so happened to be the ideally sized prey for a number of predators, including the big cats, hyenas, birds of prey and the now extinct sabertooths [385,386].

Fossil evidence from South Africa also supports the notion that early hominins were a popular menu item for predators such as the leopard. "One skull of a fossil hominid found in a South African cave has a set of puncture marks. Two round holes about the size of dimes are spaced several inches apart on the skull. If a leopard caught one of the australopiths and dragged the prize up a tree for eating, the cat's upper canines would have drilled deep into the frontal part of the brain directly above the eyes, and the lower canines would have grasped the prey on the back of the skull. When paleontologists reunited a fossil of this ancient cat with the fossil hominid skull, there was a perfect matchup between the two puncture holes in the skull and the two huge lower fangs of the cat" [235]. Similar

---

and pigs). The meat of larger animals (monkeys and pigs) is usually obtained in a cooperative team effort by a party of male hunters. The meat is shared amongst all members of the group and is sometimes used to obtain sexual favors from females. Our *Australopithecus* ancestors probably had a diet similar to that of modern-day apes. The molars of the australopithecines have a larger grinding surface, and also have thicker enamel than both chimpanzees and modern humans. Analysis of tooth size, tooth shape, enamel structure, dental microwear and jaw biomechanics indicates that *Australopithecus* might have eaten soft fruits, young leaves, herbs, grasses, and seeds, as well as coarse foods such as roots, rhizomes, and tubers. In addition, *Australopithecines* could have occasionally scavenged and hunted for small prey such as insects, lizards, small snakes and mammals (Teaford MF, 2000). One study found that around 3.5 million years ago, hominins changed their diet from the chimpanzee menu of leaves and fruits to the new menu of grasses and cereals (Sponheimer M, 2013). This finding is consistent with the hypothesis that as of 3.5 million years ago australopithecines were taking longer trips into the savanna.

telltale round holes were found in a 1.75 million year old skull recently unearthed in Dmanisi in the Republic of Georgia. "This time saber-toothed cat fangs fit neatly and perfectly into two punctures." [235] Furthermore, a taphonomic analysis of the hominin bones shows that they were chewed by carnivores.

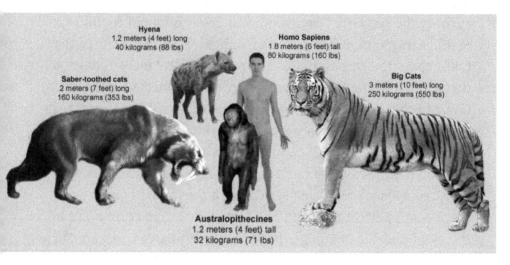

Figure 11.1 Walking prey. The small and feeble australopiths, measuring in at just 1.2 meters (4 feet) tall and weighing only 32 kilograms (71lbs), (that's the height and weight of a 4 year old!) were no match for strong predators abundant in the savanna. The big cats, hyenas, and the now extinct sabertooths were bigger and faster than the hominins. Australopiths had to avoid close encounters with the predators or risk being overpowered. Shown in the illustration:

1. Living big cats include the tiger, lion, leopard, and jaguar. These carnivores are characterized by their significant size (up to 250 kilograms (550 lbs), with a body length of up to 3 meters (10 feet)), opportunistic hunting behavior, adaptability to a variety of habitats and ability to move at high speed (up to 60 kilometers, or 37 miles, per hour).

2. The saber-toothed cats lived between 35 million and 10,000 years ago. They get their name from their saber-like teeth, which were, in some species, up to 20 centimeters (8 inches) long and extended down from the mouth even when the mouth was closed. The sabertooths were widespread in Europe, Asia, Africa and North America. They were as big as jaguars (up to

160 kilograms (353 lbs), with a body length of up to 2 meters (7 feet)) and had particularly robust front limbs (even compared to modern jaguars). This illustration shows the Smilodon painted by Charles R. Knight (The American Museum of Natural History).

3. All hyena species are efficient hunters. The spotted hyena, shown in this illustration, is the most abundant carnivore on the African continent. Spotted hyenas are powerful pack hunters. Though often labeled incorrectly as a scavenger, the majority of their nourishment is derived from live prey. Hyenas can be as heavy as 40 kilograms (88 lbs), with a body length of up to 1.2 meters (4 feet).

4. Full reconstruction of Lucy (*Australopithecus afarensis*, dating back to 3.2 million years ago) on display at the Museum of Man, San Diego, California. Compare Lucy's height to that of a modern human.

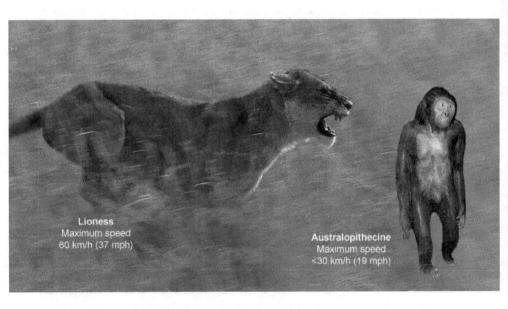

Figure 11.2 Over a short distance, the big cats and the hyenas are all considerably faster than hominins. Detecting a leopard within several meters would not help avoid a close encounter. The hominins had to detect a leopard from around fifty meters away.

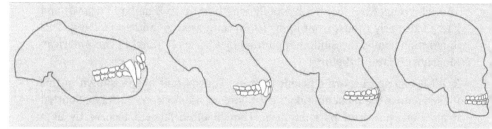

Figure 11.3 Comparative analysis of canine teeth. From left to right: a baboon, a chimpanzee, an Australopithecus, and a human. The size of the skulls is scaled to emphasize canine comparison. Male primates and other mammals often use their canine teeth to threaten and fight each other. Great apes are no exception. Baboon saber-like incisors can be as long as seven centimeters. Chimpanzee canines are as long as four centimeters. If the size of the canines could have influenced Australopithecus' success in fighting with predators, the size of their canines would be expected to increase – evolution would select individuals with longer and sharper teeth. The archeological data, on the contrary, show that the australopith canine teeth are as small as those of modern humans and significantly smaller than those of chimpanzees. This observation indicates that the larger size of canine teeth did not carry a significant enough survival benefit for the australopiths and other hominins to be favored by evolution. Just like for modern-day humans, teeth were useless for defense against a leopard and other predators.

In addition to paleontological evidence, Hart and Sussman present evidence based on observations of predation on living primates living in the wild and the recorded history of predator attacks on modern humans. In Africa and Asia where leopards exist in the wild, they are known to prey on bonobos, chimpanzees, gorillas, guenons, vervet monkeys, baboons, langurs, gibbons and humans [235]. Hart and Sussman conclude, "primates including early humans have been the prey of many carnivores, reptiles, and even birds of prey. ... Much of the human evolution has to do with the fact that we — along with other primates — are prey species. ... Hominids evolved new ways to elude predators and those adaptations include many of the most basic human behavioral traits. Predation is an important source of evolutionary change" [235].

H. Clark Barrett, the professor of Anthropology at UCLA, agrees with Hart and Sussman. "Until very recently, attack by formidable alien beast was a real and constant possibility in everyday life ... Selection to be aware of these creatures, of their plans, and intentions, as well as a strategic intelligence to take advantage of this awareness, would have been strong" [235]. The emerging scientific consensus places predation as the main evolutionary force shaping the development of hominins. The next section presents a conjecture of how this predation influenced hominin acquisition of prefrontal analysis.[kk]

11.2 Detect predators before predators detect you

In the savanna, feeble australopiths did not have much of a chance against predators: they could not run away like an antelope, they could not hide underground like mice, and pretty much had no chance of coming out victorious from a close fight. In order to survive, they had to find their own niche.[ll] A common

---

[kk] To get a feeling of the dangers in a savanna environment, imagine that one evening you and your extended family have been accidentally locked in a zoo where all the animals have escaped from their enclosures. How many of your family members would be able to survive until the daytime? ... The savanna was pretty much such a zoo with plenty of carnivores feeding on the defenseless hominins.

[ll] Some animals also rely on a high rate of reproduction to ensure the survival of the species. However this was not an option for early hominins because of relatively low reproduction rates. The hominin birth rate can be inferred by observing chimpanzees and modern humans living in hunter-gatherer societies. When food is abundant, chimpanzee females produce, on average, one offspring every three and a half years (eight months of gestation plus three years of nursing; the interval between offsprings increases when food is scarce) producing four to five offspring in their lifetime. A similar number of children is observed in primitive human hunter-gatherer societies. At such low reproduction rates, hominins could not afford losing many children to predation.

strategy used by primates is to try to detect a predator before the predator has had a chance to detect them [387]. In addition to the obvious benefit of providing greater time for escape there is also another significance of early predator detection: big cats favor an unexpected attack. If detected by prey from a distance, the cat often abandons the hunt and moves to a new location [388]. Hart and Sussman report that to discourage tiger attacks, which to this day still kill hundreds of people in the Sundarbans delta, the Indian authorities distribute plastic face masks constructed to be worn on the *back* of the head. "Locals wear them as a deterrent to tiger predation while they are boating through the swamps in the Sundarbans delta. These masks help reduce tiger attacks because big cats like to stalk prey that is unaware of impending danger. The wide-eyed, staring mask on the back of a human head is interpreted by the tiger as a fully aware prey and, therefore, not a potential meal" [235].

Robin Dunbar confirms Hart and Sussman report and explains that:

> Each predator has its own attack distance, depending on its speed and its style of attack. For a cheetah, capable of hitting 70 miles an hour within seconds from a standing start, the attack distance is 70 yards; for the slower and more bulky lion it is 30 yards, while for the lighter leopard it is just 10 yards, often less. If prey can detect a stalking predator before it can get within its attack distance, they will always be able to outrun the predator. Most predators are well enough aware of that, if only by virtue of past experience, and rarely bother to chase a prey that has already seen it. That's one reason why you will occasionally see a lion walking through a herd of wildebeest with the herd simply parting like the biblical Red Sea around the advancing predator. The wildebeest know that so long as they stay outside the lion's attack distance they are relatively safe and need do no more than keep a wary eye on it. [13]

Thus hominins had a strong evolutionary incentive to detect predators before they themselves were detected. Still, detecting a leopard[mm] within several meters would not help avoid a close encounter. The hominins had to detect a leopard from around fifty meters away: early detection would allow the hominins to scare the leopard off (e.g., by throwing stones into the leopard) or, in case hominins were chased, provide enough time advantage to run to a nearby tree.

What sensory organs could have helped hominins detect a leopard from several hundred meters away? Let's consider the olfactory system (the sense of smell), the auditory system (the sense of sound), and the visual system. The olfactory system detects volatile molecules present in the air. A specific combination of chemicals released by an organism into the air (odor) can supply a unique signature of the odor source. However, the number of volatile molecules released by a leopard into the air is limited. Furthermore, these molecules diffuse randomly in three-dimensional space around the leopard. The concentration of molecules decays with distance, at a rate proportional to the distance raised to the third power. The chances that a molecule released by a leopard will end up in the nose of a hominin who is located a hundred meters away is close to zero. No chemical sensor can ever reliably detect a leopard from a hundred meters away: neither a sophisticated modern electronic sensor, nor the bloodhounds who are bred for tracking scents. Even at a somewhat closer distance, say, 50

[mm] Here and in other parts of the book, the leopard is used as an example of a fast and agile predator from a group that includes the big cats and the now extinct saber-toothed cats, in order to help a modern reader visualize the scenario. The leopard belongs to the genus *Panthera* that evolved about five million years ago; the modern leopard did not emerge until about one million years ago.

meters (55 yards), a sensory system based on odor detection would be highly unreliable in the windy savanna.

Sound can also provide specific information about a predator. Even an immobile leopard generates sound: the heart produces a significant audio signal with every heartbeat. Doctors listen to sounds generated by the heart to detect problems such as a damaged heart valve. Some animals, like mosquitoes, use heart sounds to detect their prey (mosquitoes also use smell and heat to detect warm-blooded animals). All cars leaving US prisons are scanned for escapees with a device that is able to detect a human heartbeat. The driver must shut down the engine, step out of the car, and only then is this sensitive device able to detect any sounds produced by the heart and transmitted through the metal structure of the car. Furthermore, sound can be transmitted over great distances. On a windless day, two people standing a hundred meters away from each other on opposite sides of a lake can talk without raising their voices. The sound, reflected by the smooth surface of the water, reaches the ears without much decay. However, hominins were trying to survive in the grasslands, not on a lake, and its predators would be lurking quietly. A hunting leopard is expert at sneaking up on its prey without being heard, taking full advantage of its soft paws. The tall grasses of the savanna also do a great job at quickly dissipating sound waves, making heartbeats nearly impossible to detect from a hundred meters away.

It seems that a superior sense of smell and an improved sense of sound would not have done much to increase a hominin's chance of survival in the savanna. The sensory modality that is left is vision. In fact, light is transmitted over great distances with little decay. That's why we are able to observe stars located billions of kilometers away, and see light reflected from a golf ball flying far in the air. The hominins had to use their *sense of vision* to detect a leopard from hundreds of meters away. No other sense could have provided better protection. As Lynne Isbell, a Professor of Anthropology at University of California, Davis, put it, "Predators are consistently and universally worthy of visual attention. They are always associated with death and are thus a potentially very strong selective pressure. For that reason, most predators are best detected visually from far away" [389].

11.3 Hominin adaptation: improved visual identification of hidden, motionless predators

The most tangible adaptation of australopiths to the new environment was that of bipedalism. The Laetoli footprints confirm that as early as 3.6 million years ago, australopiths were walking upright. By allowing the head to be positioned above the grass at all times, bipedalism permitted continuous surveillance for predators. A four-legged hominin foraging with its head down in the savanna would be an all-too-easy prey for stronger and faster predators. However, being able to look over the grass provided only part of the solution. Hart and Sussman explain:

> All carnivores including big cats and hyenas use a slow and partly concealed approach to their intended prey. Their bodies are held lower than the normal position when stalking. Making considerable use of cover, the stalk is facilitated in the cat family by the sleek feline body shape and camouflaged coloration. Felids stalk their prey in elaborate fashion before rushing; they crouch down for periods from just a few minutes up to as long as an hour. For cats, a minimal distance covered in the final charge is strongly correlated with a successful kill. The closer they can get while stalking, the shorter the rush at the end and the less time the prey has to react and get away. ... The hunting strategy of the leopard is largely a matter of

lurking in likely places (water holes are always good) and approaching its prey in a stealthy manner, followed by a quick spring and swipe with the paw. [235]

Thus, hominins had to detect motionless predators hiding in the grass before being detected themselves.

Identification of motionless objects is an extremely demanding task for the brain.[nn] In fact, this task is so difficult that some animals cannot detect a still object at all. For example, a snake's visual acuity is based primarily on movement, so it has a particularly difficult time detecting motionless prey. Some animals, as a defense mechanism, take full advantage of the snake's inability to detect still targets. For example, when a rabbit detects a snake, it freezes instinctively instead of running away. There is some chance that the snake's visual system will confuse the immobile rabbit for a lifeless object, and the rabbit may escape safely.[oo] Freezing is, in fact, a common anti-predatory strategy observed in many animals including primates to avoid detection by predators [235].

Detecting stationary predators is challenging not only for

[nn] Detection of moving objects is a relatively easy process. Even when the cues normally used to identify an object are missing (outlines, contrast, or change in texture), humans and many other animals can still identify moving objects. This is so because dedicated groups of neurons specialize in detecting motion.

[oo] In a typical tit-for-tat evolutionary struggle, some snakes, including pit vipers and rattlesnakes, developed a secondary detection system capable of distinguishing immobile prey from a lifeless object over a short distance. This secondary system relies on heat radiated by warm-blooded animals. A rattlesnake, for example, has a small pit located on each side of its head composed of several thousand receptor cells specialized for heat detection. The infrared sensors are very sensitive to wavelengths of around 10 micrometers (infrared radiation). A snake can use its heat sensors to detect a warm-blooded animal even with its eyes closed.

snakes but also for other animals including mammals. Non-primate mammals often rely on movement to reliably detect predators visually and may completely miss immobile predators. An experience that many dog owners will relate to is described by Lavinia Grant in her book "On a Kenya Ranch" (2001):

> The other day they [the dogs] streamed past a huge puffadder which was lying like a log on a patch of bare ground. Its head and neck were doubled back along its body, ready to strike. Wasp, Sambu's daughter, passed within two feet of it. I called her away, but sensing from my voice that I had seen something exciting and dangerous, Wasp turned back to investigate. To my horror she passed within striking distance of the snake again without seeing it. It never moved!

Poor visual recognition of motionless predators may explain why dogs are often bitten by venomous snakes on their heads [390]. Other non-primate mammals also have a poor ability to detect immobile predators. For example, California ground squirrels often miss detecting motionless rattlesnakes amid small stones and vegetation, but they easily detect moving snakes [391].

For much of their 70 million year history as a lineage separate from other mammals, diurnal primates were under continuous selective pressure from at least one type of motionless predator: snakes [389]. In fact, it has been hypothesized that snakes acted as the primary selective pressure operating on primates to expand their brain and visual system [389]. As a result of this selection, primates are better than other mammals at detecting immobile objects [389]. However, even primates, including humans, are much slower at detecting stationary items than moving targets. The experimental paradigm for studying the effect of motion is often referred to as *live fly / dead fly* [392]. In a typical experiment, subjects see 5 to 25 identical circles presented on a display. The subjects search for either a moving circle among stationary circles (the *live-fly* condition) or a stationary circle among moving circles (the *dead-fly* condition).

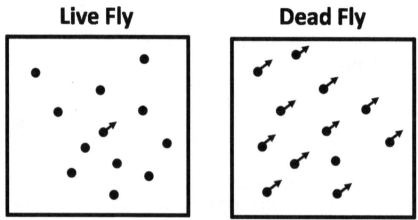

Figure 11.4 *Live fly / Dead fly* **experimental paradigm.** See description in text.

Primates, including humans, detect the moving circle (*live fly*) significantly faster than the stationary circle (*dead fly*) [393]. These experiments demonstrate that, neurologically, it is much easier to detect a moving target than an immobile one. The neuronal system necessary for detection of immobile targets is much more complex. It requires many more neurons, is energetically costly (one needs to maintain more energy-hungry neurons), and takes much longer to develop (it takes a long time for neurons to grow and establish the right connections during childhood, resulting in a longer time during which youngsters remain dependent on their parents). Note that it was "easier" for snakes to acquire a secondary, heat-based, short-range detection system for finding motionless, live objects than to improve their existing visual-based system.

Detecting motionless predators standing in the open is one problem. Detecting *camouflaged* motionless predators is an even larger problem. Camouflage effectively slows down visual detection. The detection process requires even more neurons and greater circuit sophistication to detect camouflaged predators. Consider the photographs on the next page. Notice how difficult it is to distinguish immobile objects from the background.

All ground predators, big cats, hyenas, and snakes tend to have an exterior coat that blends into the background in terms of color and pattern. This camouflage only further complicated a hominin's ability to detect motionless predators in the savanna. To make matters even worse, the tall savanna grass was perfect for partially concealing the predators, making detection that much more challenging. The visual information available to a hominin eye may have been limited to just a few fragments, such as an ear or a part of a tail sticking out just above the grass, or perhaps just a depression in the grass produced by a hiding predator.

Figure 11.5 Animal camouflage. Do you see a lizard in this picture? *Uroplatus sikorae* are experts at camouflaging themselves on wood.

Do you see an insect here? If alarmed, a Dead leaf mantis (Deroplatys desiccata) lies motionless on the rainforest floor, disappearing amongst actual dead leaves.

Can you find two birds in this picture? The Tawny Frogmouth blends in with the color and texture of tree bark.

Do you recognize a snake and a rabbit in this screenshot? I, for one, could not recognize either in the still image, but was able to identify both the snake and the rabbit momentarily once I saw them in motion. Please watch the complete video: http://www.youtube.com/watch?v=qFqseM9-mL0&

For the tree-dwelling ancestors of the australopiths (the chimpanzee-like animals that lived over six million years ago), detecting motionless stalking felines from a long distance was a bit less important since they spent most of their time in the relative safety of the treetop canopies, similar to modern day chimpanzees. Even when they ventured onto the ground near the trees, they were still much safer than the hominins in the savanna. To attack a tree-dwelling animal, a cat must MOVE itself toward the tree, making itself much easier to detect. In addition, the primates would not have to detect a predator from as far away since they could quickly escape into the safety of nearby trees. When australopiths moved away from the trees into the savannas, the situation reversed. Now the hominins were moving and the predators could remain still and blend into the background.

As discussed above, the 1.2-meter (4-foot) tall australopiths did not have much of a chance against formidable predators such as leopards, snakes, crocodiles, saber-toothed cats, or hyenas (indeed, the same can be said for unarmed modern humans). Their only chance at survival was early detection and scaring off the predators. Therefore it stands to reason that those hominins who were better and *faster* at identifying motionless stalking predators from a distance had a huge survival edge over their less developed relatives. If scientific consensus is correct that six million years ago predation was in the driving seat of evolution, then natural selection must have favored early visual detection of predators. Such selection would be expected to influence the acquisition of multiple traits directed at facilitating the visual detection of partially concealed motionless predators. It only makes sense that those hominins who were better at using visual clues to detect predators would have a greater chance to survive and pass their genes onto the next generation.

What visual system adaptations could have developed in our savanna-dwelling ancestors? What improvements to visual processing could have helped hominins see a stalking leopard through the tall savanna grasses, a motionless snake hiding in the grass, or a still crocodile submerged in a swamp?

Let's take a look at a few possible adaptations that could have facilitated identification of motionless, hidden predators:

1. A stalking leopard in a crouching position has its tail and ears perked up above the rest of the body. These parts may become visible in the swaying grass of the savanna, even if just for an instant. A hominin's ability to quickly detect a fragment of a predator's body visible above the grass would provide invaluable clues for predator identification. Therefore, it would be logical to predict that through evolution and natural selection, the hominin mind would get faster and better at serially extracting all meaningful visual cues (such as a tail or an ear sticking out above the grass) from an ambiguous visual scene and matching those visual cues to a library of predators stored in memory.

Figure 11.6 Modern humans can use a single detail to recognize an animal. Consider the following photographs: which tail belongs to a wild boar? Which tail belongs to a leopard? Humans can tell a wild boar's tail from a leopard's tail from as far away as 100 meters (300 feet), and can react accordingly, either running toward a possible food source, or running for dear life away from the predator.

2. Since the partially concealed fragments of a predator's body could have presented themselves at any angle, we would expect an improvement in a hominin's ability to perform mental rotation of visual targets for matching to those stored in memory.

3. Predators or a group of predators (e.g. a group of hyenas) hiding in the grass may have several body features exposed: a piece of ear here, a tip of a tail there. Therefore, we would expect an improvement in a hominin's ability to integrate those features into a coherent percept.

4. Even if the predator is completely concealed within the tall savanna grasses, there are still visual cues that would have made the detection of the predator possible. For example, if there is a leopard lurking in the swaying grass of the savanna, the blades of grass that are in contact with the leopard's body will remain stationary while the rest of the grass would be swaying in the wind. For an upright hominin observer who is inspecting the savanna from eye-level, these minor differences in the movement of grass would have been noticeable. Integration of this information could betray a predator. Therefore, it would be logical to predict that hominins could have acquired a better ability to search for stationary items (like those patches of still grass) amongst the uniformly moving background (the swaying grass of the savanna).

Figure 11.7 A lion hiding in the grass. Only its ear is visible through the grass.

Let's see if any of these four predictions hold water. Even though australopith subjects cannot be tested directly, researchers can instead compare human abilities with those of our closest evolutionary relative: the chimpanzee. Since the chimpanzee's habitat (the tropical forest) has not changed much since the time of our common ancestor, they have not had to adapt the way hominins did, and thus, evolutionarily speaking, have not changed much. Because of this, chimpanzees are called a conservative species. Hominins, on the other hand, had completely changed their habitat, exchanging the safety of treetop canopies for the dangers of the open savannas. If evolutionary pressure has rewired the hominin brain over the past six million years, experiments should be able to demonstrate these changes through a comparison of chimpanzees (the conservative species) and modern humans.

Before delving into the predictions, it is important to note that chimpanzees are comparable to humans in all of the following categories of basic processing of visual information:

visual acuity, perception of color and brightness, contrast sensitivity, vision temporal properties, as well as perception of basic forms, texture patterns, and perception of shape-from-shading cues [294].

Prediction 1: Evolution selected hominins who were better at detecting partially concealed predators.

Unfortunately, there are no relevant experiments comparing humans and chimpanzees as far as their ability to detect partially concealed objects. However other primates, such as the wild bonnet macaques, have been shown to recognize models of leopards partially concealed by vegetation [394]. In this experiment, the macaques were shown either the model's forequarters (the head and the front paws) or its hindquarters (the tail and the hind paws) through thick vegetation at feeding stations 25 meters away. One of the leopard models was yellow and had the common, spotted pattern of a leopard while the other model had the less common dark melanic coat with no spotted pattern. Bonnet macaques exhibited the fastest reaction times and the greatest frequency of flight after looking at the forequarters of the spotted model. The macaques' reaction times were longer and frequency of flight was lower when shown the hindquarters of the spotted model, and they were even slower when shown the forequarters of the darker model. Interestingly, when shown the hindquarters of the dark melanic model, the Bonnet macaques had no reaction, completely ignoring the model. It seems that the visual system of bonnet macaques is attuned to the leopard's head region and to its characteristic spotted yellow coat, both of which facilitate detection. The fact that Bonnet macaques paid no attention to the hindquarter of the dark model seems to indicate that they had not acquired the ability to detect a leopard based on its tail and hind paws. It would be of value to conduct a similar experiment that directly compares the human and chimpanzee ability to detect a partially concealed predator. The PFS theory predicts that most humans will be better and faster at detecting partially concealed predators.

Prediction 2: Evolution selected hominins who were better at fast mental rotation of visual targets.

Again, there are no experiments directly comparing humans and chimpanzees as far as their ability to perform mental rotation. However, in one experiment, humans were compared to rhesus monkeys as far as their ability to recognize partially occluded objects presented from different views [248]. The researchers investigated whether humans and monkeys used the same object features to identify an upright object and its rotated versions in the picture plane. The researchers found marked differences between how humans and monkeys approached this problem; while humans used the same object features independent of the object's orientation, monkeys used unique features for each orientation. In other words, rhesus monkeys basically relearned object features at each orientation rather than mentally rotating the object (the method preferred by humans). It remains to be seen if the interspecies difference exists between humans and chimpanzees.

Prediction 3: Evolution selected hominins who were better at integrating multiple local visual features into coherent percepts.

Humans have a strong propensity to group local elements into global shapes. For example when processing a large letter made of small letters, human subjects show shorter response times to identify the global form in comparison with local details [395]. This phenomenon is referred to as *global advantage*. Using geometric figures comprised of smaller geometric elements, Fagot and Tomonaga demonstrated that chimpanzees did not systematically integrate local elements into global objects and that integration was modulated by changes in the global size and the density of the local elements [396]. The clearest difference was observed at the low density of local elements. While humans readily perceived the global shape made of local elements, chimpanzees did not perceive the global shape but perceived the local elements only.

Differences between humans and chimpanzees were also shown in a study investigating the perception of illusory Kanizsa-squares [397]. The illusory square is produced by four, shaded three-quarter circles (called the inducers, or local objects) positioned in such a way that the missing quarters line up as the four corners of a square. The chimpanzees' perception of Kanizsa-squares was directly controlled by the distance between the four inducers (local objects), showing that the chimpanzees were more sensitive than humans to the separation between the local elements. For the chimpanzees, perception of a global coherent form seemed to emerge only when the local elements were close to each other. The illusory effect disappeared for the chimpanzees, but not for humans, when the distance between the inducers was enlarged [397].

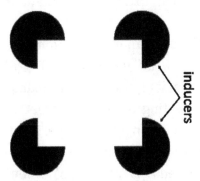

Figure 11.8 Kanizsa-square. The brain integrates local objects (inducers) to form a floating white square. Even when the four inducers are far apart humans perceive the white square. Unlike humans, chimpanzees perceive the white square only when the inducers are close to each other.

These studies show that the proximity between the local elements is critical for the chimpanzee's ability to integrate elements into a global shape. Although adult humans easily perceive shapes at the global level, chimpanzees perceive the global form more readily in high-density conditions than in low-density conditions. In fact, there is a phylogenetic trend in the ability to group local elements into global forms. Humans perceive global shapes made out of local details more readily than chimpanzees [396], and chimpanzees tend to group local features into a global form more readily than monkeys [398]. These results are consistent with the prediction that hominins were selected in the savanna for their ability to better integrate multiple local features (predator body parts exposed in the swaying savanna grass) into coherent percepts (detection and recognition of a particular predator).

Prediction 4: Evolution selected hominins who were better at searching for stationary items amongst the coherently moving background.

Matsuno and Tomonaga used the *live fly / dead fly* experimental paradigm [392] described above to study humans and chimpanzees. Both chimpanzees and humans detected the moving circle amongst the stationary circles (the *live fly* condition) significantly faster than the stationary circle amongst the moving circles (the *dead fly* condition) [393]. These results were consistent with previous studies on humans that showed a clear advantage of detecting a moving target compared to a stationary target [399]. Interestingly, the experiment also showed that chimpanzees were significantly worse at detecting the stationary target (the *dead fly* condition) when compared to humans. The interspecies difference became more striking when a greater number of circles were displayed. On average, humans needed 650 milliseconds to detect a stationary circle amongst 11 uniformly moving circles and 550 milliseconds to detect a moving circle amongst 11 stationary circles. For humans, the difference between the *dead fly* and the *live fly* display conditions was 100ms. For chimpanzees, however, the difference between the *dead fly* and the *live fly* display conditions was nearly one second (ten times greater than in humans). These results are consistent with the prediction that nature selected those hominins who were better at searching for stationary objects (concealed predators or predator body parts) amidst a coherently moving background (the uniformly swaying savanna grass, which corresponds to the moving circles in this experiment).

In another experiment, Matsuno and Tomonaga investigated whether the type of movement has an effect on performance. As in the previous *dead fly* experiment, subjects had to detect the stationary circle amongst 11 moving circles, but now the circles were moving either uniformly (all in one direction, as in the previous experiment) or randomly in multiple directions (the new condition) as shown in the illustration below.

Uniform Movement   Random Movement

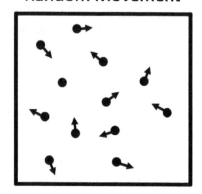

Figure 11.9 Uniform versus random movement. In this experiment subjects had to detect the stationary circle amongst 11 moving circles (*dead fly* condition), but now the circles were moving either uniformly (all in one direction) or randomly in multiple directions.

Remarkably, the human advantage observed under the uniform condition in the previous experiment (when the circles were moving in the same direction) disappeared in the new random condition (when the circles were moving in multiple directions). Again this result is easily understood in the context of natural selection. In the savanna, patches of grass sway *uniformly* under the wind with all individual grass blades swaying coherently in respect to the ground. A species selected for its ability to identify motionless predators concealed by the grass would excel at separating stationary objects against a coherently moving background (savanna grass uniformly swaying under the wind) but not against a randomly moving background.

Conclusions:

It seems that the experimental evidence is consistent with the conjecture that over the six million years of evolution in the savanna, the hominin brain was rewired to facilitate the detection of motionless predators concealed by vegetation. Humans integrate local elements better [396,397] and detect the still visual targets within uniformly moving distractors an order of magnitude faster than chimpanzees [393]. The significance of these findings cannot be overstated. The experimental evidence of interspecies differences is consistent with the conjecture that the visual detection of motionless predators concealed by the savanna vegetation was the main driving force of hominin evolution responsible for the dramatic increase in hominin brain volume necessary for detection of motionless, concealed predators. Can the same evolutionary force also be responsible for the neurobiological changes that enabled stone tool manufacturing? Exploring the neurobiological process required for identification of partially concealed and motionless objects may help answer this question.

GENERALIZATION OF THE SELECTIVE ROLE OF PREDATION IN THE EVOLUTION OF THE ENTIRE PRIMATE ORDER

Specie	Prosimians in Madagascar	New World monkeys of South America (platyrrhines)	Old World monkeys and apes (catarrhines)	*Homo habilis*	Modern Humans
Immobile Predators	Constrictor snakes.	Constrictor snakes and interrupted coexistence with venomous snakes.[A]	Constrictor snakes and continuous coexistence with venomous snakes for over 60 million years.	New stalking predators in the savanna: big cats, sabertooths, and hyenas.	Additional 2.5 million years of coexistence with snakes, big cats, sabertooths, and hyenas.
Visual System	Small brain, poor visual system, dichromatic vision.	Greater specialization of the visual system; acquisition of trichromatic vision; most males, however, retain dichromatic vision.	Greater visual and brain expansion, uniform trichromatic vision, improved short-range depth perception.	An even greater brain expansion as well as the acquisition of voluntary control of the mental template, which enabled *H. habilis* to manufacture some of the first stone tools.	Greatest visual and brain expansion; improved ability to integrate local visual elements[B]; faster detection of immobile visual targets within uniformly moving distractors[C]; acquisition of PFS.

[A] The last exposure of the New World monkeys of South America (platyrrhines) to rattlesnakes lasted for only three million years. [B] As shown by Fagot J [396,397]. [C] As shown by [393].

Table 11.10 Generalization of the selective role of predation in the evolution of the entire primate order. Lynne Isbell, a Professor of Anthropology at University of California, Davis, proposed a compelling theory of the evolution of primates [389]. She noticed that snakes were the first of the major predators of primates and that the snakes are usually camouflaged and immobile and, therefore, difficult to detect under natural conditions against a color-matched background. She hypothesized that for over 70 million years of coexistence, snakes acted as the primary selective pressure operating on primates to expand their visual system. She presents evidence that primates exposed to greater predation by snakes, i.e. primates exposed to venomous snakes, acquired a better visual system compared to primates not exposed to venomous snakes. The PFS theory picks up where the Snake Detection theory argument ends. The theory proposes that hominins foraging in the savanna were exposed to an even greater selective pressure from immobile predators partially hidden by vegetation. In addition to snakes, hominins venturing into the savanna were exposed to stalking big cats, hyenas, and the now extinct sabertooths: all fast predators that had to be detected from a distance. Not only were hominins away from the safety of treetop canopies but they were moving and therefore were easier for predators to detect. One cannot help but to see a certain "progression" in the evolution of the primate brain from the first primates to humans. According to both the Snake Detection and the PFS theories, immobile camouflaged predators continuously acted as the primary selective pressure on the evolution of the neuronal networks involved in visual recognition. The visual system is more developed in those primate species which had to detect a greater range of those immobile predators. Prosimians in Madagascar (left-most column) that have never coexisted with one of the most potent predator species, venomous snakes, have the least developed visual system among primates. New World monkeys of South America (platyrrhines, second column from the left) that have had interrupted exposure to venomous snakes have a better visual system. Old World monkeys and apes (catarrhines, middle column) that have had continuous coexistence with venomous snakes for over 60 million years have an even better visual system. Hominins (second column from the right), exposed for 3.5 million years to additional stalking predators such as big cats, hyenas, and sabertooths acquired a visual system that was better able to detect those predators and, at the same time, better capable of controlling their visual mental percept (*Homo habilis* was one of the first primate species capable of generating a mental template of a future chopper). Finally, after another 2.5 million years of predation by stalking big cats, modern humans (right-most column) acquired the best visual system for detecting immobile concealed predators; the human visual system evolved to encompass PFS, which enabled humans to generate any arbitrary mental image. A single evolutionary driving force – predation by hard-to-detect immobile predators – acting for over 70 million years on the primate visual system, created enough evolutionary pressure to acquire the strangest, energetically expensive, awkward for giving birth, and vulnerable organ: the human brain, much of which is dedicated to processing visual information in the context of our current goals.

305

11.4 The neurobiology of identifying motionless, partially concealed objects

Since the early work of the Gestalt psychologists, psychophysical research has established that scene segmentation and perceptual grouping represent important aspects of object identification. The perception of an object as a single entity within a visual scene requires that its features be segregated from the background and bound together. The neurological correlate of this segmentation process is a matter of intense research. The *binding-by-synchronization* hypothesis holds that scene segmentation and perceptual grouping is accomplished by a temporal coding mechanism using synchronization of neuronal activity as has been discussed in Chapter 2 [108,109].

Significant theoretical and experimental evidence supports the *binding-by-synchronization* hypothesis (reviewed in Refs. [109,400]). Two experiments mentioned in Chapter 2 are worth recalling. Engel and colleagues reported direct observation of the synchronicity of neurons encoding a single object. The investigators recorded from multiple neurons in the primary visual cortex of a cat. They observed that two neurons synchronized their firing *only* when their activating stimulus belonged to a single object. "These results are compatible with the hypothesis that responses to individual objects in a scene are distinguished by synchrony, whereas responses to different objects show no temporal correlation, thus allowing for the segmentation of superimposed stimuli" [110].

In another experiment Hirabayashi and Miyashita recorded the activity of pairs of neurons located in the inferior temporal cortex (responsible for face recognition) of alert monkeys [111]. The monkeys were shown pictures from two different sets. In the first set, the nose, mouse, and eyes were organized into a face-like configuration. In the second set, the facial fragments — nose, mouse, and eyes — were shown scrambled up. The neurons were selected in such a way that both cells in a pair responded significantly to facial fragments shown one at a time. Thus both neurons significantly increased their activity to both the face-like pictures and the scrambled face pictures. The researchers found no difference in the firing rate between face-like pictures and a scrambled collection of facial features. However, neurons responding to the individual features transiently synchronized their responses when the monkeys recognized that the component features of a face actually formed a face. Thus, the neuronal firing phase was modulated by the feature configuration in a face-like picture, whereas the firing rates did not reveal configuration-dependent bias. In other words, the recognition that component features of a face formed an *actual face* was associated with the synchronization of neurons encoding the individual facial features; only synchronous activation of a complete objectNE of a face resulted in perception of a face.

Armed with the *binding-by-synchronization* hypothesis, let's speculate on the neurobiology of the perception of a camouflaged animal. Consider again Figures 11.10 and 11.11 that we have first discussed in Chapter 10. When fragments 1 through 30 on Figure 11.11 are interpreted independently, all you perceive are fragments of dead leaves. Following the logic of the Hirabayashi and Miyashita experiment [111], it stands to reason that the neurons encoding these fragments fire asynchronously. According to the *binding-by-synchronization* hypothesis, to interpret fragments 17 through 21 as belonging to a frog (a single entity), neurons encoding these fragments have to be transiently organized into synchronous activity, similar to the transient synchronization of neurons encoding individual face features observed by Hirabayashi and Miyashita (2005). Thus, to perceive a frog, neurons encoding fragments 1 through 16 and 22 through 30 (which correspond to dead leaves) have to be actively phase-shifted by the lateral prefrontal cortex away from synchronization.

Figure 11.10 Can you find a camouflaged frog amongst the dead leaves in this illustration? (The color version of this photograph is shown on the back cover of the book.) The frog, motionless on the rainforest floor, disappears completely amongst the dead leaves. If you are seeing this picture for the first time, you are unlikely to find the frog. It looks like just a bunch of dead leaves, right? The dead leaves are numbered in the illustration on the next page.

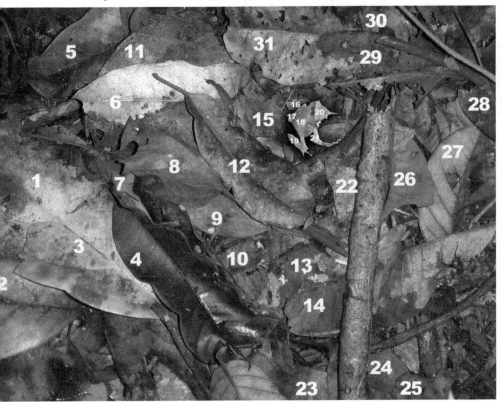

Figure 11.11 When the fragments (numbered 1 through 31) are perceived separately, each is perceived as a fragment of a dead leaf. According to the *binding-by-synchronization* hypothesis, to interpret fragments 17 through 21 as belonging to a frog (a single entity), neurons encoding these fragments have to be organized into synchronous activity. If you still do not see the frog, please turn the page to see the frog highlighted.

In the more difficult case of detecting a leopard which is almost entirely hidden in the grass, we would expect an even greater top-down influence on the neuronal phase. Perception of the leopard requires that the neurons encoding the background be phase-shifted away from synchronization. The remaining synchronized neurons form the objectNE of the leopard. Of course determining which depressions in the grass correspond to the leopard and which correspond to the background is open to a much greater number of interpretations. In this example, the physical object (the leopard) is almost entirely absent from the sensory cortex; the main visual clue would be a motionless patch of grass amongst a coherently swaying field. To perceive a leopard hiding within that patch of grass (as opposed to perceiving a wild boar or a low boulder), the mind would basically have to *imagine* the predator. In other words, the mind's percept would have to change from that of what is actually visible (the depressed grass) to an imaginary leopard (hiding in the grass). It's important to note that what is being discussed here is not the initial reaction to a patch of depressed grass. That initial reaction may be a general sense of danger, a fight-or-flight response resulting in an injection of adrenalin that increases heart rate and sharpens the senses. Rather, what is being discussed is the decision that a hominin would have to make after the initial physiological response. If the patch of motionless grass was perceived as a wild boar or a boulder, for example, then the hominin could continue his business of collecting edible plants or decide to go after the wild boar; if it was perceived as a leopard, on the other hand, the hominin would have to try to scare the predator away or make a hasty escape. The hominin, however, would have to make the correct decision in a majority of cases. The hominin who was always afraid of any motionless patch of grass would go hungry; the hominin who was never afraid would be eaten by the predator. Only the smart hominin who was capable of changing his percept to "see through the grass" would survive.pp You probably see where I am heading

---

pp The changing of the percept could have been involuntary, but it is still a change of perception.

with this. It is likely that the neurobiological mechanism of perceiving a leopard (versus a wild boar or a boulder) hiding in the grass based on a minimum number of visual clues (a depression in the grass) is very similar to perceiving a chopper inside a cobble. In both cases, top-down processes manipulate the neuronal phase of sensory neurons to reveal the unseen imaginary object. Thus, hominins selected for superior predator (and prey) detection through better top-down control of the neuronal phase of sensory neurons were also able to form a mental template of a chopper. Hominins not capable of identifying hidden predators based on the few available visual clues were eaten up by the predators and thus removed from the gene pool. This relentless evolutionary pressure was present for six million years, during which time hominins (Australopiths, *Homo habilis*, and *Homo erectus*) foraged in the African savanna while avoiding falling prey to concealed predators. I conjecture that this selection process provided an essential component for the acquisitions of PFS by *Homo sapiens*. While by itself PFS is useless in predator detection (acquisition of PFS is simply the by-product of a greater top-down control over the neuronal firing phase), it became a most powerful acquired trait, enabling mental simulation and allowing *Homo sapiens* to greatly accelerate technological process, manufacture new types of tools, and develop new hunting techniques. Furthermore PFS enabled an unprecedented level of cooperation between tribesmen through the use of a recursive communication system. A slow increase of top-down control of the neuronal phase that was building up for over six million years resulted in a disruptive change. The acquisition of PFS was a game changer: the prey became the hunter and the predator became the prey.

11.5 Seeking a comprehensive and parsimonious evolutionary theory

Many forces have been proposed as the major catalyst for the evolution of humankind: predation pressure [235], tool manufacturing [3], development of articulate speech [20], and social interactions ("social brain hypothesis" [13]). This monograph builds upon the predation pressure theory [235] and proposes that early visual identification of motionless predators partially concealed by the savanna grass was the major catalyst of the neurological development of hominins.

When our ancestors were forced into the savanna by the receding rainforest starting around ten million years ago, they encountered a new challenge. Suddenly, they were exposed to predators, such as the big cats, hyenas, and sabertooths, from whom they had previously been safe [235]. To avoid being eaten by these stronger and faster predators, our ancestors had to detect them from a significant distance. Hominins relied on their visual system to detect predators from far away, because, unlike smell and sound, visual information decays very little, even after it has been transmitted over great distances. The hominins who were best able to detect a stalking predator concealed by vegetation had a better chance to escape the encounter. Those who could not identify predators from far away were swiftly eaten by the predators and removed from the gene pool. In this way, the hominin visual system faced unrelenting natural selection for several million years, and evolved to be able to detect predators using fewer and fewer visual cues: a shadow, a pattern of moving grass, a small visible body part, etc. Simply put, the hominins with a more advanced visual system had a greater chance for survival.

It is clear that predator identification was significantly more challenging for savanna-dwelling hominins than for their tree-canopy-dwelling ancestors. While tree-dwellers mainly had to detect moving ground-dwelling predators, savanna-dwellers had to detect motionless stalking predators concealed by the grass. Computationally, the detection of stationary, partially concealed, camouflaged targets is a significantly more demanding task than the detection of a moving target [393,399]. In this monograph, I made the conjecture that the unprecedented growth of the hominin brain is primarily associated with laying down the neurological structure for detection of stationary, camouflaged predators concealed by vegetation, and I also presented a clear step-by-step evolutionary path toward modernity.

A comprehensive and parsimonious evolutionary theory should seek to explain as much of the available paleontological and experimental evidence as possible. The paleontological evidence consists of the following major trends:

(1) the development of bipedal walking in *Australopithecus afarensis* (as of 3.6 million years ago),

(2) the unprecedented and consistent increase of brain volume in hominins,

(3) the evolution of the speech apparatus, starting with the improved speech box in *Homo erectus* (2 million years ago) to the nearly modern speech box in *Homo heidelbergensis* (600,000 year ago),

(4) the evolution of a stone tools culture from Mode One stone tools manufactured by *Homo habilis* (3.3 million years ago), to the more advanced Mode Two stone tools manufactured by *Homo erectus* (2 million years ago), to Mode Three stone tools manufactured by *Neanderthals* (200,000 years ago),

(5) the production of figurative art, elaborate burials, protective dwellings, and a great acceleration of technological progress by *Homo sapiens* (as of 40,000 years ago).

The experimental evidence points to clear neurological differences between humans and chimpanzees:

(6) humans integrate multiple local features into coherent percepts better [396,397] and

(7) search the stationary visual items within uniformly moving background faster than chimpanzees [393].

The PFS theory is consistent with all of the above paleontological and experimental evidence. This monograph seeks to explain all these evolutionary milestones and experimental observations through a single parsimonious theory based on the selection of hominins for their improved ability to identify motionless predators concealed by vegetation.

I argued that improvements in the hominin visual system were based on superior top-down control over the neuronal firing phase. Initial gains in this control mechanism some 3.3 million years ago allowed *Homo habilis* to selectively shift the firing phase of neurons encoding the background to reveal the stalking predator concealed by the grass and, using the same neurological mechanism, to reveal the simple Mode One chopper inside a cobble. Around 2 million years ago, further increase in brain volume and complexity yielded even greater top-down control of the neuronal phase that improved *Homo erectus'* ability to detect stalking predators and enabled him to manufacture symmetrical Mode Two handaxes. Predation pressure didn't stop with *Homo erectus*. Continued evolutionary pressure to detect hidden, motionless predators promoted an even greater development of top-down neuronal phase regulation and has culminated in modern humans with the acquisition of PFS: an ultimate system for voluntary top-down control of perception via the neuronal phase-shift. This system not only excelled at shifting neurons *out-of-phase* with a synchronously firing ensemble (physicists would categorize this process as destructive interference), but also at shifting neurons into the-same-phase with synchronously firing ensembles, thus enabling synchronization of any number of independent objectNEs into a single mental frame (constructive interference).

In summary, upright walking enabled australopiths to see above the grass and allowed them to conduct trips into the savanna from the safety of the treetop canopies. Prefrontal analysis allowed *Homo habilis* to voluntarily form a primitive mental template of a future chopper and thus to manufacture Mode One Oldowan stone tools. Advanced *prefrontal analysis* with a well-developed mental template allowed *Homo erectus* to manufacture Mode Two Acheulean tools and to diffuse out of Africa to Asia and Europe. Finally, PFS allowed modern humans to create figurative arts, protective dwellings, advanced tools, as well as religious and philosophical thought, and to settle the entire planet at a steadfast pace. The evolution of hominins catalyzed by better detection of partially concealed predators may be all about the voluntary control of one's visual percept. Hominins progressed from being able to perceive a chopper inside a cobble using prefrontal analysis, to being able to imagine any novel object using PFS.

COMPARATIVE ANALYSIS OF			
	PALEONTOLOGICAL EVIDENCE		
Proposed primary evolutionary driving force	**(1)** development of bipedal walking	**(2)** increase in brain volume	**(3)** evolution of the speech apparatus
Motionless stalking predators concealed by vegetation (PFS theory, this monograph) [D]	✔	✔	✔
Tool manufacturing (Washburn S, 1960) [E]	✔	✔	No
Development of articulate speech (Müller M, 1861; Darwin C, 1871) [F]	No	No	✔
The "Social brain hypothesis" (Dunbar RIM, 1998) [G]	No	✔	✔
Evolution of the human hand: improved throwing and clubbing	No	✔	No

Table 11.2 Comparative analysis of hominin evolutionary theories. This table summarizes the four leading theories on the primary evolutionary driving force in *Homo sapiens*, as well as the PFS theory. The theories are being compared on the bases of their ability to explain the main paleontological and the relevant experimental evidence.

Notes:

[A] Acquisition of imagination and creativity inferred from production of figurative art, elaborate burials, protective dwellings, and acceleration of technological progress.

HOMININ EVOLUTIONARY THEORIES

PALEONTOLOGICAL EVIDENCE		EXPERIMENTAL EVIDENCE		
(4) evolution of a stone tools culture	**(5)** acquisition of imagination and creativity[A]	**(6)** integration of multiple local features [B]	**(7)** location of stationary visual items [C]	Proposed primary evolutionary driving force
✔	✔	✔	✔	Motionless concealed stalking predators
✔	No	No	No	Tool manu-facturing
No	No	No	No	Development of articulate speech
No	No	No	No	The "Social brain hypothesis"
No	No	No	No	Evolution of the human hand

[B] Humans integrate multiple local features into coherent percepts better than chimpanzees [396,397].

[C] Humans find the stationary visual items within a uniformly moving background faster than chimpanzees [393].

[D] The PFS theory is a special case of the general predation theory formulated by CK Brain [401] and refined by Hart & Sussman [235].

[E] Washburn suggested that tool manufacturing was primarily responsible for the changes in hominin evolution [3]. Can the Washburn theory explain all the paleontological and experimental evidence? The theory could explain the observed increase in brain volume (as a byproduct of tool manufacturing) as well as bipedal walking (which freed the hands for tool manufacturing), but it is hard to see how Washburn's theory could explain the evolution of the speech apparatus or the sudden proclivity towards non-utilitarian pursuits such as elaborate burials and the production of figurative art. Nor is it clear how Washburn's theory can explain the experimental observation of the neurological differences between humans and chimpanzees: humans integrate multiple local features into coherent percepts better [396,397] and search the stationary visual items within a uniformly moving background faster than chimpanzees [393].

F It is unclear how the acquisition of articulate speech alone could catalyze acquisition of any other human traits. As evidenced by multiple studies (gorilla Koko, chimpanzees Nim and Washoe), acquisition of a human communication system does not make an animal prone to understanding recursive language, manufacturing tools, or producing figurative art.

G The "social brain hypothesis" proposed by British anthropologist Robin Dunbar argues that hominin intelligence did *not* evolve primarily as a means to solve ecological problems such as predator avoidance and food foraging, but rather intelligence evolved as a means of surviving and reproducing in large and complex social groups [13]. He claims that living in large groups requires such faculties as tactical deception, coalition formation, and reciprocal altruism, all of which rely on intelligence delivered by the growing brain. Dunbar argues that when the size of a social group increases, the number of different relationships in the group may increase by orders of magnitude. Chimpanzees live in groups of about 50 individuals whereas modern humans typically have a social circle of about 150 people. According to the social brain hypothesis, when hominins started living in large groups, selection favored greater intelligence.

In fact, it is possible that hominins traveled in large groups. Better scanning for predators is one benefit of large-group living. More eyes on the lookout for a common predator increases the probability of detecting the predator before it detects its prey. If a predator attacks, a larger group provides better protection through predator confusion: "A so-called saturation effect can occur during the flight of an entire primate group from a predator in which the predator's senses are saturated and overwhelmed by so many choices" [235]. Furthermore, field observations inform us that chimpanzees form larger parties with more adult males as a defense strategy when traveling through an open, non-forested habitat in Senegal under the eyes of potential predators [402]. Although there is no direct evidence that hominins increased their group size after they split from the chimpanzee lineage, living in larger groups could certainly have benefited their survival.

The increased group size would inevitably increase the social pressure and provide some incentive to get smarter. However, it is unclear how the "social brain hypothesis" could explain the complete spectrum of the paleontological and comparative physiological evidence. The "social brain hypothesis" does not clarify the reasons for the evolution of tool culture or the multitude of developments in art, architecture, technology, and elaborate burials. The theory also does not explain the experimental evidence of the neurological differences between humans and chimpanzees (better integration of multiple local features by humans [396,397] and faster identification of stationary visual items amidst a moving background [393]). While the "social brain" hypothesis" is consistent with some paleontological evidence, such as the acquisition of a more advanced communication system based on articulate speech (to facilitate social interactions), the theory does not explain other developments, such as bipedal walking, improvements in stone tools and the visual system, as well as major advancements in tasks requiring imagination. The theory does not tie all of these major developments into one string of events driven by a single evolutionary force. Therefore the "social brain hypothesis" is unparsimonious and it is unlikely that the "social brain" selection was the primary driving force behind hominin evolution.

This is not to say that there was no selection for a better socially-adapted brain. All I am saying is that the "social brain" selection may not have been the PRIMARY driving force of human brain evolution, at least not at the early stage of hominin evolution. Selection for a better socially-adapted brain probably increased with greater demand on cooperation, once PFS had been acquired by *Homo sapiens.* Building traps for large animals, hunting, building dwellings: all of these tasks required a group effort. (Certainly PFS is advantageous, but it is less advantageous if you are the only one in possession of it... it's like working with idiots.) Eventually, those individuals who were best at figuring out ways to work and flourish (socially) in a group would certainly have been selected for. It seems that the "social brain hypothesis" might have been a major contributing factor in the evolution of *Homo sapiens* once PFS was acquired, however the "social brain" selection could only have been a minor factor in evolution leading up to PFS acquisition.

11.6 Manufacturing of stone tools was a byproduct of improved visual detection of motionless concealed predators

The co-evolution of the hominin brain volume and the stone tool culture has been a constant point of investigation since the time of Charles Darwin. The strong association between hominin species and the quality of manufactured stone tools lead Sherwood Washburn, a renowned anthropologist and primatologist, to suggest, "It was the success of the simplest tools that started the whole trend of human evolution and led to the civilizations of today" [3]. Washburn felt that tools were responsible for the changes in hominin teeth, hands, brain, and pelvises; that tools in effect changed the pressures of natural selection and thus formed the man. Washburn's view is still very popular among some anthropologists.

Contrary to Washburn's view, the PFS theory argues that the primary driving force of hominin evolution was better visual identification of motionless, partially-concealed predators and not the manufacturing of sharp-edged stone tools; advancement in stone-tool manufacturing was a byproduct of the improved cortical processing of visual information. After all, it is the visual system that allowed *Homo erectus* to avoid a leopard, a snake, a crocodile, and other camouflaged predators and, in doing so, saved his life. Sharp-edged stones, while useful for dissecting an already dead animal, are hardly helpful in direct confrontation with a leopard. How many times did *Homo erectus*, armed only with a stone tool, come out as a winner in a fight against a leopard?

Furthermore, sharp-edged stone tools are also only marginally more helpful than natural stones in food foraging. Nuts and bones can be broken with natural stones; the stone does not need to have sharp edges. Yes, the flakes are very efficient butchering instruments that could have allowed hominins to cut off pieces of steak quickly and carry them away to a safe place for consumption before they were chased away from a carcass by bigger carnivores, but that does not make the flakes critical for survival. Carcasses can be cut and flesh can be separated from bones with the use of teeth (chimpanzees do just that, often supplementing their diet with the meat of small monkeys without the use of any sharp flakes). Furthermore carcasses can be butchered with the use of just about any large stones (as well as some blunt force), albeit less efficiently.

If sharp-edged stones were not critical for survival, then why were they manufactured at all? In all likelihood, they were manufactured because *Homo erectus* was **able to manufacture** them and because sharp-edged stones were more efficient for the tasks mentioned above. Look at the market today. Why are there so many tools for slicing vegetables? All the slicing can be done with a knife. However, stores are stuffed with multiple slicers, corers, dividers, shredders, graters, squeezers, as well as electric and mechanical food processors. These tools are manufactured because humans *can* manufacture them, and because each of them makes vegetable preparation more efficient in its own way. Nobody claims that a hand knife drove evolution. By the same token, I argue that sharp-edged stones also did not drive evolution. These items are just a reflection of cortical development in general, and of progress within the visual system in particular. If one is still convinced that sharp-edged stones alone drove evolution, one needs to consider the fact that sharp-edged stones occur naturally. Rock-weathering generates nearly an unlimited number of sharp-edged stones. There are plenty of sharp stones in my backyard. If the use of sharp stones alone was so beneficial for survival, then the tribe that was better at collecting and carrying the sharp-edged stones would win the competition. Archeological evidence, however, invariably demonstrates that more advanced, bigger-brained hominins were associated with the *manufacturing* (not the collecting) of superior stone tools. It appears that sharp-edged stone tools played only a marginal role in survival, and their manufacturing was only a *reflection* of the developing visual system. *Homo habilis* won the competition over australopiths *not* because it was able to manufacture sharp-edged choppers, but because a better visual system allowed *Homo habilis* to detect predators and prey hidden in the grass. *Homo erectus* won the competition over *Homo habilis* not because it was better able to fight a leopard with a handaxe, but because it was smart enough to recognize the stalking leopard and therefore avoid an encounter more often than *Homo habilis*.

11.7 Evolutionary forces driving the improvement of the speech apparatus

To understand the catalyst for the development of the hominin speech apparatus, it may be helpful to review the timeline of the evolution of the voice box. The australopith hyoid bone discovered in Dikika, Ethiopia, closely resembles that of a chimpanzee, which indicates that there was no significant development in the Australopithecus speech apparatus [259]. There is evidence of changes in the speech apparatus starting about 2 million years ago with *Homo erectus* [139]. By about 600,000 years ago, the speech apparatus virtually reached its modern configurations as indicated by the skull of *Homo heidelbergensis* from Ethiopia [139], the Neanderthal hyoid bone from the Kebara Cave [197], and the FOXP2 gene evolution [272]. Thus, the vocal apparatus mainly developed in *Homo erectus* from about 2 million years ago to about 600,000 years ago. PFS was acquired roughly 70,000 years ago. Thus, the acquisition of a nearly modern vocal apparatus predates acquisition of PFS by at least 500,000 years. *Homo erectus* acquired articulate speech before it was able to synthesize novel objects in its own mind or in the mind of its listeners. *Homo erectus* was not able to tell or to understand a story, nor was it able to develop a complex mental plan such as building a new trap, or to explain verbally how to manufacture a tool. However, by about 600,000 year ago, *Homo heidelbergensis* (the common ancestor of Neanderthals and *Homo sapiens*) was capable of articulate speech similar to that of a three-year-old human child. What was the catalyst for the development of the speech apparatus?

Let us speculate on some of the possible benefits for *Homo erectus* in acquiring articulate speech:

1. Articulate speech could have directly helped in fighting or avoiding predators.

2. The advanced voice apparatus could have been used for superior predator warnings.

3. Articulate speech could have allowed *Homo erectus* to communicate a greater number of objects that it was now able to perceive thanks to the acquisition of prefrontal analysis.

4. A superior ability to imitate animal sounds may have facilitated hunting.

5. Being able to speak loudly could ensure that hominins did not surprise dangerous animals when moving across the savanna.

6. The modern voice apparatus could simply be a byproduct of a bigger brain.

7. Articulate speech could have increased cooperation within the hominin society.

While discussing the catalyst of voice box evolution, it's important to remember that the redesign of the modern voice box has some major disadvantages: the low position of the larynx in the throat of human adults leads to a greater chance of choking. In contrast, the larynx of chimpanzees and human babies is positioned high in the throat, which allows them to breathe and drink at the same time. The larynx descends during postnatal development in both humans and chimpanzees, but the human larynx descends significantly lower than that of the chimpanzee [403], allowing humans to produce a wider range of sounds than chimpanzees. As a result, adult chimpanzees may be limited in their vocal range, but they retain the ability to breathe and drink at the same time. Human adults trying to do both tasks at the same time would inevitably choke: a clear drawback of the modern voice box design. This effect is more than an inconvenience; the reported number of people who choke to death every year is over 2,000 in the USA alone and is even greater in some other countries (e.g. over 4,000 in Japan). It follows that the evolutionary advantage provided by articulate speech must have been more important for survival than the disadvantage of increasing one's chances of choking. With this perspective in mind, let us now discuss each of the possible benefits listed above:

1. Articulate speech could have directly helped in fighting or avoiding predators

Would articulate speech protect hominins from predators? Well, just try to use words to explain to an attacking leopard that it should not eat you! It is self-evident that words do not protect you (directly) when you encounter a leopard: predators do not understand words. No matter how many distinct sounds your speech apparatus can produce, words are not helpful as weapons for fighting off predators.

2. The advanced voice apparatus could have been used for superior predator warnings

While it is likely that vocalizations would not directly help deter an attacking leopard, what about using the superior vocalizations and vocabulary for warnings? Indeed, speech provides a method of communication superior to sign communication. Group members using sound do not need to see the speaker in order to receive a warning. Auditory warnings are often used in communications between non-human primates in the wild. The vervet monkeys of East Africa have different warnings for different threats (a leopard, a snake, an eagle, and a baboon warning). Chimpanzees in the wild use over 30 vocalizations to warn about predators and express emotions such as distress, puzzlement and excitement. Note that the majority of vocalizations are used to express emotions and only a few sounds are used as warnings. Would hominins benefit from a greater number of warning calls?

Warnings can be really helpful when they can communicate the location of a predator. "There is a snake on the big stone to the left of the tallest tree. Do not go there." However, as discussed in Part 1, the understanding of the snake's location implicit in this complex warning is only possible when hominins hearing the vocalization are able to imagine "a snake on the big stone to the left of the tallest tree," and then match the mental image to the environment in order to infer the direction toward the snake. Once the direction toward the snake is inferred, the tribesman who received the warning can avoid the snake. However to imagine "a snake on the big stone on the left of the tallest tree," one needs to synchronize the objectNEs of the big stone and the tallest tree in one mental frame. Such synchronization requires neural machinery for PFS. Judging by the lack of any external manifestations of PFS, *Homo erectus* was lacking the neuronal machinery for PFS. Without PFS, *Homo erectus* could not benefit from the complex warning containing a description of predator location.

Simple warnings which differentiate between different predators (such as the warnings used by vervet monkeys and chimpanzees) are of course helpful as well. *Homo erectus* could adjust its escape by reacting differently to different predator-warnings (hide high in a tree canopy to escape from a leopard or hide low in a tree canopy to escape from an eagle). But how many different warnings could *Homo erectus* use? With one warning for each type of predator, hominins could probably use 10 to 20 vocalizations. A voice apparatus similar to that of a chimpanzee would certainly have sufficed for a plethora of predator warnings. It follows that the ability to generate warnings was an unlikely driver of the evolution of the vocal apparatus.

3. Articulate speech could have allowed Homo erectus to communicate a greater number of objects that it was now able to perceive thanks to the acquisition of prefrontal analysis

Is it possible that the improvements in the speech apparatus of *Homo erectus* are simply associated with the species' acquisition of a greater voluntary control over perception? As evidenced by the manufacturing of stone tools, *Homo erectus* acquired the neurological capability for prefrontal analysis as early as two million years ago. *Homo erectus* was able to voluntarily form a mental template of a handaxe: it could look at a cobble but perceive a handaxe hidden inside. It is therefore likely that *Homo erectus* was capable of seeing other "invisible" objects: a wooden spear inside a tree trunk, a bone hammer, a razor sharp flake, and so on. He was likely capable of perceiving any number of "invisible" and useful objects. He was beginning to control his perception!

As prefrontal analysis was improving, so was the number of perceived objects. If there was an advantage in *Homo erectus* being able to communicate those perceived objects (such as the mental template of a handaxe), that could create evolutionary pressure on the acquisition of a better vocal apparatus. Could communicating mental templates be useful in teaching (e.g. in teaching of tool manufacturing)? Would students understand the following instructions? "To make a handaxe, mount a flint stone on an anvil and hit it on the side with a hammer stone; turn the flint stone over and hit it with hammer stone on the other side." To mentally simulate these instructions, students would have had to synchronize the image of a flint stone, an anvil, and a hammer stone in one mental frame — a neurological ability not available to *Homo erectus* students. Without PFS, *Homo erectus* was not able to verbally explain tool manufacturing to a student. Tool manufacturing would have to be demonstrated in a hands-on presentation. Lacking the ability to mentally simulate the instructions, a greater number of words would not change the effectiveness of the presentation. Even after the acquisition of articulate speech, *Homo erectus* would have had to demonstrate the tool manufacturing process to their kin in a hands-on presentation. Thus, it is not clear how prefrontal analysis could directly influence the acquisition of articulate speech. While prefrontal analysis enabled *Homo erectus* to perceive a number of objects invisible to its ancestors, the evolutionary advantage of communicating these novel perceptions is unclear.

4. A superior ability to imitate animal sounds may have facilitated hunting

Drawing on his own work with the Mbendjele forest people of Congo-Brazzaville, Jerome Lewis, an anthropologist at University College London, suggests that hominins could have acquired articulate speech by imitating natural sounds:

> [While hunting, Mbendjele] men fake animal calls to lure animals to them. Most men competently fake many key animal sounds. I [Jerome Lewis] remember watching a group of men passing time deceiving a mother hen by so perfectly

mimicking the chirping of her chicks that she would constantly attack them—to laughter and a gentle shove. Most young men are capable mimics of bay duikers and blue duikers, both very abundant game and popular food. Faking the duikers' call "come frolic with me" brings them to within a few meters of the hunter. The confused animal can return again and again, unable to understand why he is not meeting another duiker. Monkeys are drawn out of the canopy into range of crossbows or shotguns by faking the sound of a fallen infant or the call of a monkey eagle. Faking a crocodile's mating call while standing waist deep in sludgy dark water and as return calls gradually get closer requires courage. The crocodile is lured onto a small island in the marsh where prepared liana ropes are used to trap its jaws shut, before binding its limbs. Calling pigs is done when pigs are already close by and involves mimicking eating sounds so as to attract greedy animals close enough to be speared [404].

Looking elsewhere in the animal kingdom seems to provide support for the Lewis hypothesis. Humans are not the only species physically capable of generating a great number of distinct sounds. The vocal apparatus in birds evolved independently from mammals. Many singing birds use sounds for courtship, alarms, and to keep members of a flock in contact. Some birds, including African Grey Parrots and Indian Mynah birds developed the ability to mimic a wide range of sounds (including human sounds). In the wild it allows them to *imitate* other species of birds and animals.

Could natural selection of *Homo erectus* for superior faking of animal sounds lead to the acquisition of an advanced vocal apparatus? That would have been a reasonable hypothesis if the group being discussed was Mbendjele or any other forest people. However *Homo erectus* did not hunt in the forests as the Mbendjele people do. *Homo erectus* is thought to have evolved in the open African savannas. In the open savanna, where prey animals could see the hunters, it would have been nearly impossible to deceive animals through sound imitation.

5. Being able to speak loudly could ensure that hominins did not surprise dangerous animals when moving across the savanna

Jerome Lewis also notes that:

> [In the forest, Mbendjele] women walk in large groups, rarely alone, and accompany each other's speech with conventional sung sounds that contribute to increasing the volume and distinctive melodiousness of their conversations. Women talk, sing, or yodel loudly in the forest to ensure that they do not surprise dangerous animals. Menstrual odor is said to anger large dangerous animals such as gorillas, elephants, buffalo, and leopards, causing them to charge or attack people who smell of it. ... Women's fear of attack encourages them to do their daily activities in noisy groups [404].

Is it possible that *Homo erectus*, who now took longer and further trips into the savannas, acquired articulate speech to scare dangerous animals away? It's highly unlikely since the chimpanzee vocal apparatus is good enough to produce variable loud noises, certainly sufficient for scaring away and warning surrounding animals. Since the old vocal apparatus was sufficient, it doesn't seem logical that *Homo erectus* would acquire a new vocal apparatus configuration which is prone to choking just to produce loud noises.

6. The modern voice apparatus could simply be a byproduct of a bigger brain

Over time, *Homo erectus'* brain nearly doubled in volume from 850 cm^3 to 1225 cm^3. Furthermore the expanding brain was clearly associated with a greater ability to voluntarily control important cortical functions such as subjective perception and control of hand muscles: *Homo erectus* was able to voluntarily see a future handaxe in a cobble and also had enough fine motor control to create it. Could these advances spill over on their own into the cortical regions controlling fine movement of orofacial muscles responsible for articulate speech?

Acquisition of articulate speech involved more than just the fine control of orofacial muscles. As mentioned above, major morphological changes occurred in the vocal apparatus both in the position and the structure of the larynx and hyoid bone (in *Homo erectus* as compared to Australopiths). Such morphological changes are hard to understand simply as a direct consequence of an increase in brain volume.

7. Articulate speech could have increased cooperation within the hominin society

Recall that *Homo erectus* was an adventurous species: the body was built for long distance running indicating that it was constantly on the move. In fact, *Homo erectus* was moving so much that the species diffused out of Africa and settled most of Europe and Asia starting around 1.8 million years ago [405–407].

For an adventurous species like *Homo erectus*, even a small increase in cooperation was probably a big advantage. How could articulate speech facilitate cooperation within the *Homo erectus* society? *Homo erectus* lived in groups of 50 to 150 individuals in caves or other suitable natural shelters. Whether they foraged or hunted, they would have exhausted the land around their shelter within a few months. *Homo erectus* therefore must have traveled regularly from one place to another (which is consistent with the observation that *Homo erectus* diffused out of Africa about 1.8 million years ago). For such a large group, wandering around without knowing the final destination is highly inefficient. Exacerbating the problem would be the fact that most women in the group would have been either nursing or pregnant. Looking for a new shelter in the company of pregnant or nursing women and small children would have been highly dangerous. It is safer and more efficient to decide on an ideal location first, and then gather everybody together to make a quick move. Therefore, it is likely that able-bodied scouts were sent out to look for the next fertile area with a nearby shelter, while the rest of the group stayed behind in safety. Articulate speech would have allowed scouts returning from their trip to compare their observations and decide not only whose shelter was better (e.g. a bigger cave, or one with a nearby water source), but also whose shelter was best positioned as far as availability of prey animals and edible plants (grasses, herbs, seeds, roots, rhizomes, or tubers). Such discussions and comparisons do **not** require PFS; they can be based entirely on memory recall. For example, scouts could have measured the size of their caves using their own strides (the size of which is comparable in similarly-built individuals) and then used simple recall to communicate this information to help choose the largest cave.

While the scouts' presentations and ensuing negotiations may have been possible without PFS, it would have been greatly facilitated by a common verbal communication system. Scouts would need to announce that they have found a cave, and have vocabulary to communicate its size, as well as its advantages and disadvantages. They would benefit from having a vocabulary which would allow them to discuss other important features such as: the location and size of the closest water source, the types and quantities of edible plants, the names and availability of desirable prey animals, as well as possible threats and predators. A tribe capable of finding a better pasture and a better shelter would surely have a greater evolutionary advantage.

Articulate speech would also have allowed *Homo erectus* to ask for a helping hand much more efficiently. A leader could purposefully select someone more suitable for the job (he could select John, because John is stronger, or Peter because Peter is taller, or Steve who can climb trees faster, or Paul who can throw a spear with greater aim). A leader who found a cave with a prohibitively small opening would ask John to come with him and help clear the large boulders from the cave's entrance, but ask Steve to climb a tree if he has found a beehive full of honey. Since both John and Steve have seen large boulders and beehives before, they wouldn't need to synthesize any novel mental images. They could just recall the image of a stone or a beehive based on word-object association. Nor would the leader need to generate a visual plan for moving the stone with Peter or getting honey with Steve. The leader could just remember that a particular tribesman (John) was good at moving big stones in the past or that someone else (Steve) is adept at getting the honey.

An articulate communication system would also facilitate job assignment. A leader could assign specific tasks, such as collecting edible plants, flint stones (for handaxe manufacturing), wood (for spear manufacturing), or small stones (for throwing at predators) to selected tribesmen most suitable for the job. The leader could instruct the selected workers in what to take with them: handaxes for cutting trees, spears for hunting, or animal hides for carrying stones back to the shelter. Therefore, even in the absence of PFS, articulate speech would have greatly facilitated the management of an efficient *Homo erectus* society. How many words could assist in such management? First of all, every tribesman would have to be assigned a name (that's 50 to 150 words). Then, words would be necessary to describe simple actions, such as: "John, come here." Different jobs would have to have their own names:

collecting flint and small rocks, gathering wood, moving objects, and so on. Homo erectus would also benefit from naming different types of edible plants and prey animals. The total vocabulary needed to manage the *Homo erectus* society, communicate job assignments, and compare scout reports would likely consist of somewhere between several hundred and several thousand words. The chimpanzee voice apparatus is inadequate for generating even several hundred distinct words, while the modern human-like voice box is capable of generating several thousand distinct words. It follows that *Homo erectus* may have been selected for the greater ability to generate articulate speech because that would have greatly benefited cooperation within the society.

Evolutionarily speaking, even a small increase of cooperation in a social animal like *Homo erectus* would have been highly advantageous for group survival. This observation leads to a new question: if the *Homo erectus* society benefited so much from articulate speech, why is it that articulate speech was not acquired earlier by australopiths (and by the same token, by any other social animal)? Wouldn't cooperation have been equally important for Australopiths? After all, that species also lived in large groups. Even chimpanzees live in groups of about 50 individuals. Looking at the differences between the australopith and the *Homo erectus* lifestyle may provide an answer. Similar to *Homo erectus,* australopiths made trips into the savanna, but at night they returned to the safety of the forest to sleep in the treetop canopies (australopiths probably slept the same way as chimpanzees do: in individually built treetop nests). Australopiths also did not need to move around much from one area to another (which is consistent with the observation that they never diffused out of Africa). Australopiths did not have prefrontal analysis, so they did not modify the natural environment as much as *Homo erectus*. For example, since they didn't manufacture stone tools, they didn't need to collect flint stones; since they didn't live in caves, they didn't need to cooperate in searching for a suitable cave or in moving heavy stones to clear out the cave entrance. If *Homo erectus* was using fire [408], they had to carry it from one place to another and had to continuously keep the fire going once they had settled. It is also likely that *Homo erectus* hunted much more than the nearly "vegetarian" australopiths and they probably hunted larger prey [408]. A slaughtered animal would have been quickly butchered to avoid the intrusion of big cats and hyenas. Both hunting and butchering would have been greatly aided by better cooperation. Furthermore *Homo erectus* lived in a much wider variety of environments: they were continuously on the move from one place to another and were under constant pressure from predators when on the move. Any modern camper traveling in a group would appreciate the value of cooperation. In each new place, the group needed to locate a protective shelter, edible food, and a source of clean water, as well as to set up and maintain a fire; sending out and debriefing scouts is essential for the success of any expedition. In general, the timid australopiths would not have benefitted from cooperation as much as the adventurous and nomadic *Homo erectus*. Whatever small benefit they would have experienced, was probably negated by the increased chance of choking associated with a descending larynx.

It seems that the most likely explanation for the acquisition of articulate speech involves the selection for better cooperation within the *Homo erectus* society. It is likely that prefrontal analysis did not directly influence the development of the vocal apparatus. Rather, prefrontal analysis allowed *Homo erectus* to become more adventurous (as demonstrated by the species' diffusion out of Africa), flexible in its direction of movement, and confident in its ability to detect and avoid predators. The increasingly adventurous species of *Homo erectus* then significantly benefited from increased cooperation, which was, in turn, enabled by the developing vocal apparatus.

11.8 Speech acquisition summary

The evolutionary pressure for improvement of the speech apparatus was different from the evolutionary pressure driving development in the lateral prefrontal cortex. *Homo erectus* was an adventurous species with the body built for persistence hunting and long distance running [409]. Long distance traveling in a group significantly increased the value of effective communication. In each new place, a tribe needed to locate a protective shelter, edible food, a source of clean water and carry out a myriad of other location-specific projects. Any improvement in vocabulary would have allowed a *Homo erectus* chieftain to delegate jobs much more efficiently. Improved articulation probably started with a single mutation in a leader that enabled him to increase the number of distinct words from 40 (as in chimps [251-254]) to 100. Words could have been used to assign names for everyone in a group (even dolphins have life-long given names called signature whistles [410,411]). Even if no one else in the group but the leader was able to call each person by name, the leader and the group as a whole would have gained an advantage of increased cooperation and therefore better nutrition. As an alpha male, the leader would have a high number of children and thus his "improved vocal apparatus" mutation would have been fixed in a population.

After many generations another leader could acquire a different mutation that further improved his vocal apparatus and doubled his vocabulary to 300 words. The articulate leader could have been using extra words as nouns to further facilitate job assignment without the need to point to each object: two-word sentences could communicate job assignment: "John flint," meaning that John is expected to collect flint stones; "Peter sticks," meaning that Peter is expected to find sticks; "Patrick tubers," meaning that Patrick is expected to dig tuber; and so on. The leader could also instruct the selected workers in what to take with them: handaxes for cutting trees, spears for hunting, or a sack for carrying throwing stones back to the shelter.

Thousands of years later another mutation may have extended the vocabulary of the leader to 600 distinct words and enabled the leader to name more objects, tools, and actions, further improving his ability to efficiently organize the tribe's productive activities. This leader was now able to use more complex sentences: "John, come here;" "Peter, bring the handaxe;" and "Patrick, collect stones." Different types of edible plants and prey animals could have been assigned their own names and different jobs could have been assigned action words. Various geographical locations, including rivers, mountains, caves, and maybe even individual trees could be named, helping adventurous *Homo erectus* to navigate and to describe directions to other tribesmen.

Thus, I envision development of vocal apparatus as a series of beneficial mutations slowly improving the control of diaphragm, lips, tongue, chicks, vocal cords, larynx position in the trachea, and possibly hundreds of other related mutations over many millennia. When articulate speech mutations originate in a leader, they result in immediate improvement of communication (albeit one-way communication) between tribe members and consequent increase in tribe's productivity. Since leaders also had higher chances to procreate, their "improved vocal apparatus" was slowly fixed in a population over many generations.

Critically, such a communication system with many names,

nouns and verbs, while significantly benefiting traveling parties of *Homo erectus*, does not rely on voluntary imagination. In fact, apes, dogs and some other animals have been trained to follow hundreds of commands, such as "bring the ball/newspaper/slippers," "leak the hand/floor/bowl," that rely on memory of nouns and verbs, but do not require voluntary imagination.

Thus, articulate speech developed separately from voluntary imagination: their evolutionary driving forces were different and hundreds of mutations associated with improvement of each function could have been independent.

11.9 The great synergy: marriage of articulate speech and prefrontal synthesis creates modern language

While it is possible that speech apparatus and voluntary imagination were improving for several million years in parallel because of different evolutionary pressures, it doesn't mean that there was no synergy between them. Recent studies demonstrate a clear synergistic relationship between language proficiency and voluntary imagination in children. Deaf individuals communicating through a formal sign language from an early age develop normal voluntary imagination. However, in the absence of early communication, or when the sign language is lacking spatial prepositions and recursion, deaf individuals show clear deficits of voluntary imagination. Deaf individuals who had learned American Sign Language (ASL) early in life were found to be more accurate than later learners at identifying whether two complex-shape figures presented at different degrees of rotation were identical or mirror images of each other [62]. Individuals who learned ASL earlier were also faster than later learners at identifying whether two-dimensional body-shaped figures (bears with one paw raised) presented at different rotations were identical or mirror images of each other [63]. Even after decades of signing experience, the signers who learned ASL earlier were better at mental rotation accuracy [64]. Among deaf individuals who acquire sign language at the same age, the richness of "spatial" language makes a difference. Specifically, two cohorts of signers were tested with the first cohort of signers acquired the emerging sign language in Nicaragua when this language was just invented and had few spatial prepositions, while the second cohort of signers acquired the language in a more complex form with more spatial prepositions. Predictably, the second cohort of signers (tested when they were in their 20s) outperformed the first cohort of signers (tested when they were in their 30s) in several mental rotation tasks [65]. Finally, deaf individuals who are never exposed to formal sign language until puberty invariably suffer lifelong PFS paralysis despite learning significant vocabulary through intensive post-pubertal language therapy [40].

All available experimental evidence from modern-day children suggests the existence of an ontogenetic synergistic relationship between early childhood recursive language use and voluntary imagination skills. It is likely that similar synergy also existed on the phylogenetic level. Improving speech apparatus enabled better visuospatial processing and vice versa. The greatest synergy between articulate speech and voluntary imagination has been achieved with acquisition of PFS. PFS has enabled articulate speech to communicate an infinite number of novel object combinations with the use of a finite number of words, the system of communication that we call recursive language. At the same time, PFS endowed the human mind with the most efficient way to simulate the future in the neocortex: by voluntarily combining and re-combining mental objects from memory. The marriage of articulate speech and voluntary imagination 70,000 year ago resulted in the birth of a practically new species – the modern *Homo sapiens*, the species with the same creativity and imagination as modern humans.

11.10 The combination of a articulate speech with prefrontal synthesis enhanced cooperation is *Homo sapiens* to an unprecedented level

Paleontological evidence indicates that the acquisition of articulate speech by *Homo erectus* occurred at least 500,000 years prior to the acquisition of PFS by *Homo sapiens*. Thus, phonology and to some degree morphology of the communication system was already developed in *Homo sapiens'* immediate ancestors. The acquisition of PFS in *Homo sapiens* enabled the additional benefit of a flexible syntax, prepositions, adjectives, and verb tenses. The communication system flourished to its current form of a *recursive* language, capable of *high fidelity transmission* of an *infinite* number of *novel* images with the use of a *finite* number of words.

The combination of PFS with articulate speech raised cooperation in the *Homo sapiens* societies to an unprecedented level previously unseen in the animal kingdom. While other primates often cooperate [412], their cooperation is severely limited by their inability to communicate ideas and negotiate plans: skills that depend on the communicating parties being capable of PFS.

The combination of PFS with articulate speech converted a pre-PFS society to a modern human society, which relied on the highest level of cooperation. Groups of *Homo sapiens* became much better hunters: they could mentally plan a strategy using PFS and then use articulate speech to explain the plan to their companions (that is, to synthesize mental images in the minds of their peers as to where to run and how to attack a prey or an enemy). They could deceive prey animals by building a trap, making sophisticated weapons and using these weapons in novel ways. They quickly developed throwing spears, spear throwers (also called atlatls: devices that use leverage to achieve greater spear velocity) as well as the bow and arrow: all devices that facilitated hunting from a distance therefore allowing *Homo sapiens* to avoid close range (and highly dangerous) encounters with large animals [140,141].

Could a hominin tribe with no PFS build a trap? It is very unlikely. Building a sophisticated pitfall trap requires visual planning of the process. A leader has to be able to think through the plan by imagining the step-by-step process of building a trap and then communicating the plan to the tribe: "We will make a trap by digging a large pit and covering it with tree branches. A mammoth will then fall into the pit; no need to attack a mammoth head on." In fact, early modern humans are known for building traps; traps for herding gazelle, ibex, wild asses and other large animals were found in the deserts of the Near East. Some of the traps were as large as 60km (37miles) in length [227]. No, this is not a misprint: funnel-shaped traps comprising two long stone walls (up to 60 kilometers in length!) and converging on an enclosure or pit at the apex were found around the Negev desert. Animals were probably herded into the funnel until they reached the enclosure at the apex surrounded by pits, at which point the animals were trapped and killed. Some traps date back to as early as the 7th millennium BC [227].

Just think about the level of cooperation necessary for building a 60 km long trap! The building process must have been pre-planned by a tribe leader (or several leaders) and then explained to all the workers. Each worker, in turn, would have had to understand (through PFS) exactly what they needed to do: collect proper stones, assemble stones into a wall, and have the two walls meet at the apex 60 km away from where they started.

PFS and articulate speech would also have enabled humans to become better warriors. They could command a clever organized attack. For example, they could plan an encirclement of the enemy hideout followed by a simultaneous attack from all sides, they could distract the enemy and then attack them from the back, or they could entice an enemy into a trap. All these strategies require PFS to plan the attack, and articulate speech to coordinate the attack between the tribesmen.

Finally, humans could have used PFS to design and build protective shelters. Again, recursive language would have greatly facilitated the cooperation between tribesmen necessary for the planning and execution of an effective shelter.

The advantages of the *Homo sapiens'* acquisition of PFS are best appreciated when humans are compared to Neanderthals. Recall that Neanderthals spread throughout Europe between 500,000 and 200,000 years ago but were abruptly replaced by early humans about 30,000 years ago. The short time span of just 5,000 years over which the formerly ubiquitous Neanderthals were replaced by early humans raises the question: what exactly happened to the Neanderthals? Hypotheses on the fate of the Neanderthals include: the failure or inability to adapt to climate change, extinction due to parasites and pathogens, competitive exclusion, genocide by early humans, or hybridization with early humans[qq] [184,233,415].

[qq] An analysis of the Neanderthal genome shows that about one to four percent of the genes of non-African humans come from Neanderthals [184], which indicates interbreeding between the two populations. However this interbreeding may have been one-sided. First of all, no evidence for gene flow from modern humans to Neanderthals has been found. Secondly, although modern humans share some nuclear DNA with the extinct Neanderthals, the two species do not share any mitochondrial DNA, which is transmitted maternally [413]. Both observations are consistent with gene flow in one

Armed with a better understanding of the neurobiological differences between *Homo sapiens* and Neanderthals, it is possible to speculate on the Neanderthals' fate.

While Neanderthals were larger and had a more heavy-built frame than early humans, evidence seems to suggest that they did not have the capacity for PFS, and as a result could not plan a strategic defense or cooperate to the same degree as *Homo sapiens*. Therefore they were very limited in their ability to protect themselves against a group of well-coordinated early humans who were able to better plan an attack with the help of PFS and a recursive communication system.

Furthermore humans must have been better hunters since they could build a trap or attack from a distance using long-range weapons such as throwing spears. Neanderthals, on the other hand, likely hunted animals from a much closer distance, thrusting themselves as a group at an animal in an attempt to simultaneously stab it with as many spears as possible. The disproportionately large number of broken bones found in Neanderthal remains is a testament of this attack technique [139].

Both early humans and Neanderthals used spears, but humans used stone-tipped spears that were better at puncturing tough animal skin than the "big toothpicks" used by

---

direction: from Neanderthal males to modern human females. Some scientists interpreted these findings to suggest that Neanderthal males mating with human females resulted in fertile offspring, while human males mating with Neanderthal females led to infertile offspring [414]. However, there might be a simpler explanation: as Neanderthals did not possess PFS, negotiations with them were impossible. As a consequence, the inter-species sex was probably non-consensual: larger and stronger Neanderthal males taking advantage of weaker and smaller human females, while weaker human males were probably not able or not willing to take on bigger and stronger Neanderthal females.

Neanderthals.[rr] Both early humans and Neanderthals were using animal hides, but humans were stitching those hides into better fitting clothes with the use of sophisticated bone needles (equipped with an eye for threading).[ss] So, what happened to the Neanderthals? They lived in Europe and Asia for over 200,000 years and were abruptly replaced by early humans within just several thousand years. It is likely that early humans played at least some role in their extinction. Humans could have outcompeted the Neanderthals in hunting, used them as a source of food when other animals were not available[tt], or simply used their superior mental prowess to eliminate a

---

[rr] There is some evidence that hominins could have been using stone-tipped spears as early as 500,000 years ago [416], although the evidence is hotly debated.

[ss] While the Neanderthals used animal hides extensively as clothing for thousands of years, they probably did not stitch those hides, since stitching needles were never found at Neanderthal sites. It is likely that Neanderthals simply wrapped the hides around their bodies. Modern humans made clothes by stitching animal hides together. Stitching clothing is indicative of the presence of PFS. To cut and stitch an animal hide into a well-fitting garment, one first needs to mentally simulate the process: to imagine how the parts can be combined into the finished product that fits the body. This mental simulation can only be achieved through PFS.

[tt] There is strong scientific evidence that cannibalism was practiced amongst many of our ancestors. Thousands of human bones were uncovered intermixed with animal bones in settlements ranging from small villages to large towns. Human and animal bones were processed in a similar fashion. The skulls and bones were broken with stone tools for access to nutrient-rich brain and bone marrow. Dr. Tim White analyzed over 2,106 pieces of bone from at least 29 Native American men from an Anasazi site in the Mancos Canyon of southwestern Colorado. The bones invariably indicated that "people extracted the brain and cracked the limb bones for marrow after removing the muscle tissue." These findings provide convincing evidence of prehistoric cannibalism.

stronger and more muscular competitor.[uu]

If humans did contribute to the demise of the Neanderthals, it would not be the last time that humans played a role in the extinction of a species. It has been hypothesized that humans have played a role in the extinction of many other large mammals. Before modern humans arrived, North America was home to giant wooly mammoths for nearly 4.8 million years, ground sloth (a mammal the size of a modern elephant) for

---

[uu] A conversation with a Neanderthal: When two hominins are living on the same hill, it is tantalizing to speculate on how they may have interacted. I surmise that early humans were not too keen on meeting a bigger and stronger competitor one-on-one. Without PFS a Neanderthal must have appeared to them as a big and dangerous animal, capable of fighting, but not capable of conversing (or reasoning with). I think that modern human communications with Neanderthals were limited to physical interactions.

While the Neanderthal voice box and FOX2P modernity is indicative of their ability to speak many words, their communication system was non-syntactic, similar to a talking ape who has been trained to use a few hundred words (like the chimps Washoe and Nim, or the gorilla Koko). Of course the difference would be that unlike chimpanzees, who were taught to use signs and lexigrams, Neanderthals would have been able to use actual words. Imagine that an adult Neanderthal has been found and consequently trained in English for several years. What kind of conversation would we be able to conduct? With a nearly modern vocal apparatus, a Neanderthal should have no problem learning a decent-sized English vocabulary. The Neanderthal should be able to explain to you what he wants (an apple, a banana, or a piece of meat), and he should be able to express his feelings. However, he would not be able to communicate any complex concept that requires PFS. Just like a two-year-old or a talking chimp, a Neanderthal who knows the words for a cup and a keyboard would not be able to imagine "a cup on top of a keyboard." If you told a Neanderthal with a thousand word vocabulary a story about your friend John who ate a shark, and a story about the shark who ate your friend John, the Neanderthal would not be able to tell the difference: one needs to be able to synthesize novel mental images to understand flexible syntax. If you asked the Neanderthal how to make a particular tool (such as a spear), he might be able to give you a demonstration, but he would not be able to explain the complete process verbally.

about 9 million years, as well as bear-size beavers, camels, and other large mammals. The archeological evidence indicates that these animals and 70 other species disappeared around 11,000 years ago: just within a few thousand years of the arrival of modern humans in the New World (Martin PS, 1984; Martin PS, 1999). Similarly, researchers studying herbivore dung in Australia have linked the extinction of large animals, such as the three-meter tall giant kangaroos, marsupial lions, as well as giant birds and reptiles, to the arrival of humans in Australia 41,000 years ago. Scientists have concluded that hunting and human-lit fires were the cause of extinction [417].

Cooperation still plays the utmost role in modern human society. It allows for division of labor that provides individual contributors with an opportunity to focus their education. Cooperation has been credited as one of the primary reasons that the modern human society has been able to advance technological progress, build cities, and travel to space. This cooperation is made possible by PFS along with a recursive communication system.

11.11 The dual origin of human language

The origin of language has been deemed "the hardest problem in science" [418]. Approaches to the origin of language are mainly divided between those who see language mostly as an innate faculty that is largely genetically encoded (spearheaded by Noam Chomsky [419]), and those that see it as a system that is mainly cultural — that is, learned through social interactions [420]. The PFS theory conjectures that human language depends on both an innate human predisposition for PFS and a culturally acquired communication system. A quick inspection of the "innate language component" proposed by Noam Chomsky yields a conclusion that it is very similar to the innate PFS described in this monograph. Indeed, when Noam Chomsky describes the innate component of language, he is primarily describing the faculty of PFS:

> Actually you can use language even if you are the only person in the universe with language, and in fact it would even have adaptive advantage. If one person suddenly got the language faculty, that person would have great advantages; the person could think, could articulate to itself its thoughts, could plan, could sharpen, and develop thinking as we do in inner speech, which has a big effect on our lives. Inner speech is most of speech. Almost all the use of language is to oneself, and it can be useful for all kinds of purposes. [419] (page 148)

Chomsky does not use the word "language" to mean "the ability to produce sounds." In other words, "if you are the only person in the universe" who has words for a handful of objects, some basic commands and warnings (i.e. a culturally acquired communication system), this would not be much of an adaptive advantage. Chomsky clearly infuses the word "language" with additional meaning: it is something that can be used to "plan" and to "develop thinking"; it is a tool useful for reasoning (even if it's only with oneself).[vv] In that sense, Chomsky uses "language" to mean something quite similar to what I am referring to as "PFS." Although Chomsky never formally describes "language" in purely visual terms, he has written that

---

[vv] Replace "language" with "PFS" in the above paragraph and the resulting sentence makes complete sense: "Actually you can use [PFS] even if you are the only person in the universe with [PFS], and in fact it would even have adaptive advantage. If one person suddenly got the [PFS] faculty that person would have great advantages; ...."

The paragraph loses any sense if you replace "language" with "culturally acquired communication system"

"... language evolved in a way that facilitates synthesis and transmission of the synthesized mental image" (personal communications).

Noam Chomsky's definition of language is further explained in Fitch, Hauser, & Chomsky [134]:

> ... considerable confusion has resulted from the use of 'language' to mean different things. ... For many linguists, 'language' delineates an abstract core of computational operations, central to language and probably unique to humans. For many biologists and psychologists, 'language' has much more general and various meanings, roughly captured by "the communication system used by human beings."

Without a strict definition of PFS based on neuroscience, the authors struggle to describe the innate component of language. They call it "the abstract core of computational operations," "recursive mental operations," "recursive thought," and "the faculty of language in the narrow sense (FLN)." They explain:

> Ultimately, we think it is likely that some bona fide components of FLN—mechanisms that are uniquely human and unique to language—will be isolated and will withstand concerted attempts to reject them by empirical research. An understanding of such mechanisms from the genetic, neural and developmental perspectives will illuminate our understanding of our own species.

The authors use every opportunity to differentiate *the innate faculty of language* from a *communication system* :

> ... it seems clear that the current utility of recursive mental operations is not limited to communication. ... recursive thought would appear to be quite useful in such functions as

planning, problem solving, or social cognition.

The example that the authors bring up to describe "recursive thought" portrays the process of PFS:

> As an example of how recursion plausibly functions in spatial reasoning and navigation, consider such concepts as ((((the hole) in the tree) in the glade) by the stream) and ask whether there is an obvious limit to such embedding of place concepts within place concepts (... in the forest by the plain between the mountains in the north of the island...).

Clearly the description of the innate component of language by Fitch, Hauser, & Chomsky [134] is very close, if not identical, to the definition of PFS. Chomsky argues that a single chance mutation that occurred in one individual about 70,000 years ago triggered the 'instantaneous' emergence of this innate faculty of language [i.e. PFS].

On the other hand, Charles Darwin envisioned the origin of language as the acquisition of a mechanical ability to produce sounds that provide the basis for a communication system:

> I cannot doubt that language owes its origin to the imitation and modification, aided by signs and gestures, of various natural sounds, the voices of other animals, and man's own instinctive cries. [20]

In his view, Darwin followed Max Müller who assumed that once hominins had stumbled upon the appropriate mechanism for producing articulate speech, words would automatically link with meanings, a communication system would develop, and language would evolve.

Armed with the understanding that human language relies on both articulate speech (as the most common communication system) and PFS, let's now re-examine the story of the origin of language. It appears that PFS was developing independently of the vocal apparatus. The acquisition of PFS was catalyzed by predation: from the time the hominin branch split off from the chimpanzees some 6 million years ago, hominins were selected for the superior ability to detect motionless predators concealed by vegetation. That selection was actively occurring until 70,000 years ago when PFS was acquired. The acquisition of the modern vocal apparatus, on the other hand, was catalyzed by social factors: hominins were selected for their ability to better cooperate using articulate speech. That system was developing (separately) starting around 2 million years ago, and continuing until about 600,000 years ago. These two independent traits converged in *Homo sapiens* and enabled the human use of a recursive language. Therefore the PFS theory unites the polarized views on the origin of language by explaining that language relies on both the innate and cultural components: the innate delayed prefrontal cortex maturation and prolonged critical period along with the culturally acquired recursive language.

11.12 Improvement of voluntary imagination defined the pace of language evolution

In this book, I have presented multiple theoretical and experimental observations that argue for dichotomy of language: 1) The neurological apparatus for articulate speech (the Broca's and Wernicke's areas) is distinct from the neurological apparatus for voluntary imagination (the lateral prefrontal cortex control over the visual areas in the posterior cortex). 2) Double dissociation of PFS and articulate speech in patients with brain lesions: patients with PFS paralysis do not demonstrate changes in articulate speech and patients with expressive aphasia can have normal PFS. 3) Double dissociation of PFS and articulate speech in childhood language development: some children acquire normal articulate speech while showing clear deficits in voluntary imagination, while others can have trouble in articulate speech, but attain normal PFS. 4) Our recent data from a large group of children with autism demonstrate that children improve their language following a course of voluntary imagination exercises [15]. All these observations point to the dichotomy of recursive language and the importance of the visuospatial component of language.

The dichotomy of recursive language poses a dilemma: which of the two components of language was hampering language acquisition in hominins? Since articulate speech is so obviously different between humans and apes, this question has been commonly answered in favor of the articulate speech (e.g., by Darwin [20]). However, as clearer understanding of differences in voluntary imagination between humans and apes emerges, this conventional wisdom is put in doubt. Apes who learned hundreds of words do not show any improvement of their voluntary imagination: they cannot integrate modifiers or juxtapose various mental objects at will to demonstrate PFS ability.

In this chapter, I propose a radical idea that evolutionary acquisition of recursive language was primarily limited not by the capacities of the speech apparatus, but by the slow progress in the development of the lateral prefrontal cortex-dependent visuospatial mechanisms i.e., voluntary imagination. Voluntary imagination is mediated via some of the longest fibers in the brain (arcuate fasciculus and superior longitudinal fasciculus). Fine-tuning of these fibers by experience-dependent myelination is a far more complex and slower task than acquisition of vocabulary; typically-developing children commonly acquire articulate speech by the age of 2, but do not acquire PFS until 4 years [37].

In fact, the argument in favor of the speech apparatus

limiting the acquisition of recursive language is fundamentally weak, as speech is not an obligatory component of language at all. If hominins had neurological machinery for voluntary imagination, they could have invented sign language. A sign language does not require hundreds of mutations necessary for an articulate speech apparatus and apes easily learn hundreds of signs [421,422]. All formal sign languages include spatial prepositions and other recursive elements. In a largest natural experiment of language origin, four hundred Nicaraguan deaf children assembled in two schools in the 1970s (genetically modern children, with the propensity for normal voluntary imagination) spontaneously invented a new recursive sign language in just a few generations [129]. Thus, the capacities of the speech apparatus could not have been a limiting factor in the acquisition of recursive language. The only possible explanation for not acquiring recursive language earlier is the insufficiency of voluntary imagination mechanisms. The lack of PFS in our premodern ancestors (before 70,000ya) must have prevented their acquisition of recursive language.

Additional supporting evidence for this hypothesis comes from the observation of the variety of sound boxes in birds and the uniqueness of human voluntary imagination. Articulate sounds can be generated by Grey parrots and thousands of other songbird species [423]. This shows that improving sound articulation is, evolutionarily speaking, a simpler process than improving voluntary imagination.

On the bases of neurological observations, archeological findings, children studies, the sign language argument, and variety of sound boxes in birds, I argue that the evolution of hominin speech apparatus must have followed (rather than led to) the improvements in voluntary imagination. Contrary to Darwin's prediction, not speech, but voluntary imagination appears to define the pace of language evolution.

11.13 Conclusions

Hominin evolution in the savannas of Africa was primarily driven by predation. Hominins relied on their visual system rather than on speed or strength as their primary means of protection. The selection favored hominins who were better able to detect stalking predators concealed by vegetation. As a result of 3 million years of selection, hominins acquired prefrontal analysis for more reliable predator-recognition. *Homo habilis* was better able to control its visual percept; it was able to *see* a predator hidden by vegetation as well as to *see* a chopper hidden inside a cobble. In the next 3 million years, predation further selected hominins for their ability to analyze the savanna scenery for the presence of motionless, stalking predators concealed by vegetation. Developing analytical capabilities of the visual system allowed *Homo erectus* to detect "invisible" predators and see an "invisible" handaxe inside a flint stone. Better predator detection and avoidance emboldened *Homo erectus* to become more adventurous (as evidenced by *the species'* diffusion out of Africa) as well as flexible in its direction of movement. The more adventurous *Homo erectus* significantly benefited from increased cooperation. Greater cooperation was enabled by the acquisition of articulate speech made possible by a slowly changing vocal apparatus (which occurred from 2 million to 600,000 years ago).

Increased voluntary top-down control over perception culminated in *Homo sapiens*. *Homo sapiens* acquired an ability to voluntarily integrate unrelated visual elements into a single imaginary percept (PFS), making it possible to voluntarily generate mental movies. Being able to create mental movies allowed humans to simulate multiple plans and select the best solution for any problem. Tribesmen with PFS transformed an archaic non-recursive communication system into a recursive language. PFS coupled with a recursive communication system created the ultimate hunting machine with unmatched abilities for strategizing, planning and execution of attacks. Recursive language enabled an unprecedented level of cooperation between individuals and allowed human society to develop culture and build cities. *Homo sapiens* were no longer primarily driven by predation; we became predators ourselves.[ww]

[ww] It's important to note that the evolutionary pressure acted VERY slowly over ten million years. As the African climate changed, the rainforest was slowly replaced by patches of forest separated by expanses of grassland, then by savannas, and later by open grasslands. Had the climate change been more abrupt, hominins may have been wiped out from the planet by faster and stronger predators. With a reproduction rate of just four to five offsprings in a female's lifetime, hominins could not afford losing even half of their offspring. To grow the population, a female could only afford to lose one or two of her offspring. How could hominins have lived in such a hostile environment and lose so few offsprings? I think that the answer is that hominins never lived in an environment that was too hostile: ten million years ago our chimpanzee-like ancestors were protected from predators in treetop canopies. As the patches of forest reduced in size, hominins increased the time they spent foraging in grasslands, but they retained the safety provided by the treetop canopies nearby. At the same time natural selection improved the hominin ability of detecting stalking predators. As forests shrank further, hominins acquired a greater ability to detect and avoid predators. Around one million years ago, when patches of forest disappeared, hominins evolved into a respectable species with modern-level predator recognition, prefrontal analysis, and some control of fire [408]. The whole game of evolution reminds me of my son's gymnastics training when he was learning to walk on his hands. To assist him in this process, the coach initially allowed him to use a soft ball for support. As he was improving, the coach used a smaller and smaller ball until one day my son didn't need the ball any more. As far as I can see, evolution acted as a gentle coach: it slowly increased the distance to the next patch of forest just as hominins were improving in their skill of detecting concealed predators. Eventually hominins did not need the next patch of forest just like my son no longer needed the support of a ball.

This logic has bearing on an intriguing (and often asked) question: can chimpanzees be selectively bred into an intelligent species with the ability to use PFS? I don't see any reason why the answer should be "no." Selectively breeding chimpanzees with greater top-down control over their percept should eventually result in acquisition of PFS. The time of breeding would probably be shorter than six million years as artificial selection should be faster than natural selection but it may still take a long time.

What about selectively breeding chimpanzees for their ability to acquire a human communication system? As discussed in Part 1, Chapter 5, there have been several scientists who have attempted to train a chimpanzee in a human communication system. These scientists believed that chimpanzees would be able to acquire flexible syntax (and therefore PFS) as a result of grasping a human communication system. This belief is based on observations of human development: children normally acquire PFS concurrently with the communication system, and children who fall behind in grasping a communication system (e.g. deaf linguistic isolates or feral children) often fall behind in developing PFS (discussed in detail in Part 3). Thus many scientists believe that the lack of flexible syntax and the associated lack of external manifestations of PFS in chimpanzees is the result of an underdeveloped communication system. They believe that if they could improve the communication system, the PFS system would develop automatically. I think it is a bit naive to expect chimpanzees to acquire PFS simply as a result of learning a communication system. So far, all the recorded attempts to prove this theory have failed, and have resulted in chimps who can speak many words, but who do not exhibit PFS. While a communication system enables external communication, this skill on its own is not sufficient to lay down neurological structural changes necessary for PFS in chimpanzees.

Part 5: What chimpanzees are thinking about?

Chapter 12. The uniqueness of human language and imagination

... almost all of the phenomena that are central to the humanities are puzzling anomalies from an evolutionary perspective. Chief among these are the human attraction to fictional experience (in all media and genres) and other products of the imagination. (We will be using the word fiction in its broadest sense, to refer to any representation intended to be understood as nonveridical, whether story, drama, film, painting, sculpture, and so on.) If these phenomena did not exist, no evolutionary psychologist, at our present level of understanding, would have felt compelled to look for or predict them.

JOHN TOOBY & LEDA COSMIDES, *Does beauty build adapted minds? Toward an evolutionary theory of aesthetics, fiction, and the arts* (2001)

12.1 Problem solving by animals

What components of imagination are available to animals? PFS has never been demonstrated in non-human animals. Even simpler components of voluntary imagination [145], such as modifier integration seem to be out of reach for animals. Animals which know the names of objects, colors and sizes are not capable of integrating the objects and modifiers together – they are incapable of finding "the long red pencil" or "the short blue crayon" among multi-colored, multi-sized pieces of Lego, crayons, and pencils. These limitations in voluntary imagination should not be surprising. We have previously determined that voluntary imagination is mediated by the lateral prefrontal cortex and its long frontoposterior fibers. The lateral prefrontal cortex is much smaller in non-human primates and absent in non-primate mammals [202]. The long frontoposterior fibers (mediating all the aspects of voluntary imagination in humans) are much smaller or absent in non-human primates [361].

Despite these limits in voluntary imagination, mammals can clearly play out future scenarios in their dreams as we had seen in Chapter 1.6. What else can animals imagine in their mind? After reading the first edition of this book, Noam Chomsky remarked: "I like the idea of mental synthesis very much (but how do we know a dog can't think of a bone and mentally synthesize the image with its favorite spot under the couch?)..."

The Neuronal Ensembles Synchronization (NES) hypothesis [123] predicts that mammals can spontaneously synthesize novel mental images. The NES hypothesis explains that objectNEs that spontaneously activate *in-synchrony* are perceived together as novel combined objects or scenes. In other words, the objectNEs firing spontaneously and asynchronously from each other are perceived as *separate* objects; however, if by accident, two disparate objectNEs fire in-sync with each other, they are perceived as a *novel* hybrid object. In this process, an unlimited number of hybrid mental images can form during REM-sleep or day-dreaming and the animal can envision a solution to a problem (Chapter 4.5). This phenomenon of spontaneously seeing a solution is called an insight or the "Aha! moment."

History provides many examples of dream-inspired discoveries. Otto Loewi dreamed of an experiment that proved chemical transmission of nerve impulses. He immediately went to his lab to perform the experiment and later received the Nobel Prize for this discovery. Elias Howe, the inventor of the first sewing machine, has claimed that the main innovation, placing the thread hole near the tip of the needle, came to him in a dream. The chemist Friedrich Kekulé discovered the ring shape of the benzene molecule after having a dream of a snake seizing its own tail. The memory of a dream is short-lived, but if one wakes up during an insight, they can consolidate the "vision" into long-term memory and come up with an important discovery. I am sure you can recall events when solutions spontaneously popped up into your mind when walking in the woods or taking a shower.

There is no structure in the brain that could preclude mammals from REM-sleep or day-dreaming insights. The dog "can't think of a bone and mentally synthesize the image with its favorite spot under the couch" voluntarily, on purpose, but can happen to envision "a bone ... at its favorite spot under the couch" spontaneously during REM-sleep or day-dreaming insight.

Many solutions to problems demonstrated by animals could have been found using spontaneous insight. Wolfgang Köhler showed that chimpanzees who could not reach fruit hanging from a high ceiling, could spontaneously figure out how to stack boxes in order to reach higher. Some chimpanzees were also able to use long sticks to reach food outside of their enclosure [424]. When first encountering bananas hanging out of reach, the animals all tried to obtain the food by leaping at it. Köhler explains: "Sultan soon relinquished this attempt, paced restlessly up and down, suddenly stood still in front of the box, seized it . . ." (p. 38, 1925/1959) and moved it to a position from which he jumped and tore down the bananas. During early tests, sticks were used only when they were lying in the same field of view as the food, as if the animal had to see how the stick filled the gap between hand and food. Only with experience did animals readily fetch sticks from elsewhere."

Daniel Hanus was able to demonstrate that some chimpanzees were able to pull a peanut from a tube, using water from a nearby container [425]. An excellent Nova movie "Ape Genius" (2008) documents an amazing range of problems that can be solved by chimpanzees.

In primates, the lateral prefrontal cortex significantly facilitates the process of insight. As discussed in Chapter 4.5, the lateral prefrontal cortex encodes categories of objects and can prime selected categories into spontaneous firing (category-primed spontaneous imagination), thus focusing spontaneous imagination on the category of interest.

Figure 12.1 This chimpanzee is using a stick to get food from a tree.

12.2 Animal signs and vocalizations

All human languages are optimized for synthesizing novel images in the mind of a listener. PFS allows the speaker to synthesize an infinite number of images in the mind of a listener using a limited number of words: "a dog ate a cat," "a cat ate a dog," "a cat was eaten by a dog," "a cat was not eaten by a dog," "a cat was not uneaten by a dog," and so on. Since animals are known to use signs and vocalizations in the wild, let us see how these communication systems compare to human recursive language. Do animal communication systems have flexible syntax, prepositions or any other elements that facilitate *high fidelity transmission* of an *infinite* number of *novel* images with the use of a *finite* number of words?

Bees. Many species of bees use dance to communicate the direction and distance to a food source. Karl von Frisch correlated the runs and turns of the dance to the distance and direction of the food source from the hive. The orientation of the dance correlates to the relative position of the sun to the food source, and the length of the waggle portion of the run is correlated to the distance from the hive. Karl von Frisch was awarded the Nobel Prize in Medicine in 1973 for his study of the language and dialects of bees.

Birds. Bird songs play a role in mating as well as identification of the singing bird. Experiments suggest that the quality of a bird's singing may be a good indicator of the bird's health as diseases can degrade song quality. Individual birds may be sensitive enough to identify each other through their calls.

Whales. Two groups of whales, the Humpback whale and

the Blue whale, produce repetitive sounds at varying frequencies known as whale songs. Humpbacks make a sound called the feeding call (10 second long sounds of near constant frequency). Since Humpbacks generally feed in groups, it is likely that feeding calls help whales assemble into groups. Male Humpbacks are also known to perform songs during the mating season, probably for attracting a mating partner.

Dolphins. Dolphins emit two very distinct kinds of acoustic signals, which are called whistles and clicks. There is strong evidence that some specific whistles, called signature whistles, are used by dolphins to identify and call each other, just like humans call each other by name. In one study, researchers played signature whistles of animals within the group and also played other whistles in their repertoire as well as signature whistles of different groups. Individual dolphins only responded to their own calls, by sounding their whistle back. Dolphins develop their own unique signature-whistle early on in life. It was documented that dolphins both generate other dolphins' signature whistles as well as their own, and remember signature whistles for their entire lifetime.

Vervet Monkeys. The Vervet monkeys of East Africa sound different warnings for different threats: a leopard warning that sends the monkeys climbing into trees, an eagle warning that makes them hide under bushes, a snake warning that makes them stand on their hind legs, and a baboon warning that sends them rushing to treed areas. Recently, Dorothy Cheney and Robert Seyfarth, conducting research at the Amboseli Reserve in Kenya, identified even more predator-specific alarm calls for small carnivores, and unfamiliar humans.

Figure 12.2 Vervet monkeys of East Africa

Chimpanzees. Chimpanzees in the wild use over 30 vocalizations and signs. Here are some signs described by Jane Goodall, who has studied chimpanzees in the wild for over 45 years:

- Enjoying social interaction: Soft grunt
- Enjoying food: "Aaaaaa"
- Enjoyment of body contact: Lip smack
- Excitement: Pant - hoot
- Puzzlement: "Huuuu"
- Annoyance: Soft bark
- Distress: "Hoooo"
- Anger: "Waa" - bark
- Fear: "Wraaa"
- If one chimpanzee sees a snake, it makes a low, rumbling noise, signaling to all the other chimpanzees to climb into nearby trees.

- When a food source is located, the chimps can vocalize with loud calls to inform other chimps that food has been found.
- When seeing a leopard, chimpanzees give loud alarm calls described as 'waa barks.'

These are just a few examples of animals in the wild using signs and acoustic calls to communicate information. These examples indicate that the communicated information is limited to a description of feelings, a few danger codes, and, in the case of bees, information about distance to the food source. The limited scope and lack of recursive elements (such as spatial prepositions) in animal communications highlight the difference between the animal and human communication systems.

Like any other trait, animal communication skills were acquired to enhance their chance of survival. For example, a low, rumbling noise produced by a chimpanzee when it sees a snake (a snake call) increases the chimpanzees' chance of survival by allowing the group to quickly climb nearby trees where they are safe from the snake. A reasonable question to ask is: why is chimpanzee vocabulary limited to just a few danger codes? For example, if one chimpanzee could explain to other chimpanzees the direction from which a snake is approaching, that would clearly increase the group's chance of survival. Instead of running in all directions, chimpanzees could run in the direction away from the snake. Suppose that in addition to specific predator calls (for a leopard, a snake, or a lion), chimpanzees also possessed signs that described objects in their environment: "tall tree," "short tree," "green tree," "tree with big leaves," "big stone," "white stone," "river," etc. Now suppose that a snake is approaching from the direction of the tall tree near the big stone. One of the chimpanzees detects the snake and warns the group with a call: "a snake — the tall tree — the big stone" ("a snake [is approaching from the direction of] the tall tree [near] the big stone"). That call would only make sense if the chimpanzees hearing the call were able to imagine a snake near the tall tree near the big stone, and then match the mental image to the environment in order to understand the location of the snake. However, imagining such an image requires neural machinery for PFS. Animals can associate words with objects, feelings and actions and recall those based on a call or a sign. Humans, on the other hand, can use PFS to combine objects together into a novel scene following the rules specified in a recursive sentence.

Stephen Anderson, a linguist at Yale University arrived at a similar conclusion:

> What gives human language its power and its centrality in our lives is its capacity to articulate a range of novel expressions, thoughts, and ideas, bounded only by imagination. In our native language, you and I can produce and understand sentences we have never encountered before. Human languages have the property of including such a potentially infinite number of distinct sentences with discrete meanings because they are organized in a hierarchical and recursive fashion. Words are not just strung out one after another. Rather, they are organized into phrases, which themselves can be constituents of larger phrases, and so on - in principle, without any limit. ... What gives us the power to talk about an unlimited range of things even though we only know a fixed set of words at any one time, is our capacity for putting those words together into larger structures, the meanings of which are a function of both the meaning of the individual words and the way the words are put together. Thus we can make up new expressions of arbitrary complexity (such as the preceding sentence!) by putting together known pieces in regular ways. Furthermore, the system of combination is recursive. What that means is that language users only need to know how to construct a limited number of different kinds of structures,

because those structures can be used repeatedly as building blocks. Recursion enables speakers to build linguistic entities of unlimited complexity from a few basic patterns. Among animals in the wild, there is simply no evidence that their communication incorporates any of these structures. Instead, communication is limited to a rather small, fixed set of "words." Vervet monkeys, for instance, distinguish among a small number of different predators (eagle, leopard and snake) and warn their fellow monkeys with a few distinct calls of alarm. Some groups have even adapted certain calls to announce something like "unfamiliar human coming"; others have developed a call for warning of dogs accompanying human hunters. Impressive as those behaviors may be, such an augmentation of the call system happened slowly, and the system itself remains limited. What's more, vervets have no way of saying anything about "the leopard that almost sneaked up on us yesterday."[426]

Animal communication systems are effective for warning, attracting attention, and describing some feelings, but, unlike human languages, they lack recursive elements essential for transmission of an infinite number of *novel* images from a speaker's mind to a listener's mind.

12.3 Can animals be taught a human language?

The most intriguing studies of animal linguistic capabilities come not from observing animals in the wild, but from attempting to teach various species to communicate via a set of signs (i.e. sign language or lexigrams).

Parrots. Parrots are famous for their ability to mimic human language. I am always reminded of this fact when visiting Manhattan where I usually stay with friends who own an African Grey Parrot named Kaipo. Kaipo likes ice cream and apples. Whenever he feels like eating dessert, Kaipo loudly and clearly says, "Kaipo wants ice cream" or "Kaipo wants an apple."

Another African Grey Parrot, Alex (acronym for Avian Learning EXperiment), learned about 150 words and was able to answer a number of simple questions about objects. Trained by animal psychologist Irene Pepperberg, Alex appeared to have an understanding of what he said. For example, Alex could identify fifty different objects, was able to distinguish seven colors and five shapes, and several materials (wood, plastic, metal and paper). He also understood the concepts of "bigger," "smaller," "same," and "different." When Alex was asked about the difference between two objects, he was able to answer correctly. When there was no difference between two objects, Alex said "none." Alex was also able to recognize quantities up to six. In 2005, Dr. Pepperberg reported that Alex understood the concept of zero.

When Alex was tired of being tested, he would say "I'm wanna go back," and if the researcher displayed annoyance, Alex tried to defuse it with the phrase, "I'm sorry." If he said, "wanna banana" but was offered a nut instead, he stared in silence, asked for the banana again, or took the nut and threw it at the researcher.

Chimpanzees. The vocal apparatus of non-human primates is very primitive. For that reason, the number of different vocalizations is greatly limited. For example, the chimpanzee Vicki, who was raised from infancy in the household of two psychologists and subjected to rigorous training aimed at getting her to speak English words, was hardly able to whisper four words (up, cup, mama, and papa) even after years of training. To circumvent the problem of limited vocalizations, sign language and lexigrams (symbols that represent words) are used to teach language to primates.

Project Washoe. Washoe was the first chimpanzee to learn American Sign Language and she could reliably use about

250 signs. Washoe also displayed the ability to combine signs in novel and meaningful ways. For example, she referred to the refrigerator as "open food drink," even though the scientists always called it a "cold box."

Alan and Beatrix Gardner used conditioning to teach Washoe sign language. After several years, Washoe could learn new sign language gestures without conditioning, simply by observing humans signing amongst themselves. For example, the scientists signed "toothbrush" to each other while they brushed their teeth near Washoe. On a later occasion, Washoe reacted to the sight of a toothbrush by spontaneously producing the correct sign, thereby showing that she had in fact learned the sign from observation.

Clearly some animals can be taught a great number of signs. They can use those signs to express their desires and to interpret human commands. The next logical question is whether an animal taught a great number of words develops the capacity for PFS.

12.4 Do animals taught a human-like communication system develop the capacity for prefrontal synthesis?

Project Nim. Project Nim was an attempt to go further than Project Washoe. Dr. Herbert S. Terrace led a study at Columbia University of a chimpanzee whom he named Nim Chimpsky, a play on Dr. Noam Chomsky, the foremost theorist of human language structure and grammar. Project Nim was conceived as a challenge to Chomsky's thesis that only humans can grasp a complex language. From birth, Nim lived with his human family and learned about 125 signs from American Sign Language. He was able to "say" short sentences like "Yogurt Nim eat," "Play me Nim," and "Tickle me Nim." After many years of training, Dr. Terrace concluded that Nim hadn't acquired "real language." Terrace also reviewed the reports of other researchers trying to teach chimpanzees human language and concluded the same thing: apes are not able to come up with complex sentences [8].[xx]

Koko: A Talking Gorilla. Koko was a lowland gorilla. She had been trained in American Sign Language (ASL) since the age of one by Dr. Francine Patterson [9]. By the time Koko was 10, Dr. Patterson had assessed Koko's vocabulary at over 1,000 signs, which places her among the most proficient non-human users of language. She also understood approximately 2,000 words of spoken English. According to Patterson's account, Koko had "really learned" sign language, using it the way humans do: swearing, using metaphors, telling jokes, and making puns. Dr. Patterson has even documented Koko inventing new signs that were never taught to her. For example, Koko combined the words "finger" and "bracelet" to describe a ring, invented "drink-fruit" to describe a melon, and invented "water-bird" to describe a swan. In August 2004, Koko communicated that she had a toothache. Several documentaries have been made about Koko, including "Koko: A Talking Gorilla" (1977).

Unfortunately, I must agree with Stephen Anderson who notes, "we have nothing but Patterson's word for any of that. She says she has kept systematic records, but no one else has been able to study them. And without a way to assess Koko's behavior independently, the project is the best illustration imaginable of the adage that "the plural of 'anecdote' is not 'data.'"

[xx] It is important to note that Dr. Terrace originally set out to disprove Chomsky's thesis. He believed that through exposure to a suitable communication system, such as ASL, chimpanzees would acquire the full human language. By the end of the experiment, Dr. Terrace has reversed his mind [8].

The information obtained about Koko from publicly available sources does not inspire great confidence. Here is dialogue from a NOVA program filmed when Koko was about ten years old: (Translations for Koko's and Patterson's signing are presented in capital letters.)

KOKO: YOU KOKO. LOVE DO KNEE YOU
PATTERSON: KOKO LOVE WHAT?
KOKO: LOVE THERE CHASE KNEE DO
OBSERVER: The tree, she, wants to play in it!
PATTERSON: No, the girl behind the tree!

Stephen Anderson concludes from this dialog that "Patterson's interpretation, that Koko wanted to chase the girl behind the tree, is not self-evident, to say the least."

Bonobo Kanzi. One of the most interesting studies of an ape's linguistic abilities was conducted by primatologist Dr. Sue Savage-Rumbaugh and her colleagues from the Georgia State University's Language Research Center [10]. Dr. Savage-Rumbaugh taught Kanzi, a male bonobo, an artificial symbolic system based on associations between meanings and arbitrary graphic designs called lexigrams. To "say a word" Kanzi was expected to press the keys corresponding to that word. Stephen Anderson explains:

> In his subsequent training, the keyboard was carried around, and the trainers would press lexigrams as they spoke in English about what they and the animals were doing. While tickling Kanzi, the teacher said, "Liz is tickling Kanzi," and pressed the three keyboard keys LIZ TICKLE KANZI. Kanzi himself used the keyboard to freely express objects he wanted, places he wanted to go and things he wanted to do. ... By the time he was about four years old, Kanzi had roughly forty-four lexigrams in his productive vocabulary and he could recognize the corresponding spoken English words. He performed almost flawlessly on double-blind tests that required him to

match pictures, lexigrams, and spoken words. He also used his lexigrams in ways that clearly showed an extension from an initial, highly specific reference to a more generalized one. COKE, for instance, came to be used for all dark liquids, and BREAD for all kinds of bread-including taco shells. [426]

By the age of ten, Kanzi had a good handle on several hundred words. Kanzi had no problem following simple commands such as: "put the ball on the pine needles," "put the ice water in the potty," "give the lighter to Rose," and "take the ball outdoors." Furthermore many of the actions requested (squeezing hot dogs, washing the TV) were entirely novel, so Kanzi could not succeed simply by doing what one normally does with the object named. Even more striking is the fact that Kanzi was able to arrange stuffed animals in the position requested by the caretaker. The request "make the doggie bite the snake" and "make the snake bite the doggie" resulted in a different arrangement of the stuffed animals. It appears that Kanzi could understand the difference between the two sentences despite the fact that they use identical words and only differ in the word order. Understanding the difference in word order is equivalent to understanding syntax. Therefore, Patricia Greenfield, a linguist from UCLA who analyzed the Savage-Rumbaugh data, concluded that Kanzi had acquired an understanding of the syntactic structure of multiword combinations.

Stephen Anderson, however, remains unconvinced. He points out that Kanzi has poor understanding of the difference between *in*, *on*, and *next to*, as well as between conjunctions such as *and*, *that*, and *which*. Dr. Savage-Rumbaugh, in turn, complains that linguists keep raising the bar:

> First the linguists said we had to get our animals to use signs in a symbolic way if we wanted to say they learned language. OK, we did that, and then they said "No that's not language,

because you don't have syntax." So we proved our apes could produce some combinations of signs, but the linguists said that wasn't enough syntax, or the right syntax. They'll never agree that we've done enough.

What is going on between linguists and primatologists? Why can't they agree on a set of rules that define a "human language"? Can Kanzi understand syntax or can't he? Let's explore these questions a bit deeper.

Formally, we have to agree with Patricia Greenfield. Kanzi understood the difference between "Make the doggie bite the snake" and "Make the snake bite the doggie" and since the only difference between those sentences is the word order, Kanzi must have understood syntax. However, if you dig deeper, you will see that Kanzi's understanding of syntax may be limited to the understanding of a rigid word order. In both sentences, "Make the doggie bite the snake" and "Make the snake bite the doggie," the first noun names the biter. Kanzi can use that information to correctly build the scenery by linearly processing the rigid syntax: "Make the doggie bite the snake." In the first mental frame Kanzi recalls the doggie and picks up the stuffed doggie. The first noun is always the biter, therefore Kanzi opens the doggie's mouth. The doggie is placed on the sofa with its mouth open. In the second mental frame Kanzi recalls the snake, picks up the stuffed animal and places it on the sofa next to the stuffed doggie. Kanzi does not need to use PFS to integrate the doggy and the snake in his mind. The integration of the doggie and the snake has occurred on the sofa, after the stuffed animals were placed next to each other. Therefore, understanding of sentences with fixed word order is a poor indicator of the grasp of syntax, and thus of PFS.

Similar logic applies to Kanzi's processing of novel requests such as "put the ball on the pine needles," "put the ice water in the potty," "give the lighter to Rose," and "take the ball outdoors." All these requests can be processed linearly by recalling word-object associations from memory: "take the ball outdoors". Kanzi does not need to mentally synthesize the "ball" and "outdoors" in one mental frame. Rather, Kanzi can process "take the ball" in one mental frame (Kanzi finds the ball) and "outside" in another mental frame (Kanzi goes outside). These experiments simply do not prove that Kanzi synthesized any novel mental images. Therefore we have to agree with Stephen Anderson and Herbert S. Terrace who concluded that none of the apes were ever able to grasp a complex human language. As primatologist Mark Hauser notes: "It seems relatively clear, after nearly a century of intensive research on animal communication, that no species other than humans has a comparable capacity to recombine meaningful units into an unlimited variety of larger structures, each differing systematically in meaning" [128].

12.5 Storytelling

Humans are prolific storytellers. Whenever we meet other people we are eager to tell them a story, an anecdote, our impression of the latest movie or some gossip about a mutual friend. Parents stimulate PFS acquisition in children with conversations and reading them fairy tales. Have you noticed that most fairy tales are cruel and brutal?

In "The Three Little Pigs", the pigs cook the wolf in the cauldron alive: "...Then the wolf ... declared he would eat up the little pig, and that he would get down the chimney after him. When the little pig saw what he was about, he hung on the pot full of water, and made up a blazing fire, and, just as the wolf was coming down, took off the cover, and in fell the wolf; so the little pig put on the cover again in an instant, boiled him up, and ate him for supper... My son Benny cried in his sleep after listening to "three pigs" the night before as he was afraid that our house would be blown away by the wind.

In "The Wolf and the Seven Young Goats:" the wolf eats the goats. The mother goat cuts open the wolf's belly and the six children spring out miraculously unharmed. What does she do? She fills the wolf's belly with rocks, and the mother sews it back up again. When the wolf wakes up, he is very thirsty. He goes to the river to drink, but falls in and drowns under the weight of the rocks.

In "Hansel and Gretel" the stepmother decides to take the children into the woods and leave them there to fend for themselves, so that she and her husband do not starve to death. Then the witch lures children to eat her house of candy so that she can then eat them.

In "Cinderella", the sisters are punished for their deception by having their eyes pecked out by birds.

When children turn 5, we start reading them Greek myths, that are even more cruel and evolved. The Minotaur with the head and tail of a bull and the body of a man lives at the center of the Labyrinth, which was built on the command of King Minos of Crete, so that the Minotaur cannot escape. Why so much cruelty? Because the Minotaur is his son. Pasiphaë, Minos's wife, fell deeply in love with the bull. They mated. The offspring was the monstrous Minotaur. Pasiphaë nursed him, but he grew and became ferocious, being the unnatural offspring of a woman and a beast; he had no natural source of nourishment and thus devoured humans for sustenance. Minos, after getting advice from the oracle at Delphi, had Daedalus construct a gigantic labyrinth to hold the Minotaur. Its location was near Minos' palace in Knossos. Minos required that seven Athenian youths and seven maidens, drawn by lots, be sent every seventh year to be devoured by the Minotaur.

Why parents read their children cruel and brutal fairy tales and myths? To stimulate their PFS. It is not enough to provide children with tools to exercise their brain (recursive language). It is essential to make children exercise their PFS by clearly imagining novel scenes in their mind.

What is the best way to accomplish this? Apparently, the solutions that our civilization has found is to involve children's emotional brain (the ventromedial prefrontal cortex); make the newly created scenes emotionally relevant with cruelty and brutality (at the expense of making children cry and lose sleep).

Developing PFS in children was always the goal of tribe leaders. Without PFS, people could not hunt effectively or use stratagem to fight an enemy tribe. Thus, it would be chieftains and priests whose task would be to flurry children's imagination in order to set in place synchronous frontoposterior connections.

Animals, as far as it is known, do not tell stories to each other. Even animals that have been taught hundreds of words have never been observed conversing with their offsprings, parents, or other conspecifics familiar with the communication system, nor do these trained animals normally entertain their caregivers with a story.

12.6 Active teaching

Unlike humans who commonly use mental simulation for teaching other humans, animals mainly learn from each other through observation and mimicking. To discuss this question, let's first establish that animals can learn through observation and then turn our attention to the relationship between a teacher and a pupil in the animal kingdom.

One classic example of animals learning through observation occurred between the macaques on Koshima Island in Japan [427]. In 1952, scientists began feeding sweet potatoes to the monkeys while observing their social behavior. The potatoes were cut into pieces and tossed on the ground. Monkeys, who understandably do not like to eat sand, used their hands to rub the sand off the potatoes. One day, a juvenile female named Imo took her sandy potatoes to the water's edge and washed them clean. By 1958, potato washing had been adopted by 14 of 15 juveniles and 2 of 11 adults. The original washing monkeys have all since died, but the macaques at Koshima Island continue to wash potatoes to this very day. Since the behavior was transmitted through observation rather than genetics, Lee Dugatkin concluded that it was a result of cultural transmission.

Another example of animals learning from each other through observation occurred amongst a group of wild dolphins living along the south Australian coast near Adelaide. In the 1980s, Billie, one of the females in the group, spent a few weeks in a dolphinarium recovering from an illness, a consequence of having been trapped in a marina lock. Billie received no training while at the dolphinarium, but may have observed other (trained) dolphins tail-walking during her stay. After Billie was returned to the wild, she along with other females in her group picked up the tail-walking behavior. Since tail-walking is rarely seen in the wild, the obvious conclusion is that Billie learned it from observing trained dolphins, and the rest of the wild pack learned it from Billie. "This indicates that they do learn from each other, which is not a surprise really, but it does also seem that they exhibit elements of what in humans we would call 'cultural' behavior. These are things that groups develop and are passed between individuals and that come to define those groups, such as language or dancing; and it would seem that among the Port River dolphins we may have an incipient tail-walking culture," concluded Dr. Bossley from the Whale and Dolphin Conservation Society, who studied the group of

Australian tail-walking dolphins (Whale and Dolphin Conservation Society, 2010).

Figure 12.3 Dolphins demonstrate tail-walking in a dolphinarium.

Animals are also able to transfer newly acquired knowledge in a controlled environment. A team headed by Victoria Horner at the Yerkes National Primate Research Center, created an experiment to test how chimpanzees learn different techniques by observing other members of their community [428]. The researchers created a box that could be opened either by sliding the door or by lifting it. The team then trained one chimp to get fruit from the box by sliding the door and another chimp by lifting the door. Each animal showed their learned technique to another generation of chimpanzees, which, in turn demonstrated it to another generation, and so on. In total, a chain of six chimpanzees exclusively lifted the door to get fruit, and a chain of five chimpanzees exclusively slid the door to get fruit. The researchers concluded that cultural learning can determine the problem solving technique used by chimpanzees.

Having established that animals can learn from each other through observation, let's now turn to the second question and examine the relationship between the teacher and the pupil. At the core of the definition of teaching as proposed by Caro and Hauser are the following questions: Does the teacher adapt its behavior to the pupil's progress? Does the teacher slow down? In most cases, the answer seems to be "no." To date, studies have provided evidence of animal teachers adapting their behavior for the sake of their pupils in only three species [429]. Tandem-running ants that know the route to a food source modify their journeys when accompanied by a novice follower, allowing the follower to investigate landmarks en route, and continue the run only when tapped by the follower's antennae. Meerkats, small mammals from the mongoose family, use a form of teaching to help pups learn to handle difficult prey. Young meerkat pups are primarily given dead or disabled prey by older group members but are gradually introduced to live, intact prey as they grow older. In pied babblers, a group-living bird species, adults actively condition nestlings to associate a specific purr call with food by giving the call during feeding visits.

However, these three examples seem to be the exception rather than the rule and are perhaps a result of complex reflexes. A great deal of experimental data shows that animals normally do not modify their behavior for the sake of their pupils. Bennett Galef and colleagues investigated whether rat dams (mothers) would modify their food choices to teach their young which of two foods was safe to eat [430]. The scientists "examined food choices of rat dams trained to eat one of two foods that their young could access when the dams could also access a third, more palatable food that their pups could not reach. These dams spent no more time eating the safe food available to their young than did control dams ... providing no evidence of teaching by rat dams" [430].

Termite fishing is a common behavior among chimpanzees. It provides important nutrients at a time when other food sources are scarce. Acquisition of this behavior by the young, however, seems to be slow and inefficient. Youngsters require a prolonged learning period (i.e. 4-5 years) to gain proficiency in this technique [431] but chimp adults don't seem to slow down their actions for the sake of educating their youngsters in this technique. Rather, the young chimps learn by observing the adults. They first learn that they need a termite mound; then they learn that they need a stick. At first, they simply roll the stick over the mound; only later, do they learn to put the stick into the hole. At the beginning, they often have difficulty figuring out the correct size of the tool, trying to use a stick that is too thick. Clearly, the chimp learning method looks more like trial-and-error aided by observing adults. When the youngsters finally stumble upon the correct solution, they are able to remember the actions that brought them the yummy reward (termites).

In contrast, the human learning method usually involves PFS. We use language to first simulate the process in the mind of the students, and, only after this PFS exercise, are students invited to proceed on their own.

12.7 Animal art

Humans are prolific artists capable of producing hybrid objects such as lion-men, dragons, cyclopes, and centaurs. Let's take a look at what is known about the painting abilities of other animals.

Chimpanzees are inquisitive animals. When given an opportunity, captive great apes scribble with markers, paintbrushes, or with their fingers without any food reward. Their drawings include scribbles of lines, curves and loops. Chimpanzees familiar with drawing have begged for art supplies when they saw them in the possession of their caregivers and some have even complained vigorously when their painting-time was stopped or interrupted. There is no doubt about it: some chimpanzees love to paint! Spontaneous drawing by nonhuman primates may reflect an intrinsic interest in exploratory play. Similarly, elephants, particularly Asian elephants (*Elephas maximus*), also seem to possess an innate impulse to draw. Unprompted, an Asian elephant in captivity will often pick up a pebble or a stick with the tip of her trunk and casually doodle on the floor of her enclosure. Researchers, however, agree that both the great ape and elephant subjects remain at the scribbling stage and do not (naturally) progress to show figurative drawings. In fact, none of the animal subjects investigated by scientists moved to the figurative drawing stage on their own [432].

Figure 12.4 A dolphin painting at a sanctuary in Florida. There is a whole industry which trains animals to paint and then sells their drawings. In most cases, animals are provided with a brush or markers. Animals then apply several colors in strokes to the canvas. These drawings, however, are abstract and cannot be considered figurative art by any stretch of the imagination. For example, the chimpanzee Congo has been able to produce a number of paintings. A series of three paintings by Congo recently sold at auction for twelve thousand pounds (BBC News, June 20, 2005; You can watch a video of the chimpanzee Congo drawing here: http://www.youtube.com/watch?v=uvzGV3LnWIE). However even Congo was not as good with colors as his paintings might suggest. If left alone with the paints, he would mix them all together and then use that brown mixture to paint. To avoid that, he would be handed brushes, which had been preloaded with a particular color, one at a time. He would not be given the next colored brush until the previous color had dried up. Without such external pacing, Congo would not allow one color to dry before slapping on the next paint and the strokes would inevitably become a muddy mess. Desmond Morris, who worked with Congo, concluded that the chimpanzees he studied "never managed to produce a recognizable pictorial image" and that their paintings were "abstract compositions" (Daily Mail, 2009).

Figure 12.5 An example of a dolphin drawing.

However, perhaps animals can be *taught* to draw recognizable objects? During a recent trip to Thailand, a friend of mine was fascinated by the public performance of an elephant who used her trunk to paint a small elephant holding a rose. My friend was convinced that this particular elephant was a master artist.[yy] Unfortunately, I had to disappoint my friend and tell her

---

[yy] You can watch a video of an elephant performance here. Note the human handlers who are obviously aiding the elephants by holding their trunk or tusk: http://www.youtube.com/watch?v=Cy9kKxJJpug
http://www.youtube.com/watch?v=SsPb-Rep9Ds
http://www.youtube.com/watch?v=ajM-9OIu1Ow
http://www.youtube.com/watch?v=HXhhdkOc9Bo
Without a handler's assistance, the elephants only manage to paint abstract drawings as in the following videos:
http://www.youtube.com/watch?v=4KW5y7SmQq4
http://www.youtube.com/watch?v=RV4cDEH9RUo

that the elephant that she saw was a performance animal and not an artist. The elephant had spent her entire life training and then performing this specific routine for show. The elephant's repertoire would be limited to a single picture. Furthermore it takes years to train an elephant to paint just that one picture. It is therefore likely that the elephant is simply exhibiting the result of instrumental training (a variation of Pavlovian training) that has painstakingly engraved every little move of the performance into the elephant's muscle memory. In the same way that this elephant can memorize a complex routine in the circus, it can also memorize a complex set of movements with her trunk that result in a painting. A mouse can similarly be trained to run a maze in a predetermined sequence (Squire & Kandel, 2008). If a dripping paint box was then attached to the tail, the mouse would leave behind a footprint with a drawing of the predetermined design. However we will be hard pressed to find anyone who thinks that this procedure constitutes the normal process of painting a figurative image.

Even animals that grew up with humans and who were taught hundreds of words cannot draw more than a few random lines. Consider the male gorilla Michael who had a vocabulary of over 600 signs. Michael greatly enjoyed painting, and painted a number of drawings. Furthermore Michael often reported to his caregivers what he saw in these paintings. One painting in particular is cited as an indication that Michael was able to produce figurative drawings.

Michael used to own a pet dog called Apple. Apple and Michael often chased each other. Sometime after Apple's death, Michael drew a black and white painting that he called "Apple Chase."[zz] While the painting lacks any fragments with a shape

---

[zz] You can view "Apple Chase" and other paintings by gorilla Michael on this

(eyes, ears, nose, or mouth), it is still possible for a human observer to discern a dog in the painting. So, not only did Michael name the painting after his pet dog, but it was actually possible to see a dog in the painting. As you can imagine, this caused quite a sensation! Many people credited Michael with creating a figurative drawing. However, before jumping to the same conclusion ourselves, let's consider some comparisons between Michael and an average human child:

1. Sometime between the ages of three and four, most children develop the ability to make a figurative drawing. If you have ever witnessed this for yourself then you will know that as soon as a child is capable of drawing a recognizable object, the child will not stop. In fact, they will start to create a great number of different figurative pictures, often producing a dozen or more realistic looking animals in half an hour. Conversely, "Apple Chase" is the only one of Michael's drawings with a somewhat recognizable animal (or object). In all his other paintings, Michael seems to favor the abstract school of art.

2. In addition, once a child is capable of painting a figurative picture, he or she will include some details in the drawing. A picture of a person will often include a circular head with symmetrical eyes and legs, the so-called "head-feet representation" [433] (page 222). In contrast, *all* of Michael's paintings are completely abstract and definitely lack *any* recognizable details. Even "Apple Chase" lacks any discernible facial features.

After considering *all* of Michael's paintings and comparing them to the paintings of an average child, it is reasonable to conclude that Michael was not able to intentionally paint a figurative drawing. So, if Michael was not making a figurative

---

website: http://www.koko.org/world/art_portraits.html

drawing, then what is the explanation for "Apple Chase"? I would argue that "Apple Chase" was just a lucky combination of strokes that, once created, could be interpreted as a dog. Just like human observers, Michael could have simply recognized his pet dog Apple in the painting. Once he recognized the dog in the painting, Michael could have simply recalled playing chase with Apple, and then described his memory of chasing Apple when he called the drawing "Apple Chase." In other words, it is possible that once Michael had put a few strokes on paper, he was able to appreciate the image, recognize a familiar object and name that object to his caregivers. Though this is certainly sophisticated behavior, it does not require PFS.[aaa]

Michael Gazzaniga, a Professor of Psychology and the Director for the SAGE Center for the Study of Mind at the University of California Santa Barbara, sums it up quite elegantly:

... the creation of art is new to the world of animals. It is now

---

[aaa] Note that art appreciation has little to do with art production. Neurologically speaking, art appreciation is channeled through object recognition. Even in a completely abstract drawing one can often recognize a familiar object. The perceived object may trigger emotions that will be associated with the drawing. Thus art can be appreciated even in the complete absence of mental synthesis.

Can animals appreciate art? I don't see why not. Many animals are good at object recognition. Nothing precludes a dog from recognizing a cat in a drawing and then being emotional about that cat. It is likely that many animals can appreciate art in a similar fashion to humans.

In other words, art appreciation does not necessarily involve mental synthesis of new visual objects. Art appreciation can be entirely based on object recognition. Therefore art appreciation is completely irrelevant to the discussion of figurative art *production*. It is perfectly reasonable to assume that art can be appreciated by a creature that has no ability to produce figurative art.

being recognized that this uniquely human contribution is firmly based in our biology. We share some perceptual processing abilities with other animals, and therefore we may even share what we call aesthetic preferences. But something more is going on in the human brain — something that has allowed us to engage in pretense, as Alan Leslie suggests, some connectivity change that has allowed us to decouple the true from the imaginary. ... Our imaginative ability allowed one of us thousands of years ago to look at a wall of an empty cave in France and decide to spruce it up with a little fresco, another to tell the story of the odyssey of Ulysses, another to look at a chunk of marble and see David trapped inside, and another to look at a strip of bay-front property and envision the Sydney Opera House. [434]

So animals are not capable of drawing recognizable objects, in the normal sense of drawing, but how about simply *copying* a figurative picture? Can an animal copy a picture of a horse, a cow or even something as simple as a triangle without first going through a regiment of instrumental training? It looks like even this task is beyond the abilities of any animal. Tetsuro Matsuzawa has been studying the great apes at Kyoto University for over 30 years. The chimpanzees in Dr. Matsuzawa's research center have learned many fascinating skills including recognizing the numbers from 1 to 9 and arranging them in ascending or descending order, often faster and more accurately than humans [11]. However, these chimpanzees have not been able to learn how to copy any complex figure (Tetsuro Matsuzawa, personal communications). After multiple training sessions and only when given several attempts to redraw, the chimpanzees were able to copy a single line and draw it parallel to a given model line [432]. Just a single line! Copying anything as sophisticated as a triangle or a square seems to be beyond the chimpanzees' ability.

In summary, animals do not come close to humans in their ability to create figurative art. The fact that chimpanzees are able to copy a model line and that elephants can be trained to paint with their trunk indicates that it is not a lack of motor skills that inhibits animals' art expression, but rather it is a fundamental difference in the organization of their brain. Without PFS one can draw a line, an arc or a circle, but one is not able to organize several lines into a coherent figurative drawing.

12.8 Creativity and innovation

Human creativity and innovation are primarily the result of PFS. How often is machinery designed by trial-and-error? Instead of the inefficient trial-and-error process, humans commonly simulate the process mentally. This mental simulation has greatly facilitated creativity and innovation over the past 70 thousand years. Instead of roaming the savanna by foot like our ancestors, we drive cars and send robots to distant planets. Animals, on the other hand, are not known for their creativity. Tool use is uncommon, although primates, birds and even fish have been observed to use tools occasionally. For example, chimpanzees are well known to use tools to break nuts and hunt for termites. Chimps have to carefully prepare sticks used for termite fishing by trimming twigs. Younger chimps learn the craft by observing older chimps use the tools. Jane Goodall and other scientists reported an extensive list of over thirty types of tools used in the wild by chimpanzees [5,6,251].

Figure 12.6 A bonobo "fishing" for termites

Even birds and fish have been observed using tools. Green herons frequently lure fish by throwing an object into the water. Cichlid fish often use leaves to carry their eggs as in a baby carrier.

Tool use is conserved within a given population of chimpanzees [6]. Innovation is either lacking or extremely slow, indicating that tool use is likely being acquired through trial and error rather than through mental simulation. Chimpanzees in the wild have never been observed to intentionally flake a stone to *make* a tool [241].

12.9 Natural sciences

As early as the age of three or four, humans seek explanations and form hypotheses for unobservable forces. Do chimpanzees seek explanations for unobservable forces the way humans do? Daniel J. Povinelli and Sarah Dunphy-Lelii of University of Louisiana at Lafayette set out to investigate this very question. They write:

> Like other species, chimpanzees clearly learn about the observable features and propensities of the objects and entities they encounter. Given their perceptual and cognitive similarities to us, they might be expected to generate additional concepts related to perceptually nonobvious phenomena – concepts that could provide a unified account of why such regularities exist in the first place. However, in the absence of language, these concepts might be difficult to identify. The current studies were designed to present chimpanzees (and young children) with scenarios in which their efforts to complete a simple task (standing up wooden blocks) were unexpectedly frustrated (e.g., by presenting them with a [sham] block that could not stand)... In order to create the two different types of blocks, small lead weights were placed inside each block. In the case of the functional blocks, the weights were positioned over the long axes of the blocks so that they would easily stand in their inverted orientation; in the case of the sham block, the weight was positioned so that the block was unstable. We [researchers] sought to determine whether they [the chimpanzees] would engage in behaviours designed to explore the source of the problem. We reasoned that if the chimpanzee's general system for object exploration is modulated by a subsystem that seeks explanations for events, then they could be expected to attempt to diagnose the cause of unexpected events. [435]

The results of the experiments were rather striking. When functional and sham blocks were visually identical, 61% of the 3 to 5 year old children engaged in at least one form of inspection of the bottom of the sham block, and 50% engaged in both visual and tactile inspections. There was not one instance in which the apes (seven chimpanzees) performed either of the inspection tasks, nor were there any instances in which the apes unambiguously inspected the blocks by some other means (e.g., orally) [435]. All seven chimpanzees spent all the allotted time trying to get the sham block to stand up properly. Over and over again, the chimpanzees lifted the sham block and tried to stand it up without ever forming a theory of why the block kept falling down, and without even investigating the source of the problem! The researchers concluded that, "when there were no detectable perceptual differences between the sham blocks and the functional blocks, only the children inspected the sham blocks." Now you know why you've never seen a chimpanzee employed as a lab scientist: they don't seem to be able to form a visual model of something that they don't see!

12.10 Discussion of Part 5

The uniqueness of human imagination has been pondered by scientists and philosophers for ages. Ovid sets the imagination at the center of human uniqueness, as he deals with the Prometheus legend in Metamorphosis (Ovid, 8AD; interpretation by Gaylin W [436]). Lev Vygotsky, the renowned developmental psychologist, argues that "Imagination is a new formation that is not present in the consciousness of the very young child, is totally absent in animals, and represents a specifically human form of conscious activity" [437]. Karl Marx wrote in 1867: "A spider conducts operations that resemble those of a weaver, and a bee puts to shame many an architect in the construction of her cells. But what distinguishes the worst architect from the best of bees is this, that the architect raises his structure in imagination before he erects it in reality." Joseph Carroll, an English professor at the University of Missouri writes: "the modern human mind, alone among all minds in the animal kingdom ... is free to organize the elements of its perception in an infinitely diverse array of combinatorial possibilities" [438]. Michael Gazzaniga, a professor of psychology at the University of California writes: "... Our imaginative ability allowed one of us thousands of years ago to look at a wall of an empty cave in France and decide to spruce it up with a little fresco, another to tell the story of the odyssey of Ulysses, another to look at a chunk of marble and see *David* trapped inside, and another to look at a strip of bay-front property and envision the Sydney Opera House" [434]. Ian Tattersall, the eminent paleoanthropologist and curator at the American Museum of Natural History writes: "... if there is one single thing that distinguishes humans from other life-forms, living or extinct, it is the capacity for symbolic thought: the ability to generate complex mental symbols and to manipulate them into new combinations. This is the very foundation of imagination and creativity: of the unique ability of humans to create a world in the mind..." [139]. The insight of Lev Vygotsky, Ian Tattersall, Joseph Carroll, Michael Gazzaniga and many others has been born out of neuroscience. The uniqueness of human imagination is the ability to combine and recombine mental objects in the process of PFS. On the neurological level, this process is mediated by the lateral prefrontal cortex and its long frontoposterior connections, such as arcuate fasciculus.

Figure 12.7 The anthropomorphic belief that animals are capable of imagining the consequences of their actions was even stronger in the past. Until the eighteenth century in Europe, animals were put on trial when they violated the laws of men. Just like common criminals, they would be arrested, jailed, accused of wrongdoing and forced to stand trial. Offences alleged against them ranged from murder to criminal damage. The court would even appoint lawyers who would defend the animals at the trial. In addition, animals could be tortured for confession and if convicted, it was usual for an animal to be executed, or exiled. The earliest surviving record of an animal trial involves a pig that was executed in 1266 at Fontenay-aux-Roses. Because animals were treated as peers with humans in judicial proceedings, it was considered improper to consume any animal that had been capitally punished. Many different animals had their day in court: pigs, dogs, horses, and even bulls. Some animals were even believed to possess magic powers. In 1692 and 1693 twenty people were accused of witchcraft and executed in Salem, Massachusetts. Along with people two dogs were also sentenced to death: dogs were believed to possess and exercise witchcraft – quite a high mark for the dogs. This illustration from Chambers Book of Days depicts a sow and her piglets being tried for the murder of a child. The trial allegedly took place in 1457, the mother being found guilty and the piglets acquitted.

Part 5: Human Uniqueness

Book Conclusions

I quite agree that language evolved in a way that facilitates synthesis and transmission of the synthesized mental image. ... I don't think there can be much doubt, purely conceptually, that language was a late arrival. Whatever mutation provided the key to it would have had no selectional advantage at all, and would have just been a useless "organ," if it could not have linked up to pre-existing thought systems.

NOAM CHOMSKY, *Review of the 1st edition of this book* (2009)

The neurological mechanism of prefrontal synthesis: new hypothesis vs. established facts

This monograph presents a parsimonious theory of the evolution of the human mind and suggests experiments that could be done to test, refute, or validate the hypothesis. To propose this evolutionary theory, I focused on the question of the uniqueness of the human mind. I noticed that while there is continuity of most neurological functions amongst all primates, including the communicative function [355] and the ability to recall images from memory [439], there is a discontinuity between modern humans and all their ancestors in the ability to intentionally imagine *novel* objects. I called the process of juxtaposition of mental objects that have never been seen together into a novel image *prefrontal synthesis* (PFS) and have proposed the neurological mechanism for this process.

There is scientific consensus that previous experiences are encoded in the primate brain in the form of object-encoding neuronal ensembles (objectNEs). Enhanced connections between neurons in an objectNE enable the self-organization property of an ensemble and form the basis of memory. Synchronous re-activation of an objectNE during the process of memory recall recreates a conscious experience of an object or an event. To a large extent, the same neurons are activated during a conscious experience of physical objects and a conscious experience of imaginary objects [440]. During their lifetime, both humans and non-human primates accumulate conscious experiences that can be recalled from memory. However, humans have the unique ability to not only recall previous experiences, but also to construct new conscious experiences in the process of PFS. This allows humans to conduct mental simulation of their future behavior, before executing the behavior in the physical world. Once we, humans, acquired PFS 70,000 years ago, we dramatically changed our behavior; we invented animal traps, spear throwers, kiln-baked ceramics, figurative arts and religious mythology. Other primates remained limited in their reliance on reflex and memory to organize their behavior.

The basic gist of this proposal is hardly new. Numerous scientists and philosophers have noticed that humans are significantly more imaginative and creative than animals. These scientists and philosophers, however, spoke of the uniqueness of human imagination in purely phenomenological terms, not delving into the possible neurological mechanisms responsible for human uniqueness. In neuroscience circles, however, studying or even discussing *imagination* is much less popular. Owing to the subjective nature of the process, *imagination* is difficult to study in a precise way using neurological techniques. Researchers rarely enter a live human brain with electrodes except in special cases such as epilepsy treatment. The usual scientific backup — animal subjects — are ill-suited for studying the mechanism of a uniquely human phenomenon. With the invention of the functional MRI technique in the early 1990s, scientists gained the ability to peek inside the human brain noninvasively, but fMRI remains a crude method for studying imagination. Its low spatial and temporal resolution are not very useful for separating PFS from simple memory recall. Since both phenomena are mediated by overlapping cortical areas, fMRI is largely inept for revealing the neurological differences between the two phenomena. Furthermore the time resolution of fMRI is prohibitively low to study the effect of synchronization. As a result, PFS, simple memory recall and other components of mental imagery remained bound together under the title of imagination; PFS has never made a separate entry into the realm of neuroscience.

My path towards understanding the neurological mechanism of imagination started with reading literature describing the general neurological mechanism of a conscious experience. Over two decades ago, Francis Crick, Rodolfo Llinás and other scientists suggested that a *conscious experience* may be based on synchronous activation of neurons. While reading Francis Crick's *Astonishing hypothesis* (1995), I realized that while some neural systems can activate into synchronous activity spontaneously, others must be actively pushed into synchronization. The neurons of an objectNE are trained by the synchronously incoming sensory stimulation imposed by external physical objects. This sensory stimulation binds neurons of an ensemble into neural networks with enhanced synapses ready to activate into synchronous resonant activity that results in a conscious experience (either recognition or recall) of that familiar object. This hypothesis came to be known as the binding-by-synchronization hypothesis (reviewed by Singer [441]). I also realized that the infinite number of novel objects that humans can voluntarily imagine cannot jump into spontaneous synchronized activity on their own since the parts forming those novel images have never been seen together. It occurred to me that to account for voluntary imagination, the binding-by-synchronization hypothesis would need to be extended to include the phenomenon of PFS whereby the brain actively and intentionally synchronizes independent objectNEs into one morphed image. This PFS hypothesis allowed me to think of human imagination in neurological terms for the first time. Once I formulated the neurological mechanism of imagination and realized the uniqueness of this mechanism in humans, the evolutionary theory of the human mind fell into place.

ObjectNEs storing sensory memories are located in the posterior cortex (temporal, parietal and occipital lobes), while the temporal organization of behavior is a function of the frontal cortex. Single neuron recordings in monkeys (reviewed by Miyashita [150]) and functional brain imaging studies in humans (reviewed by Fuster [21]) demonstrated that memory recall is associated with activation of objectNEs in the posterior sensory cortex and is under the executive control of the prefrontal cortex (part of the frontal cortex located just behind one's forehead). I hypothesized that juxtaposition of mental objects is performed by the prefrontal cortex, which activates and synchronizes independent objectNEs *in-phase* with each other. When two or more independent objectNEs are activated to fire synchronously in one mental frame they are consciously experienced as one unified object or scene. In this process humans can intentionally manufacture an unlimited number of novel mental images and plan their future actions through mental simulation of the physical world.

The association of the prefrontal cortex with future planning is not new. Based on his research of patients with lesions in their prefrontal cortex, Aleksandr Luria wrote nearly forty years ago: "The role of prefrontal cortex in the synthesis of systems of stimuli and the creation of plan of action is manifested not only in relation to currently acting stimuli, but also in the formation of active behavior directed towards the future" [36]. In addition to studies of frontal patients, brain functional imaging studies of healthy subjects demonstrate the role of the prefrontal cortex in all tests that rely on PFS for future planning, complex mathematics, and reasoning tasks [21,152], but not in simpler tasks that do not involve PFS [442]. The PFS theory proposes a neurological mechanism with which the prefrontal cortex accomplishes future planning. The prefrontal cortex can be viewed as a puppeteer controlling its puppets (memories encoded in objectNEs stored in the posterior cortex). By pulling the strings that connect the puppeteer to its puppets, the prefrontal cortex activates and changes the firing phase of the objectNEs retrieved into working memory. Phase-synchronized objectNEs are consciously experienced as a novel whole object or scene. For example, to imagine something you have never seen before, such as your favorite cup on top of your computer's keyboard, your prefrontal cortex (1) activates the objectNE of the cup, (2) activates the objectNE of the keyboard, and then (3) synchronizes the two ensembles in time. In this process the prefrontal cortex relies on isochronous connections between the neurons of the prefrontal cortex and the neurons of the posterior sensory cortex. Without isochronous connections it would be impossible to synchronize the objectNE puppets located at varying physical distances from the puppeteer. I presented evidence that the isochronicity of the connections between the puppeteer and its puppets may be accomplished by experience-dependent differential myelination of those connections. Additional axonal isolation provided by multiple layers of the myelin sheath can dramatically increase conduction velocity and compensate for the uneven distance between the puppeteer and its puppets. The experience essential for training the isochronous connections is provided by using a recursive communication system during early childhood.

The dual origin of human language

Acquisition of language is commonly cited as the reason that humans dramatically changed their behavior around 70,000 years ago. The PFS theory concurs with that explanation. Language as we know it was acquired by hominins around 70,000 years ago. However, to this day, there is vigorous scientific discussion around the following two questions: what part of language was acquired 70,000 years ago and why was language acquired so abruptly [128]? Charles Darwin envisioned the origin of language simply as the acquisition of a mechanical ability to produce sounds, which provides the basis for a communication system. A modified version of that hypothesis claims that a culturally acquired communication system enabled language acquisition [420]. Opponents of the "nurture" hypothesis argue that human recursive language cannot be taught to animals and therefore humans must be unique in their genetic predisposition to language. Spearheading the "nature" hypothesis is Noam Chomsky who argues that a genetic mutation, which took place 70,000 years ago, enabled the innate faculty of language. Both parties agree that hominin behavior changed dramatically some 70,000 years ago, but the nurture party argues that a communication system was culturally acquired at that time, while the nature party argues that a genetic mutation predisposed humans to language acquisition. Neither hypothesis, however, adequately explains the dramatic and sudden change in human behavior: the appearance of figurative drawings and sculpture, unprecedented technological progress, and lightning-fast expansion of settlements to all habitable regions of the planet. It is relatively easy to imagine how a single mutation could have increased the brain volume by 10% or the number of synapses by 10% or the number of glial cells by 10% but it is unclear how that relatively small change in neurology could have resulted in such an abrupt change of behavior. If it was not a genetic mutation but solely the acquisition of a communication system that was acquired 70,000 years ago, then it is unclear why the communication system that had been developing for close to two million years (as evidenced by the developing speech apparatus) generated such a dramatic change in behavior 70,000 years ago but not earlier. My research led me to the conclusion that the nurture and nature theories are not mutually exclusive and that, in fact, both theories are correct. Sometime around 70,000 years ago, there was a genetic mutation that predisposed humans to the acquisition of PFS, the innate component of language, and there was a change from a non-recursive to a recursive communication system, which completed the giant step of language acquisition. Humans now possessed both components of language: a communication system complete with spatial prepositions and flexible syntax and the ability to synthesize words into an infinite number of novel mental images. Humans now possessed both components of language: a communication system complete with spatial prepositions and flexible syntax and the ability to synthesize words into an infinite number of novel mental images.

Until 70,000 years ago, the two components of language developed slowly and independently for several million years. Natural selection mandated that our ancestors should be in groups in order to survive. Cooperation was in high demand for the highly social and very adventurous *Homo erectus*, and it was aided by the verbal communication system, which improved in *Homo erectus* starting some two million years ago. The archeological [139] and genetic (FOX2P [186]) evidence unequivocally points to the fact that, as of 600,000 years ago, hominins had acquired a nearly modern speech apparatus. Noam Chomsky is absolutely right: the *Homo erectus* species that existed 600,000 years ago lacked the innate part of human language – the long critical period. Accordingly, the species lacked PFS and was thus unable to intentionally synthesize novel mental objects. Without PFS, *H. erectus* could not use flexible syntax, verb tenses or spatial prepositions. Their communication system was a non-recursive, finite communication system, similar to the communication system of chimpanzees, but with a larger vocabulary enabled by the nearly modern articulate vocal apparatus. Even in the absence of PFS, the large number of words provided a significant advantage for the mobile *Homo erectus* who was often relocating from one place to another. The recursive communication system acquired by humans 70,000 years ago grew out of this non-recursive communication system of *Homo erectus*.

Concurrently, another independent evolutionary force was preparing the hominin brain for acquisition of voluntary imagination. In their new habitat, hominins were continuously selected for their superior ability to recognize motionless, stalking predators partially obscured by the tall savanna grass. A hypothesis put forth in this book is that predator recognition in the savanna became significantly more difficult for hominins and that the selection of hominins capable of faster and better predator recognition became a major evolutionary force. While their chimpanzee-like ancestors were safe from most ground-dwelling predators in the treetop canopies, hominins venturing into the open savanna were exposed to many new predators including big cats, hyenas, and the now extinct sabertooths. Unable to fight off the bigger and faster predators, the four-foot-tall hominins had only one option for survival: long-distance recognition and scaring off the stalking, motionless predators. All primates, including humans, recognize motionless objects slower than moving objects [393,399]. For our tree-dwelling chimpanzee-like ancestors, fast recognition of motionless stalking felines was not such a big deal: to attack, a cat had to *move* itself toward a tree, making itself much easier to detect. However, when hominins moved away from the trees into the savannas, the situation reversed. Now the hominins were moving and the camouflaged predators could remain motionless and blend into the background. Recognition of stationary ambiguous visual stimuli is not a trivial matter. The hominin brain was rewired to facilitate the detection of motionless predators concealed by vegetation. As a result of these neurological changes, modern humans detect stationary visual targets an order of magnitude faster than chimpanzees [393] and integrate local elements significantly better than chimpanzees [396,397]. The prefrontal cortex plays an active role in the visual processing of ambiguous stimuli [295]. It is likely that the increased control by the prefrontal cortex of objectNEs in the posterior cortex resulting in an improved recognition of hidden, stalking predators began in australopiths and improved continuously over the next six million years of hominin evolution. Stone tools manufactured by hominins indicate that as of 3.3 million years ago, the hominin visual system was able to actively and intentionally control its percept. The prefrontal cortex of *Homo habilis* was able to voluntarily shift neurons representing flakes *out-of-phase* with the rest of the objectNE in order to reveal the mental template of a chopper inside. In the next 3 million years, predation further selected hominins for their ability to *analyze* the savanna scenery for the presence of motionless stalking predators concealed by vegetation. The improvement of stone tools followed the improvement of the visual system. Improving top-down control of the prefrontal cortex over its conscious percept allowed *Homo erectus* to detect "invisible" predators concealed by vegetation and to see an "invisible" handaxe inside a flint stone. Better predator detection and avoidance emboldened *Homo erectus* to become more adventurous as well as flexible in its direction of movement as evidenced by the species' diffusion out of Africa. As of 600,000 years ago, *Homo erectus* had a nearly modern speech apparatus and was able to intentionally control its perception by desynchronizing parts of existing objectNEs. However the species was not yet capable of synchronizing independent objectNEs into novel mental images; it was not capable of PFS. Two events separated *Homo erectus* from acquiring PFS and an infinite recursive communication system, one genetic and one cultural: a genetic mutation that would slow down maturation of the prefrontal cortex and the concurrent cultural acquisition of a recursive communication system.

Maturation of the prefrontal cortex in modern humans is delayed dramatically compared to chimpanzees and monkeys [372]. Overall, humans are born with a less mature brain [374] and develop 1.5 to 2 times slower than chimpanzees: molar teeth erupt three years later and humans become sexually active roughly five years after the chimps do [374]. However, the delay in synaptic maturation in the prefrontal cortex from a few months in chimpanzees and macaques to more than five years in humans [372] and the delay in axon myelination in the prefrontal cortex [373] are much more dramatic compared to this overall delay in maturation. The PFS theory connects a specific genetic mutation to language acquisition and describes the neurological mechanism affected by the mutation. I became convinced that the genetic mutation that triggered the dramatic delay of the maturation of the prefrontal cortex was the mutation, which triggered recursive language acquisition. This conviction was based on the following logic: on its own, without the simultaneous acquisition of a recursive language, the genetic mutation that caused this dramatic delay in the maturation schedule of the prefrontal cortex is deleterious and therefore highly unlikely to become "fixed" within a population. A recipient of this mutation would have had a significantly longer childhood when the brain was still immature and was incapable of fully assessing risk; such an individual was prone to early death as a consequence of its cognitive immaturity. This mutation becomes advantageous only with the concurrent acquisition of a recursive communication system, in which case the mutation would have aided in the ontogenetic development of isochronous connections between the prefrontal cortex and the posterior cortex. Extending the period of neuroplasticity would have provided the prefrontal cortex puppeteer extra time to fine-tune its voluntary control over the firing phase of the objectNE puppets located in the posterior sensory cortex. This fine control of the firing phase of the objectNEs is crucial for synchronization of those neural ensembles (remember that voluntary synchronization of independent objectNEs lies at the basis of humans' ability to synthesize any novel mental images in the process of PFS). The physical length of connections between the prefrontal cortex and the memory storage areas in the posterior cortex varies at least ten-fold. As discussed in Chapter 10.3, the development of isochronous connections to objectNEs located in the posterior cortex likely involves adjustment of the conduction velocity in individual fibers via experience-dependent differential myelination of those fibers. This experience is normally provided by recursive communications. Without early exposure to recursive communications, modern children do not acquire PFS (reviewed in Chapter 10.5). A non-recursive communication system (e.g. home-sign) is inadequate for ontogenetic acquisition of isochronous connections between the prefrontal cortex puppeteer and the objectNE puppets located in the posterior cortex. A modern child who is linguistically deprived during the critical period is unable to convert a finite non-recursive communication system (e.g. home-sign) into an infinite recursive communication system on his or her own. However, as has been seen in the case of deaf children in Nicaragua, it is possible for a group of children to spontaneously invent a recursive communication system [275,277]. It follows that a recursive communication system must have been invented by at least two children who were living together during their critical period of the prefrontal cortex maturation (The Romulus and Remus hypothesis). Once the two children (most likely siblings or twins) who were both carriers of the mutation that delayed the maturation of their prefrontal cortex, invented a few prepositions, they would have converted their tribe's non-recursive finite communication system into an infinite recursive communication system. With just a few spatial prepositions, their normal conversations with each other would have trained the isochronous connections between their prefrontal and posterior cortical areas, thus allowing them to attain PFS. A mutation that was deleterious in the absence of a recursive communication system became a highly advantageous mutation due to the simultaneous acquisition of a culturally transmitted recursive communication system and PFS. This mutation gave the prefrontal cortex puppeteer the time it needed to adjust the connections to its neuronal-ensemble puppets. This fine-control of the firing phase of objectNEs would allow for the ability to combine disparate images into novel, never-before-seen configurations: the foundation of what is called "imagination."

The PFS theory proposes that the two parts of language were propelled by unrelated evolutionary forces until about 70,000 years ago: the communication system developed independently of the prefrontal cortex' ever-increasing control of perception (future PFS); there was little synergy in their development. This separation explains why the process was so slow until 70,000 years ago. Neither slowly increasing top-down control of perception by the prefrontal cortex, nor the improving speech apparatus were enough on their own to trigger acquisition of either PFS and a recursive communication system. However, their combination was.

Increased top-down control of perception and improvements in speech accumulated a necessary critical mass and colluded 70,000 years ago to produce the uniquely human ability of PFS. Their synergistic combination can be compared to the effect of a spark on gunpowder. The finite, non-recursive communication system of *Homo erectus* was converted into an infinite, recursive language that we know today.

Once the recursive communication system was invented, it was transmitted culturally from generation to generation to train the ontogenetic acquisition of PFS in all developing children through establishment of isochronous connections between the prefrontal cortex and the posterior cortex. The nurture and nature components came together to enable a dramatic change in human behavior. Art, technology, and religious beliefs exploded over a very short period of time indicating that the acquisition of PFS along with a full recursive language was a revolutionary event. This event completely separated the pre-PFS hominins, who were animal-like creatures relying primarily on reflex and memory to organize their behavior, from the morphologically similar but behaviorally different breed of hominins who possessed a full recursive language and who relied on mental simulation to plan their behavior before executing it in the physical world. The acquisition of a recursive language resulted in what was now in essence a behaviorally new species: the first *behaviorally modern Homo sapiens*. This evolutionary synergy between speech and PFS resulted in a revolutionary change in the relationship between humans and nature. The newly acquired power for mental simulations led to dramatic improvement in hunting (with stratagem, projectiles, and animal traps); the human population exploded and humans quickly settled most habitable areas of the planet. The humans diffusing out of Africa 65,000 years ago were very much like us. They were now in possession of both components of human language: the culturally acquired recursive communication system along with the innate predisposition towards PFS. Armed with the ability to mentally simulate any plan and then to communicate it to their companions, humans were poised to become the dominant species.

A wish list of experiments

Dubito, ergo cogito, ergo sum
(I doubt, therefore I think, therefore I am)
After RENÉ DESCARTES, *Principles of Philosophy* (1644)

An important component of a theory is that it should be falsifiable. A theory must make predictions that were not used in the construction of the theory initially but are now available for inspection. If the predictions are borne out, the theory would be strengthened. If not, then the original theory ought to be modified or abandoned. During the development of the PFS theory, I had a major concern: how do I make a theory about mainly subjective phenomena (internal thoughts) falsifiable? In this chapter, I discuss some testable predictions from the theory and provide an accompanying "wish list" of experiments that could be done to refute or validate those predictions. This "wish list" of experiments is followed by a complete set of predictions that follow from the PFS theory.

1. The theory can be falsified by proving that animals can acquire prefrontal synthesis

The PFS theory predicts that humans are unique in their genetic predisposition to acquisition of PFS. Thus, the easiest way to falsify this theory is to prove that other primates are capable of acquiring PFS. For example, if an animal could learn to flexibly use spatial prepositions, such as "put a {cup|ball|stick|towel} {on|under|in front of|behind} a {sofa|chair|table}," this would indicate that the creature has mentally simulated the final structure by morphing independent objectNEs into a novel mental image in the process of PFS. Additional tests of PFS have been published in Ref. [37].

2. The theory predicts that prefrontal synthesis involves synchronization of independent objectNEs

The theory predicted that the mechanism of PFS involves synchronization of independent objectNEs. The lateral prefrontal cortex, acting as puppeteer, actively and intentionally synchronizes independent objectNEs, the puppets, into one mental frame. Once the two objectNEs are firing synchronously they are perceived as a single whole object. It may actually be possible to confirm the process of synchronization of the objectNEs with a single-cell recording technique. The experimental paradigm developed by Itzhak Fried and colleagues allows for the simultaneous recording from a multitude of very selective neurons [83,84,92]. The researchers were able to identify neurons selective to Bill Clinton, Jennifer Aniston, the Sydney Opera House, baseball, animals and many other animate and inanimate objects. These selective neurons fire at a high rate when a subject observes or recalls the object associated with that cell but does not fire when the subject is shown any other image [81,92]. For example, the neuron selective to Bill Clinton fires at a rate of over 30 action potentials per second only when the subject observes or recalls the image of Bill Clinton, independent of Bill Clinton's posture or position in the picture. The neuron does not fire when the subject is shown photographs of other people. To conduct the proposed experiment, two or more very selective neurons would be identified: for example, a neuron that is part of the Bill Clinton neuronal ensemble, and another neuron that is part of the objectNE of a lion. As in the Gabriel Kreiman experiment (2000), when the subject recalls Bill Clinton, the Clinton neuron is expected to fire at a high rate; when the subject recalls the lion, the lion neuron is expected to fire at a high rate. This proposed experiment, however, would aim to answer the following question: what happens when the subject imagines Bill Clinton holding the lion on his lap? If the PFS theory is correct, both the Clinton neuron and the lion neuron will increase their firing rate and their activity will be **synchronized** when the subject imagines Bill Clinton holding the lion on his lap.

At the end of the experiment, a picture of Bill Clinton holding a lion could be shown to the subject to test what happens when the subject sees Bill Clinton holding the lion on his lap. Again, both the Clinton neuron as well as the lion neuron are expected to increase their activity. In addition, their action potentials are expected to synchronize.

Since researchers can often identify several object-selective neurons in a subject, multiple novel pairing of objects can be studied. Furthermore, morphing of more than two objects into one mental frame can be investigated. For example, if researchers happen to identify selective neurons for Bill Clinton, the Sydney Opera house, and a lion, the subject can be asked to imagine Bill Clinton sitting next to the Sydney Opera house and holding the lion. In this case, all three neurons would be expected to fire synchronously. This paradigm also paves the way for many other interesting experiments studying the neuroscience of imagination. For example, what would happen on the neuronal level if: Bill Clinton was imagined as a monument rather than as a human being?; the lion was seen fighting Bill Clinton, rather than sitting on his lap?; the subject was to imagine the lion swallowing Bill Clinton?; etc.

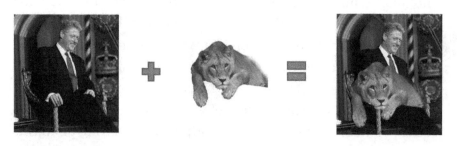

Figure E.1 PFS of Bill Clinton holding a lion. Once selective neurons for Bill Clinton and the lion are identified, the patient can be asked to imagine Bill Clinton holding the lion on his lap. The PFS theory predicts that both the Clinton neuron and the lion neuron will increase their firing rate and that their activity will be synchronized.

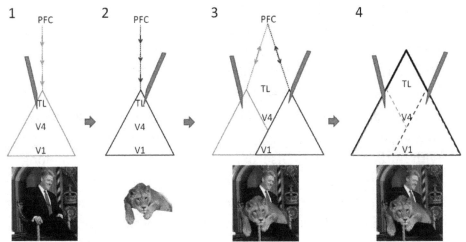

Figure E.2   On a neurological level, mentally forming the image of Bill Clinton and the lion consists of the following steps:

Step 1 - Recall of Bill Clinton: The prefrontal cortex (PFC) activates the ensemble of neurons representing Bill Clinton to fire synchronous actions potentials. Bill Clinton is perceived by the patient. The electrode implanted into the temporal lobe (TL) records an increased rate of action potentials.

Step 2 - Recall of the lion: The prefrontal cortex activates the ensemble of neurons representing the lion to fire synchronous actions potentials. The lion is perceived. The second electrode implanted into the temporal lobe records an increased rate of action potentials.

Step 3 - The patient mentally synthesizes the images of Bill Clinton and the lion. The prefrontal cortex synchronizes the two objectNEs in time.

Step 4 - When synchronization is achieved a new, never-before-seen mental image of Bill Clinton holding the lion on his lap is perceived. The two implanted electrodes record synchronous action potentials.

3. The prefrontal synthesis theory predictions for autism therapy

Children with autism often have difficulties in imaginative play, Theory of Mind, and playing out different scenarios in their minds. Therapists, researchers, and caregivers working with children exhibiting language comprehension problems, appreciate the challenges of PFS acquisition. Even when language therapy is administered daily, some children never build up their frontoposterior connections essential for PFS. Failure to acquire the PFS ability results in a lifelong inability to understand semantically-reversible sentences, spatial prepositions, recursion, and fairytales (that require the listener to imagine unrealistic situations). Among individuals diagnosed with Autism Spectrum Disorder (ASD), the prevalence of lifelong PFS paralysis is 30 to 40% [66] and can be as high as 60% among children enrolled into special ASD schools [37]. These individuals are frequently referred to as having low-functioning ASD. They usually exhibit full-scale IQ below 70 [163,443] and typically perform below the score of 85 in non-verbal IQ tests, see Ref. [163].

The PFS theory predicts that early focus on PFS exercises at the expense of vocabulary, memory, logic and other executive functions training can significantly improve the outcome [444]. Unlike PFS that has short and strong critical period, new vocabulary can be learned at any age. To test this hypothesis, we wrote a software application with PFS exercises disguised as games. We called it Mental Imagery Therapy for Autism or MITA. The games automatically adjust to each child's ability, increasing in difficulty as the child gains skill. And none of the games repeat—ever! So, there's no chance for a child to simply memorize the correct answer. Every minute is spent "flexing" the mind's eye.

We made MITA available to parents free of charge on the condition that they complete an evaluation every three months to let us know how their child is doing. In 2015, we launched a three-year study of the language therapy embodied in the app. 6,454 children between the ages of two and twelve completed our study. It became the largest and the longest study of language intervention in autistic children [15]. At the end of the three-year period, the children who regularly completed MITA exercises scored 120 percent higher on the language test than the children with matching initial scores who did not!

4. The prefrontal synthesis theory predicts far greater variation of myelination of cortical connections in humans than in other primates

Despite the three-fold difference in brain volume, the structure of the human brain is not very different from that of a chimpanzee. In fact, for all practical purposes, the human brain looks like a scaled up version of the chimpanzee brain; despite decades of research, no new cortical areas or unique connections have been reported. Even the language-specific Broca's and Wernicke's areas have been homologized morphologically and functionally to non-human primates (Ref. [355]; also discussed in Figure: 10.7 Evolution of Broca's area and Wernicke's area). The homologue of the left lateralized Broca's area in chimpanzees is involved in intentional communicative gestures and vocal signals [358]. The homologue of Wernicke's area in the left and right hemispheres has been demonstrated to be involved in the processing of conspecific vocalizations in macaques [359] and chimpanzees [358].

The morphological and functional continuity between humans and other great apes on the neurological level contrasts sharply with behavioral discontinuity. The PFS theory explains this conundrum by arguing that the behavioral discontinuity comes from acquisition of PFS. Neurologically, PFS is based on isochronous neural connections between the prefrontal cortex and the posterior sensory cortex. Isochronous neural networks, in turn, are developed during ontogenesis primarily as a result of differential myelination of those connections. Thus, the major difference between humans and great apes is probably not in the structure or organization of the brain, but rather in the

413

degree of differential myelination. Investigation of such differences is much more difficult but nevertheless possible. Electron microscopy allows direct observation as well as the counting of myelin layers in brain slices. A comparison of myelination maps between the human brain and the chimpanzee brain may be most useful for uncovering the secret of human uniqueness. The PFS theory predicts that there is a significantly greater amount of differential myelination in the human brain.

5. Detection of partially concealed predators

Humans are better than chimpanzees at integration of multiple local visual features [396,397] and faster at searching for stationary visual items [393]. The PFS theory explains these findings by hypothesizing that during the six million years of evolution in the savanna, our forebears were evolutionarily selected for their ability to better detect partially concealed motionless predators: the human brain was tweaked to better detect a stalking leopard based on only a few, small visual cues: a leopard's tail or an ear perked up above the swaying grass of the savanna. An experiment similar to the one conducted by Coss RG [394] (in which macaques were shown to recognize models of leopards partially concealed by vegetation; discussed in Chapter 11.3) may be able to compare human detection of motionless predators to that of chimpanzees. A model of a stalking leopard of dark melanic color[bbb] can be hidden in thick vegetation at some distance from feeding stations. By observing the chimpanzees' reaction to the partially concealed model, the

---

[bbb] To avoid recognition of a leopard based solely on the skin coloration, a dark-colored, melanic model can be used (see Coss RG, 2005).

researchers can determine whether a chimpanzee can recognize an object based on minimal visual cues. If the chimpanzees show no reaction when only a small part of the tail is visible, then a greater portion of the tail could be revealed. If this does not result in recognition, then more (and more) of the model can be revealed until the leopard is recognized. It is predicted that naive chimpanzees (ones not specifically trained to recognize the tail) would not recognize a motionless leopard based on its tail alone, while most humans would be able to recognize the leopard. Similar experiments can be conducted with other small, visible body parts, such as the leopard's ears or back. I would expect humans to outperform chimpanzees on any and all variations of this 'leopard recognition task.'

It may be possible to conduct a simpler version of this experiment with computer-generated images. A chimpanzee can be trained to report the presence of a leopard on a computer screen. Following 100% recognition of the complete leopard image on the screen, the leopard image would be hidden behind a layer of virtual grass with only a small piece of a tail or an ear peaking out above. The PFS theory predicts that humans will outperform chimpanzees: they will not only be able to recognize a leopard faster, but also based on a smaller visual cue (the visible body part). The difference in performance between a human and a chimpanzee should decrease or disappear entirely when faced with detecting a *moving* leopard (based on the same small body part).

Another variation of the above experiment could test the human ability to perform mental rotation of visual targets. Since the partially concealed fragments of a predator's body could have presented themselves at any angle, the PFS theory would predict an improvement in a human's ability to perform mental rotation of visual targets for matching to those stored in memory. An experiment similar to that performed by Nielsen KJ

(2008) (discussed in Chapter 9.3 of this monograph) could compare humans and chimpanzees in their ability to recognize partially occluded objects presented from different views.

6. Dissociation of working memory and prefrontal synthesis

Working memory is defined as the system that actively holds multiple pieces of transitory information in the mind, where they can be manipulated. For example, you use working memory to remember a telephone number for as long as you visually imagine the written number or verbally repeat the number to yourself over and over again. In other words working memory is used to transiently store an internal representation of an object in the mind's eye. Joaquin M. Fuster aptly defined working memory as the "sustained attention focused on an internal representation" [21].

The neural basis of working memory has been primarily derived from lesion experiments and single-neuron recordings in animals. In a classical animal experiment testing the delayed response mediated by working memory, a monkey is shown how the experimenter places a bit of food under one of two identical looking cups. A shutter is then lowered for a variable delay period, screening off the cups from the monkey's view. After the delay, the shutter opens and the monkey is allowed to retrieve the food from under the correct cup. In this paradigm, the monkey has to remember which of the two cups is covering the food. The emerging consensus is that this feat is accomplished by the prefrontal cortex, as it continuously stimulates the objectNE of the cup located in the posterior cortex: the prefrontal cortex puppeteer holds the cup's objectNE puppet active during the delay period. In the 1930s, Jacobsen and Fulton first showed that lesions in the prefrontal cortex impaired monkeys' performance in working memory tasks. Joaquin M. Fuster later found neurons in the prefrontal cortex that fired mostly during the delay period, suggesting that they were involved in representing the food location while it was invisible [445]. Later research has shown similar delay-active neurons in the posterior cortex. These neurons are likely part of the objectNE puppet actively stored in working memory (reviewed by Ashby [446]). The central role of the prefrontal cortex in working memory tasks is also consistent with memory interference experiments. Disruption of delay-active neurons (using microelectrodes) in the prefrontal cortex in animals or temporary virtual lesions produced by transcranial magnetic stimulation of the prefrontal cortex in humans produces an impairment in the performance of tasks which involve working memory (reviewed by Mottaghy [447]).

The neural mechanisms of working memory have been elucidated primarily through animal studies. Non-human primates can hold "pieces of transitory information" in working memory for tens of seconds [21] but they do not manipulate those "pieces." Humans, however, in addition to holding objects in working memory can actively manipulate those objects. The theory presented in this monograph hypothesizes that the manipulation part primarily comes from the prefrontal cortex that not only activates but also shifts the phase of objectNE firing. Destructive interference in the process of prefrontal analysis shifts parts of the objectNE *out-of-phase* with the rest of the ensemble, which remains in working memory and is consciously perceived as the partial object. Constructive interference in the process of PFS shifts several objectNEs held in working memory *in-phase* with each other whereby they are perceived as a single whole object. Working memory is therefore an important component of both prefrontal analysis and PFS.

Attempts to dissociate working memory from PFS have been conducted in the past. The majority of these studies have used the Finke and Slayton "creative synthesis" paradigm, which involves presenting the subject with an array of verbally described shapes. For example, the shapes may be the capital letters J and D, and the subject would then be asked to combine them into as many objects as possible, with size being flexible. A suitable answer in this example would be: an umbrella (Finke and Slayton, 1988). The performance in this task is quantified by counting the number of legitimate patterns that participants construct using the presented shapes. A study conducted by Pearson DG and colleagues found that concurrent continuous tapping of a series of keys (spatial tapping) significantly reduces a subject's performance in the creative synthesis task [448]. In contrast, there was only a marginal effect of spatial tapping on a working memory task in which subjects had to recall the presented shapes.

While the dissociation of PFS and working memory using spatial tapping is encouraging, understanding the neurological mechanism of PFS allows conduction of a more precise set of experiments that may dissociate working memory from PFS both in terms of cortical localization and in terms of their temporal organization. Both PFS and working memory engage the lateral prefrontal cortex [21], but as discussed in Chapter 9.2, more complex PFS tasks tend to recruit the anterior lateral prefrontal cortex (the part of the lateral prefrontal cortex located right behind the forehead, also called the frontopolar cortex or Brodmann area 10). Thus, temporal suppression of area 10 with transcranial magnetic stimulation (TMS) may result in significant deterioration of performance in PFS tasks, but not in working memory tasks.

Furthermore, while both working memory and PFS rely on continuous activation of objectNEs by the prefrontal cortex, the theory predicts that only PFS involves precise manipulation of its firing phase. This observation can be exploited in an experiment that disrupts the ability of the prefrontal cortex to precisely control the timing of its neurons. For example, transcranial magnetic stimulation of the prefrontal cortex by weak randomly spaced pulses may differentially interfere with PFS but not with working memory.

An equally interesting experiment would involve temporary suppression of the cerebellum in order to prevent the prefrontal cortex from receiving the precise timing information.

7. Cloning of a Neanderthal

In January of 2013, George Church, a Professor of Genetics at Harvard Medical School, said in an interview with the German magazine "Der Spiegel" that it could be possible to clone a Neanderthal baby from ancient DNA if he could find a woman willing to act as a surrogate: "I have already managed to attract enough DNA from fossil bones to reconstruct the DNA of the human species largely extinct. Now I need an adventurous female human." While currently it is hard to imagine cloning of a Neanderthal for ethical reasons, history teaches us that eventually intellectual curiosity will win over and the Neanderthal will be cloned. How different will it be? George Church suggests, "Neanderthals might think differently than we do. We know that they had a larger cranial size. They could even be more intelligent than us."

Is it possible that the cloned Neanderthal will be more intelligent than us? Let us investigate. As was discussed in Chapter 6.3, the archeological record (lack of "grave goods," constructed dwellings, figurative art, complex tools, etc.) indicates that Neanderthals did not have the ability for PFS. Lack of PFS in Neanderthals can be explained by either a lack of the innate ability to acquire PFS (i.e. the lack of genetic mutations necessary for PFS) or by the lack of a culturally acquired recursive communication system (after all, PFS does not develop even in modern children deprived of exposure to normal recursive communication) or by the lack of both the genetic and the cultural components.

The PFS theory predicts that the genetic mutation, which dramatically delayed maturation of the prefrontal cortex (and enabled PFS), occurred concurrently with the acquisition of the infinite recursive communication system and resulted in the acquisition of PFS by the first generation of mutation carriers. It follows that the lack of PFS in Neanderthals is associated with the lack of both the genetic mutation as well as a culturally transmitted recursive communication system. There is little doubt that Neanderthals possessed a nearly modern speech apparatus. However their communication system was a finite non-recursive communication system that lacked prepositions, verb tenses and other elements of grammar that make our communication system infinite.

The previous discussion, however, concerns extinct Neanderthals. The question posed by George Church, on the other hand, concerns the cloned Neanderthal who would be reared by humans and exposed to a recursive communication system from birth. Will this child acquire PFS and full human language? The answer would depend on the duration of the critical period in the cloned Neanderthal. If the critical period is similar to that of a chimpanzee, then it is highly unlikely that the cloned child would be able to acquire much ability for PFS. However, if the critical period is similar to that of a modern human, then the child will acquire normal PFS and the hypothesis that Neanderthals lacked the "trigger" mutation would be incorrect. This would mean that the genetic mutation that caused the delay in the maturation of the prefrontal cortex was acquired earlier in hominid evolution than the recursive communication system. It would also imply that modern humans and Neanderthals shared the mutation that delays the maturation of the prefrontal cortex and that the only reason Neanderthals did not have PFS is because they did not invent a recursive language. I suspect however that the delay in maturation of the prefrontal cortex is somewhat longer in Neanderthals than in chimpanzees but still significantly shorter than in humans. Neanderthals likely did not have that "trigger" genetic mutation that dramatically slowed down maturation of the prefrontal cortex, but they had other mutations that delayed it somewhat compared to chimpanzees (after all, the volume of the Neanderthal brain was nearly four times greater than that of the chimpanzee; some delay of the prefrontal cortex maturation could have been a direct result of increase in brain volume). I predict that under purposeful linguistic training the cloned Neanderthal would acquire some PFS but probably less than a modern human. The cloned Neanderthal adult would likely not be able to keep up a conversation that relies heavily on PFS. In other words, you shouldn't expect to be able to discuss human evolution or nuclear physics with a Neanderthal. Contrary to George Church's proposition, the Neanderthal would likely be significantly less intelligent than the reader of this book. Furthermore the experiment with a cloned Neanderthal raised by modern humans and exposed to recursive communication from the time of birth still would not answer the main question concerning the cognitive level of extinct Neanderthals. As mentioned above, even if Neanderthals had acquired all the right mutations, but had not invented an infinite recursive communication system, they would have likely developed similarly to linguistically deprived children, acquiring no capability for PFS during ontogenesis.

8. Searching for the mutation that triggered acquisition of prefrontal synthesis

The PFS theory proposed that Neanderthals' prefrontal cortex developed faster; they did not possess the mutation which extended the critical period. Thus, a comparison of the Neanderthal genome to the modern human genome should reveal the genetic basis of PFS. In fact, Liu X and colleagues identified four transcription factors that could play a role in regulating the timing of the development of the prefrontal cortex: myocyte enhancer factor 2A (MEF2A), early growth response 1 (EGR1), early growth response 2 (EGR2) and early growth response 3 (EGR3) [372]. These four transcription factors have been previously shown to be involved in the regulation of neuronal functions [449]. Furthermore MEF2A is predicted to regulate the three EGR genes, as well as several other signal transduction genes [449]. Deleterious mutations of MEF2A were also observed in a significant number of individuals with severe mental retardation [450], which may be the result of mental-synthesis-disability. Mehmet Somel and colleagues concluded that MEF2A may have a master role in the regulation of the human-specific delay of the prefrontal cortex maturation [2]. Furthermore, there are indications that human-specific changes in the expression of MEF2A might have occurred after the human–Neanderthal split [2]. If confirmed, the mutation in MEF2A could be a candidate for the "trigger" mutation that triggered acquisition of PFS in humans.

9. Correlation between the age of maturation of the prefrontal cortex and propensity for prefrontal synthesis

The PFS theory argues that PFS is ontogenetically acquired via an experience-dependent mechanism limited in time by the duration of the period of plasticity of the prefrontal cortex. It follows that a significantly shortened period of plasticity may be associated with a reduced propensity for PFS in adulthood. Nature often experiments with genetic mutations. Modern humans who have a significantly shortened period of maturation of the prefrontal cortex may be investigated to study the correlation between the duration of the period of plasticity and PFS ability in adulthood. As was discussed in Chapter 10.5, based on cases of linguistically deprived children, the critical period for acquiring PFS seems to be limited by puberty. Thus, reaching puberty early, at four to five years of age, may significantly limit the ability of the prefrontal cortex connections to attain isochronicity as a result of an abnormally shortened period of experience, which is so critical for sculpting isochronous networks. Puberty that occurs at an unusually early age (called *precocious puberty*) affects hundreds of individuals, and studying PFS in those adults may yield interesting correlational results.

10. An artificial extension of the period of plasticity of the prefrontal cortex may increase propensity for prefrontal synthesis in animals

If genetic regulators of the period of plasticity of the prefrontal cortex were found, researchers could devise a way to extend the period of plasticity. Chimpanzees with an extended period of prefrontal cortex plasticity can then be exposed to a recursive communication system through lexigrams or sign language. If scientists succeed in stretching out the critical period from several months to several years, these artificially modified animals may be prone to acquisition of some PFS.

11. A possible biological marker of prefrontal synthesis: the size of the corpus callosum

PFS relies on the isochronic axonal projections to synchronize independent objectNEs. The isochronicity of connections is achieved by fine-tuning the axonal conduction velocity in the experience-dependent manner via differential myelination of axonal fibers. The experience is primarily provided by exercising PFS with recursive language. Lack of experience is therefore expected to be associated with reduced myelination of relevant axonal projections. The corpus callosum is the largest and most prominent bundle of axonal projections in the brain. It consists of approximately 200 million axons connecting the left and right cerebral hemispheres. The number of axonal fibers in the corpus callosum decreases shortly after birth but continuous myelination of the remaining fibers results in a slow increase of the size of the corpus callosum from birth to adulthood.[ccc]

The corpus callosum is not essential for survival. Humans born with agenesis of the corpus callosum often grow into fully functional adults and patients who have had the corpus callosum severed as a treatment for epilepsy (a procedure called callosotomy) are able to recover most of their functions. However, in people born with a normal corpus callosum, its

---

[ccc] The myelination of the corpus callosum is relatively slow. It is one of the last areas of the brain to undergo myelination, and myelination is not complete until at least the time of puberty. As a result, the brain of a young child is similar to that of a split-brain patient: some types of interhemispheric signal transfer are significantly inferior to that in an adult brain. For example, children have a greater difficulty matching tactile designs between hands than within hands. In addition, children younger than 10 months are not able to recognize a face shown to only one hemisphere with the use of the other hemisphere, which indicates an inability to transfer information about the face over the corpus callosum.

myelination pattern may tell the story of the person's upbringing just as tree rings reflect the pattern of the tree's annual growth. The PFS theory predicts a reduction of the myelination of the corpus callosum in all conditions associated with a reduction of PFS and an increase in myelination of the corpus callosum in high-intelligence individuals with more developed PFS.

One crude measure of the level of myelination of the corpus callosum is its thickness, which can be easily assessed with a noninvasive MRI test. Consistent with the predictions of the PFS theory, an increased thickness of the corpus callosum has been positively correlated with intelligence, creativity, and other hallmarks of PFS [ddd], while a reduction in the thickness of the corpus callosum has been observed in patients with PFS paralysis: those diagnosed with mental retardation, Down's syndrome, autism, as well as children suffering from abuse and neglect who showed on average a 17% reduction in myelination of the corpus callosum [321]. Thus, in humans born with a normal corpus callosum, the thickness of the corpus callosum may be a useful morphological biomarker of myelination associated with ontogenetic acquisition of PFS. It would be particularly informative to study the corpus callosum of linguistically deprived children. In these children, PFS paralysis is expected to be associated with a significant reduction in the thickness of the corpus callosum.

[ddd] Albert Einstein, for example, whose thought experiments in which he'd imagine himself riding alongside a beam of light are well known, had a thicker corpus callosum than age-matched controls [451].

Predictions of the prefrontal synthesis theory

Core theory
1. **Core neurological hypothesis:** The basis of the theory is a simple, yet fundamental question: what happens neurologically when two objects, never before seen together (say, an apple on top of a whale), are imagined together for the first time? The scientific consensus is that a familiar object, such as an apple or a whale, is represented in the brain by thousands of neurons dispersed throughout the posterior cortex (occipital, temporal, and parietal lobes). When one sees or recalls such an object, the neurons of that object's objectNE tend to activate into synchronous resonant activity. The objectNE binding mechanism, based on the Hebbian principle "neurons that fire together, wire together," came to be known as the *binding-by-synchronization* hypothesis (Singer & Gray, 1995). However, while the Hebbian principle explains how we perceive a familiar object, it does not explain the infinite number of novel objects that humans can voluntarily imagine. The objectNEs encoding those objects cannot jump into spontaneous synchronized activity on their own since the parts forming those novel images have never been seen together. I propose that to account for unlimited human imagination, the *binding-by-synchronization* hypothesis would need to be extended to include the phenomenon of prefrontal synthesis (PFS) whereby the prefrontal cortex (PFC) actively and intentionally synchronizes independent objectNEs into one morphed image. Thus, the *apple objectNE* is synchronized with the *whale neuronal ensemble*, and the two disparate objects are perceived together. The synchronization mechanism of *PFS*

is likely responsible for many imaginative and creative traits that philosophers and scientists have recognized as being uniquely human, despite not having a precise neurological understanding of the process.

2. **Core evolutionary hypothesis:**
   As of 70,000 years ago, hominins had already evolved both a greater control of perception by the PFC and a nearly modern speech-production apparatus. However the connections between the PFC and the posterior cortex remained asynchronous; the PFC was unable to synchronize independent objectNEs, the communication system remained finite and non-recursive: one word was only able to communicate one image. At that time, a single mutation delayed the ontogenetic development of the PFC and permitted the newly invented recursive speech to train the synchronous connections between the PFC and the posterior cortex. This allowed the acquisition of PFS and propelled humans to behavioral modernity.

A. Core neurological predictions [a]	Status [b]
1. PFS is orchestrated by the PFC.	Prediction supported by neuropsychological, functional imaging, and lesion data.
2. To conduct PFS, the PFC activates and synchronizes independent objectNEs in time.	Novel prediction
3. Only synchronously firing objectNEs are experienced in one mental frame as one morphed image; objectNEs firing asynchronously are experienced as independent objects.	Novel prediction
4. The PFC in humans is capable of synchronizing objectNEs located at physically different distances from the	Novel prediction

PFC, because of isochronous connections between the PFC and the objectNEs.	
5. These isochronous connections are developed ontogenetically in an experience-dependent manner. The experience is provided by the infinite recursive communication system.	Novel prediction
6. The isochronicity of the connections is accomplished by experience-dependent differential myelination of those connections. Additional axonal isolation provided by multiple layers of the myelin sheath can dramatically increase conduction velocity and compensate for the uneven physical distance between the PFC and the neurons in the posterior cortex.	Novel prediction
Corollary neurological predictions [c]	
7. Humans have greater differential myelination of cortical pathways between the PFC and the posterior cortex than other primates.	Novel prediction

B. Core evolutionary predictions	**Status**
1. Acquisition of PFS has two evolutionary precursors: greater voluntary control of the visual percept by the PFC and the nearly modern speech apparatus.	Novel hypothesis
2. Greater control of the visual percept by the PFC evolved as a result of selective pressure from immobile predators. Hominins were selected for their ability to better detect and therefore avoid stalking predators	Novel hypothesis

	occluded by vegetation.	
3.	A nearly modern speech apparatus evolved in hominins long before 70,000 years ago.	Prediction supported [197]
4.	The two precursor changes combined synergistically around 70,000 years ago, which allowed the acquisition of PFS and propelled humans to behavioral modernity.	Novel hypothesis
5.	The infinite recursive communication system was acquired concomitantly with PFS about 70,000 year ago. Prior to the acquisition of PFS, the communication system of hominins was finite and non-recursive: one word was only able to communicate one image. That finite non-recursive communication system was lacking spatial prepositions, verb tenses and a flexible syntax.	Novel hypothesis
6.	External manifestations of PFS – figurative art, religious beliefs, construction of complex protective dwellings, invention of animal traps, kiln-baked ceramics, bow and arrow, bone needles with an eye and other similarly complex tools – could not have been expressed by hominins lacking PFS. Therefore, these artifacts cannot appear in the archeological record before acquisition of PFS 70,000 years ago.	Prediction supported (e.g. Ref. [139])
7.	External manifestations of PFS – figurative art, religious beliefs, construction of complex protective dwellings, and invention of multiple types of complex tools – are expected to appear in the archeological record	Prediction supported (e.g. Ref. [139])

at approximately the same time, since all are a direct result of the acquisition of PFS.	
8. The symbolic use of objects does not necessarily involve PFS and therefore could have been practiced by hominins before the acquisition of PFS. For example, the use of red ochre may have been highly symbolic due to its association with blood. However, this association may be entirely based on memory of an emotional event such as a bloody battle and may not involve production of any novel images in the process of PFS. Therefore the use of red ochre by hominins does not by itself signify the acquisition of PFS and is not adequate evidence of behavioral modernity.	Novel hypothesis
9. As the visual system makes up about half of the entire cortex [82], the larger brain is primarily an indication of hominin adaptation to better visually detect stalking immobile predators occluded by the tall grass of the savanna.	Novel hypothesis
10. As a result of six million years of evolution in the savanna, modern humans detect immobile partially occluded predators faster, and/or more reliably, and/or from a greater distance than other primates.	Novel hypothesis
11. Modern humans detect immobile visual targets faster than other primates.	Prediction supported [393]
12. Modern humans are better than other primates at mental rotation of visual targets (such as predator body parts,	Prediction supported [248]

like an ear or a tail, sticking out just above the grass).	
13. Modern humans are better than other primates at integrating multiple local visual features (such as predator body parts) into coherent percepts.	Prediction supported [396,397]
14. Modern humans are better than other primates at searching for immobile visual items (such as predator body parts) amongst the coherently moving background (such as grass blades swaying *uniformly* in the wind).	Prediction supported [393]
15. Increased control by the PFC of objectNEs in the posterior cortex resulting in an improved recognition of hidden, stalking predators began in australopiths and improved continuously over the next six million years of hominin evolution.	Novel hypothesis
16. The flaking of a stone tool requires active intentional modification of the objectNE of a cobble into a mental template of a future handaxe.	Novel prediction
17. This modification is accomplished by the PFC in the process of *prefrontal analysis*, the voluntary process of reducing a synchronously firing objectNE by shifting a part of the ensemble *out-of-phase* with the rest of the ensemble.	Novel prediction
18. Prefrontal analysis (PFA) was acquired by hominins around 3.3 million years ago and resulted in the manufacturing of the first stone tools (Mode One chopper).	Novel hypothesis
19. PFA improved from *Homo habilis* (manufacturer of Mode One tools) to	Novel hypothesis

Homo erectus (manufacturer of Mode Two tools) to Neanderthals (manufacturer of Mode Three tools). The succeeding species were capable of desynchronizing finer and finer fragments of an objectNE and therefore exhibiting better voluntary control of their percept (mental template).	
20. PFA evolved as a result of selective pressure from immobile predators. Hominins were selected for their ability to better "see" stalking predators occluded by vegetation and, as a result, were better able to "see" a chopper "hidden" inside a cobble.	Novel hypothesis
21. Prefrontal analysis, which entails a greater control of the visual percept, was a stepping stone toward PFS: the unlimited control of the visual percept.	Novel hypothesis

C. Core ontogenetic predictions	Status
1. Modern children acquire PFS as a result of external and internal recursive speech, using this speech to continuously create novel mental images, to examine those images and then to use the ensuing feedback mechanism to fine-tune the connections between the PFC and the objectNEs in the posterior cortex.	Novel prediction
2. A lack of recursive communication during the critical period of PFC plasticity (which lasts until puberty), results in PFS paralysis, which reveals itself as poor comprehension of	Prediction supported [165,326,329–331,452]

complex sentences, poor understanding of spatial prepositions, and a lack of complex expressive speech.	
3. PFS paralysis in linguistically deprived children is the result of underdevelopment of isochronous connections between the PFC and the objectNEs in the posterior cortex.	Novel prediction
4. The conduction velocity in fibers connecting the PFC and the posterior cortex cannot be significantly changed after the closure of the period of the PFC plasticity around puberty.	Novel prediction
5. The finite non-recursive communication system such as home-sign is unable to drive the development of PFS. Only an infinite recursive communication system is capable of developing PFS.	Prediction supported [329-331,452]
6. A child communicating using a home-sign system is unable to invent an infinite recursive communication system on his or her own and therefore is unable to acquire PFS.	Prediction supported [329-331,452]
7. A group of modern children using a home-sign system are likely to spontaneously convert a finite non-recursive communication system into an infinite recursive communication system by inventing spatial prepositions, verb tenses and other grammar elements.	Prediction supported [132,133,275,277]
8. Neurotypical children acquire PFS from about three to five years of age. Children rescued from linguistic deprivation after seven years of age may recover completely, but require a	Prediction supported [37,333-336]

focused multi-year training with a speech pathologist. Children rescued from linguistic deprivation after 12 years of age (i.e. after puberty) cannot acquire much PFS even after multi-year training with a speech pathologist.	
9. Neurotypical children acquire PFS after the age of three and exhibit it externally through understanding of complex recursive communication, reasoning, figurative drawings, seeking explanations for invisible phenomena, construction of complex structures, and predilection to strategy games.	Prediction supported
10. Before the age of three, children lack PFS; they cannot precisely imagine an image described by a complex novel sentence.	Prediction supported
11. In congenitally deaf children, the age of exposure to the first recursive sign language negatively correlates with the extent of PFS development. Children exposed to a formal recursive sign language from birth often acquire better PFS; those children who are linguistically deprived even only during the initial part of the critical period, could end up with some PFS paralysis.	Prediction supported [338,339]
Corollary ontogenetic predictions 12. Modern children who have a significantly shortened period of PFC plasticity (possibly as a result of reaching puberty early, particularly	Novel prediction

before the age of five) may have a reduced propensity towards PFS in adulthood especially if they were not involved in many recursive conversations during their short period of PFC plasticity.	
13. A greater involvement of such children into PFS-stimulating activities such as discussions, storytelling, book reading, etc. before the closure of the PFC plasticity period should increase their propensity for PFS in adulthood.	Novel prediction
14. A child with a significant speech delay (lacking both internal and external speech until 5-7 years of age) does not receive the necessary input for development of synchronous PFC – posterior cortex connections and may end up with PFS paralysis unless PFS is actively trained by other mental-synthesis-developing activities that do not depend on knowing words (e.g. visual puzzles, figurative drawing, construction of complex structures).	Novel prediction
15. In linguistically deprived children, PFS paralysis is likely associated with under-myelination of long-range cortical fibers between the PFC and the posterior cortex and the diminished size of the corpus callosum.	Novel prediction
D. Core animal cognition predictions	**Status**
1. Humans are unique in their genetic predisposition to ontogenetic acquisition of PFS. Animals cannot	Others have suggested that animals have a

	acquire PFS and therefore cannot voluntarily imagine novel objects in their mind.	comparatively weaker imagination; the complete lack of PFS in animals is a novel prediction
2.	Animals cannot conduct intentional mental simulations of their future behavior.	Suggested by others
3.	Animals cannot mentally simulate tool manufacturing: the tools that animals do manufacture are the result of memory, reflex, and innate abilities, but not the result of the voluntary synchronization of independent objectNEs.	Novel prediction
4.	Primates introduced to recursive language from birth (under focused training) learn the meaning of many words but cannot develop understanding of complex recursive language.	Prediction supported (e.g. Refs. [8,10,421,426]
5.	Understanding of complex recursive language relies on PFS which, in turn, relies on isochronous connections between the PFC and the posterior cortex. A shorter period of PFC plasticity (a few months in chimpanzees and macaques compared to more than five years in humans [372]), among other things, prevents other primates from developing isochronous connections even when they are exposed to recursive communications from birth and are able to learn hundreds of words.	Novel prediction

E. Core molecular biological predictions	Status
1. The "trigger" mutation that resulted in human behavioral modernity was the mutation that delayed the ontogenetic development of the PFC around 70,000 years ago and significantly increased the duration of the period during which the mutation carriers exposed to recursive language could acquire PFS.	Novel hypothesis
2. Once the two children (most likely siblings or twins) who were both carriers of the mutation that delayed the maturation of the PFC invented a few prepositions, they would have converted their tribe's non-recursive finite communication system into an infinite recursive communication system. The infinite recursive communication system would, in turn, trained acquisition of PFS in these individuals. Successive generations improved the communication system by increasing the number of grammar elements and in the process enhanced their PFS (providing an additional mechanism for humans to become smarter, more imaginative and creative generation after generation).	Novel hypothesis
3. The mutation that delayed the ontogenetic development of the PFC was deleterious on its own before it was combined with the acquisition of PFS. It was deleterious because a recipient of this mutation had a significantly longer childhood when	Novel hypothesis

the brain was still immature and was incapable of fully assessing risk; such individual was prone to early death as a consequence of its cognitive immaturity. This mutation may have occurred many times before 70,000 years ago, but its carriers could not have developed PFS without the cultural exposure to a recursive language during the period of PFC plasticity.	
4. The "trigger" mutation became advantageous only after the first mutation-carrying children invented a recursive communication system and, as a result, trained their brains in PFS.	Novel hypothesis
5. The significant delay from the time when a nearly modern speech apparatus emerged 600,000 years ago to the time when PFS was acquired 70,000 years ago, is explained primarily by the low probability of the event of birth of two carriers of the mutation (likely twins or siblings) living under one roof at the same time during their childhood (so that they could invent a few spatial prepositions in their conversations).	Novel hypothesis
Corollary molecular biological predictions	
6. If genetic regulators of the period of plasticity of the PFC were found, researchers could devise a way to extend the period of plasticity. Chimpanzees with an extended period of PFC plasticity could then be exposed to a recursive communication system through lexigrams or sign	Novel prediction

| language. If scientists succeed in stretching out the developmental window from several months to several years, these artificially modified animals may be capable of acquisition of some PFS. | |

[a] Core predictions are those that should be essential to confirm in order for the hypothesis to be supported.

[b] Under the category "Status," predictions that are supported are those with direct or indirect evidence. Predictions or hypotheses that are novel are suggested here for the first time and require investigation. Some predictions or hypotheses are not novel and have been suggested by others.

[c] Corollary hypotheses and predictions are those that are not essential to the core hypothesis if they are refuted but would support the core hypothesis if they are confirmed.

Appendix

Appendix 1. Glossary

Action potentials are short 1 millisecond (0.001 seconds) spikes in voltage from a resting membrane potential of negative 70 millivolt (0.070 Volt) to positive 40 millivolt. Action potentials are the primary mechanism used to exchange information between neurons.

Consciousness — In this book, *consciousness* is used in its colloquial connotation, meaning awareness.

Conscious experience — In this book, *conscious experience* is used in its colloquial connotation, that is, any experience of which a subject is aware. A conscious experience includes many states ranging from passive awareness to voluntary intentional PFS.

Hippocampus — The hippocampus is a group of specialized neurons located deep inside the temporal lobe. The hippocampus is essential for forming long-term memories of people, places and events. Once formed, these memories reside in cerebral cortices and do not depend on the hippocampus. Long-term memories of people, places and events cannot form when the hippocampi are surgically removed from both hemispheres as was demonstrated in the seminal case of the patient "HM".

Hominins — members of the group that includes modern humans and their extinct ancestors (all of the *Homo* species, all of the australopiths and other ancient forms like Paranthropus and Ardipithecus).

Mental image — The easiest way to experience a visual mental image is to close your eyes and recall an object from memory. (When the eyes are open, we usually experience a *visual percept*; although sometimes our thoughts drift away and we experience a mental image even when the eyes are open). Neurologically, experiencing a mental image of an object is associated with the activation of the objectNE.

Prefrontal synthesis (PFS) — PFS is defined as the ability to juxtapose mental visuospatial objects at will. The Neuronal Ensembles Synchronization hypothesis predicts that, neurologically, PFS is mediated by synchronization of two or more objectNEs. For example, you can imagine your favorite cup standing on top of your favorite keyboard. On a neurological level, mentally forming the image of *the cup on top of the keyboard* consists of the following steps:

Step 1 - Recall of the cup: The prefrontal cortex (PFC) activates the ensemble of neurons representing the cup to fire synchronous actions potentials. The cup is perceived.

Step 2 - Recall of the keyboard: The prefrontal cortex activates the ensemble of neurons representing the keyboard to fire synchronous actions potentials. The keyboard is perceived.

Step 3 - The prefrontal cortex synchronizes the two objectNEs in time. When synchronization is achieved, a new, never-before-seen mental image of the cup on top of the keyboard is perceived.

Step 4 - The connections between the synchronously activated neurons are strengthened and, thus, the new objectNE representing the cup on top of the keyboard is formed (black pyramid). This ensemble will be stored in memory and can be activated at a later time as one unit.

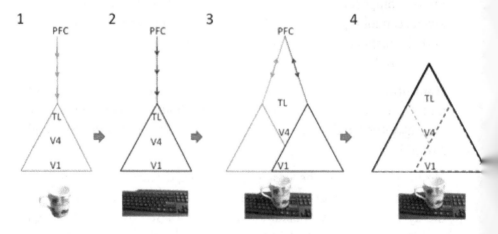

Figure G.1 The process of PFS. Please see the text (above) for a detailed description of the process.

Do not confuse intentional voluntary PFS with spontaneous involuntary dreaming, day-dreaming, and categorically-primed spontaneous imagination.

Mental template — A mental template is an image formed in the mind by means of a decomposition of a larger image from memory or from a visual percept. The process of mental-template-formation is different from PFS: while PFS involves integration of two or more objectNEs together into one synchronously firing unit, mental template formation entails desynchronization and/or deactivation of part of an objectNE in order to experience a "smaller" object. The mental template is formed in the process of *prefrontal analysis* (PFA).

According to the theory put forth in this book, PFA was acquired by the first stone-tool makers around 3.3 million years ago. As a result, *Homo habilis* gained the ability to manufacture simple stone choppers. When looking at a natural cobble, the prefrontal cortex of the *Homo habilis* was able to identify the objectNE encoding a chopper (*mental template* for a chopper) and to shift the neurons encoding the flakes *out-of-phase* with the chopper ensemble, enabling *Homo habilis* to consciously experience the mental template of the chopper, that is, to "see" the chopper inside the cobble.

Before 3.3 million years ago, australopithecines had likely not yet acquired the ability to **voluntarily** shift parts of an objectNEs *out-of-phase* with the rest of the ensemble in order to concentrate on one visual detail: they were not able to see a future chopper inside a cobble.

Mental template formation is a precursor to PFS. While mental template formation involves shifting some neurons *out-of-phase* with the rest of the ensemble, PFS involves shifting neurons of several objectNEs *in-phase* with each other.

Myelin — The conduction velocity is significantly greater in axons that have multiple extra layers of electrical isolation provided by an oily substance called myelin. Myelin increases conduction velocity through axons by fundamentally changing the way action potentials are propagated. Rather than an uninterrupted wave of depolarization amplified continuously along the axon, the action potentials in myelinated axons are amplified at isolated points along the axon, called nodes of Ranvier. Conduction velocity in myelinated axons can be as much as 100-fold faster than conduction velocity in unmyelinated fibers. The degree of myelination varies greatly, with some of the fastest axons having up to 160 layers of myelin. In fact, myelin occupies the bulk part of white matter, which, in turn, comprises over half of the human brain, a far greater proportion than in other animals (Fields RD, 2008).

Appendix 2: Organization of the Human Brain

Understanding the evolution of the human mind is impossible without knowing the fascinating and complex way in which our brain is organized. To do justice to this topic could take many volumes. There is much that neuroscientists already know, and probably quite a bit more that is yet to be discovered. However, let's get acquainted with some of the basics which will be essential for the purposes of our discussion.

The human brain contains more than 100 billion neurons and each neuron can be linked to as many as 10,000 other neurons. To appreciate the complexity of the brain, imagine that your brain is a planet, and that each neuron is a person. Planet Brain has a population that is 10 times that of planet Earth, and on top of that, almost every person on Planet Brain is connected to 10,000 other people. This is the conversation that neuroscientists are trying to understand. The analogy goes even further. Similar to a person's sensory receptors on the skin and in the internal organs, a neuron also has millions of receptors both on its surface and inside the cell. These receptors are sensitive to hundreds of chemicals that can affect a neuron's communication, spur growth, or trigger apoptosis (controlled death). No one expects to describe the workings of the brain in the same elegant format as ideal gas thermodynamics, or to develop a probabilistic description of the brain similar to quantum mechanics. Both of these theories benefit from the selfsameness of their constituent units: the molecules of ideal gas are identical for the purposes of thermodynamics and electrons are also identical for the purposes of quantum mechanics. Neurons, on the other hand, are all different. They have different receptors, different shapes, and different connections. Every neuron in the brain is special both morphologically and functionally. Despite these obvious differences, neurons do share many common characteristics.

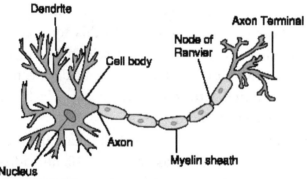

Figure B.1 Schematic representation of a neuron.

Figure B.2 An action potential visualization. An action potential traveling along an axon can be visualized as a flame racing along a fuse, each Node of Ranvier igniting the next until the action potential reaches the end of the axon, referred to as the *axon terminal*.

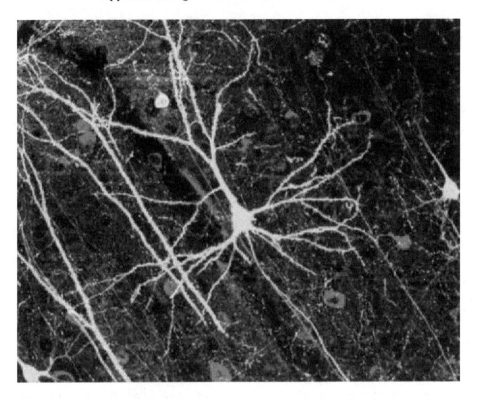

Figure B.3   Image of pyramidal neurons in the cerebral cortex expressing green fluorescent protein. Source: PLoS Biology.

All neurons are small cells with a cell body that is about 0.02 millimeters wide (that's just a bit thinner than an average human hair) and long, branch-like projections up to one meter in length. These long projections allow neurons to exchange information over long distances. Neurons exchange information by firing action potentials, which are short 1 millisecond (0.001 seconds) spikes in voltage from a resting membrane potential of negative 70 millivolt (0.070 Volt) to positive 40 millivolt. Some neurons fire action potentials as often as 100 times per second, while others can go minutes without firing.

When a neuron in the motor cortex fires an action

potential, the muscle cell connected to the neuron twitches. Action potentials travel between the neuron and the muscle via a long branch of the neuron called an axon. Action potentials travel along the axon quite slowly. The speed varies from 0.3 meters per second (m/s) to 100 m/s. (Compare that to the speed of electrical transmission along a copper wire, which is about one trillion m/s.) One reason for the relatively slow transmission rates is that action potentials have to be amplified every millimeter or so. The amplification stations are located at the so-called Nodes of Ranvier. You can visualize an action potential traveling along an axon as a flame racing along a fuse, each Node of Ranvier igniting the next until the action potential reaches the end of the axon, referred to as the *axon terminal.*

Between the amplification stations, the axons of most neurons are insulated from the extracellular fluid by up to 160 extra layers of lipid known as myelin. The cell membrane and the additional myelin sheath prevents the electrical charges from leaking out of the axon and increases the conduction velocity (the speed with which an action potential is conducted along the axon). The lowest conduction velocity is observed in unmyelinated fibers. The highest conduction velocity is observed in thickly myelinated axons. For example, temperature receptors in the skin are mostly unmyelinated. The conduction velocity in these fibers is approximately 1 m/s. Therefore, it can take over a second for the action potential to traverse the 1 meter distance from the receptors in your hand to the spinal cord and the brain. This is why we are often so slow at removing our hand from a hot surface.

Pain receptors (called nociceptors) on the other hand, primarily conduct their signals via myelinated axons with a much swifter conduction velocity of up to 30 m/s. When you step on a nail, the pain signal is quickly transmitted to the spinal cord (it only takes around 0.03 seconds for the action potential to travel 1 meter) which quickly activates the crossed extensor reflex: the leg that is stepping on the nail pulls away, while the other leg takes the weight of the whole body. Thanks to the extra layers of myelin, the reflex is activated so quickly that the nail rarely penetrates the skin before the leg is withdrawn.

The contact between an axon terminal and the target cell is called a synapse. When an action potential reaches the axon terminal, a chemical, called a neurotransmitter, is released from the axon terminal into the space between the axon terminal and the target cell. This neurotransmitter acts upon the target cell to evoke a response. If the target cell is a muscle, the response is a contraction of the muscle. If the target cell is a neuron, the response is a change of voltage in that neuron. The voltage change in response to activity at a single synapse is usually relatively small. Stimuli at multiple synapses are normally required to induce the neuron to fire an action potential. The process is analogous to voting. The synapses can vote for the action potential (excitatory synapses) or against the action potential (inhibitory synapses). (Recall that there may be as many as 10,000 voting synapses on each neuron.) When enough synapses vote for the action potential, they depolarize the neuron from -70 mV (millivolt) to above the critical threshold, which is approximately -55 mV. At this point the neuron will respond with an action potential. Once activated, the action potential travels along the axon all the way to the axon terminals where it stimulates other neurons or muscle cells connected to this axon.

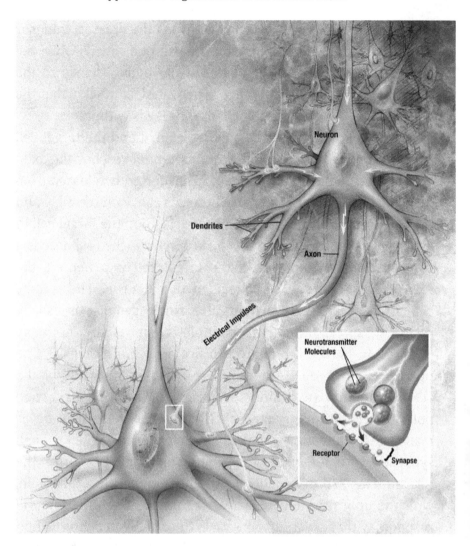

Figure B.4 A signal propagates from one neuron along its long branch (the axon) to the cell body and dendrites of a second neuron. The contact between the axon and the second neuron is called a synapse. One synapse is marked by a white square and expanded in the right lower corner. When an action potential reaches the synapse, a chemical, called a neurotransmitter, is released from the axon into the synapse. These neurotransmitter molecules bind to the receptors located on the surface of the second neuron and evoke a response. A response can be a change in the membrane potential from -70 mV to -65 mV. Normally stimuli at multiple synapses are required to depolarize the neuron to -55 mV, thus inducing the neuron to fire an action potential.

The brain is divided into the left and right cerebral hemispheres, which are interconnected by about 200 million axons laid out in a structure called the *corpus callosum*. There are two groups of specialized neurons deep inside the brain that will be referred to in the text: the thalamus and the hippocampus (plural: hippocampi). The thalamus is a relay station for a number of sensory signals including visual and auditory sensory information. The hippocampus is a group of specialized neurons essential for forming long-term memories of people, places and events. Long-term memories of this kind cannot form when the hippocampi are surgically removed from both hemispheres, as was demonstrated in the seminal case of the patient "HM". Since the age of 10, HM suffered from increasing epileptic seizures. Eventually the seizures became so intense and frequent that by the age of 27 his doctors suggested removing the parts of the brain that were thought to be responsible for his disorder.

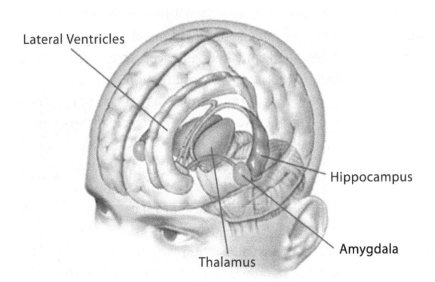

Figure B.5 The thalamus and the hippocampi are structures deep inside the brain. They are symmetrically located in the right and left hemispheres.

The surgical removal of both hippocampi and the surrounding tissue stopped the debilitating seizures but induced a serious side effect: an inability to form new memories of people, places and events and a partial retrograde amnesia. The operation, however, had no effect on early memories, personality, general intelligence, speech and comprehension, or short-term memory.

The outermost, convoluted layer of each hemisphere, which is about 2 to 4 millimeters thick, is called the cerebral cortex (Latin for bark), and it contains a lot of neuronal cell bodies. (Neuronal cell bodies appear gray in preserved brains, hence the name 'grey matter.' Under the layer of neuronal cell bodies lies a layer of myelinated axons, which connect neurons to their target cells. Myelinated axons are white in appearance, hence the name 'white matter'). The cerebral cortex plays a key role in voluntary muscle control, sensory perception, memory, speech and comprehension. Neurons in the cortex are organized territorially based on their function: motor neurons are located in the motor cortex, neurons sensitive to touch in the somatosensory cortex, neurons responsible for language comprehension are concentrated in Wernicke's area, and neurons responsible for language production are located in Broca's area. If you think of a brain as a company, then functional cortical areas correspond to different departments. Each department minds its own business. The departments often exchange information but the bulk of the decisions are made within each department. In the brain, sending an action potential from one department to another takes anywhere from 3 to 20 milliseconds. Within each department, the shorter distance between neurons allows for faster communication: anywhere from 1 to 3 milliseconds. Thus, the neuronal organization based on function reduces the distance between neurons in one department, and, consequently, allows for a faster decision-making process within the department.

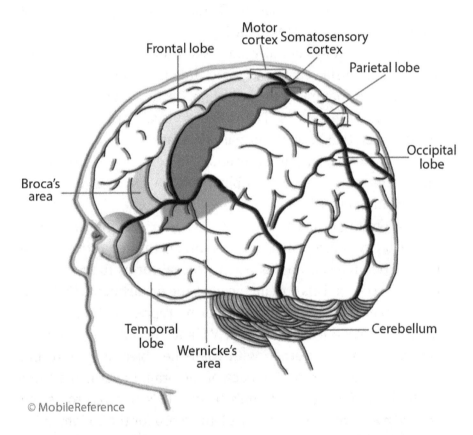

© MobileReference

Figure B.6 Neurons in the brain are organized territorially based on their function. Motor neurons that control muscle movement are located in the motor cortex (yellow). Neurons sensitive to touch are located in the somatosensory cortex (red). Language areas responsible for comprehension are located in Wernicke's area (violet). Language areas responsible for generating speech are located in Broca's area (blue).

When a disease such as a stroke destroys one functional area of the cortex, the patient loses control over that function. Damage to the motor area results in loss of motor control over the part of the body controlled by the damaged cortex. Damage to the somatosensory area results in loss of sensations within the body part connected to the damaged cortex. Damage to Wernicke's area results in loss of auditory comprehension (sensory aphasia). Damage to Broca's area results in loss of productive speech (motor aphasia).

The visual system also consists of multiple departments. The primary visual cortex, V1, is located in the occipital lobe. It receives information from the retina via the lateral geniculate nucleus in the thalamus. The primary visual cortex is the first cortical area that receives visual information. Bilateral damage to the primary visual cortex results in blindness; this disorder is often referred to as cortical blindness, to distinguish it from retinal blindness.

From the primary visual cortex, the visual information is passed in two directions, or streams. In the first stream, the information flows from the primary visual cortex to the inferior temporal cortex. This stream includes the departments that deal with object recognition and form representation. These departments, which include V2, V4 and the inferior temporal cortex (IT), are concerned with *what* the object is. Due to the stream's direction from the back of the brain towards the front of the brain (along "the brain's belly"), it is referred to as the *ventral pathway* from *venter*, the Latin word for the abdomen.

The second stream deals with an object's position in space. The departments along this stream process information about *where* the object is positioned. These departments are concerned with an object's motion, location, as well as controlling the eyes and arms in the specialized tasks of grasping nearby objects. For example, the perception of motion is the major function of visual area V5, also known as visual area MT. Damage to V5 leads to a specific deficit in motion perception. Due to the stream's direction from the back of the brain towards the parietal lobe (along the "the brain's back"), it is referred to as the *dorsal pathway* from *dorsum,* the Latin word for the back. The dorsal stream has been described as providing "vision for action."

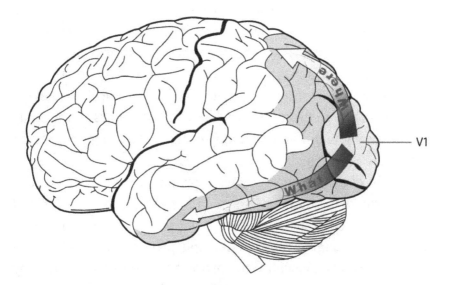

Figure B.7 Visual information processing in the cortex. From the primary visual cortex (V1, shown in yellow), the visual information is passed in two streams. The neurons along the ventral stream (shown in purple) are primarily concerned with *what* the object is. The neurons along the dorsal stream (shown in green) are primarily concerned with *where* the object is.

There is a specialization hierarchy along the visual information pathways. The departments become more specialized the farther the information moves along the visual pathway. As mentioned above, images from the retina at the back of each eye are first channeled to the lateral geniculate nuclei in the thalamus. Neurons in the lateral geniculate nuclei can be activated by visual stimulation from either one eye or the other but not both eyes. They respond to any change in activity of the retinal neuron that they are connected to. From the lateral geniculate nuclei, visual information moves to the primary visual cortex (V1). Neurons in V1, which can usually be activated by either eye, are sensitive to specific attributes, such as the orientation of line segments, color, and binocular disparity. Visual information is transmitted from V1 to cortical areas with greater specificity. Neurons in V2 respond to short lines and corners, contours, small spots of color within larger receptive fields and to synchronized movement of contrast borders and rows of spots against a background. Neurons in V4 respond selectively to aspects of visual stimuli critical to shape identification. Neurons in the inferior temporal lobe may respond only when an entire object (such as a face) is present within the visual field.

The entire cerebral cortex is primarily a memory system. Long-term visual memory is stored in the cortex in the form of connections between neurons (synapses). A new memory is formed by changing the number and properties of millions of synapses. You can visualize the process of memory formation by thinking of a neuron as a tree. When making new synapses, the tree (neuron) grows its branches to reach other trees (neurons) in the forest (brain). While you are reading this book, your neurons are growing their branches and making millions of new connections.

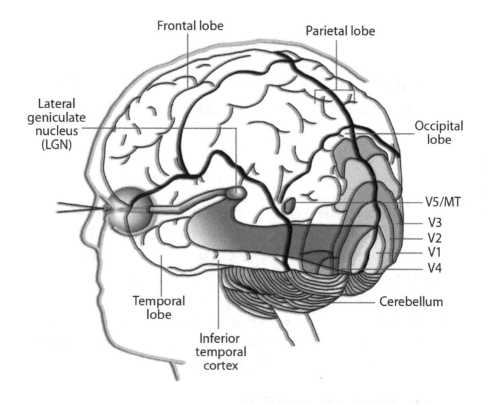

Figure B.8 Organization of the visual system. The primary visual cortex (V1, located in the occipital lobe) receives information from the retina via the lateral geniculate nucleus in the thalamus. The primary visual cortex is the first *cortical* area that receives visual information. There is a specialization hierarchy along the visual information pathways. The departments become more specialized the farther the information moves along the visual pathway. Neurons in the lateral geniculate nuclei can be activated by visual stimulation from either one eye or the other but not both eyes. They respond to any change in activity of the retinal neuron that they are connected to. Neurons in V1, which can usually be activated by either eye, are sensitive to specific attributes, such as the orientation of line segments, color, and binocular disparity. Visual information is transmitted from V1 to cortical areas with greater specificity. Neurons in V4 respond selectively to aspects of visual stimuli critical to shape identification. Neurons in the inferior temporal lobe may respond only when an entire object (such as a face) is present within the visual field. The perception of motion is the major function of the visual area V5, also known as visual area MT.

Appendix 3. Observations from the direct stimulation of the cerebral cortex

Neurosurgeon Wilder Penfield invented a procedure in which he treated patients with severe epilepsy by destroying nerve cells in the brain where the seizures originated. Before operating, Penfield stimulated the brain with electrical probes while the patients were conscious on the operating table, and observed their responses. In this way he could more accurately target the areas of the brain responsible for the seizures, reducing the side effects of the surgery.

Temporal lobe stimulation

In order to avoid damaging language areas, Penfield had to explore the specialization of the temporal lobe (although the general pattern of cortical organization is common in all people, each of us has a unique map of functional specialization in the cortex). Accordingly, Penfield stimulated the temporal lobe neurons in 520 patients. Stimulation of the temporal lobe triggered vivid recall of memories in 40 of the patients.

Here are some quotes from Wilder Penfield's book, "The Mystery of the Mind," describing responses of patient M.M. (a young, 26-year-old woman) upon stimulation of several points in the right temporal lobe (Penfield W [89], pages 24-26). The point numbers are in bold:

11 - "I heard something, I do not know what it was."

11 - (stimulation repeated without warning) "Yes, Sir, I think I heard a mother calling her little boy somewhere. It seemed to be something that happened years ago." When asked to explain, she said, "It was somebody in the neighborhood where I live." Then she added that she herself "was somewhere close enough to hear."

12 - "Yes. I heard voices down along the river somewhere - a man's voice and a woman's voice calling... I think I saw the river."

15 - "Just a tiny flash of a feeling of familiarity and a feeling that I knew everything that was going to happen in the future."

17c - (a needle is insulated except at the tip, and inserted to the superior surface of the temporal lobe, deep in the fissure of Sylvius, and the current is switched on) "Oh! I had the same very, very familiar memory, in an office somewhere. I could see the desks. I was there and someone was calling me, a man leaning on a desk with a pencil in his hand."

I warned her I was going to stimulate, but I did not do so. "Nothing."

18a - (stimulation without warning) "I had a little memory - a scene in a play - they were talking and I could see it - I was just seeing it in my memory."

Penfield goes on to say (page 21):

> It was evident at once that these [patient's recollections] were not dreams. They were electrical activations of the sequential record of consciousness, a record that had been laid down during the patient's earlier experience. The patient "re-lived" all that he had been aware of in that earlier period of time as in a moving-picture "flashback."
>
> On the first occasion when one of these flashbacks was reported to me by a conscious patient (1933), I was incredulous. On each subsequent occasion, I marveled. For example, when a mother told me she was suddenly aware, as my electrode touched the cortex, of being in her kitchen listening to the voice of her little boy who was playing outside in the yard. She was aware of the neighborhood noises, such as passing motorcars, that might mean danger to him.
>
> A young man stated he was sitting at a baseball game in a small town and watching a little boy crawl under the fence to join the audience. Another was in a concert hall listening to music. "An orchestration," he explained. He could hear the different instruments...
>
> D.F. could hear instruments playing a melody. I re-stimulated the same point thirty times (!) trying to mislead her, and dictated each response to a stenographer. Each time I re-stimulated, she heard the melody again. It began at the same place and went on from chorus to verse. When she hummed an accompaniment to the music, the tempo was what would have been expected.

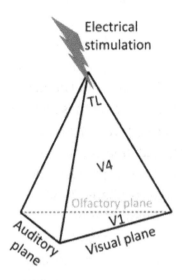

Figure P.1 The objectNE activated by the stimulation of the temporal lobe can be depicted as a pyramid. Each side of the pyramid represents one sensual modality. The neurons at the base of the pyramid are the least selective; these are the neurons located in the primary visual area, primary auditory area and so on. The neurons in the temporal lobe stimulated by Penfield are located at the tip of the pyramid. They are the most selective. These neurons have a high probability of triggering synchronous activity of a complete neuronal ensemble.

Let us attempt to understand Penfield's observations within the context of the PFS theory. Electrical stimulation of the temporal lobe in conscious patients triggered a recall of a series of memory frames that included both visual ("I think I saw the river," "I could see the desks") and auditory ("mother calling her little boy," "instruments playing a melody") sensations. Each conscious frame described by the patient was represented by an increased activity of a large group of neurons (neuronal ensemble) firing in synchrony with each other. The objectNE likely included neurons located in the visual cortex (V1, V2, V4, ITL, MT), as well as in the auditory cortex. It is likely that these were the same parts of the cortex that were active during the original conscious experience of the event's occurrence in the physical world.

An objectNE activated by the stimulation of the temporal lobe can be depicted as a pyramid. Each side of the pyramid represents one sensual modality. The neurons at the base of the pyramid are the least selective; these are the neurons located in the primary visual area, primary auditory area and so on. The neurons in the temporal lobe stimulated by Penfield are located at the tip of the pyramid. They are the most selective. These neurons have a high probability of triggering synchronous activity of a complete neuronal ensemble; they are binding the ensemble together. The memory of an event is not located in any single neuron; it is encoded in the connections between the hundreds of thousands of neurons comprising the *complete* ensemble. Thus the memory is distributed throughout the cerebral cortex. The activity of the complete ensemble can be triggered by activity in any part of the ensemble. However, activity in the binding neurons located in the temporal lobe has the greatest probability of activating the complete neuronal ensemble. Damage to a part of the cortex may interfere with the memory of one aspect of the event. However, damage to the binding neurons of the temporal lobe makes it especially hard for the patient to activate the complete neuronal ensemble. Thus, damage to the temporal lobe can be especially detrimental to a patient's memory (not because memory is located in the temporal lobe, but because the binding neurons are located there).

Finally, I should mention that humans can voluntarily modify any part of the objectNE representing the memory of an event. Humans can use PFS to change any characteristic of an event: we can change the color of the objects, or even replace them with other objects; we can change the auditory memory; etc.

Stimulation of the speech cortex

Here is one more quote from Penfield's "The Mystery of the Mind" (pages 50-51), describing the responses of patient C.H. upon stimulation of Wernicke's area in his left temporal lobe:

> ... We have found that a gentle electrical current interferes with the function of the speech mechanism. One touches the cortex with a stimulating electrode and, since the brain is not sensitive, the patient does not realize that this has made him aphasic until he tries to speak, or to understand speech, and is unable to do so.
>
> One of my associates began to show the patient a series of pictures on the other side of the sterile screen. C.H. named each picture accurately at first. Then, before the picture of a butterfly was shown to him, I applied the electrode where I supposed the speech cortex to be. He remained silent for a time. Then he snapped his fingers as though in exasperation. I withdrew the electrode and he spoke at once:
>
> "Now I can talk," he said. "Butterfly. I couldn't get that word 'butterfly,' so I tried to get the word 'moth!'"
>
> It is clear that while the speech mechanism was temporarily blocked he could perceive the meaning of the picture of a butterfly. He made a conscious effort to "get" the corresponding word. Then, not understanding why he could not do so, he turned back for a second time to the interpretive mechanism, which was well away from the interfering effect of the electrical current, and found a second concept that he considered the closest thing to a butterfly. He must then have presented that to the speech mechanism, only to draw another blank.

This experiment suggests that the visual recognition faculty (visual department) can function independently from the speech cortex (auditory/ linguistic department). The patient C.H. was obviously able to recognize the butterfly without any help from the speech cortex. When the linguistic department was not able to name the butterfly, C.H. was able recall the image of a moth (which he associated with a butterfly), again with no help from the speech cortex. The neuronal activation pattern in C.H. can be depicted as follows:

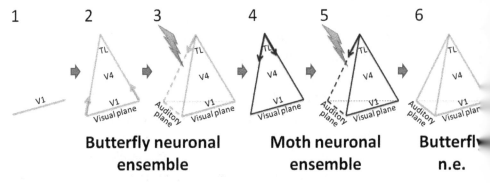

Butterfly neuronal ensemble   **Moth neuronal ensemble**   **Butterfly n.e.**

Figure P.2 The neuronal activation pattern in patient C.H. following presentation of a butterfly.

(1) A picture of a butterfly is shown. Neurons in V1 (green/light line) are activated.

(2) The butterfly is recognized. The part of the objectNE representing the butterfly in the visual cortex is activated.

(3) However, the auditory neurons that are part of the butterfly ensemble (located in the speech cortex) are inactivated by electrical current. These neurons are represented here by the auditory plane of the green pyramid. Consequently, this part of the ensemble is not activated and the patient is unable to utter the word 'butterfly.'

(4) The patient searches for a different objectNE that is closely associated with the objectNE of the butterfly. The objectNE representing a moth is activated and the patient experiences the mental image of a moth (blue/dark).

(5) Normally such a recollection would also activate the auditory plane of the neuronal ensemble. However the speech cortex is still inactivated by electrical current and the patient fails to speak the word 'moth'.

(6) As soon as the electrical stimulation of the speech cortex is stopped, the complete neural ensemble that includes the auditory neurons can form and the patient is able to speak.

Appendix 4. Additional experimental data supporting the hypothesis that the mental activity involved in the process of viewing an object and recalling the same object with eyes closed is largely the same

In addition to the five experiments mentioned in Chapter 2.3, I would like to go over four other experiments supporting the hypothesis that the mental activity involved in the process of viewing an object (visual perception) and recalling the same object with eyes closed (mental imagery) is largely the same:

1. A 1992 experiment showed that mental images can interfere with visual perception and this interference is location specific: the interference is greatest when the mental image is formed directly over the visual percept [453].

2. Parallel deficits were reported in mental image formation and in visual perception in patients with brain damage (see Ganis [103], for review). First, patients with unilateral damage in the occipital lobe who had lost visual perception in half of the visual field had trouble forming mental images in that part of space [454]. Second, patients with damage localized in one hemisphere, who neglect half of the space during visual perception, also neglect the same half of the space when forming a mental image. A stroke in the right hemisphere can lead to neglect of the left side of the visual field, causing a patient to behave as if the left side of the sensory space were nonexistent.

In extreme cases, a patient with neglect may fail to eat the food on the left half of the plate, even though the patient may complain of being hungry. If a patient with neglect is asked to draw a clock, the drawing may show only the numbers 12 to 6, with the other side of the clock left blank. Patients with neglect may also ignore one side of their body, shaving or applying makeup only to the non-neglected side.

Finally, damage to the visual cortex (due to exposure to toxins such as carbon monoxide) often leads to a patient's inability to recognize objects (object agnosia) while other visual functions, such as acuity, color vision, and brightness discrimination, may still be intact. Patients with object agnosia have trouble visually recognizing, copying, or discriminating between different objects. Often, such patients also have difficulties imagining those objects. For example, patients who are impaired at face recognition often have difficulty imagining faces [101,102].

3. Transcranial magnetic stimulation is a noninvasive method to excite neurons in the brain. Electromagnetic induction from a coil of wire (encased in plastic) triggers some neurons to fire action potentials. When transcranial magnetic stimulation is applied repetitively, it can desensitize (inactivate) a patch of neurons under the coil. Kosslyn and colleagues used transcranial magnetic stimulation to temporarily desensitize small patches of the cortex [455]. Following the desensitization of the visual cortex, the performance of subjects in both visual imagery and visual perception tests was degraded. Statistical calculations indicated that not only was the performance degraded, but that it was degraded by the same degree in visual imagery and visual perception. Desensitization of the cortex outside of the visual cortex did not degrade a subject's performance in either test. The fact that desensitization of the visual cortex degrades performance in mental imagery tasks

indicates that the visual cortex plays an active role in performing the task.

4. Cortical activity measured by Positron emission tomography, functional MRI, and single photon emission computed that the tomography during visual perception overlaps with brain activity measured during mental imagery. The evidence of cortical activity measured during mental imagery is summarized in the book "The Case for Mental Imagery" [440]. The book also provides an excellent in-depth discussion of the physical properties of mental images. The authors conclude that visual percepts and mental images share underlying neural processes.

Appendix 5: Mental imagery in blind patients

Blindness (the inability to visually recognize objects), can be caused by (1) visual information not reaching the cortex (for example due to damage to both eyes or to a pathway from the eyes to the cortex) or (2) damage to the visual cortex.

In the first case, completely blind patients may still be able to use the visual cortex to recall mental images and conduct PFS (note that these patients cannot visually recognize objects). Using positron emission topography, Sadato and colleagues compared the brain activity in blind and sighted subjects who were reading text using the Braille system [456]. Each Braille character is made up of six raised dots, arranged in a rectangle containing two columns of three dots each. The brain activity of blind subjects reading Braille text showed an activation of the visual cortical areas. The sighted subjects performing the same task showed a deactivation of visual cortical areas. The authors concluded that "in blind subjects, cortical areas normally reserved for vision may be activated by other sensory modalities" [456].

In the second case, damage to the visual cortex may be associated with a specific deficit in mental imagery. In the most profound case of bilateral damage to the visual cortex, patients are cortically blind. These patients cannot visually recognize objects and the majority of these patients have difficulty forming visual mental images.

However, there are reports that some of these patients can

solve visual-based tasks. How can these patients solve visual-based tasks without the ability to form mental images? Here is an insight provided by Kosslyn and colleagues [440] (page 116):

> One possible account for this result rests on the idea that the tasks may not have required object-based imagery. For example, one of us once saw a patient who had a major damage to her occipital lobes. When asked whether the uppercase letter A had any curved lines, she literally drew it in the air, and then responded, "No." She clearly was using kinesthetic feedback to answer. Her ability to draw need not have been guided by visual imagery; rather, purely spatial or motoric information would have been sufficient to allow her to make the response.
>
> Another account focuses on the fact that topographically organized areas are present not only in the occipital and parietal lobes, but at many levels of hierarchy in the pathways within these systems.

Thus, patients with damage to the visual cortex can sometimes draw upon other cortical areas for the tasks normally solved in the visual cortex. This should not come as a surprise since redundancy is a hallmark of the cerebral cortex. It is likely that some tasks that are normally solved in the visual cortex can be solved in the motor cortex, or maybe even in the somatosensory cortex. After all, both motor and somatosensory cortices are organized topographically. In addition, the brain can often reprogram its hardware, especially when the damage occurs at a young age. In this case, the brain area normally reserved for one task can be rewired to perform a very different task. One demonstration of such cortical plasticity was done by Mriganka Sur, a Professor of Neuroscience and the Director of the Simons Center for the Social Brain at MIT. In 2000, he redirected visual input in newborn ferrets from the visual cortex to the auditory cortex [457]. Could ferrets see with their auditory cortex? It turns out that the rewired cortex could "mediate visual behavior. When light stimuli are presented in the portion of the visual field … ferrets respond as though they perceive the stimuli to be visual rather than auditory" [457]. Cortical neurons show an amazing plasticity.

Appendix 6: Additional discussion of Genie's cognitive abilities

While there is scientific consensus that Genie was not able to acquire recursive language expressed by her inability to understand prepositions and to comprehend complex sentences, Genie was deemed cognitively developed on the bases of several tests.

> "... [Genie] shows a profile of primitive recursive and morphological ability combined with relatively well-developed semantic ability. Genie's semantic sophistication suggests a conceptual level far surpassing what one would imagine from her otherwise rather primitive utterance. This impression is borne out through testing. In 1977, at the age of 20 she was in the concrete operational stage, performing at or above a 10-year-level on stereognosis, on figure-ground tasks, on a test of topographical and Euclidean relations, and on a test for decentrism of visual perspective. She conserved for area, length, and (questionably) number. Her drawing was at a 6- to 7-year level. She was able to perform all nesting operations tested and effortlessly constructed stick and block structures involving several layers of hierarchical structure, including Greenfield's models as well as several more complex structures. She performed all classification tasks perfectly (sorting on the principles of gender, animacy, and others), and sequenced all "picture-stories" correctly" [165].

Based on these experiments, one may conclude that Genie was capable of PFS. After all, our common experience dictates that a typical child capable of sequencing "picture-stories" correctly, would also be capable of PFS. However Genie is anything but a typical person. To make a judgment of her PFS capabilities, it is important to understand which tests require PFS for completion and which can be completed without forming any novel mental images. For example, sequencing picture-stories does not rely on PFS. If picture A shows a boy running, picture B shows the boy falling, and picture C shows the boy crying, then, one does not need to use PFS to realize that picture C follows picture B which follows picture A. Understanding causality between events shown in the pictures does not necessarily involve synthesis of any novel mental images. The inference of the order of events can be made from a memory of similar events or a personal experience of running, falling and crying thereafter. On all language tests that unambiguously test PFS, such as spatial prepositions, Genie didn't rise up above random performance.

Additionally, Genie was tested with Raven's Matrices and Wechsler Intelligence Scale for Children (WISC). Fromkin *et al.* report that 1.5 years into rehabilitation Genie's "performance on the Raven Matrices could not be scored in the usual manner but corresponded to the 50th percentile of children aged 8.5 to 9 years" [458]. Curtiss *et al.* report that 2 years into rehabilitation "on WISC... performance subtests ... she has achieved subtest scaled scores as high as eight and nine" [459]. In addition, Curtiss reports that 5 years into rehabilitation "Genie was given the Coloured Progressive Matrices Test. ... Genie's overall score was 29." [326]. In all three nonverbal tests that Genie was administered up to five years into rehabilitation Genie has invariably failed to demonstrate the capacity for PFS [145].

Genie's capacity for figurative drawing is harder to dissect. After all, figurative drawing in a typical child is often a manifestation of developing PFS. How can the dissociation between Genie's ability to draw figurative images "at a 6- to 7-year level" and her lack of understanding of spatial prepositions (normally developed between the ages of 3 and 4) be explained? Let's first discuss Genie's drawings: 10 drawings spanning the period of seven years after Genie's rescue are published in Susan Curtiss' 1977 book, *Genie: A Psycholinguistic Study of a Modern Day Wild Child*. To get an expert opinion, I showed the drawings to several specialists in child development and, without much explanation, asked them to guess the age of the child who made each drawing. The specialists' guesses ranged from three to seven years of age. Genie's earliest drawings made during the first year after isolation (e.g. the "head feet representation" made on 12/22/1971) were comparable, according to the specialists, to those made by a 3 to 4 year old child. Thus, at least during the first year after captivity, there may not have been much dissociation between Genie's figurative drawings and her language: both approximately corresponded to a level typical of a 3 to 4 year old child (Genie's age at the time was 14).

Genie was encouraged to draw and her later drawings clearly show more proficiency. The specialists I interviewed guessed that these later drawings were produced by a 4 to 7 year old but noticed that there was something atypical about these drawings. The specialists were particularly startled by the apparent discontinuity of lines. All of Genie's drawings are performed with short light strokes consisting of straight lines and circles. Long strong lines are nearly completely absent. There is some uncertainty in location of the eyes, ears, hands, and other features: the nose, eyes, ears, hands, and feet are all depicted with multiple circular lines. A drawing of a typical 7-year old shows intentionality in placement of each feature. As was discussed in Chapter 3.11, each feature placement is probably rehearsed mentally and only then performed on paper (that is, PFS provides feedback for the correct placement of each feature). When looking at Genie's drawings, one has a feeling that **Genie was synthesizing features on paper rather than in her mind**. For example, it seems that to draw a nose, Genie would repeat circular motions until the nose appeared to be in the correct location on the face (that is, until Genie's sensory system recognized that the nose was being drawn in the right place). This drawing style is consistent with Genie being unsure where to draw the nose initially; the feedback seems to be provided not through mental simulation, but by the sensory signal from the actual drawing on the paper.

Consider Genie's most complex drawing, made in 1977 when she was 20 years old, showing her mother holding her as a baby. The caption written by Curtiss explains:

> At first she only drew a picture of her mother and then labeled it "I miss Mama." She then suddenly began to draw more. The moment she finished she took my hand, placed it next to what she had just drawn, motioning me to write, and said "Baby Genie." [Genie added a baby to the drawing] Then she pointed under her drawing and said, "Mama hand." I dictated all the letters. Satisfied, she sat back and stared at the picture. There she was, a baby in her mother's arms. She has created her own reality.

Note that Genie did not create "her own reality" mentally, she did not set out to draw her mother holding baby Genie from the beginning. Genie initially drew the mother and then after a pause decided to add a baby. The synthesis occurred on paper.

To sum up, there may be no dissociation between Genie's figurative drawings and her language skills — both manifest PFS at the level of a 3-4 year old child. Genie's drawings during the first post-captivity year clearly correspond to a level of a 3-4 year old child, while in later drawings Genie has found a method to add features to a drawing with minimal reliance on PFS. (This later methodology may be akin to thinking on paper. Compare the addition of three digit numbers conducted on paper to those conducted mentally. Clearly arithmetic on paper (365+257=?) is much easier than finding the solution mentally: when synthesis occurs on paper, one does not need to use as many mental resources. Solving algebraic, geometrical, and logical problems is often much easier on paper than in the mind.)

Acknowledgments

I am indebted to Rita Dunn for scrupulous editing of the book, enlightened suggestions and productive discussions. I am grateful to my wife Olga for putting up with occasional periods of melancholy as well as constructive discussions about sections of the book that I was struggling with. I would like to thank Yulia Dumov and my wife Olga for illustrating this book. I would also like to express the greatest appreciation for my teachers: Dr. Jen-Wei Lin, who introduced me to Experimental Neurophysiology; Dr. Raymond Murphy, who mentored me in Medicine for over a decade at Stethographics; Dr. Efim Levin, who mentored me in Physics; Dr. Sergei P. Preobrazensky, who trained me in Mathematics and taught me patience; and many others. I have to thank my friends and colleagues for numerous discussions on the subject and invaluable critique of the ideas. I'd like to especially notice the contributions of Dr. Fred Wasserman, Dr. Maria K. Houtchens, Dr. Irene Piryatinsky, Dr. Julia Braverman, Mikhail Tselman, Dane Wolf, Dr. Ilya Pevzner, and Edward Khokhlovich.

Bibliography

1. Darwin's, C. On the origin of species. *Publ. On* **24**, (1859).
2. Somel, M., Liu, X. & Khaitovich, P. Human brain evolution: transcripts, metabolites and their regulators. *Nat. Rev. Neurosci.* **14**, 112–127 (2013).
3. Washburn, S. L. Tools and human evolution. *Sci. Am.* **203**, 62–75 (1960).
4. van Lawick-Goodall, J. The behaviour of free-living chimpanzees in the Gombe Stream Reserve. *Anim. Behav. Monogr.* **1**, 161IN1-311IN12 (1968).
5. McGrew, W. C. *Chimpanzee material culture: implications for human evolution.* (Cambridge University Press, 1992).
6. Whiten, A. *et al.* Cultures in chimpanzees. *Nature* **399**, 682–685 (1999).
7. Pruetz, J. D. & Bertolani, P. Savanna chimpanzees, Pan troglodytes verus, hunt with tools. *Curr. Biol.* **17**, 412–417 (2007).
8. Terrace, H. S., Petitto, L. A., Sanders, R. J. & Bever, T. G. Can an ape create a sentence? *Science* **206**, 891–902 (1979).
9. Patterson, F. & Linden, E. The education of Koko. (1981).
10. Savage-Rumbaugh, E. S. *et al.* Language comprehension in ape and child. *Monogr. Soc. Res. Child Dev.* i–252 (1993).
11. Inoue, S. & Matsuzawa, T. Working memory of numerals in chimpanzees. *Curr. Biol.* **17**, R1004–R1005 (2007).
12. Luncz, L. V., Mundry, R. & Boesch, C. Evidence for cultural differences between neighboring chimpanzee communities. *Curr. Biol.* **22**, 922–926 (2012).
13. Dunbar, R. & Dunbar, R. I. M. *Grooming, gossip, and the evolution of language.* (Harvard University Press, 1998).
14. Poincaré, H. Sur la valeur objective de la science. *Rev. Métaphys. Morale* **10**, 263–293 (1902).
15. Vyshedskiy, A. *et al.* Novel prefrontal synthesis intervention improves language in children with autism. *Healthcare* **8**, 566 (2020).
16. Pearson, J. The human imagination: the cognitive neuroscience of visual mental imagery. *Nat. Rev. Neurosci.* 624–634 (2019).
17. Braun, A. R. *et al.* Regional cerebral blood flow throughout the sleep-wake cycle. *Brain* **120**, 1173–1197 (1997).
18. Siclari, F. *et al.* The neural correlates of dreaming. *Nat. Neurosci.* **20**, 872 (2017).
19. Solms, M. *The neuropsychology of dreams: A clinico-anatomical study.* (L. Erlbaum, 1997).
20. Darwin, C. *The Descent of Man and Seletion in Relation to Sex.* (John Murray, 1871).
21. Fuster, J. *The Prefrontal Cortex, Fourth Edition.* (Academic Press, 2008).

22. Li, N., Chen, T.-W., Guo, Z. V., Gerfen, C. R. & Svoboda, K. A motor cortex circuit for motor planning and movement. *Nature* **519**, 51–56 (2015).

23. Christoff, K. & Gabrieli, J. D. The frontopolar cortex and human cognition: evidence for a rostrocaudal hierarchical organization within the human prefrontal cortex. *Psychobiology* **28**, 168–186 (2000).

24. Waltz, J. A. *et al.* A system for relational reasoning in human prefrontal cortex. *Psychol. Sci.* **10**, 119–125 (1999).

25. Duncan, J., Burgess, P. & Emslie, H. Fluid intelligence after frontal lobe lesions. *Neuropsychologia* **33**, 261–268 (1995).

26. Luria, A. *Higher cortical functions in man.* (Springer Science & Business Media, 2012).

27. Baker, S. C. *et al.* Neural systems engaged by planning: a PET study of the Tower of London task. *Neuropsychologia* **34**, 515–526 (1996).

28. Friederici, A. D. The brain basis of language processing: from structure to function. *Physiol. Rev.* **91**, 1357–1392 (2011).

29. Jay, T. *Why we curse: A neuro-psycho-social theory of speech.* (John Benjamins Publishing, 1999).

30. Harari, Y. N. *Sapiens: A brief history of humankind.* (Random House, 2014).

31. Atance, C. M. & O'Neill, D. K. Episodic future thinking. *Trends Cogn. Sci.* **5**, 533–539 (2001).

32. Suddendorf, T. & Redshaw, J. The development of mental scenario building and episodic foresight. *Ann. N. Y. Acad. Sci.* **1296**, 135–153 (2013).

33. MacKay, D. G. & Goldstein, R. Creativity, Comprehension, Conversation and the Hippocampal Region: New Data and Theory. *AIMS Neurosci.* **3**, 105 (2016).

34. Shallice, T. Specific impairments of planning. *Phil Trans R Soc Lond B* **298**, 199–209 (1982).

35. Zago, L. *et al.* Neural correlates of simple and complex mental calculation. *Neuroimage* **13**, 314–327 (2001).

36. Luria, A. R. Traumatic aphasia. Mouton. *The Hague* (1970).

37. Vyshedskiy, A. *et al.* Novel Linguistic Evaluation of Prefrontal Synthesis (LEPS) test measures prefrontal synthesis acquisition in neurotypical children and predicts high-functioning versus low-functioning class assignment in individuals with autism. *Appl. Neuropsychol. Child* (2020) doi:https://doi.org/10.1080/21622965.2020.1758700.

38. Berardi, N., Pizzorusso, T. & Maffei, L. Critical periods during sensory development. *Curr. Opin. Neurobiol.* **10**, 138–145 (2000).

39. Romeo, R. R. *et al.* Language exposure relates to structural neural connectivity in childhood. *J. Neurosci.* **38**, 7870–7877 (2018).

40. Vyshedskiy, A., Mahapatra, S. & Dunn, R. Linguistically deprived children: meta-analysis of published research underlines the importance of early syntactic language use for normal brain development. *Res. Ideas Outcomes* (2017) doi:10.3897/rio.3.e20696.

41. Schreibman, L. Diagnostic features of autism. *J. Child Neurol.* **3**, S57–S64 (1988).

42. Lovaas, O. I., Koegel, R. L. & Schreibman, L. Stimulus overselectivity in autism: A review of research. *Psychol. Bull.* **86**, 1236–1254 (1979).

43. Ploog, B. O. Stimulus overselectivity four decades later: A review of the literature and its implications for current research in autism spectrum disorder. *J. Autism Dev. Disord.* **40**, 1332–1349 (2010).

44. American Speech-Language-Hearing Association. Scope of practice in speech-language pathology. *Available from www.asha.org/policy/* (2016).

45. Axe, J. B. Conditional discrimination in the intraverbal relation: A review and recommendations for future research. *Anal. Verbal Behav.* **24**, 159–174 (2008).

46. Michael, J., Palmer, D. C. & Sundberg, M. L. The multiple control of verbal behavior. *Anal. Verbal Behav.* **27**, 3–22 (2011).

47. Eikeseth, S. & Smith, D. P. An analysis of verbal stimulus control in intraverbal behavior: implications for practice and applied research. *Anal. Verbal Behav.* **29**, 125–135 (2013).

48. Lowenkron, B. Joint control and the selection of stimuli from their description. *Anal. Verbal Behav.* **22**, 129–151 (2006).

49. Hartshorne, J. K., Tenenbaum, J. B. & Pinker, S. A critical period for second language acquisition: Evidence from 2/3 million English speakers. *Cognition* **177**, 263–277 (2018).

50. Kral, A. Auditory critical periods: a review from system's perspective. *Neuroscience* **247**, 117–133 (2013).

51. Kuhl, P. K., Williams, K. A., Lacerda, F., Stevens, K. N. & Lindblom, B. Linguistic experience alters phonetic perception in infants by 6 months of age. *Science* **255**, 606–608 (1992).

52. Wartenburger, I. *et al.* Early setting of grammatical processing in the bilingual brain. *Neuron* **37**, 159–170 (2003).

53. Kim, K. H., Relkin, N. R., Lee, K.-M. & Hirsch, J. Distinct cortical areas associated with native and second languages. *Nature* **388**, 171–174 (1997).

54. Snow, C. E. & Hoefnagel-Höhle, M. The critical period for language acquisition: Evidence from second language learning. *Child Dev.* 1114–1128 (1978).

55. Tallal, P. *et al.* Language comprehension in language-learning impaired children improved with acoustically modified speech. *Science* **271**, 81–84 (1996).

56. Kilgard, M. P. & Merzenich, M. M. Plasticity of temporal information processing in the primary auditory cortex. *Nat. Neurosci.* **1**, 727 (1998).

57. Sherman, S. M. & Spear, P. D. Organization of visual pathways in normal and visually deprived cats. *Physiol. Rev.* **62**, 738–855 (1982).

58. Bateson, P. Brief exposure to a novel stimulus during imprinting in chicks and its influence on subsequent preferences. *Anim. Learn. Behav.* **7**, 259–262 (1979).

59. Knudsen, E. I., Knudsen, P. F. & Esterly, S. D. A critical period for the

recovery of sound localization accuracy following monaural occlusion in the barn owl. *J. Neurosci.* **4**, 1012–1020 (1984).

60.   Lenneberg, E. H. The biological foundations of language. *Hosp. Pract.* **2**, 59–67 (1967).

61.   Bick, J. *et al.* Effect of early institutionalization and foster care on long-term white matter development: a randomized clinical trial. *JAMA Pediatr.* **169**, 211–219 (2015).

62.   Emmorey, K., Kosslyn, S. M. & Bellugi, U. Visual imagery and visual-spatial language: Enhanced imagery abilities in deaf and hearing ASL signers. *Cognition* **46**, 139–181 (1993).

63.   Martin, A. J. Does age of language acquisition affect the relation between American sign language and mental rotation? (UNIVERSITY OF MINNESOTA, 2009).

64.   Martin, A., Senghas, A. & Pyers, J. Age of acquisition effects on mental rotation: evidence from Nicaraguan sign language. in *BUCLD 37: proceedings of the 37th Boston university conference on language development* 241–250 (2013).

65.   Pyers, J. E., Shusterman, A., Senghas, A., Spelke, E. S. & Emmorey, K. Evidence from an emerging sign language reveals that language supports spatial cognition. *Proc. Natl. Acad. Sci.* **107**, 12116–12120 (2010).

66.   Fombonne, E. Epidemiological surveys of autism and other pervasive developmental disorders: an update. *J. Autism Dev. Disord.* **33**, 365–382 (2003).

67.   Webb, S. J., Jones, E. J. H., Kelly, J. & Dawson, G. The motivation for very early intervention for infants at high risk for autism spectrum disorders. *Int. J. Speech Lang. Pathol.* **16**, 36–42 (2014).

68.   Dunn, L. M. & Dunn, D. M. *PPVT-4: Peabody picture vocabulary test.* (Pearson Assessments, 2007).

69.   Williams, K. T. Expressive vocabulary test second edition (EVT^{TM} 2). *J Am Acad Child Adolesc Psychiatry* **42**, 864–872 (1997).

70.   Thakkar, M. M. & Datta, S. The evolution of REM sleep. *Evol. Sleep Phylogenetic Funct. Perspect. Camb. Univ. Press N. Y.* 197–215 (2010).

71.   Hobson, J. A. REM sleep and dreaming: towards a theory of protoconsciousness. *Nat. Rev. Neurosci.* **10**, 803 (2009).

72.   Ólafsdóttir, H. F., Barry, C., Saleem, A. B., Hassabis, D. & Spiers, H. J. Hippocampal place cells construct reward related sequences through unexplored space. *Elife* **4**, e06063 (2015).

73.   Vyshedskiy. Language evolution to revolution: the leap from rich-vocabulary non-recursive communication system to recursive language 70,000 years ago was associated with acquisition of a novel component of imagination, called Prefrontal Synthesis, enabled by a mutation that slowed down the prefrontal cortex maturation simultaneously in two or more children – the Romulus and Remus hypothesis. *Res. Ideas Outcomes* **5**, e38546 (2019).

74.   Irwin, S. O. Embodied being: Examining tool use in digital storytelling. *Tamara J. Crit. Organ. Inq.* **12**, 39–49 (2014).

75. Andrews-Hanna, J. R. The brain's default network and its adaptive role in internal mentation. *The Neuroscientist* **18**, 251–270 (2012).
76. Diamond, A. & Lee, K. Interventions shown to aid executive function development in children 4 to 12 years old. *Science* **333**, 959–964 (2011).
77. Fuster, J. *Cortex and mind: Unifying cognition.* (Oxford university press, 2003).
78. Dobbs, A. R. & Rule, B. G. Prospective memory and self-reports of memory abilities in older adults. *Can. J. Psychol. Can. Psychol.* **41**, 209 (1987).
79. Ingvar, D. H. ' Memory of the future': an essay on the temporal organization of conscious awareness. *Hum. Neurobiol.* **4**, 127–136 (1985).
80. Suddendorf, T. TWO KEY FEATURES CREATED THE HUMAN MIND INSIDE OUR HEADS. *Sci. Am.* **319**, 43–47 (2018).
81. Kreiman, G., Koch, C. & Fried, I. Imagery neurons in the human brain. *Nature* **408**, 357–361 (2000).
82. Barton, R. A. Visual specialization and brain evolution in primates. *Proc. R. Soc. Lond. B Biol. Sci.* **265**, 1933–1937 (1998).
83. Quiroga, R. Q., Kreiman, G., Koch, C. & Fried, I. Sparse but not 'grandmother-cell' coding in the medial temporal lobe. *Trends Cogn. Sci.* **12**, 87–91 (2008).
84. Quiroga, R. Q., Kraskov, A., Koch, C. & Fried, I. Explicit encoding of multimodal percepts by single neurons in the human brain. *Curr. Biol.* **19**, 1308–1313 (2009).
85. Waydo, S., Kraskov, A., Quiroga, R. Q., Fried, I. & Koch, C. Sparse representation in the human medial temporal lobe. *J. Neurosci.* **26**, 10232–10234 (2006).
86. Hebb, D. O. *The organization of behavior: A neuropsychological approach.* (John Wiley & Sons, 1949).
87. Squire, L. R. & Kandel, E. R. *Memory: From mind to molecules.* vol. 69 (Macmillan, 2003).
88. Sacks, O. W. *The man who mistook his wife for a hat and other clinical tales. 1st Touchstone edn.* (New York, NY: Simon & Schuster, 1998).
89. Penfield, W. *Mystery of the mind: A critical study of consciousness and the human brain.* (Princeton University Press, 2015).
90. Kastner, S., Demmer, I. & Ziemann, U. Transient visual field defects induced by transcranial magnetic stimulation over human occipital pole. *Exp. Brain Res.* **118**, 19–26 (1998).
91. Kosslyn, S. M., Ganis, G. & Thompson, W. L. Neural foundations of imagery. *Nat. Rev. Neurosci.* **2**, 635–642 (2001).
92. Gelbard-Sagiv, H., Mukamel, R., Harel, M., Malach, R. & Fried, I. Internally generated reactivation of single neurons in human hippocampus during free recall. *Science* **322**, 96–101 (2008).
93. Reddy, L., Tsuchiya, N. & Serre, T. Reading the mind's eye: decoding category information during mental imagery. *Neuroimage* **50**, 818–825 (2010).
94. Cichy, R. M., Heinzle, J. & Haynes, J.-D. Imagery and perception share

cortical representations of content and location. *Cereb. Cortex* **22**, 372–380 (2012).

95. Klein, I. *et al.* Retinotopic organization of visual mental images as revealed by functional magnetic resonance imaging. *Cogn. Brain Res.* **22**, 26–31 (2004).

96. Danker, J. F. & Anderson, J. R. The ghosts of brain states past: remembering reactivates the brain regions engaged during encoding. *Psychol. Bull.* **136**, 87 (2010).

97. Jeannerod, M. & Frak, V. Mental imaging of motor activity in humans. *Curr. Opin. Neurobiol.* **9**, 735–739 (1999).

98. Meister, I. G. *et al.* Playing piano in the mind—an fMRI study on music imagery and performance in pianists. *Cogn. Brain Res.* **19**, 219–228 (2004).

99. Crick, F., Koch, C., Kreiman, G. & Fried, I. Consciousness and neurosurgery. *Neurosurgery* **55**, 273–282 (2004).

100. Zatorre, R. J., Halpern, A. R., Perry, D. W., Meyer, E. & Evans, A. C. Hearing in the mind's ear: a PET investigation of musical imagery and perception. *J. Cogn. Neurosci.* **8**, 29–46 (1996).

101. Shuttleworth Jr, E. C., Syring, V. & Allen, N. Further observations on the nature of prosopagnosia. *Brain Cogn.* **1**, 307–322 (1982).

102. Levine, D. N., Warach, J. & Farah, M. Two visual systems in mental imagery: Dissociation of "what" and "where" in imagery disorders due to bilateral posterior cerebral lesions. *Neurology* **35**, 1010–1010 (1985).

103. Ganis, G., Thompson, W. L., Mast, F. W. & Kosslyn, S. M. Visual imagery in cerebral visual dysfunction. *Neurol. Clin.* **21**, 631–646 (2003).

104. O'Craven, K. M. & Kanwisher, N. Mental imagery of faces and places activates corresponding stimulus-specific brain regions. *J. Cogn. Neurosci.* **12**, 1013–1023 (2000).

105. Uhlhaas, P. J. & Singer, W. Neural synchrony in brain disorders: relevance for cognitive dysfunctions and pathophysiology. *Neuron* **52**, 155–168 (2006).

106. Gray, C. M., König, P., Engel, A. K., Singer, W., & others. Oscillatory responses in cat visual cortex exhibit inter-columnar synchronization which reflects global stimulus properties. *Nature* **338**, 334–337 (1989).

107. Bartos, M., Vida, I. & Jonas, P. Synaptic mechanisms of synchronized gamma oscillations in inhibitory interneuron networks. *Nat. Rev. Neurosci.* **8**, 45–56 (2007).

108. Singer, W. & Gray, C. M. Visual feature integration and the temporal correlation hypothesis. *Annu. Rev. Neurosci.* **18**, 555–586 (1995).

109. Uhlhaas, P. *et al.* Neural synchrony in cortical networks: history, concept and current status. *Front. Integr. Neurosci.* **3**, 17 (2009).

110. Engel, A. K., Konig, P., & others. Interhemispheric synchronization of oscillatory neuronal responses in cat visual cortex. *Science* **252**, 1177 (1991).

111. Hirabayashi, T. & Miyashita, Y. Dynamically modulated spike correlation in monkey inferior temporal cortex depending on the feature configuration

within a whole object. *J. Neurosci.* **25**, 10299–10307 (2005).
112. Fries, P. A mechanism for cognitive dynamics: neuronal communication through neuronal coherence. *Trends Cogn. Sci.* **9**, 474–480 (2005).
113. Meador, K. J., Ray, P. G., Echauz, J. R., Loring, D. W. & Vachtsevanos, G. J. Gamma coherence and conscious perception. *Neurology* **59**, 847–854 (2002).
114. Nakatani, C., Ito, J., Nikolaev, A. R., Gong, P. & Leeuwen, C. van. Phase synchronization analysis of EEG during attentional blink. *J. Cogn. Neurosci.* **17**, 1969–1979 (2005).
115. Doesburg, S. M., Kitajo, K. & Ward, L. M. Increased gamma-band synchrony precedes switching of conscious perceptual objects in binocular rivalry. *Neuroreport* **16**, 1139–1142 (2005).
116. Fries, P., Schröder, J.-H., Roelfsema, P. R., Singer, W. & Engel, A. K. Oscillatory neuronal synchronization in primary visual cortex as a correlate of stimulus selection. *J. Neurosci.* **22**, 3739–3754 (2002).
117. Buzsáki, G. Large-scale recording of neuronal ensembles. *Nat. Neurosci.* **7**, 446–451 (2004).
118. Llinás, R., Ribary, U., Contreras, D. & Pedroarena, C. The neuronal basis for consciousness. *Philos. Trans. R. Soc. Lond. B. Biol. Sci.* **353**, 1841–1849 (1998).
119. Sehatpour, P. *et al.* A human intracranial study of long-range oscillatory coherence across a frontal–occipital–hippocampal brain network during visual object processing. *Proc. Natl. Acad. Sci.* **105**, 4399–4404 (2008).
120. Rodriguez, E., George, N., Lachaux, J.-P., Martinerie, J., & others. Perception's shadow: long-distance synchronization of human brain activity. *Nature* **397**, 430 (1999).
121. Hipp, J. F., Engel, A. K. & Siegel, M. Oscillatory synchronization in large-scale cortical networks predicts perception. *Neuron* **69**, 387–396 (2011).
122. Vyshedskiy & Dunn, R. Mental synthesis involves the synchronization of independent neuronal ensembles. *Res. Ideas Outcomes* **1**, e7642 (2015).
123. Vyshedskiy, A. Voluntary and Involuntary Imagination: Neurological Mechanisms, Developmental Path, Clinical Implications, and Evolutionary Trajectory. *Evol. Stud. Imaginative Cult.* **4**, 1–17 (2020).
124. Diamond, A. Executive functions. *Annu. Rev. Psychol.* **64**, 135–168 (2013).
125. Barbey, A. K., Krueger, F. & Grafman, J. Predictions in the Brain: Using our Past to Prepare for the Future. (2011).
126. Pinker, S. *Words and rules: The ingredients of language.* (Basic Books, 2015).
127. Hockett, C. F. Refurbishing our foundations. *Elem. Linguist. Adv. Point View* (1987).
128. Hauser, M. D., Chomsky, N. & Fitch, W. T. The faculty of language: what is it, who has it, and how did it evolve? *science* **298**, 1569–1579 (2002).
129. Senghas, A. & Coppola, M. Children creating language: How Nicaraguan

Sign Language acquired a spatial grammar. *Psychol. Sci.* **12**, 323–328 (2001).

130. Morgan, G. & Kegl, J. Nicaraguan sign language and theory of mind: The issue of critical periods and abilities. *J. Child Psychol. Psychiatry* **47**, 811–819 (2006).

131. Kocab, A., Senghas, A. & Snedeker, J. The emergence of temporal language in Nicaraguan Sign Language. *Cognition* **156**, 147–163 (2016).

132. Groce, N. E. *Everyone here spoke sign language: Hereditary deafness on Martha's Vineyard.* (Harvard University Press, 1985).

133. Sandler, W., Meir, I., Padden, C. & Aronoff, M. The emergence of grammar: Systematic structure in a new language. *Proc. Natl. Acad. Sci.* **102**, 2661–2665 (2005).

134. Fitch, W. T., Hauser, M. D. & Chomsky, N. The evolution of the language faculty: clarifications and implications. *Cognition* **97**, 179–210 (2005).

135. Hernadi, P. Literature and evolution. *SubStance* **30**, 55–71 (2001).

136. Humphreys, G. W. & Riddoch, M. J. *To see but not to see: A case study of visual agnosia.* (Psychology Press, 1987).

137. Pike, A. W. *et al.* U-series dating of Paleolithic art in 11 caves in Spain. *Science* **336**, 1409–1413 (2012).

138. Dalton, R. *Lion man takes pride of place as oldest statue.* (Nature Publishing Group, 2003).

139. Tattersall, I. *Becoming human: Evolution and human uniqueness.* (Houghton Mifflin Harcourt, 1999).

140. Lombard, M. Quartz-tipped arrows older than 60 ka: further use-trace evidence from Sibudu, KwaZulu-Natal, South Africa. *J. Archaeol. Sci.* **38**, 1918–1930 (2011).

141. McClellan III, J. E. & Dorn, H. *Science and technology in world history: an introduction.* (JHU Press, 2015).

142. Viereck, G. What life means to Einstein: an interview. (1929).

143. Gopnik, A. Conceptual and semantic development as theory change: The case of object permanence. *Mind Lang.* **3**, 197–216 (1988).

144. Gabay, S., Kalanthroff, E., Henik, A. & Gronau, N. Conceptual size representation in ventral visual cortex. *Neuropsychologia* **81**, 198–206 (2016).

145. Vyshedskiy, A., Dunn, R. & Piryatinsky, I. Neurobiological mechanisms for nonverbal IQ tests: implications for instruction of nonverbal children with autism. *Res. Ideas Outcomes* **3**, e13239 (2017).

146. Wierzynski, C. M., Lubenov, E. V., Gu, M. & Siapas, A. G. State-dependent spike-timing relationships between hippocampal and prefrontal circuits during sleep. *Neuron* **61**, 587–596 (2009).

147. Lewis, P. A., Knoblich, G. & Poe, G. How memory replay in sleep boosts creative problem-solving. *Trends Cogn. Sci.* **22**, 491–503 (2018).

148. Hobson, R. & McCarley, J. *Theory of Dreaming.* (1977).

149. Solms, M. Dreaming and REM sleep are controlled by different brain mechanisms. *Behav. Brain Sci.* **23**, 843–850 (2000).

150. Miyashita, Y. Cognitive memory: cellular and network machineries and their top-down control. *Science* **306**, 435–440 (2004).
151. Sidtis, J. J., Volpe, B. T., Holtzman, J. D., Wilson, D. H. & Gazzaniga, M. S. Cognitive interaction after staged callosal section: evidence for transfer of semantic activation. *Science* **212**, 344–346 (1981).
152. Christoff, K., Irving, Z. C., Fox, K. C., Spreng, R. N. & Andrews-Hanna, J. R. Mind-wandering as spontaneous thought: a dynamic framework. *Nat. Rev. Neurosci.* **17**, 718 (2016).
153. Vyshedskiy, A. Neuroscience of imagination and implications for hominin evolution. *J. Curr. Neurobiol.* **10**, 89–109 (2019).
154. Seli, P., Risko, E. F., Smilek, D. & Schacter, D. L. Mind-wandering with and without intention. *Trends Cogn. Sci.* **20**, 605–617 (2016).
155. Bowden, E. M., Jung-Beeman, M., Fleck, J. & Kounios, J. New approaches to demystifying insight. *Trends Cogn. Sci.* **9**, 322–328 (2005).
156. Sternberg, R. J. & Davidson, J. E. *The nature of insight.* (The MIT Press, 1995).
157. Weisberg, R. W. *Creativity: Understanding innovation in problem solving, science, invention, and the arts.* (John Wiley & Sons, 2006).
158. Salvi, C., Bricolo, E., Kounios, J., Bowden, E. & Beeman, M. Insight solutions are correct more often than analytic solutions. *Think. Reason.* **22**, 443–460 (2016).
159. Miller, E. K. & Cohen, J. D. An integrative theory of prefrontal cortex function. *Annu. Rev. Neurosci.* **24**, 167–202 (2001).
160. Miller, E. Earl K. Miller. *Neuron* **95**, 1237 (2017).
161. Nir, Y. & Tononi, G. Dreaming and the brain: from phenomenology to neurophysiology. *Trends Cogn. Sci.* **14**, 88–100 (2010).
162. Cole, M., Levitin, K. & Luria, A. R. *The autobiography of Alexander Luria: A dialogue with the making of mind.* (Psychology Press, 2014).
163. Boucher, J., Mayes, A. & Bigham, S. Memory, language and intellectual ability in low-functioning autism. *J Boucher DM Bowler Eds Mem. Autism Camb. CUP* (2008).
164. Cheng, Q., Roth, A., Halgren, E. & Mayberry, R. I. Effects of early language deprivation on brain connectivity: Language pathways in deaf native and late first-language learners of American Sign Language. *Front. Hum. Neurosci.* **13**, 320 (2019).
165. Curtiss, S. Dissociations between language and cognition: Cases and implications. *J. Autism Dev. Disord.* **11**, 15–30 (1981).
166. Curtiss, S. Abnormal language acquisition and the modularity of language. *Linguist. Camb. Surv.* **2**, 96–116 (1988).
167. Mayberry, R. I. Cognitive development in deaf children: The interface of language and perception in neuropsychology. *Handb. Neuropsychol.* **8**, 71–107 (2002).
168. Skeide, M. A., Brauer, J. & Friederici, A. D. Brain functional and structural predictors of language performance. *Cereb. Cortex* **26**, 2127–2139 (2015).
169. Voss, M. W., Nagamatsu, L. S., Liu-Ambrose, T. & Kramer, A. F.

Exercise, brain, and cognition across the life span. *J. Appl. Physiol.* **111**, 1505–1513 (2011).

170. Broad, K. D., Curley, J. P. & Keverne, E. B. Mother–infant bonding and the evolution of mammalian social relationships. *Philos. Trans. R. Soc. B Biol. Sci.* **361**, 2199–2214 (2006).

171. Horn, E. R. ' Critical periods' in vestibular development or adaptation of gravity sensory systems to altered gravitational conditions? *Arch. Ital. Biol.* **142**, 155–174 (2004).

172. Cunningham, M. A. & Baker, M. C. Vocal learning in white-crowned sparrows: Sensitive phase and song dialects. *Behav. Ecol. Sociobiol.* **13**, 259–269 (1983).

173. Vyshedskiy, A. *The Emergence of Dreaming: Mind-Wandering, Embodied Simulation, and the Default Network.* (JSTOR, 2020).

174. Dragoy, O., Akinina, Y. & Dronkers, N. Toward a functional neuroanatomy of semantic aphasia: A history and ten new cases. *Cortex* **97**, 164–182 (2017).

175. Chomsky, N. On phases. *Curr. Stud. Linguist. Ser.* **45**, 133 (2008).

176. Lee, K. H. *et al.* Neural correlates of superior intelligence: stronger recruitment of posterior parietal cortex. *Neuroimage* **29**, 578–586 (2006).

177. Goodale, M. A. & Milner, A. D. Separate visual pathways for perception and action. *Trends Neurosci.* **15**, 20–25 (1992).

178. Zacks, J. M. Neuroimaging studies of mental rotation: a meta-analysis and review. *J. Cogn. Neurosci.* **20**, 1–19 (2008).

179. Cohen, M. S. *et al.* Changes in cortical activity during mental rotation A mapping study using functional MRI. *Brain* **119**, 89–100 (1996).

180. Schendan, H. E. & Stern, C. E. Mental rotation and object categorization share a common network of prefrontal and dorsal and ventral regions of posterior cortex. *Neuroimage* **35**, 1264–1277 (2007).

181. Scally, A. *et al.* Insights into hominid evolution from the gorilla genome sequence. *Nature* **483**, 169–175 (2012).

182. Kumar, S., Filipski, A., Swarna, V., Walker, A. & Hedges, S. B. Placing confidence limits on the molecular age of the human–chimpanzee divergence. *Proc. Natl. Acad. Sci.* **102**, 18842–18847 (2005).

183. Becquet, C., Patterson, N., Stone, A. C., Przeworski, M. & Reich, D. Genetic structure of chimpanzee populations. *PLoS Genet* **3**, e66 (2007).

184. Green, R. E. *et al.* A draft sequence of the Neandertal genome. *science* **328**, 710–722 (2010).

185. Green, R. E. *et al.* A complete Neandertal mitochondrial genome sequence determined by high-throughput sequencing. *Cell* **134**, 416–426 (2008).

186. Krause, J. *et al.* The derived FOXP2 variant of modern humans was shared with Neandertals. *Curr. Biol.* **17**, 1908–1912 (2007).

187. Veizer, J., Godderis, Y. & François, L. M. Evidence for decoupling of atmospheric CO2 and global climate during the Phanerozoic eon. *Nature* **408**, 698–701 (2000).

188. Green, D. J. & Alemseged, Z. Australopithecus afarensis scapular

ontogeny, function, and the role of climbing in human evolution. *Science* **338**, 514–517 (2012).

189. Harmand, S. *et al.* 3.3-million-year-old stone tools from Lomekwi 3, West Turkana, Kenya. *Nature* **521**, 310–315 (2015).
190. Semaw, S. *et al.* 2.5-million-year-old stone tools from Gona, Ethiopia. *Nature* **385**, 333 (1997).
191. Graves, R. R., Lupo, A. C., McCarthy, R. C., Wescott, D. J. & Cunningham, D. L. Just how strapping was KNM-WT 15000? *J. Hum. Evol.* **59**, 542–554 (2010).
192. Lalueza-Fox, C. *et al.* A melanocortin 1 receptor allele suggests varying pigmentation among Neanderthals. *Science* **318**, 1453–1455 (2007).
193. Klein, R. G. & Edgar, B. *The dawn of human culture.* (Wiley New York, 2002).
194. Thieme, H. Die ältesten Speere der Welt-: Fundplätze der frühen Altsteinzeit im Tagebau Schöningen. *Archäol. Nachrichtenblatt* **10**, 409–417 (2005).
195. Thieme, H. Altpaläolithische Holzgeräte aus Schöningen, Lkr. Helmstedt: Bedeutsame Funde zur Kulturentwicklung des frühen Menschen. *Ger. Anz. Röm.-Ger. Komm. Dtsch. Archäol. Inst.* **77**, 451–487 (1999).
196. Churchill, S. E. & Rhodes, J. A. The evolution of the human capacity for "killing at a distance": the human fossil evidence for the evolution of projectile weaponry. in *The evolution of hominin diets* 201–210 (Springer, 2009).
197. D'Anastasio, R. *et al.* Micro-biomechanics of the Kebara 2 hyoid and its implications for speech in Neanderthals. *PloS One* **8**, e82261 (2013).
198. Vargha-Khadem, F., Watkins, K., Alcock, K., Fletcher, P. & Passingham, R. Praxic and nonverbal cognitive deficits in a large family with a genetically transmitted speech and language disorder. *Proc. Natl. Acad. Sci.* **92**, 930–933 (1995).
199. Aiello, L. C. & Wheeler, P. The expensive-tissue hypothesis: the brain and the digestive system in human and primate evolution. *Curr. Anthropol.* **36**, 199–221 (1995).
200. Clarke, D. D. Circulation and energy metabolism of the brain. *Basic Neurochem. Mol. Cell. Med. Asp.* (1999).
201. Mink, J. W., Blumenschine, R. J. & Adams, D. B. Ratio of central nervous system to body metabolism in vertebrates: its constancy and functional basis. *Am. J. Physiol.-Regul. Integr. Comp. Physiol.* **241**, R203–R212 (1981).
202. Striedter, G. F. *Principles of Brain Evolution.* (Sinauer Associates, 2004).
203. Falk, D. Brain evolution in Homo: The "radiator" theory. *Behav. Brain Sci.* **13**, 333–381 (1990).
204. O'Neill, M. C., Umberger, B. R., Holowka, N. B., Larson, S. G. & Reiser, P. J. Chimpanzee super strength and human skeletal muscle evolution. *Proc. Natl. Acad. Sci.* **114**, 7343–7348 (2017).
205. McHenry, H. M. & Coffing, K. Australopithecus to Homo: transformations in body and mind. *Annu. Rev. Anthropol.* **29**, 125–146

(2000).

206. Soares, P. *et al.* Correcting for purifying selection: an improved human mitochondrial molecular clock. *Am. J. Hum. Genet.* **84**, 740–759 (2009).

207. Poznik, G. D. *et al.* Sequencing Y chromosomes resolves discrepancy in time to common ancestor of males versus females. *Science* **341**, 562–565 (2013).

208. Francalacci, P. *et al.* Low-pass DNA sequencing of 1200 Sardinians reconstructs European Y-chromosome phylogeny. *Science* **341**, 565–569 (2013).

209. Zhivotovsky, L. A., Rosenberg, N. A. & Feldman, M. W. Features of evolution and expansion of modern humans, inferred from genomewide microsatellite markers. *Am. J. Hum. Genet.* **72**, 1171–1186 (2003).

210. Macaulay, V. *et al.* Single, rapid coastal settlement of Asia revealed by analysis of complete mitochondrial genomes. *Science* **308**, 1034–1036 (2005).

211. Thorne, A. *et al.* Australia's oldest human remains: age of the Lake Mungo 3 skeleton. *J. Hum. Evol.* **36**, 591–612 (1999).

212. Hublin, J.-J. *et al.* New fossils from Jebel Irhoud, Morocco and the pan-African origin of Homo sapiens. *Nature* **546**, 289 (2017).

213. Zilhão, J. *et al.* Symbolic use of marine shells and mineral pigments by Iberian Neandertals. *Proc. Natl. Acad. Sci.* **107**, 1023–1028 (2010).

214. Klein, R. G. *The human career: human biological and cultural origins*. (University of Chicago Press, 2009).

215. McBrearty, S. & Brooks, A. S. The revolution that wasn't: a new interpretation of the origin of modern human behavior. *J. Hum. Evol.* **39**, 453–563 (2000).

216. Bouzouggar, A. *et al.* 82,000-year-old shell beads from North Africa and implications for the origins of modern human behavior. *Proc. Natl. Acad. Sci.* **104**, 9964–9969 (2007).

217. Henshilwood, C., d'Errico, F., Vanhaeren, M., Van Niekerk, K. & Jacobs, Z. Middle stone age shell beads from South Africa. *Science* **304**, 404–404 (2004).

218. d'Errico, F., Henshilwood, C., Vanhaeren, M. & Van Niekerk, K. Nassarius kraussianus shell beads from Blombos Cave: evidence for symbolic behaviour in the Middle Stone Age. *J. Hum. Evol.* **48**, 3–24 (2005).

219. Henshilwood, C. S., d'Errico, F. & Watts, I. Engraved ochres from the middle stone age levels at Blombos Cave, South Africa. *J. Hum. Evol.* **57**, 27–47 (2009).

220. Mania, D. & Mania, U. Deliberate engravings on bone artefacts of. *Homo Erectus Rock Art Res.* **5**, 91–107 (1988).

221. Gargett, R. H. *et al.* Grave Shortcomings: The Evidence for Neandertal Burial [and Comments and Reply]. *Curr. Anthropol.* **30**, 157–190 (1989).

222. Kolen, J. Hominids without homes: on the nature of Middle Palaeolithic settlement in Europe. *Middle Palaeolithic Occup. Eur.* 139–75 (1999).

223. Higham, T. *et al.* Testing models for the beginnings of the Aurignacian

and the advent of figurative art and music: The radiocarbon chronology of Gei\s senklösterle. *J. Hum. Evol.* **62**, 664–676 (2012).

224. Toro-Moyano, I. *et al.* The oldest human fossil in Europe, from Orce (Spain). *J. Hum. Evol.* **65**, 1–9 (2013).

225. Swisher III, C. C., Curtis, G. H. & Lewin, R. *Java man: how two geologists changed our understanding of human evolution.* (University of Chicago Press, 2001).

226. Gibbons, A. Who were the Denisovans? *Science* **333**, 1084–1087 (2011).

227. Holzer, A., Avner, U., Porat, N. & Horwitz, L. K. Desert kites in the Negev desert and northeast Sinai: Their function, chronology and ecology. *J. Arid Environ.* **74**, 806–817 (2010).

228. Barnosky, A. D., Koch, P. L., Feranec, R. S., Wing, S. L. & Shabel, A. B. Assessing the causes of Late Pleistocene extinctions on the continents. *science* **306**, 70–75 (2004).

229. Smith, F. A., Smith, R. E. E., Lyons, S. K. & Payne, J. L. Body size downgrading of mammals over the late Quaternary. *Science* **360**, 310–313 (2018).

230. Bar-Yosef, O. The upper paleolithic revolution. *Annu. Rev. Anthropol.* **31**, 363–393 (2002).

231. Botha, R. & Knight, C. *The cradle of language.* vol. 12 (OUP Oxford, 2009).

232. Harari, Y. N. & Perkins, D. *Sapiens: A brief history of humankind.* (Harvill Secker London, 2014).

233. Diamond, J. *The third chimpanzee.* (Oneworld Publications, 2014).

234. Underhill, P. A. *et al.* Y chromosome sequence variation and the history of human populations. *Nat. Genet.* **26**, 358–361 (2000).

235. Hart, D. & Sussman, R. W. Man the Hunted: Primates. *Predat. Hum.* (2005).

236. Vyshedskiy, A. Development of behavioral modernity by hominins around 70,000 years ago was associated with simultaneous acquisition of a novel component of imagination, called prefrontal synthesis, and conversion of a preexisting rich-vocabulary non-recursive communication system to a fully recursive syntactic language. *bioRxiv* 166520 (2019) doi:https://doi.org/10.1101/166520.

237. Amos, W. & Hoffman, J. I. Evidence that two main bottleneck events shaped modern human genetic diversity. *Proc. R. Soc. Lond. B Biol. Sci.* **277**, 131–137 (2010).

238. Sanz, C. M. & Morgan, D. B. Chimpanzee tool technology in the Goualougo Triangle, Republic of Congo. *J. Hum. Evol.* **52**, 420–433 (2007).

239. Trinkaus, E. *The shanidar neandertals.* (Academic Press, 2014).

240. Trinkaus, E. & Villemeur, I. Mechanical advantages of the Neandertal thumb in flexion: a test of an hypothesis. *Am. J. Phys. Anthropol.* **84**, 249–260 (1991).

241. Mithen, S. The prehistory of the mind. *Camb. Archaeol. J.* **7**, 269–269 (1997).

242. Birnholz, J. C. The development of human fetal eye movement patterns. *Science* **213**, 679–681 (1981).

243. Kanizsa, G., Renzi, P., Conte, S., Compostela, C. & Guerani, L. Amodal completion in mouse vision. *Perception* **22**, 713–721 (1993).

244. Fagot, J., Barbet, I., Parron, C. & Deruelle, C. Amodal completion by baboons (Papio papio): contribution of background depth cues. *Primates* **47**, 145–150 (2006).

245. Kellman, P. J. & Arterberry, M. E. Infant visual perception. *Handb. Child Psychol.* (2006).

246. Petrides, M. & Pandya, D. N. Comparative cytoarchitectonic analysis of the human and the macaque ventrolateral prefrontal cortex and corticocortical connection patterns in the monkey. *Eur. J. Neurosci.* **16**, 291–310 (2002).

247. Lillard, A. S., Pinkham, A. M. & Smith, E. Pretend play and cognitive development. *Wiley-Blackwell Handb. Child. Cogn. Dev.* **32**, 285 (2011).

248. Nielsen, K. J., Logothetis, N. K. & Rainer, G. Object features used by humans and monkeys to identify rotated shapes. *J. Vis.* **8**, 9–9 (2008).

249. Fitch, W. T., de Boer, B., Mathur, N. & Ghazanfar, A. A. Monkey vocal tracts are speech-ready. *Sci. Adv.* **2**, e1600723 (2016).

250. Crystal, D. *The Cambridge Encyclopedia of Language*. (Cambridge Univ. Pres, 2003).

251. Goodall, J. Chimpanzees of the Gombe Stream Reserve. in *PRIMATE BEHAVIOR FIELD STUDIES OF MONKEY AND APES* 425–473 (Holt, Rinehart & Winston, 1965).

252. Slocombe, K. E., Townsend, S. W. & Zuberbühler, K. Wild chimpanzees (Pan troglodytes schweinfurthii) distinguish between different scream types: evidence from a playback study. *Anim. Cogn.* **12**, 441–449 (2009).

253. Slocombe, K. E. & Zuberbühler, K. Chimpanzees modify recruitment screams as a function of audience composition. *Proc. Natl. Acad. Sci.* **104**, 17228–17233 (2007).

254. Mitani, J. C., Hasegawa, T., Gros-Louis, J., Marler, P. & Byrne, R. Dialects in wild chimpanzees? *Am. J. Primatol.* **27**, 233–243 (1992).

255. Tattersall, I. An evolutionary context for the emergence of language. *Lang. Sci.* **46, Part B**, 199–206 (2014).

256. Frayer, D. W. Talking Hyoids and Talking Neanderthals. in *Human Paleontology and Prehistory* 233–237 (Springer, 2017).

257. Dediu, D. & Levinson, S. C. On the antiquity of language: the reinterpretation of Neandertal linguistic capacities and its consequences. *Front. Psychol.* **4**, 397 (2013).

258. Frayer, D. W. & Nicolay, C. 14 Fossil Evidence for the Origin of Speech Sounds. (2000).

259. Alemseged, Z. *et al.* A juvenile early hominin skeleton from Dikika, Ethiopia. *Nature* **443**, 296–301 (2006).

260. Capasso, L., Michetti, E. & D'Anastasio, R. A Homo erectus hyoid bone: possible implications for the origin of the human capability for speech. *Coll. Antropol.* **32**, 1007–1011 (2008).

261. Arensburg, B. *et al.* A Middle Palaeolithic human hyoid bone. *Nature* **338**, 758–760 (1989).

262. Rodríguez, L., Cabo, L. & Egocheaga, J. *"Breve nota sobre el hioides Neandertalense de Sidrón (Piloña, Asturias)," in Antropología y Diversidad.* vol. 1 (Barcelona: Edicions Bellaterra, 2003).

263. Martınez, I., Quam, R. M. & Rosa, M. Auditory capacities of human fossils: a new approach to the origin of speech. in *Proceedings of the 2nd ASA-EAA Joint Conference Acoustics* 4177–4182 (2008).

264. Laitman, J. T., Heimbuch, R. C. & Crelin, E. S. The basicranium of fossil hominids as an indicator of their upper respiratory systems. *Am. J. Phys. Anthropol.* **51**, 15–33 (1979).

265. Laitman, J. T. & Reidenberg, J. S. Advances in understanding the relationship between the skull base and larynx with comments on the origins of speech. *Hum. Evol.* **3**, 99–109 (1988).

266. Laitman, J. T. & Heimbuch, R. C. The basicranium of Plio-Pleistocene hominids as an indicator of their upper respiratory systems. *Am. J. Phys. Anthropol.* **59**, 323–343 (1982).

267. Laitman, J. T. The anatomy of human speech. *Nat. Hist.* **93**, 20–27 (1984).

268. MacLarnon, A. M. & Hewitt, G. P. The evolution of human speech: The role of enhanced breathing control. *Am. J. Phys. Anthropol.* **109**, 341–363 (1999).

269. Martínez, I. *et al.* Auditory capacities in Middle Pleistocene humans from the Sierra de Atapuerca in Spain. *Proc. Natl. Acad. Sci.* **101**, 9976–9981 (2004).

270. Kojima, S. Comparison of auditory functions in the chimpanzee and human. *Folia Primatol. (Basel)* **55**, 62–72 (1990).

271. Quam, R. & Rak, Y. Auditory ossicles from southwest Asian Mousterian sites. *J. Hum. Evol.* **54**, 414–433 (2008).

272. Enard, W. *et al.* Molecular evolution of FOXP2, a gene involved in speech and language. *Nature* **418**, 869–872 (2002).

273. Reich, D. *et al.* Genetic history of an archaic hominin group from Denisova Cave in Siberia. *Nature* **468**, 1053 (2010).

274. Maricic, T. *et al.* A recent evolutionary change affects a regulatory element in the human FOXP2 gene. *Mol. Biol. Evol.* **30**, 844–852 (2012).

275. Kegl, J., Senghas, A. & Coppola, M. *Creation through contact; sign language emergence and sign language change in nicaragua.* (na, 1999).

276. Senghas, A. The development of Nicaraguan Sign Language via the language acquisition process. in *Proceedings of the 19th annual Boston University conference on language development* 543–552 (Boston: Cascadilla Press, 1995).

277. Senghas, A., Kita, S. & Özyürek, A. Children creating core properties of language: Evidence from an emerging sign language in Nicaragua. *Science* **305**, 1779–1782 (2004).

278. Roese, N. J. Counterfactual thinking. *Psychol. Bull.* **121**, 133 (1997).

279. Owen, A. M., Downes, J. J., Sahakian, B. J., Polkey, C. E. & Robbins, T.

W. Planning and spatial working memory following frontal lobe lesions in man. *Neuropsychologia* **28**, 1021–1034 (1990).

280. Klingberg, T., O'Sullivan, B. T. & Roland, P. E. Bilateral activation of fronto-parietal networks by incrementing demand in a working memory task. *Cereb. Cortex* **7**, 465–471 (1997).

281. De Pisapia, N., Slomski, J. A. & Braver, T. S. Functional specializations in lateral prefrontal cortex associated with the integration and segregation of information in working memory. *Cereb. Cortex* **17**, 993–1006 (2007).

282. Kroger, J. K. *et al.* Recruitment of anterior dorsolateral prefrontal cortex in human reasoning: a parametric study of relational complexity. *Cereb. Cortex* **12**, 477–485 (2002).

283. Prabhakaran, V., Smith, J. A., Desmond, J. E., Glover, G. H. & Gabrieli, J. D. Neural substrates of fluid reasoning: an fMRI study of neocortical activation during performance of the Raven's Progressive Matrices Test. *Cognit. Psychol.* **33**, 43–63 (1997).

284. Stuss, D. T. *et al.* Language functioning after bilateral prefrontal leukotomy. *Brain Lang.* **28**, 66–70 (1986).

285. Wallesch, C. W., Kornhuber, H. H., Köllner, C., Haas, H. C. & Hufnagl, J. M. Language and cognitive deficits resulting from medial and dorsolateral frontal lobe lesions. *Arch. Für Psychiatr. Nervenkrankh.* **233**, 279–296 (1983).

286. Freeman, W. Psychosurgery. *Am. J. Psychiatry* **116**, 601–604 (1960).

287. Tomita, H., Ohbayashi, M., Nakahara, K., Hasegawa, I. & Miyashita, Y. Top-down signal from prefrontal cortex in executive control of memory retrieval. *Nature* **401**, 699 (1999).

288. Wilson, S. M. *et al.* Neural correlates of syntactic processing in the nonfluent variant of primary progressive aphasia. *J. Neurosci.* **30**, 16845–16854 (2010).

289. Wilson, S. M. *et al.* Syntactic processing depends on dorsal language tracts. *Neuron* **72**, 397–403 (2011).

290. Whishaw, I. Q. Did a change in sensory control of skilled movements stimulate the evolution of the primate frontal cortex? *Behav. Brain Res.* **146**, 31–41 (2003).

291. Isbell, L. A. & Etting, S. F. Scales drive detection, attention, and memory of snakes in wild vervet monkeys (Chlorocebus pygerythrus). *Primates* **58**, 121–129 (2017).

292. Kaas, J. H. & Huerta, M. F. The subcortical visual system of primates. *Comp. Primate Biol.* **4**, 327–391 (1988).

293. Preuss, T. M. Human brain evolution: from gene discovery to phenotype discovery. *Proc. Natl. Acad. Sci.* **109**, 10709–10716 (2012).

294. Matsuno, T. & Fujita, K. A comparative psychophysical approach to visual perception in primates. *Primates* **50**, 121–130 (2009).

295. Windmann, S., Wehrmann, M., Calabrese, P. & Güntürkün, O. Role of the prefrontal cortex in attentional control over bistable vision. *J. Cogn. Neurosci.* **18**, 456–471 (2006).

296. Stephan, H., Frahm, H. & Baron, G. New and revised data on volumes of

brain structures in insectivores and primates. *Folia Primatol. (Basel)* **35**, 1–29 (1981).

297. Holloway, R. L. The failure of the gyrification index (GI) to account for volumetric reorganization in the evolution of the human brain. *J. Hum. Evol.* **22**, 163–170 (1992).

298. Semendeferi, K., Armstrong, E., Schleicher, A., Zilles, K. & Van Hoesen, G. W. Prefrontal cortex in humans and apes: a comparative study of area 10. *Am. J. Phys. Anthropol. Off. Publ. Am. Assoc. Phys. Anthropol.* **114**, 224–241 (2001).

299. Brodmann, K. Neue Ergebnisse über die vergleichende histologische Lokalisation der Grosshirnrinde mit besonderer Berücksichtigung des Stirnhirns. *Anat Anz* **41**, 157–216 (1912).

300. Semendeferi, K., Lu, A., Schenker, N. & Damásio, H. Humans and great apes share a large frontal cortex. *Nat. Neurosci.* **5**, 272–276 (2002).

301. Schoenemann, P. T., Sheehan, M. J. & Glotzer, L. D. Prefrontal white matter volume is disproportionately larger in humans than in other primates. *Nat. Neurosci.* **8**, 242–252 (2005).

302. Krubitzer, L. The organization of neocortex in mammals: are species differences really so different? *Trends Neurosci.* **18**, 408–417 (1995).

303. Bennett, M. V. Comparative physiology: electric organs. *Annu. Rev. Physiol.* **32**, 471–528 (1970).

304. Stanford, L. R. Conduction velocity variations minimize conduction time differences among retinal ganglion cell axons. *Science* **238**, 358–360 (1987).

305. Sugihara, I., Lang, E. J. & Llinas, R. Uniform olivocerebellar conduction time underlies Purkinje cell complex spike synchronicity in the rat cerebellum. *J. Physiol.* **470**, 243 (1993).

306. Chomiak, T., Peters, S. & Hu, B. Functional architecture and spike timing properties of corticofugal projections from rat ventral temporal cortex. *J. Neurophysiol.* **100**, 327–335 (2008).

307. Kimura, F. & Itami, C. Myelination and isochronicity in neural networks. *Front Neuroanat* **3**, (2009).

308. Pelletier, J. G. & Paré, D. Uniform range of conduction times from the lateral amygdala to distributed perirhinal sites. *J. Neurophysiol.* **87**, 1213–1221 (2002).

309. Salami, M., Itami, C., Tsumoto, T. & Kimura, F. Change of conduction velocity by regional myelination yields constant latency irrespective of distance between thalamus and cortex. *Proc. Natl. Acad. Sci.* **100**, 6174–6179 (2003).

310. Tessitore, C. & Brunjes, P. C. A comparative study of myelination in precocial and altricial murid rodents. *Dev. Brain Res.* **43**, 139–147 (1988).

311. Szalay, F. Development of the equine brain motor system. *Neurobiol. Bp. Hung.* **9**, 107–135 (2000).

312. Toga, A. W., Thompson, P. M. & Sowell, E. R. Mapping brain maturation. *Focus* (2006).

313. Bartzokis, G. *et al.* Age-related changes in frontal and temporal lobe

volumes in men: a magnetic resonance imaging study. *Arch. Gen. Psychiatry* **58**, 461–465 (2001).

314. Szeligo, F. & Leblond, C. P. Response of the three main types of glial cells of cortex nad corpus callosum in rats handled during suckling or exposed to enriched, control and impoverished environments following weaning. *J. Comp. Neurol.* **172**, 247–263 (1977).

315. Tauber, H., Waehneldt, T. V. & Neuhoff, V. Myelination in rabbit optic nerves is accelerated by artificial eye opening. *Neurosci. Lett.* **16**, 235–238 (1980).

316. Gyllensten, L. & Malmfors, T. Myelinization of the optic nerve and its dependence on visual function—a quantitative investigation in mice. *Development* **11**, 255–266 (1963).

317. Barres, B. A. & Raff, M. C. Proliferation of oligodendrocyte precursor cells depends on electrical activity in axons. *Nature* **361**, 258 (1993).

318. Stevens, B., Tanner, S. & Fields, R. D. Control of myelination by specific patterns of neural impulses. *J. Neurosci.* **18**, 9303–9311 (1998).

319. Stevens, B. & Fields, R. D. Response of Schwann cells to action potentials in development. *Science* **287**, 2267–2271 (2000).

320. Als, H. *et al.* Early experience alters brain function and structure. *Pediatrics* **113**, 846–857 (2004).

321. Teicher, M. H. *et al.* Childhood neglect is associated with reduced corpus callosum area. *Biol. Psychiatry* **56**, 80–85 (2004).

322. Bengtsson, S. L. *et al.* Extensive piano practicing has regionally specific effects on white matter development. *Nat. Neurosci.* **8**, 1148–1150 (2005).

323. Fields, R. D. White matter in learning, cognition and psychiatric disorders. *Trends Neurosci.* **31**, 361–370 (2008).

324. Barth, M., Hirsch, H. V., Meinertzhagen, I. A. & Heisenberg, M. Experience-dependent developmental plasticity in the optic lobe of Drosophila melanogaster. *J. Neurosci.* **17**, 1493–1504 (1997).

325. Lorenz, K. *Evolution and modification of behavior.* (1965).

326. Curtiss, S. Genie: A Psycholinguistic Study of a Modern-Day"" Wild Child""(Perspectives in. (1977).

327. Rymer, R. Genie: A scientific tragedy. (1993).

328. Itard, J. M. G. The wild boy of Aveyron (G. Humphrey & M. Humphrey, trans.). *N. Y. Appleton-Century-CroftsOriginal Work Publ. 1806* (1962).

329. Grimshaw, G. M., Adelstein, A., Bryden, M. P. & MacKinnon, G. E. First-language acquisition in adolescence: Evidence for a critical period for verbal language development. *Brain Lang.* **63**, 237–255 (1998).

330. Morford, J. P. Grammatical development in adolescent first-language learners. *Linguistics* **41**, 681–722 (2003).

331. Hyde, D. C. *et al.* Spatial and numerical abilities without a complete natural language. *Neuropsychologia* **49**, 924–936 (2011).

332. Ramírez, N. F., Lieberman, A. M. & Mayberry, R. I. The initial stages of first-language acquisition begun in adolescence: when late looks early. *J. Child Lang.* **40**, 391–414 (2013).

333. Mason, M. K. Learning to speak after six and one-half years of silence. *J.*

Speech Disord. **7**, 295–304 (1942).

334. Davis, K. Final note on a case of extreme isolation. *Am. J. Sociol.* **52**, 432–437 (1947).

335. Koluchová, J. Severe deprivation in twins: A case study. *J. Child Psychol. Psychiatry* **13**, 107–114 (1972).

336. Koluchová, J. The further development of twins after severe and prolonged deprivation: A second report. *J. Child Psychol. Psychiatry* **17**, 181–188 (1976).

337. Fujinaga, T., Kasuga, T., Uchida, N. & Saiga, H. Long-term follow-up study of children developmentally retarded by early environmental deprivation. *Genet. Soc. Gen. Psychol. Monogr.* (1990).

338. Mayberry, R. I. & Eichen, E. B. The long-lasting advantage of learning sign language in childhood: Another look at the critical period for language acquisition. *J. Mem. Lang.* **30**, 486–512 (1991).

339. Newport, E. L. Maturational constraints on language learning. *Cogn. Sci.* **14**, 11–28 (1990).

340. Penfield, W. & Roberts, L. *Speech and brain mechanisms.* (Princeton: Princeton University Press, 1959).

341. Chomsky, N. A review of BF Skinner's Verbal Behavior. *Language* **35**, 26–58 (1959).

342. Boatman, D. *et al.* Language recovery after left hemispherectomy in children with late-onset seizures. *Ann. Neurol.* **46**, 579–586 (1999).

343. Basser, L. S. Hemiplegia of early onset and the faculty of speech with special reference to the effects of hemispherectomy. *Brain* **85**, 427–460 (1962).

344. Krashen, S. & Harshman, R. Lateralization and the critical period. *J. Acoust. Soc. Am.* **52**, 174–174 (1972).

345. Pulsifer, M. B. *et al.* The cognitive outcome of hemispherectomy in 71 children. *Epilepsia* **45**, 243–254 (2004).

346. Bakker, P. Autonomous languages of twins. *Acta Genet. Medicae Gemellol. Twin Res.* **36**, 233–238 (1987).

347. Moodie, P. M. Mortality and morbidity in Australian aboriginal children. *Med. J. Aust.* **1**, 180–85 (1969).

348. Kuperman, V., Stadthagen-Gonzalez, H. & Brysbaert, M. Age-of-acquisition ratings for 30,000 English words. *Behav. Res. Methods* **44**, 978–990 (2012).

349. King, M.-C. & Wilson, A. C. Evolution at two levels in humans and chimpanzees. *Science* **188**, 107–116 (1975).

350. Varki, A. & Nelson, D. L. Genomic comparisons of humans and chimpanzees. *Annu. Rev. Anthropol.* **36**, (2007).

351. Wetterbom, A., Sevov, M., Cavelier, L. & Bergström, T. F. Comparative genomic analysis of human and chimpanzee indicates a key role for indels in primate evolution. *J. Mol. Evol.* **63**, 682–690 (2006).

352. Gibbs, R. A. & Pachter, L. Genome sequence of the Brown Norway rat yields insights into mammalian evolution. *Nature* **428**, 493–521 (2004).

353. Harris, E. E. Nonadaptive processes in primate and human evolution. *Am.*

J. Phys. Anthropol. **143**, 13–45 (2010).

354. Burbano, H. A. *et al.* Targeted investigation of the Neandertal genome by array-based sequence capture. *science* **328**, 723–725 (2010).

355. Spocter, M. A. *et al.* Wernicke's area homologue in chimpanzees (Pan troglodytes) and its relation to the appearance of modern human language. *Proc. R. Soc. B Biol. Sci.* **277**, 2165–2174 (2010).

356. Petrides, M., Cadoret, G. & Mackey, S. Orofacial somatomotor responses in the macaque monkey homologue of Broca's area. *Nature* **435**, 1235–1238 (2005).

357. Preuss, T. M. & Goldman-Rakic, P. S. Architectonics of the parietal and temporal association cortex in the strepsirhine primate Galago compared to the anthropoid primate Macaca. *J. Comp. Neurol.* **310**, 475–506 (1991).

358. Taglialatela, J. P., Russell, J. L., Schaeffer, J. A. & Hopkins, W. D. Communicative signaling activates 'Broca's' homolog in chimpanzees. *Curr. Biol.* **18**, 343–348 (2008).

359. Poremba, A. *et al.* Species-specific calls evoke asymmetric activity in the monkey's temporal poles. *Nature* **427**, 448–451 (2004).

360. Buxhoeveden, D. P., Switala, A. E., Litaker, M., Roy, E. & Casanova, M. F. Lateralization of minicolumns in human planum temporale is absent in nonhuman primate cortex. *Brain. Behav. Evol.* **57**, 349–358 (2001).

361. Rilling, J. K. *et al.* The evolution of the arcuate fasciculus revealed with comparative DTI. *Nat. Neurosci.* **11**, 426–428 (2008).

362. Evans, P. D., Anderson, J. R., Vallender, E. J., Choi, S. S. & Lahn, B. T. Reconstructing the evolutionary history of microcephalin, a gene controlling human brain size. *Hum. Mol. Genet.* **13**, 1139–1145 (2004).

363. Jackson, A. P. *et al.* Identification of microcephalin, a protein implicated in determining the size of the human brain. *Am. J. Hum. Genet.* **71**, 136–142 (2002).

364. Bundey, S. *Genetics and neurology*. (Elsevier, 2014).

365. Evans, P. D. *et al.* Microcephalin, a gene regulating brain size, continues to evolve adaptively in humans. *science* **309**, 1717–1720 (2005).

366. Evans, P. D. *et al.* Adaptive evolution of ASPM, a major determinant of cerebral cortical size in humans. *Hum. Mol. Genet.* **13**, 489–494 (2004).

367. McLean, C. Y. *et al.* Human-specific loss of regulatory DNA and the evolution of human-specific traits. *Nature* **471**, 216–219 (2011).

368. Suzuki, I. K. *et al.* Human-specific NOTCH2NL genes expand cortical neurogenesis through Delta/Notch regulation. *Cell* **173**, 1370–1384 (2018).

369. Florio, M. *et al.* Human-specific gene ARHGAP11B promotes basal progenitor amplification and neocortex expansion. *Science* **347**, 1465–1470 (2015).

370. Dennis, M. Y. *et al.* Evolution of human-specific neural SRGAP2 genes by incomplete segmental duplication. *Cell* **149**, 912–922 (2012).

371. Charrier, C. *et al.* Inhibition of SRGAP2 function by its human-specific paralogs induces neoteny during spine maturation. *Cell* **149**, 923–935 (2012).

372. Liu, X. *et al.* Extension of cortical synaptic development distinguishes humans from chimpanzees and macaques. *Genome Res.* **22**, 611–622 (2012).

373. Miller, D. J. *et al.* Prolonged myelination in human neocortical evolution. *Proc. Natl. Acad. Sci.* **109**, 16480–16485 (2012).

374. Zollikofer, C. P. & de León, M. S. P. The evolution of hominin ontogenies. in *Seminars in cell & developmental biology* vol. 21 441–452 (Elsevier, 2010).

375. Robson, S. L. & Wood, B. Hominin life history: reconstruction and evolution. *J. Anat.* **212**, 394–425 (2008).

376. Leigh, S. R. Brain growth, life history, and cognition in primate and human evolution. *Am. J. Primatol. Off. J. Am. Soc. Primatol.* **62**, 139–164 (2004).

377. Sakai, T. *et al.* Differential prefrontal white matter development in chimpanzees and humans. *Curr. Biol.* **22**, 171 (2012).

378. Thompson-Schill, S. L., Ramscar, M. & Chrysikou, E. G. Cognition without control: When a little frontal lobe goes a long way. *Curr. Dir. Psychol. Sci.* **18**, 259–263 (2009).

379. Smith, T. M. *et al.* Dental evidence for ontogenetic differences between modern humans and Neanderthals. *Proc. Natl. Acad. Sci.* **107**, 20923–20928 (2010).

380. Xu, J. Unintentional drowning deaths in the United States. *1999–2010 NCHS Data Brief* 1–8 (2014).

381. Bortolus, R. *et al.* The epidemiology of multiple births. *Hum. Reprod. Update* **5**, 179–187 (1999).

382. Xue, Y. *et al.* Human Y chromosome base-substitution mutation rate measured by direct sequencing in a deep-rooting pedigree. *Curr. Biol.* **19**, 1453–1457 (2009).

383. Belle, E. M., Benazzo, A., Ghirotto, S., Colonna, V. & Barbujani, G. Comparing models on the genealogical relationships among Neandertal, Cro-Magnoid and modern Europeans by serial coalescent simulations. *Heredity* **102**, 218 (2009).

384. Chomsky, N., Larson, R. K., Déprez, V. & Yamakido, H. *Chomsky, N. 'Some simple evo-devo theses: How true might they be for language' in 'The evolution of human language'.* (Cambridge University Press Cambridge, 2010).

385. Hayward, M. W. Prey preferences of the spotted hyaena. *Crocuta Crocuta* (2006).

386. Hayward, M. W. *et al.* Prey preferences of the leopard (Panthera pardus). *J. Zool.* **270**, 298–313 (2006).

387. Sigg, H. Differentiation of female positions in hamadryas one-male-units. *Z. Für Tierpsychol.* **53**, 265–302 (1980).

388. Schaller, G. B. *The Serengeti lion: a study of predator-prey relations.* (University of Chicago Press, 2009).

389. Isbell, L. A. *The fruit, the tree, and the serpent: Why we see so well.* (Harvard University Press, 2009).

390. Hackett, T. B., Wingfield, W. E., Mazzaferro, E. M. & Benedetti, J. S. Clinical findings associated with prairie rattlesnake bites in dogs: 100 cases (1989–1998). *J. Am. Vet. Med. Assoc.* **220**, 1675–1680 (2002).

391. Coss, R. & Owings, D. Restraints on ground squirrel anti-predator behavior: adjustments over multiple time scales. in *Issues in the Ecological Study of Learning* (Lawrence Erlbaum Associates, 1985).

392. Verghese, P. & Pelli, D. G. The information capacity of visual attention. *Vision Res.* **32**, 983–995 (1992).

393. Matsuno, T. & Tomonaga, M. Visual search for moving and stationary items in chimpanzees (Pan troglodytes) and humans (Homo sapiens). *Behav. Brain Res.* **172**, 219–232 (2006).

394. Coss, R. G., Ramakrishnan, U. & Schank, J. Recognition of partially concealed leopards by wild bonnet macaques (Macaca radiata): The role of the spotted coat. *Behav. Processes* **68**, 145–163 (2005).

395. Navon, D. Forest before trees: The precedence of global features in visual perception. *Cognit. Psychol.* **9**, 353–383 (1977).

396. Fagot, J. & Tomonaga, M. Global and local processing in humans (Homo sapiens) and chimpanzees (Pan troglodytes): Use of a visual search task with compound stimuli. *J. Comp. Psychol.* **113**, 3 (1999).

397. Fagot, J. & Tomonaga, M. Effects of element separation on perceptual grouping by humans (Homo sapiens) and chimpanzees (Pan troglodytes): perception of Kanizsa illusory figures. *Anim. Cogn.* **4**, 171–177 (2001).

398. Hopkins, W. D. & Washburn, D. A. Matching visual stimuli on the basis of global and local features by chimpanzees (Pan troglodytes) and rhesus monkeys (Macaca mulatta). *Anim. Cogn.* **5**, 27–31 (2002).

399. Royden, C. S., Wolfe, J. M. & Klempen, N. Visual search asymmetries in motion and optic flow fields. *Percept. Psychophys.* **63**, 436–444 (2001).

400. Miller, E. K. & Wilson, M. A. All my circuits: using multiple electrodes to understand functioning neural networks. *Neuron* **60**, 483–488 (2008).

401. Brain, C. K. *The hunters or the hunted?: an introduction to African cave taphonomy.* (University of Chicago Press, 1983).

402. Tutin, C. E., McGrew, W. C. & Baldwin, P. J. Social organization of savanna-dwelling chimpanzees, Pan troglodytes verus, at Mt. Assirik, Senegal. *Primates* **24**, 154–173 (1983).

403. Nishimura, T., Mikami, A., Suzuki, J. & Matsuzawa, T. Descent of the larynx in chimpanzee infants. *Proc. Natl. Acad. Sci.* **100**, 6930–6933 (2003).

404. Lewis, J. As well as words: Congo Pygmy hunting, mimicry, and play. *Cradle Lang.* **12**, 236 (2009).

405. Broadfield, D. C. *et al.* Endocast of Sambungmacan 3 (Sm 3): a new Homo erectus from Indonesia. *Anat. Rec. Off. Publ. Am. Assoc. Anat.* **262**, 369–379 (2001).

406. Carbonell, E. *et al.* Lower Pleistocene hominids and artifacts from Atapuerca-TD6 (Spain). *Science* **269**, 826–830 (1995).

407. Lordkipanidze, D. *et al.* A complete skull from Dmanisi, Georgia, and the evolutionary biology of early Homo. *Science* **342**, 326–331 (2013).

408. Wrangham, R. & Conklin-Brittain, N. Cooking as a biological trait. *Comp. Biochem. Physiol. A. Mol. Integr. Physiol.* **136**, 35–46 (2003).
409. Bramble, D. M. & Lieberman, D. E. Endurance running and the evolution of Homo. *Nature* **432**, 345 (2004).
410. Barton, R. A. Animal communication: do dolphins have names? *Curr. Biol.* **16**, R598–R599 (2006).
411. Janik, V. M., Sayigh, L. S. & Wells, R. S. Signature whistle shape conveys identity information to bottlenose dolphins. *Proc. Natl. Acad. Sci.* **103**, 8293–8297 (2006).
412. Melis, A. P., Hare, B. & Tomasello, M. Engineering cooperation in chimpanzees: tolerance constraints on cooperation. *Anim. Behav.* **72**, 275–286 (2006).
413. Krings, M. *et al.* Neandertal DNA sequences and the origin of modern humans. *cell* **90**, 19–30 (1997).
414. Mason, P. H. & Short, R. V. Neanderthal-human hybrids. *Hypothesis* **9**, e1 (2011).
415. Boule, M. *Les hommes fossiles: éléments de paléontologie humaine.* (Masson, 1921).
416. Wilkins, J., Schoville, B. J., Brown, K. S. & Chazan, M. Evidence for early hafted hunting technology. *Science* **338**, 942–946 (2012).
417. Rule, S. *et al.* The aftermath of megafaunal extinction: ecosystem transformation in Pleistocene Australia. *Science* **335**, 1483–1486 (2012).
418. Christiansen, M. H. *Languages Evolution: the Hardest Problem in Science?, in «Language Evolution», M. Christiansen and S. Kirby.* (Oxford University Press, 2003).
419. Chomsky, N. *On nature and language.* (Cambridge University Press, 2002).
420. Ulbaek, I. The origin of language and cognition. *Approaches Evol. Lang.* 30–43 (1998).
421. Patterson, F. G. & Gordon, W. Twenty-seven years of Project Koko and Michael. in *All apes great and small* 165–176 (Springer, 2002).
422. Segerdahl, P., Fields, W. & Savage-Rumbaugh, S. *Kanzi's primal language: The cultural initiation of primates into language.* (Springer, 2005).
423. Pepperberg, I. M. Vocal learning in Grey parrots: A brief review of perception, production, and cross-species comparisons. *Brain Lang.* **115**, 81–91 (2010).
424. Köhler, W. *The mentality of apes.* (Harcourt, Brace & Co., Inc. London, 1925).
425. Hanus, D. & Call, J. Chimpanzee problem-solving: contrasting the use of causal and arbitrary cues. *Anim. Cogn.* **14**, 871–878 (2011).
426. Anderson, S. R. A telling difference. *Nat. Hist.* **113**, 38–43 (2004).
427. Dugatkin, L. A. *The imitation factor: Evolution beyond the gene.* (Simon and Schuster, 2000).
428. Horner, V. & De Waal, F. B. Controlled studies of chimpanzee cultural transmission. *Prog. Brain Res.* **178**, 3–15 (2009).

429. Thornton, A. & Raihani, N. J. Identifying teaching in wild animals. *Learn. Behav.* **38**, 297–309 (2010).
430. Galef Jr, B. G., Whiskin, E. E. & Dewar, G. A new way to study teaching in animals: despite demonstrable benefits, rat dams do not teach their young what to eat. *Anim. Behav.* **70**, 91–96 (2005).
431. Teleki, G. Chimpanzee subsistence technology: materials and skills. *J. Hum. Evol.* **3**, 575–594 (1974).
432. Iversen, I. H. & Matsuzawa, T. Model-guided line drawing in the chimpanzee (Pan troglodytes). *Jpn. Psychol. Res.* **39**, 154–181 (1997).
433. Lowenfeld, V. Creative and mental growth. (1957).
434. Gazzaniga, M. S. *The Science Behind What Makes Us Unique. New York, Ecco.* (HarperCollins, 2008).
435. Povinelli, D. J. & Dunphy-Lelii, S. Do chimpanzees seek explanations? Preliminary comparative investigations. *Can. J. Exp. Psychol. Can. Psychol. Expérimentale* **55**, 185 (2001).
436. Gaylin, W. In defense of the dignity of being human. *Hastings Cent. Rep.* 18–22 (1984).
437. Vygotsky, L. S. Play and its role in the mental development of the child. Translated by Catherine Mulholland from Voprosy psikhologii 1933. *Sov. Psychol.* **5**, 6–18 (1967).
438. Carroll, J. *Reading human nature: Literary Darwinism in theory and practice.* (SUNY Press, 2011).
439. Martin-Ordas, G., Berntsen, D. & Call, J. Memory for distant past events in chimpanzees and orangutans. *Curr. Biol.* **23**, 1438–1441 (2013).
440. Kosslyn, S. M., Thompson, W. L. & Ganis, G. *The case for mental imagery.* (Oxford University Press, 2006).
441. Singer, W. Binding by synchrony. *Scholarpedia* **2**, 1657 (2007).
442. De Jong, B. M., Van Zomeren, A. H., Willemsen, A. T. M. & Paans, A. M. J. Brain activity related to serial cognitive performance resembles circuitry of higher order motor control. *Exp. Brain Res.* **109**, 136–140 (1996).
443. Beglinger, L. J. & Smith, T. H. A review of subtyping in autism and proposed dimensional classification model. *J. Autism Dev. Disord.* **31**, 411–422 (2001).
444. Vyshedskiy, A. *This Way to Language: Four Things to Do at the First Sign of Autism.* (LuLu, 2021).
445. Fuster, J. M. & Alexander, G. E. Neuron activity related to short-term memory. *Science* **173**, 652–654 (1971).
446. Ashby, F. G., Ell, S. W., Valentin, V. V. & Casale, M. B. FROST: A distributed neurocomputational model of working memory maintenance. *J. Cogn. Neurosci.* **17**, 1728–1743 (2005).
447. Mottaghy, F. M. Interfering with working memory in humans. *Neuroscience* **139**, 85–90 (2006).
448. Pearson, D. G. & Logie, R. H. Working memory and mental synthesis: A dual task approach. *Spat. Cogn. Found. Appl.* **347**, 359 (2000).
449. Flavell, S. W. *et al.* Genome-wide analysis of MEF2 transcriptional

program reveals synaptic target genes and neuronal activity-dependent polyadenylation site selection. *Neuron* **60**, 1022–1038 (2008).

450. Zweier, M. *et al.* Mutations in MEF2C from the 5q14. 3q15 microdeletion syndrome region are a frequent cause of severe mental retardation and diminish MECP2 and CDKL5 expression. *Hum. Mutat.* **31**, 722–733 (2010).

451. Men, W. *et al.* The corpus callosum of Albert Einstein's brain: another clue to his high intelligence? *Brain* **137**, e268–e268 (2014).

452. Ferjan Ramirez, N. *et al.* Neural language processing in adolescent first-language learners. *Cereb. Cortex* **24**, 2772–2783 (2013).

453. Craver-Lemley, C. & Reeves, A. How visual imagery interferes with vision. *Psychol. Rev.* **99**, 633 (1992).

454. Butter, C. M., Kosslyn, S., Mijovic-Prelec, D. & Riffle, A. Field-specific deficits in visual imagery following hemianopia due to unilateral occipital infarcts. *Brain J. Neurol.* **120**, 217–228 (1997).

455. Kosslyn, S. M. *et al.* The role of area 17 in visual imagery: convergent evidence from PET and rTMS. *Science* **284**, 167–170 (1999).

456. Sadato, N. *et al.* Activation of the primary visual cortex by Braille reading in blind subjects. *Nature* **380**, 526–528 (1996).

457. Von Melchner, L., Pallas, S. L. & Sur, M. Visual behaviour mediated by retinal projections directed to the auditory pathway. *Nature* **404**, 871–876 (2000).

458. Fromkin, V., Krashen, S., Curtiss, S., Rigler, D. & Rigler, M. The development of language in genie: a case of language acquisition beyond the "critical period". *Brain Lang.* **1**, 81–107 (1974).

459. Curtiss, S., Fromkin, V., Rigler, D., Rigler, M. & Krashen, S. An update on the linguistic development of Genie. *Georget. Univ. Round Table Lang. Linguist.* 145–157 (1975).

Illustration credits

The author and publisher have exerted every effort to contact illustration copyright holders.

http://en.wikipedia.org/wiki/File:AltamiraBison.jpg
http://en.wikipedia.org/wiki/File:Lascaux_painting.jpg
http://upload.wikimedia.org/wikipedia/commons/thumb/8/86/Atom-struc.svg/2000px-Atom-struc.svg.png
http://en.wikipedia.org/wiki/File:Samuel_Reshevsky_versus_the_World.JPG
http://commons.wikimedia.org/wiki/Image:Vervet_monkeys_Manyara.jpg
http://commons.wikimedia.org/wiki/Image:Dolphin-intelligence.jpg
http://commons.wikimedia.org/wiki/Image:BonoboFishing05.jpeg
http://en.wikipedia.org/wiki/Image:Chimpanzee_and_stick.jpg
http://commons.wikimedia.org/wiki/Image:Human_brain_NIH.jpg
http://en.wikipedia.org/wiki/Image:Pencil_in_a_bowl_of_water.png
http://en.wikipedia.org/wiki/File:Archerfish_(PSF).png
http://en.wikipedia.org/wiki/Image:ComparitiveBrainSize.jpg
http://upload.wikimedia.org/wikipedia/commons/9/94/Chopper_of_Dmanisi.png
http://en.wikipedia.org/wiki/Image:Chopping_tool.gif
http://en.wikipedia.org/wiki/Image:Bifaz_abbevillense.png
http://en.wikipedia.org/wiki/Image:Hand_axe_spanish.gif
http://commons.wikimedia.org/wiki/File:Sapiens_neanderthal_comparison_en.png
http://upload.wikimedia.org/wikipedia/commons/7/70/Venus-de-Laussel-vue-generale-noir.jpg
http://en.wikipedia.org/wiki/Image:HyenaTanzania.JPG
http://en.wikipedia.org/wiki/ Image:Serengeti_Lion_Running_saturated.jpg
http://en.wikipedia.org/wiki/File:Trial_of_a_sow_and_pigs_at_Lavegny.png
http://commons.wikimedia.org/wiki/Image:Oldupai_gorge.jpg
http://commons.wikimedia.org/wiki/Image:Musculi_coli_base.svg.
http://commons.wikimedia.org/wiki/File:Camouflage_DSC05383_-_Original_image.JPG
http://en.wikipedia.org/wiki/File:Myelinated_neuron.jpg
http://biology.plosjournals.org/perlserv/?request=get-document&doi=10.1371/journal.pbio.0040029)]
http://www.nia.nih.gov/NR/rdonlyres/4E12F6CF-2436-47DB-8CC5-607E82B2B8E4/2372/neurons_big1.jpg
http://en.wikipedia.org/wiki/Image:Ventral-dorsal_streams.svg

http://commons.wikimedia.org/wiki/Image:Bristol.zoo.dead.leaf.mantis.arp.
jpg
http://commons.wikimedia.org/wiki/Image:Tawny_Frogmouth_camouflage.j
pg
http://commons.wikimedia.org/wiki/File:Children_playing_with_Campbell_K
id_dolls.jpg

About the author

Andrey Vyshedskiy, Ph.D., is an Adjunct Professor at Boston University. Dr. Vyshedskiy was trained in astrophysics, biomedical engineering, and neuroscience. He received a Ph.D. in Neuroscience from Boston University, and has conducted research in neuroscience, cardiopulmonary acoustics, and optical vibrometry. He has co-founded several successful companies, received numerous awards from the NSF, the NIH, and the DOD, and directed the development of several FDA approved medical devices. He has been teaching Human Physiology to BU students for nearly two decades. He has also periodically taught Tufts Medical School students. He has authored over 100 scientific publications, book chapters, and conference presentations. His work has appeared in the New England Journal of Medicine, Thorax, Chest, the Journal of Neuroscience and other leading scientific journals. Dr. Vyshedskiy currently lives in Boston with his wife and two children.

The frog from the illustration on the cover is highlighted.

A zoomed in view of the frog from the illustration on the cover.

CPSIA information can be obtained
at www.ICGtesting.com
Printed in the USA
LVHW011257010821
694126LV00008B/439